For its leaders, the German Democratic Republic was founded on the legacy of communist resistance to Nazism. They laid particular emphasis on events at Buchenwald, where communist-led prisoners allegedly threw off the fascist yoke in a heroic act of self-liberation (although in reality they were liberated by the American army). A key strand in the Buchenwald narrative was the tale of the rescue by communist prisoners of a three-year-old Jewish prisoner, Stefan Jerzy Zweig. His story became a powerful focus for the country's celebration of its antifascist past. Bruno Apitz's novel *Naked among Wolves,* which describes Zweig's rescue, was published in 1958 and became an immediate bestseller. It was later adapted into a highly successful cinema film, and became a staple of the school curriculum. In 1963, a campaign to find Zweig — by this time a grown man — met with success when he was located in Lyon and offered the chance to study in the GDR.

Bill Niven sets out to establish what really happened to Zweig in Buchenwald. How was he protected by adult prisoners, and at what price? (There is evidence that a Sinto boy was sent to Auschwitz in Zweig's place, perhaps as a result of the influence of the communist prisoners, evidence that was suppressed in the GDR.) Niven explores how Zweig's story was presented in East Germany and examines what that reveals about the country's understanding — and use of — the Nazi past and the Holocaust. He then examines the postunification reception of Zweig's story: in a unified Germany dominated by west Germans, the GDR's deployment of the story has come in for heavy criticism — which in turn serves the politicized end of condemning East Germany's approach to the Nazi past.

THE BUCHENWALD CHILD

THE BUCHENWALD CHILD

TRUTH, FICTION, AND PROPAGANDA

BILL NIVEN

CAMDEN HOUSE
Rochester, New York

First published 2007
by Camden House

Camden House is an imprint of Boydell & Brewer Inc.
668 Mt. Hope Avenue, Rochester, NY 14620, USA
www.camden-house.com
and of Boydell & Brewer Limited
PO Box 9, Woodbridge, Suffolk IP12 3DF, UK
www.boydellandbrewer.com

ISBN-13: 978-1-57113-339-7
ISBN-10: 1-57113-339-9

Library of Congress Cataloging-in-Publication Data

Niven, William John
    The Buchenwald child: truth, fiction, and propaganda / William Niven.
        p. cm. — (Studies in German literature, linguistics, and culture)
Includes bibliographical references and index.
ISBN-13: 978-1-57113-339-7 (hbk.: alk. paper)
ISBN-10: 1-57113-339-9 (hbk.: alk. paper)
    1. Buchenwald (Concentration camp)   2. Zweig, Stefan Jerzy, 1941–
— Imprisonment.   3. World War, 1939–1945 — Concentration camps
— Liberation — Germany — Weimar (Thuringia)   4. Anti-fascist
movements — Germany (East)   5. Collective memory — Germany (East)
6. Apitz, Bruno. Nackt unter Wölfen.   I. Title.   II. Series.

D805.5.B83N58 2007
940.53′15092—dc22

                                                                    2006030221

A catalogue record for this title is available from the British Library.

This publication is printed on acid-free paper.
Printed in the United States of America.

CONTENTS

ILLUSTRATIONS

(The photographs in this book are reproduced courtesy of the Gedenkstätte Buchenwald unless otherwise noted.)

ACKNOWLEDGMENTS

I HAVE MANY PEOPLE to thank for the help and support they gave to me when I was undertaking the research for this book. Above all, I would like to thank Stefan Jerzy Zweig himself, not just for being prepared to provide what were important interviews, but also for his general helpfulness in so many other respects. He knows as well as I do that our conversations were not always easy. In trying to find out more, I asked many questions, perhaps too many. I was always aware that I was writing a book about the exploitation of a victim of Nazi anti-Semitism in East Germany and contemporary Germany, and that I did not want to fall into the same trap of "using" Stefan. Yet still I had to ask those questions. I am deeply grateful to him for his patience with me. I am also grateful to various archivists for their support, not least Frau Sabine Stein of the Buchenwald Archive, whose knowledge, not just of the archive, but also of the role played by Buchenwald during the GDR proved invaluable. As ever, I am indebted to Grit Ullrich in the Federal Archives (Berlin) for her advice and guidance. I also benefited enormously from E-mail exchanges and meetings with Susanne Hantke, Evelyn Preuss, and Thomas Taterka, all of whom are also working to varying degrees on Bruno Apitz and Buchenwald. Evelyn and I never agreed, and airing our disagreements — on so many issues — animated us to even more disagreement. Yet had it not been for Evelyn's determined refusal to see things my way, I might not have been so consistently inspired to review my own position. If my views in the course of researching the book became more complex, that is not least because of Evelyn (even though I am sure she will still disagree with me). I am very grateful, too, to Kikki Apitz, Frank Beyer, and Gisela Karau for allowing me to interview them. The most important person in helping me to develop the ideas for this book, apart from Stefan himself, is Ken Waltzer of Michigan State University. I would like to express my deepest thanks to Ken for sharing my passion for researching the fate of Buchenwald's youngest inmates, even if my interest was always more in the post-1945 period. The countless E-mail discussions and the talks we had in East Lansing and Milwaukee fed into this book in so many ways that it would take me too long to enumerate them here.

I should also like to express my thanks first, to the British Academy for its generous support in funding the research trips to Germany that were a prerequisite for the writing of this book, and second, to the Arts and Humanities Research Council, without whose equally generous support I would never have been able to find the time to write it. My thanks are due also to the Buchenwald Memorial Site, The German Historical Museum (Berlin), and the Film Archive of the Federal Archives (Berlin) for granting me permission to reproduce the photographs that appear in this book. Last but not least, I should like to thank my editor Jim Walker for his invaluable support and advice, and my copyeditor Sue Innes for her careful reading of the manuscript, and her advice on how it might be improved.

Bill Niven
October 2006

ABBREVIATIONS

BBF/DIPF/Archiv = Archiv der Bibliothek für Bildungsgeschichtliche Forschung des Deutschen Instituts für Internationale Pädagogische Forschung, Berlin (archive reference for material held by the German Institute for International Pedagogical Research)

BStU = Bundesbeauftragte für die Unterlagen des Staatssicherheitsdienstes der ehemaligen Deutschen Demokratischen Republik (Archive reference for the files of the GDR's State Security Service, or *Stasi*)

BwA = Archiv der Gedenkstätte Buchenwald (Buchenwald Archive, Buchenwald)

BZ am Abend = *Berliner Zeitung am Abend* (roughly, *Berlin Evening Mail*)

CDU = Christlich-Demokratische Union (Christian Democratic Party)

DEFA = Deutsche Film-Aktiengesellschaft (German Film Corporation)

DHM = Deutsches Historisches Museum (German Historical Museum)

DRA = Deutsches Rundfunkarchiv (German Radio Archives, Berlin)

FDJ = Freie Deutsche Jugend (Free German Youth)

FRG = Federal Republic of Germany

GDR = German Democratic Republic

IGM = IG Metall (West German Trade Union)

IKBD = Internationales Komitee Buchenwald-Dora (International Buchenwald-Dora Committee)

ILK = Internationales Lagerkomittee (International Camp Committee, Buchenwald)

IML = Institut für Marxismus-Leninismus (Institute for Marxism-Leninism)

IMO = Internationale Militärorganisation (International Military Organization, Buchenwald)

KAG = Künstlerische Arbeitsgruppe (Artistic Working Group, part of DEFA)

KdAW = Komitee der Antifaschistischen Widerstandskämpfer (Committee of Antifascist Resistance Fighters)

KPD = Kommunistische Partei Deutschlands (Communist Party of Germany)

KPO = Kommunistische Partei — Opposition (Communist Party Opposition)

LHASA = Landeshauptarchiv Sachsen-Anhalt (Main Regional Archive for Saxony-Anhalt)

MDR = Mitteldeutscher Rundfunk (Central German Radio and Television)

MDV = Mitteldeutscher Verlag (Central German Publishing Company)

MELS = Marx-Engels-Lenin-Stalin-Institut

MfDG = Museum für Deutsche Geschichte (Museum for German History)

MfK = Ministerium für Kultur (Ministry for Culture)

ND = Neues Deutschland (*New Germany*, SED Party newspaper)

NMGB = Nationale Mahn- und Gedenkstätte Buchenwald (National Site of Warning and Commemoration, Buchenwald)

OSE = Oeuvre de Secours aux Enfants (Agency for Helping Children)

PWD = American Psychological Warfare Division

SAdK = Stiftung Archiv Akademie der Künste (Academy of Arts Archive, Berlin)

SAPMO-BArch = Stiftung Archiv der Parteien und Massenorganisationen der DDR im Bundesarchiv (Archive of the Parties and Mass Organizations of the GDR at the Federal Archives, Berlin)

SED = Sozialistische Einheitspartei Deutschlands (Socialist Unity Party of Germany)

SPD = Sozialdemokratische Partei Deutschlands (Social Democratic Party of Germany)

StadtA Weimar = Stadtarchiv Weimar (Weimar Town Archive)

Stasi = Staatssicherheitsdienst (GDR State Security Service)

UNRRA = United Nations Relief and Rehabilitation Agency

USHMM = United States Holocaust Memorial Museum

VEB = Volkseigener Betrieb (People's Own Industry)

VVN = Vereinigung der Verfolgten des Naziregimes (Association of Those Persecuted by the Nazi Regime)

ZDF = Zweites Deutsches Fernsehen (Second German Television)

ZK = Zentralkomitee (Central Committee)

ZPKK = Zentrale Parteikontrollkommission (Central Commission for Control of the Party)

NOTE ON TRANSLATIONS

U NLESS OTHERWISE STATED, all translations of quotations into English are my own. Only in two cases have I provided the original German quotations in the footnotes. First, in my discussion in chapter 3 of the changes made to Bruno Apitz's typescript of his novel *Naked among Wolves* (*Nackt unter Wölfen*); and, second, in my discussion in chapter 6 of the changes made to the plaque at Buchenwald commemorating Stefan Jerzy Zweig's rescue. In each case, because the changes to the German were so significant, I wanted to provide scholars of the GDR with the opportunity to appreciate this for themselves. Generally, though, I have not provided the original German. The book, being based principally on archival research, contains many endnotes as it is, and I did not want to try the reader's patience by providing even more. I also wanted to make the text as a whole accessible to the ordinary reader, given that the topic is one of general as well as academic interest.

INTRODUCTION

T HE POLISH JEW STEFAN JERZY ZWEIG was one of just over 900 children whom American forces liberated at Buchenwald concentration camp on 11 April 1945. Up until that point, his entire short life had been spent in Nazi captivity: born in the Cracow ghetto on 28 January 1941, he survived incarceration in a series of Nazi camps in Poland before being transported to Buchenwald in the late summer of 1944. Without the perseverance, imagination, and resourcefulness of his father, Zacharias, Stefan would never have survived; at Buchenwald, a number of other prisoners, notably communists, were also involved in his rescue. This book, for the most part, is about the story of this rescue as it was told in the German Democratic Republic (1949–90); the final chapter considers changes in the telling of the rescue story since 1990. It is, therefore, not in first instance a book about the rescue itself. The opening chapter does provide an overview of Zacharias's report of his son's rescue, and it examines other sources that also shed light on the circumstances of that rescue; all later representations need to be measured for their accuracy against these facts. But by and large this is a monograph about the way the rescue of Stefan at Buchenwald was remembered. While the diary of Anne Frank was well known in the GDR, it did not have the significance it did in the West. In East Germany, it was the story of Stefan Jerzy Zweig, filtered through a variety of media and usually seen through a communist lens, that captured the public imagination more. In contrast to Anne Frank, Stefan Zweig survived the Holocaust; the story of Stefan Zweig's experience under Nazism as narrated in the GDR was one that emphasized its happy ending. It was also one that foregrounded not Jewish suffering or German perpetration but the travails and the courage of a particular set of German victims, namely the communist inmates of Buchenwald.

What I set out to explore in this book, by example of Buchenwald and Stefan Jerzy Zweig, is the molding of the past in the interests of collective identity in the present. Much recent work on memory, not least by Jan Assmann, takes its cue from Maurice Halbwachs, the French sociologist who developed the idea that the way we remember is a function of social frameworks, which themselves serve to underpin the collective memory of any given group, be this the family, a religious community, or the professional environment in which we work.[1] Maurice Halbwachs wasted away in the Small Camp ("Kleines Lager") at Buchenwald in 1945.[2] For all the significance of Halbwachs for contemporary memory studies, no attempt has so far been made to apply his ideas to the memory of the concentration camps.[3] And yet — cruel coincidence of history — his ideas seem to anticipate the cult of memory built up around Buchenwald in East Germany between 1951, when the camp was passed over to the GDR by the Soviet authorities, and 1990, when German unification brought an end to what is now disparagingly referred to as "prescribed antifascism."

Initially, it was the former Buchenwald prisoners themselves who set about developing this cult. The social framework was the male collective of those communist prisoners who had either played their part in the communist underground at Buchenwald or had taken on functions within the camp's SS-imposed "self-administration." In the immediate postwar period, members of this collective found themselves occupying important political and administrative positions in the Soviet-occupied zone. In the course of 1946 and 1947, however, as a result of rumors that charges might be brought against communist camp functionaries at the Buchenwald trials in Dachau for complicity in SS crimes, the collective came under pressure to justify its conduct, especially when subjected to an internal investigation by the SED (Socialist Unity Party).[4] This led to an essentially defensive program of self-glorification. Former Buchenwald prisoners in east Germany (as of 1949, the GDR) set about exaggerating the extent, effectiveness, and probity of communist resistance at Buchenwald; the apogee of this exaggeration was the framing of the liberation of Buchenwald as a self-liberation (*Selbstbefreiung*).[5] A narrative of heroic resistance was generated, a narrative that, in confirmation of the theories of Halbwachs, was born of the exigencies of the present.

This narrative, of course, can be seen as part of a wider antifascist narrative in eastern Germany, one that was cultivated, disseminated, and vigorously maintained through organizations such as the Association of Those Persecuted by the Nazi Regime (*Vereinigung der Verfolgten des Naziregimes*, or VVN), and particularly the Committee of Antifascist Resistance Fighters (*Komitee der Antifaschistischen Widerstandskämpfer*, or KdAW). Before its dissolution and replacement by the KdAW in 1953, the VVN did much to promote the idea of a qualitative difference between "fighters against fascism" and "victims of fascism." The "fighters against fascism" encompassed all those — generally communists — who were adjudged to have been engaged in active resistance to fascism, whether in the Spanish Civil War, in German towns and cities, in concentration camps, in the National Committee for a Free Germany (*Nationalkomitee Freies Deutschland*), or in exile. However, within this greater antifascist collective, it was the communist ex-prisoners of Buchenwald who came to regard themselves as the supreme resistance heroes. After all, as prisoners in an SS-run camp, their resistance had, as it were, been staged in the lion's den itself, and therefore in the most adverse conditions imaginable. At no other

Nazi camp, moreover, had the communist underground been so tightly organized as at Buchenwald, and no other group of antifascists could even conceivably lay claim to having helped to overcome the murderous SS system.

The defensive self-promotion of Buchenwald's communists after 1945 did not silence their opponents. They had to face continued criticism, not only from the West, but also from other antifascists within the GDR. The greater antifascist memory collective was not as harmonious as it often appeared; tensions existed between former prisoners of different concentration camps, not least between those of Sachsenhausen and Buchenwald. Exile communists, such as SED General Secretary Walter Ulbricht, who had sat out the war in Moscow, resented attempts on the part of former concentration-camp prisoners, especially those who had been in Buchenwald, to lay claim to a special moral status; and they were particularly reluctant to countenance attempts on the part of such former prisoners to derive from this self-conferred status a right to *political* authority in the present. Because the SED investigation of 1946/47 into the conduct of the communists at Buchenwald had revealed evidence of their possible corruption and possible complicity in the SS system, it provided Ulbricht with the opportunity to exclude them from positions of real power; further investigations and exclusions followed in the early 1950s.[6] Moreover, with the disbanding of the VVN in 1953, Buchenwald's ex-prisoners appeared to lose their strong influence on the public image of their past. But the decline in their political fortunes did not result in a diminution of the significance of Buchenwald as a *lieu de mémoire*. On the contrary.

In fact, as chapter 2 will demonstrate, between 1955 and 1958 the collective memory of Buchenwald's communist prisoners was transformed into the official memory of the SED. A massive memorial complex was erected on the south-facing slope of the Ettersberg hill near Buchenwald — under the guiding hand of GDR Minister-President Otto Grotewohl. Following the end of hopes of German reunification, the signing of the Paris Treaties by West Germany, and the threat of rearmament, the two Germanys seemed implacably pitched against one another. Under such circumstances, it became more important than ever for each German state to seek to legitimize its claim to be the better Germany by laying exclusive claim to positive traditions in German history. In this respect, the propaganda potential of the communist prisoners' version of Buchenwald's history for the SED was considerable; the GDR could be presented as heir to the spirit of resistance that had overthrown the mighty SS, and as the state that had taken up the pledge of Buchenwald's prisoners in April 1945 to go on fighting fascism, which of course was now believed to be located in West Germany. But for the SED, this resistance narrative was to be understood as expressive of the courage and effectiveness of antifascist resistance as a whole, as *pars pro toto*, not as a narrative that singled out the achievements of Buchenwald's communists over those of other antifascists.

The assimilation of the heroic Buchenwald resistance narrative into official memory again confirms Halbwachs's argument that the past is being continually molded to fit the exigencies of the present. Indeed, it appears to bear out his observations quite precisely. Halbwachs has argued that family memories often focus on a certain day or event, although this day or event is rarely remembered as it was: "We compose it anew, and introduce elements borrowed from several periods which preceded or followed the scene in question."[7] The memory of Buchenwald for the GDR state and for former Buchenwald prisoners themselves also coalesced around certain events and days. Two of these were the murder of the German communist leader Ernst Thälmann by the Nazis in Buchenwald's crematorium on 18 August 1944 and the liberation of Buchenwald on 11 April 1945. Both of these events were represented in the GDR as staging posts in the dynamic progress of communism. Thälmann's murder was remembered in the context of the secret commemorative ceremony organized by the prisoners that followed it, a ceremony that supposedly helped to strengthen resistance.[8] And Buchenwald's liberation was remembered as a self-liberation, to make it appear as the inevitable outcome of the long-term and laborious planning of an uprising that had preceded it.

A third focal point of collective memory of Buchenwald in the GDR was the rescue of Stefan Jerzy Zweig. The latter half of chapter 2 explores references to the rescue story in eastern Germany/the GDR between 1946 and 1958, references made particularly in exhibitions and documentation about Buchenwald. These references were brief, but they were not without significance.[9] Indeed, the very brevity of early references to Zweig in the GDR enabled an iconic image to be established. The claim that a very young child, the personification of innocence and vulnerability, had survived thanks to antifascist solidarity was simultaneously a claim that the communists at Buchenwald had acted in a truly paternal, altruistic, and courageous manner, and that they had triumphed over death even when it was at its most imminent. The memorial complex near Buchenwald dedicated in 1958 includes two representations of a child. One of these is on a stela titled "Arrival in the Camp," sculpted by Waldemar Grzimek. Fritz Cremer's monumental sculpture showing a group of prisoners liberating the camp also features a small child. That Grzimek or Cremer took their inspiration from the rescue of Zweig rather than from stories of the rescue of other children cannot be clearly established, but it is more than possible.

Certainly Bruno Apitz's novel *Naked among Wolves* (*Nackt unter Wölfen*), published in mid-1958, was significantly inspired by the story of Zweig's rescue. Chapter 3 examines the genesis of the novel, which began life in 1954 as a proposal for a film.[10] In many ways, *Naked among Wolves* is the literary counterpart to Cremer's memorial, given that the whole action is directed toward the self-liberation of Buchenwald, with which the novel ends. But Apitz's novel, as text, is much more explicit and expansive in its praise of communist resistance at the camp, and the story of the child's rescue becomes bound up with the history of that resistance in a much more intimate way than had been the case prior to the novel's appearance. Apitz, however, as his 1954 film proposal makes clear, also had the Cold War in mind:[11] his novel was designed as an implicit critique of West Germany, in which, so Apitz believed, fascism was still rife. Thus it was that *Naked among Wolves* served both to reinforce a heroic view of Buchenwald's communists — Apitz, himself a former Buchenwald prisoner, will have been aware of their disempowerment in the early 1950s — and to provide a propaganda weapon for the SED against West Germany.

Thanks to *Naked among Wolves*, the desired view of Buchenwald as a site of heroic resistance, hitherto largely a feature of the collective memory of former Buchenwald prisoners and of "official" memory, established itself in the consciousness of the GDR's population as a whole. Visits to Buchenwald's National Site of Warning and Commemoration, established in 1958, by tens of thousands of young Thälmann Pioneers or Free German Youth members, of course, also did much to anchor this view in the minds of East German youth. But it was above all thanks to the influence of *Naked among Wolves*, which sold hundreds of thousands of copies in the GDR within a few years of its publication and soon became a staple of the school curriculum, that the heroic picture of Buchenwald became a feature of national collective memory. This influence was strengthened by the TV film (1960) and DEFA film (1963) of Apitz's novel. That *Naked among Wolves* was genuinely popular with the GDR's reading public had much to do with its dramatic and sentimental account of a child's rescue from the brutality of the SS. But in the GDR Apitz's fable was popular for another, albeit largely subconscious, reason. GDR readers, in identifying with the image it projected of antifascist solidarity, were able to reimagine themselves as belonging to a victim and resistance collective, and to associate Nazi criminality exclusively with the SS.

It would be reasonable to claim that the molding of history by collective memory identified by Maurice Halbwachs leads to myth-building — not least because what results is a tendentious and distortive version of the past. In adapting history, myth irons out its inconsistencies and contradictions, exaggerates certain of its aspects while downplaying or ignoring others, streamlines it so that it acquires a sense of shape and direction, and even adds to it entirely invented episodes. In the GDR, it could be said, there existed a myth of antifascist resistance — not because there never was such resistance during the Third Reich, but because the picture of it disseminated to GDR citizens adapted history in the way described above. Thus, for example, too little mention was made of non-communist groupings in the resistance, of tensions between antifascist groupings between 1933 and 1945, or their limited efficacy, or limited collaboration. Even less mention was made of the fact that the norm in Nazi Germany was not resistance but passivity or collaboration. In exactly the same way, the East German view of communist resistance at Buchenwald had much in common with a myth because, while this resistance certainly took place, it did not result in a self-liberation, and the glorification of it overlooks the problem that some communist camp functionaries may have been morally implicated in the SS system.[12] The emphasis on resistance, moreover, obscured the basic fact that, at Buchenwald, suffering and death predominated — and German perpetration. Finally, the story of Stefan Zweig's rescue as presented in the GDR was also a myth, because, for instance, it played up the role of the communists in Stefan's rescue, played down that of his father, and overlooked the fact that that rescue was only possible because someone else was deported from the camp in his place.[13] But at no point, of course, did the GDR acknowledge that its view of antifascist history, generally or in the specific instance, was a myth. On the contrary, this view was presented as absolutely authentic.

Naked among Wolves is a novel, not a documentary report. Chapter 4 begins by examining the process by which its fictional status was nevertheless increasingly disavowed. Because the constructs of collective memory and myth often stand in contrast to the facts of history, they are vulnerable and are in constant need of corroboration. Chapter 4, accordingly, argues that the making of the 1963 DEFA film of *Naked among Wolves* was the result, not just of the wish to popularize Apitz's tale even more, but also of the desire to reinforce its canonical status by underpinning its supposed authenticity. The making of the film was informed by a programmatic commitment to "recreating the original atmosphere." Behind this almost fetishistic concern for authenticity of milieu was the hope that it, in turn, would authenticate the image of resistance the film conveyed. From today's perspective, there adheres to this concern the same defensive overcompensation that characterized the self-glorification of Buchenwald's communist former prisoners in the late 1940s. Was there concern that the GDR public doubted the heroic image of communist resistance, or at least the details of the child's rescue? I believe, and will seek to demonstrate, that there were such doubts.

Nor will the DEFA film have fully dispelled any such doubts. As chapter 4 also demonstrates, the international reception of this film was problematic. At the Moscow Film Festival in 1963, *Naked among Wolves* failed to win the main prize (in part, at least) precisely because one member of the international jury, the Pole Jan Rybkowski, was indignantly dismissive of its "glossing over of reality."[14] The GDR population was never informed as to this reason for the film's failure in Moscow. Not that the Moscow Film Festival had been all bad news for the GDR delegation; contact was established to relatives of Stefan Zweig and, through them, to his father Zacharias and then to Stefan himself. Chapter 5 traces the search to find

Stefan and the efforts to bring him to the GDR, where he studied and lived between 1964 and 1972. While there is no indication of highest-level SED involvement in these efforts — which were undertaken largely by the GDR newspaper *Berliner Zeitung am Abend* — there can be little doubt that Stefan's return to Buchenwald and his reunion with some of those communists involved in rescuing him, as well as his temporary adoption by the GDR, served to authenticate Apitz's tale. Its credibility, damaged in Moscow, was restored.

However, as chapter 5 also sets out to show, this act of authentification was only possible by means of a concerted campaign, particularly in the GDR media. Stefan Zweig's presence in the GDR was framed as the conclusive proof of the absolute effectiveness and humanity of communist resistance as depicted by Apitz. Again and again, his experience of Buchenwald was presented to the GDR public as identical to that of the fictional Stefan Cyliak in *Naked among Wolves*. This campaign of equivalence could be maintained only by suppressing the full facts of Zweig's rescue. In late 1963, a copy of Zacharias Zweig's own account of Stefan's rescue was made available to the *BZ am Abend* (among others). Yet rather than publish this account in its entirety, which would have drawn attention to discrepancies between it and *Naked among Wolves*, *BZ am Abend* serialized it in truncated form. Zacharias's testimony was thereby distorted, the distortion presented as truth, and this pseudo-truth used to corroborate Apitz's version. The lesson of this is that myths, which need to carry historical conviction to retain their force, can generally only do this by means of a masquerade of authenticity.

That Zacharias and Stefan Zweig tolerated the suppression of disparities and the exploitation of the streamlined story of Stefan's rescue in the GDR resulted from a mixture of impulses, such as genuine thankfulness for what some communists at Buchenwald had done for Stefan, and understandable opportunism (Stefan was offered a unique chance to study film in Babelsberg). There was a further motive. Zacharias — who visited East Germany briefly in 1964 — and Stefan hoped they might be able to use their stay in the GDR to bring about the emigration of Zacharias's brother Heinrich from Moscow, who, as a Jew, was possibly under threat.[15] Stefan Zweig left the GDR in 1972; for various reasons, he opted to live in Vienna, where he still resides today. Despite his departure, the rescue story remained well-known in the GDR, and Apitz's novel was a staple of the school curriculum right up until 1989/90, as the first part of the final chapter, chapter 6, will show.

Chapter 6 also shows that, to a limited degree, there developed in the GDR a literary reception of *Naked among Wolves*. Erich Maria Remarque's Buchenwald novel *Spark of Life* (*Der Funke Leben*, 1952) and Ernst Wiechert's Buchenwald memoir *The Forest of the Dead* (*Der Totenwald*, 1946) had been the literary reference points for Apitz. In turn, *Naked among Wolves* became a point of intertextual reference for subsequent literary works dealing with ghettos and concentration camps, such as Jurek Becker's *Jacob the Liar* (*Jakob der Lügner*, 1969) and Fred Wander's *The Seventh Well* (*Der siebente Brunnen*, 1971). Such critical intertextuality, however, never seriously perturbed the canonical status in the GDR of Apitz's novel and its image of communist resistance. This changed radically with the fall of the Wall, and particularly with German unification. As chapter 6 will demonstrate, the typical view in united Germany is that Buchenwald's communists, far from being heroes, were utterly complicit in the SS system.[16] The GDR's glorified image of Buchenwald has also come in for heavy criticism. Nor has criticism spared the version of the Zweig rescue story propagated in the GDR particularly through *Naked among Wolves*. Transport lists demonstrating that a Sinto boy was sent to Auschwitz in place of Stefan — probably as a result of the intervention of communist prisoners — can now be seen at the Buchenwald Memorial Site. The literary critic Wilfried Schoeller has done much to discredit the supposed authenticity of *Naked among Wolves*, as has Hans Joachim Schädlich in his recent novel *Different* (*Anders*, 2003).

The post-1990 period, then, as chapter 6 shows, has seen a complete deconstruction of the GDR's version of Zweig's rescue based on *Naked among Wolves*. A story about rescue has become a story about protection at the cost of another boy's life, so effectively a story about death, even murder. It has become a story about collaboration between communists and the SS — in essence, then, a totalitarianist tale about similarities between fascist and communist ideologies and practices, overlooking the rather obvious fact that communists at Buchenwald were prisoners — however privileged in relative terms the position of some of them, and however dubious their role in the camp's self-administration. As such, the cloth of the tale has been cut to fit the group interests of the fundamentally *west* German memory collective, which, in the process of building a new national German identity on the basis of West German points of historical reference, is keen to discredit east German antifascism. The result is that the deconstruction of a GDR myth has gone hand in hand with a remythification. For the post-1990 view of communist resistance at Buchenwald and of Zweig's rescue is in some respects as distorted as the GDR view it has ousted. In the concluding part of chapter 6, I also consider the effect of the ongoing deployment of the Zweig rescue story on Zweig himself. Arguably, his reactions and feelings have never been properly respected. In 2005, just after I had submitted what I thought would be the final typescript of the current book, Zweig's own book, *Tears Alone Are Not Enough* (*Tränen allein genügen nicht*), appeared in print.[17] In a brief epilogue, I consider the content and arguments of *Tears Alone Are Not Enough*. It is, in many respects, a Holocaust survivor's angry riposte to decades of exploitation.

Notes

[1] See Maurice Halbwachs, *On Collective Memory*, ed. and trans. by Lewis A. Coser (Chicago and London: U of Chicago P, 1992).

[2] Another of Buchenwald's inmates, the famous Spanish-French writer Jorge Semprun, talked frequently to Halbwachs at Buchenwald, and has given moving testimony to his death. See Jorge Semprun, *Der Tote mit meinem Namen* (Frankfurt am Main: Suhrkamp, 2002).

[3] Although reference is made to Halbwachs in Wolfgang Sofsky, *Die Ordnung des Terrors: Das Konzentrationslager* (Frankfurt am Main: Fischer, 1997).

[4] See Lutz Niethammer, ed., *Der "gesäuberte" Antifaschismus: Die SED und die roten Kapos von Buchenwald* (Berlin: Akademie Verlag, 1994), 71–77. See also chapter 1.

[5] The ambivalence of the circumstances of the camp's liberation will be discussed in chapter 1.

[6] For more on this, see Niethammer, *Der "gesäuberte" Antifaschismus*, 403–7.

[7] Halbwachs, *On Collective Memory*, 61.

[8] The commemorative ceremony was organized by the KPO, a communist splinter group formed during the Weimar Republic. In the GDR, the ceremony was increasingly remembered as a KPD event, thus enabling it to be more easily streamlined (see Niethammer, *Der "gesäuberte" Antifaschismus*, 61–62).

[9] See, for instance, Karl Barthel, *Die Welt ohne Erbarmen* (Rudolstadt: Greifenverlag zu Rudolstadt, 1946), 150–51; and *KL Bu: Konzentrationslager Buchenwald: Bericht des internationalen Lagerkomitees Buchenwald* (Weimar: Thüringer Volksverlag, 1945), 43–45.

[10] Stiftung Archiv der Parteien und Massenorganisationen der DDR im Bundesarchiv (henceforth SAPMO-BArch), DR1/8745: Letter from Apitz to Hans Rodenberg (DEFA), undated (probably late 1954).

[11] SAPMO-BArch, DR1/8745: Letter from Apitz to Rodenberg.

[12] See chapter 1 for further discussion of this.

[13] See chapter 1 for an account of this exchange.

[14] SAPMO-BArch, DR1/8907: Hans Rodenberg, "Bericht über das Internationale Moskauer Filmfestival," 24 July 1963.

[15] Interview with Stefan Zweig, 30 March 2004.

[16] See particularly Niethammer, *Der "gesäuberte" Antifaschismus*, and Manfred Overesch, *Buchenwald und die DDR oder die Suche nach Selbstlegitimation* (Göttingen: Vandenhoeck & Ruprecht, 1995).

[17] See Zacharias Zweig and Stefan Zweig, *Tränen allein genügen nicht* (Vienna: Eigenverlag, 2005).

CHAPTER ONE

THE PROTECTION OF
STEFAN JERZY ZWEIG

Introduction

MOST OF THIS BOOK is about constructions of Buchenwald's past in the interests of the present, both in the GDR and in contemporary Germany. But before examining the manner in which this past was and is represented, it is important to try to present it as it "really was," or at least to get as close to this reality as possible on the basis of available sources. Only against the background of such a presentation will the discrepancy between the complex character of communist resistance at Buchenwald and the equally complex circumstances of Zweig's rescue on the one hand and the simplified, tendentious versions of these constructed in East Germany and indeed in post-unification Germany on the other become apparent. This chapter, therefore, after providing a brief general history of Buchenwald concentration camp, examines the role played by Buchenwald's communist prisoners within the camp and the question of their contribution to the rescue of children at Buchenwald. This examination provides the general context for the specific story of the rescue of Stefan Jerzy Zweig, as related by his father Zacharias, which then follows. The chapter concludes with a section in which other prisoners' memories of Stefan's rescue, and the evidence provided by archival documents, are set in relation to Zacharias's in order to fill in the gaps in his account and also to point out and investigate any inconsistencies. Not all of these can be conclusively resolved. Nevertheless, I hope that a generally reliable picture will emerge of the essentials of the process by which Stefan Zweig came to survive "the brown apocalypse."[1]

Death and Survival at Buchenwald

Buchenwald concentration camp was built in 1937. Initially, about half of its prisoners were men who had been incarcerated on political grounds, many of them communists. The other half was made up of what were known in the camp as "professional criminals"[2] — men who had already served sentences for criminal activities but had to endure further incarceration for "preventive" purposes. The majority of the first cohorts of prisoners in 1937 were Germans. In time, the composition of the prisoners changed.

These changes were the direct result of an intensification of discriminatory Nazi politics. Thus in 1938, the numbers of prisoners swelled following the rounding up of those considered to be "arbeitsscheu," an elastic concept used to justify the imprisonment of any number of supposed delinquents — not least Jews. After the Reich Pogrom Night in November 1938, some 26,000 Jews were brought to Dachau, Sachsenhausen, and Buchenwald, where they were brutally treated.[3] Most of the Jews imprisoned in November 1938 were subsequently released — having been pressured into emigration.

But it was really with the start of the German war campaign in September 1939 that the most significant changes in the numbers and composition of Buchenwald's prisoners occurred. Gradually, Buchenwald became an "international" concentration camp: the numbers of Czech, Polish, French, and Soviet prisoners soon far outstripped the numbers of Germans and Austrians. If, prior to 1942, the reason for incarceration was still primarily that of "protective custody," the need for slave labor as the war wore on meant that Buchenwald soon became a vast collection and distribution point of labor resources. Buchenwald was also used to imprison Russian forced laborers working in Germany who had fled from their place of work or refused orders; they were brought to the camp in large numbers in 1942 and 1943.[4] Toward the end of the war, as the Germans retreated and dissolved camps in the occupied areas, hundreds of thousands of concentration-camp prisoners were transported back into camps within the borders of the old Reich, such as Buchenwald. By the end of September 1944, the number of prisoners in Buchenwald had already reached 84,505. Between October 1944 and April 1945, the mortality rate increased sharply. The Americans were able to liberate 21,000 prisoners;[5] but between 1937 and 1945, 56,000 had been murdered at Buchenwald by various means, such as hanging, beating, shooting, strangulation, or — by far the most common methods of murder — slave labor,[6] starvation, illness, and disease.

Those imprisoned in Buchenwald in 1937 and 1938 had a far better chance of survival than the prisoners in the camp in the final chaotic months, when disease was more rife, and death transports more frequent, than at any other time. Imprisonment in the main camp meant a chance of survival; the chance of survival in the Small Camp, or Quarantine Camp, where prisoners were first sent after their arrival at Buchenwald before being reallocated, was so slight as to make survival there something of a miracle.[7] Survival depended, too, on which work detail a prisoner was allocated to. Those sent out to work in the underground rocket factory at Mittelbau-Dora, for instance, suffered greatly and had little prospect of survival.[8] By contrast, those who worked within the camp itself, perhaps in the building detail under Kapo Robert Siewert[9] — of whom more below — had a greater chance of survival.

Fig. 1: Buchenwald concentration camp in 1944. Courtesy of Gedenkstätte Buchenwald.

Writing of concentration camps in general, sociologist Wolfgang Sofsky has claimed that they were characterized by a hierarchized prisoner society set up at the whim of the SS, with the criminal prisoners ("Greens") and political prisoners ("Reds") at the top of the system of classification, the western, northern, and southern Europeans in the middle, the Poles and Russians near the bottom, and the Gypsies and Jews at the bottom.[10] Buchenwald was in many ways exemplary of this system. Given that the Reich German nationals held at Buchenwald were generally either "Reds" or "Greens," their chances of survival were better, not least because the SS preferred to use these prisoner groups for the camp's self-administration, but also because they shared a common language with the SS, and, in the case of the politicals, a common history beyond all ideological differences. The Poles and the Soviets, regarded by the SS as subhuman, were much worse off by comparison. 8,000 Soviet POWs brought to Buchenwald in 1942, for instance, were killed in a manner that seems appallingly treacherous and heinous even by SS standards. When they stood with their backs to the wall, having been told they were to have their height measured, a hidden marksman on the other side of the wall murdered them one after one with a single, precisely-aimed bullet to the neck.[11]

But it was the Jewish and the Sinti and Roma prisoners who had to endure the worst fate. The prisoner category "Jew" was introduced by the SS in Buchenwald at the end of April 1938, after the first arrests in the course of the "Work-shy Reich" (ASR) action. In June 1938, 1,256 Jews were incarcerated in Buchenwald as ASR inmates; a further 2,400 Jews were then brought to Buchenwald from Dachau in September 1938, while 12,000 were incarcerated in Buchenwald following the notorious anti-Jewish pogroms in November 1938. The SS concentrated the Jews in a so-called "Sonderlager" (special camp), where they were exposed to mal-treatment, theft, and murder. By December 1938, when most of them were released, 233 Jews had lost their lives in the "Sonderlager."[12] After the beginning of the war, Buchenwald camp became a trap for many Jews: only 114 Jewish prisoners were released between 1940 and 1942. Jews were continually subject to gratuitous, often murderous violence. Thus SS Sturmbahnführer Hüttig had 30 Jewish prisoners aged between twenty and twenty-five summarily shot after Georg Elser's failed attempt on Hitler's life in November 1939.[13] The first systematic acts of annihilation of large numbers of Buchenwald Jews took place within the framework of the euthanasia program: of the 187 prisoners selected for transport to the gas chamber at Pirna-Sonnenstein in the early summer of 1941, about half were Jews.[14] In March 1942, after the planned deportation of Jews to Lublin had been delayed as a result of the Wannsee Conference, about 400 Jews in Buchenwald adjudged "sick" or "not capable of work" by SS doctor Waldemar Hoven were sent to the notorious euthanasia center at Bernburg, where they were murdered by means of gas.[15] Following Hitler's decision in October 1942 to make Germany "free of Jews" ("judenfrei"), the SS transported most of Buchenwald's remaining 650 Jews to Auschwitz.[16] Two hundred thirty-four remained. Until mid-1944, the number of Jewish prisoners at Buchenwald was very low.

It increased rapidly again with the transportation into the camp of Hungarian Jews in May 1944. Many Jews were either sent on to murder-ous satellite camps, or, if deemed unfit to work, transported to Auschwitz, where they were murdered. In late 1944, too, some 1,800 Sinti and Roma prisoners were brought from Auschwitz to Buchenwald, from where they were transported to murderous work details in Mittelbau-Dora. By the beginning of 1945, following the dissolution of Auschwitz and Groß-Rosen, the Jews represented the largest group of prisoners at Buchenwald. The SS set about evacuating them in large numbers in April 1945. As Elie Wiesel writes in his record of a childhood spent in Auschwitz and Buchenwald: "every day, several thousand prisoners went through the camp gate and never came back."[17]

Self-Administration and Resistance at Buchenwald

For all the frequency of death and the omnipresence of suffering, it is impor-tant to be aware that the experience of Buchenwald could nevertheless take different forms depending on when a prisoner was in Buchenwald, how long he was there, where he was located within the camp, which work detail or satellite-camp he was allocated to, his nationality, and the color of the triangle that he, like every prisoner, had to wear on his chest and on his right leg. Given that the Nazis favored the "Greens" and the "Reds" for the camp's internal administration, and given too that both the criminal and political prisoners realized that their survival depended on securing an influence within this administration, there ensued a protracted power struggle between these very different sets of prisoners. Particularly the criminal, but to a degree also the political prisoners — the latter dominated by the communists — did not shrink from using murderous methods in this struggle.[18] In the end, the communists gained the upper hand, but only because the SS allowed them to. As the war wore on and Buchenwald became important as a producer of armaments-related materials, the SS needed good organization within the camp, something the communist prisoners, of whose networks throughout Buchenwald the SS was well aware, could be relied on to provide (in contrast to the unorganized "Greens").[19] The SS's wish to exploit the communists' organizational abilities increased as more and more SS men were called up for active duty at the front. For all this, the tensions between the "Reds" and the "Greens" never ceased, nor did the SS wish them to. The SS fomented these internal divisions on the assumption that the more the prisoners were fighting amongst themselves, the more they would strive to collaborate and curry favor with the SS. *Divide et impera* — the principle according to which, in the view of structuralist historians, Hitler ruled during the Third Reich — was also a process whose effectiveness could be observed at Buchenwald.

The communists had to succeed in gaining control of the main centers of the camp's self-administration in order to improve their chances of survival. The Storage Building (*Kammergebäude*), where personal effects and prisoners' clothes were stored and where the politicals Heinz Bausch and then Willi Bleicher (of whom more later) were Kapos, was an important area to administer, not least because survival was more often than not a question of what prisoners wore. The Work Statistics Office, where the communist Willi Seifert was Kapo as of 1941, was a vital area of self-administration, because the prisoners working there could directly influence transport and work-detail lists — a matter of life and death. Equally important was the sick bay, where the communist Ernst Busse was Kapo as of 1942.[20] Allocation to the sick bay and access to medication could prove life-saving. In securing a modicum of influence over clothes, food, medication, work details, and transports, the communists were, in the first instance, concerned with protecting their own cadres. Inevitably, then, that influence was used to reinforce the social classification identified by Sofsky, because it resulted in the privileging of political prisoners, who received more food and better clothes than the majority, and were allocated to blocks and work details where chances of survival were relatively good.[21]

Several former prisoners have testified to the fact that, at Buchenwald, the communists exercised considerable control and possessed privileges. Walter Poller describes how, when he came to Buchenwald in December 1938, he was immediately given privileged treatment, along with other newly arrived politicals. This included being issued with better-quality boots than the non-political prisoners, and being asked if he needed a pullover or woolen jacket — which, according to Poller, were offered only to political prisoners. It also included allocation to a better block, in the main camp.[22] Poller is not the only prisoner to distinguish between an "elite" among Buchenwald's prisoners and a "large, strangely uniform, depersonalized mass."[23] The Jewish-Hungarian prisoner Eugene Heimler, for instance, who was imprisoned in Buchenwald in 1939 and then again in late summer 1944, described the communists as "the *élite* of society at Buchenwald."[24] The Austrian prisoner Benedikt Kautsky — a Buchenwald prisoner from 1938 until October 1942, then again as of January 1945 — also refers to the communist camp functionaries as "an aristocracy" that watched over its own privileges and asserted its position vis-à-vis other prisoners as well as the SS.[25]

From prisoner testimonies, it becomes clear that the acute desire to protect these privileges — reinforced by traditional communist prejudices — often meant discriminating quite actively against other prisoners. Heimler makes the point that the non-communist political prisoners "were under suspicion by the communists," particularly the social democrats and the "political prisoners who came from the Church."[26] Benedikt Kautsky also mentions the communists' suspiciousness, indeed, hatred, of the social democrats — a hatred that could take a "quite practical" expression in the allocation to particular work details and in the way social democrats were treated in the sick bay.[27] Kautksy further refers to the notorious "Lagerfeme" (kangaroo courts), a term used to describe the summary justice dispensed by communists against primarily the criminal prisoners.[28] A British Buchenwald prisoner, Christopher Burney, roundly accuses the German communists of unscrupulously manipulating transport lists to dispose of potential opposition to their power. More often than not, Burney writes, it was the French prisoners who were disposed of in this way, not least because the German communists feared their independence of mind.[29] Interesting too, in Kautsky's account, is his reference to divisions among the communist prisoners themselves. Thus "dissident" communists, including Trotskyists and trade unionists, were treated even worse by the communists than were social democrats.[30]

Udo Dietmar, a political prisoner liberated at Buchenwald, found the fact that there were also communists among those Kapos and functionaries who maltreated and even murdered prisoners "all the more reprehensible because they claimed to possess a political creed and yet were basically indulging in sheer egoism."[31] Yet it would be unjust to claim that all the communists were merely acting in their own interests. Kautsky makes a distinction between the "narrow-minded and fanatical" majority of communist prisoners and the more cultivated and humane group of communists who "in effect ran the camp from 1939 up till liberation."[32] He gives credit to this group for its "extraordinary services" to the prisoners of Buchenwald.

There can be little doubt that the replacement of the "Greens" by the "Reds" as the dominant force in the prisoner self-administration in 1942 led to a general improvement in camp conditions; the setting up in 1942 of a Camp Police, manned by political prisoners, to keep order in the camp reduced the number of SS men and, accordingly, the degree of brutality endured by prisoners.[33] Although quite prepared to dispose of those they regarded as opponents, ideological deviants, spies, or simply as undesirables, the communists were not as corrupt, nor as routinely and gratuitously brutal, as the "Greens." And for all their commitment to protecting their own, the communists, or at least some of them, genuinely did try to alleviate conditions for non-politicals, including, in some cases, Jews. Nor should it be overlooked that acts of solidarity toward those with whom the communists felt an obvious affinity, such as the Soviet POWs who arrived at Buchenwald in October 1941, also required great courage and involved enormous risks.[34]

There can be little doubt, either, that the well-organized communists did seek to use their organization to conspire against the SS. From the very moment Buchenwald was set up, the German communist prisoners began to build up KPD regional cells within the camp. Their organizational rigor, initially, was a key weapon in the power struggle with the much more disparate "Greens."[35] With the outbreak of war, Buchenwald became much more international in its prisoner composition, and soon the communists among the French, Belgian, Dutch, Polish, and Soviet prisoners, for instance, began to form their own national Party groups. In the summer of 1943, the illegal International Camp Committee (ILK) was formed, bringing together representatives of Buchenwald's different national communist constituencies, and making possible a coordinated policy for communist survival and self-assertion.[36] It was flanked by an International Military Organization (IMO) entrusted with preparing for a possible rebellion against the SS, and much effort was invested in planning for this and gathering weapons.[37] While members of the ILK itself were not involved directly in the camp's self-administrative structures, preferring to operate in the background, the committee nevertheless played a significant part in influencing the way these functioned. Certain work details, such as the Prisoner Fire Brigade (set up in February 1943) and the Sanitary

Troop (from late 1943), had access to areas of the camp outside the prisoner compound and were therefore used by the ILK to gather intelligence about the SS.[38] In addition to planning a possible uprising, the ILK did much to orchestrate various forms of sabotage in the weapons-related industries at Buchenwald, such as the Gustloff Works. Indeed, because stealing material from the SS factories was a prerequisite for secretly building and stockpiling weapons, sabotage and preparations for the uprising went hand in hand.[39]

In the first days of April, as the Americans approached, the ILK debated whether or not the time was right for an uprising but decided against it, as the SS was still much too powerful. What the resistance organization was able to do in those days, however, was delay the mass evacuations of Jews from Buchenwald. Elie Wiesel writes that "the camp resistance organization had decided not to abandon the Jews and was going to prevent their being liquidated."[40] A young Jewish prisoner, Thomas Geve, wrote in his memoir that, following the evacuation order, his Block Elder was issued with a parcel of red, black, and green triangles, and within minutes "the boys from the ghettos" became "Poles and Russians — political, unsocial, or criminal ones." As Geve puts it, "the ones that were said to be on the alert without us ever noticing them had acted."[41] Ultimately, the SS did force through the evacuation of tens of thousands of Jews, but many lives were nevertheless saved by the delays. Of course it was in the interests of the resistance organization to delay the evacuation of Jews, because as long as they had not been evacuated, the SS would not evacuate the other prisoners, and certainly not the politicals, upon whom they depended for assisting with those very evacuations that the ILK simultaneously tried to hinder. Nevertheless, the attempts by the resistance to help Jews in the final days were its greatest deed to date.

And they remained its greatest deed, for the uprising planned over many years never transpired. While it is difficult to be entirely sure of the precise circumstances of the liberation of the camp — not least because of diverging accounts — it is clear that "American troops ended SS rule" at Buchenwald, as Buchenwald Memorial Site puts it in a volume published in 1999.[42] It was about 1:00 P.M. on 11 April 1945 that American tanks became embroiled in an exchange of fire with Buchenwald's SS troops before taking control of the SS area of the camp by about 2:30 P.M. By this time, most of the SS men had fled. Before the Americans reached the prisoner area of the camp, however, prisoners were able to open the gates of Buchenwald — albeit quite peacefully by electronic means.[43] There is little doubt, too, that prisoners cut their way through the barbed-wire around the camp, that they took control of the entire prisoner area, and that they were able to capture some individual SS men. But there was no fighting with the SS, which had fled, and therefore no uprising. In the afternoon of 11 April, the ILK had indeed distributed weapons that it had been hoarding.

However, the intention behind this distribution was to enable prisoners to *defend* the camp in the event of an attempt by the SS to liquidate the camp's prisoners before taking to its heels.[44] After taking control of the camp on 11 April — the Americans having moved on toward Weimar — the Camp Committee issued a proclamation in which it claimed that Buchenwald's "international antifascists" had helped to liberate the camp, a claim which, while still exaggerated, approximates to the reality.[45] On 1 May 1945, however, the ILK then sent a letter to American unions claiming that the Americans had assisted in the camp's self-liberation.[46] Within a few weeks, a process of inflation of the ILK's role in liberation on the one hand and of minimalization of the American role on the other set in, a process that would be intensified in the GDR. In fact in Apitz's novel *Naked among Wolves* (*Nackt unter Wölfen*, 1958), the Americans play no direct part in the liberation.[47]

In sum, Kautsky's claim that "nothing is more wrong than providing a simple, black-and-white representation of camp life and the prisoners" certainly applies to the communists.[48] They fought for and enjoyed privileges, yet to a degree ameliorated conditions in the camp for all prisoners; they arguably collaborated with the SS to a degree by taking over camp functionary positions, yet at the same time did seek to build up a resistance network and plan an uprising; they did not shrink from wielding what power they had to protect their own and dispose of those by whom they felt threatened, yet were capable of using that power to protect others who did not belong to their cadres. It was only by securing privileges for themselves that the communists, or at least many of them, were able to keep relatively well-fed while others wasted away in their thousands in the Small Camp. Equally, only by keeping themselves relatively strong and by setting up camp networks were they able to organize the resistance they staged. Communist group egoism, then, was tempered by moments and acts of genuine selflessness and altruism. In later years, Buchenwald's communists referred particularly to the assistance they provided to children as evidence of this altruism. What were conditions like for children at Buchenwald? Were they helped, and, if so, how?

Children at Buchenwald

At Buchenwald, age was a decisive factor for chances of survival. The SS could be particularly brutal toward children, regarding them as "useless eaters." Older people and very young prisoners were less resistant to illness and disease. Many of those incarcerated at Buchenwald were certainly young; indeed, in December 1944 more than a third of the camp's inmates were under twenty years of age.[49] According to the German communist prisoner Robert Siewert, the age of the 200 youngest Polish prisoners on one transport to the camp ranged between eight and sixteen.[50] Children under the age of sixteen were frequently transported back out of Buchenwald to Auschwitz or Bergen-Belsen, where they were murdered. Some of Buchenwald's children entered the camp without a single relative to protect them. While whole families or parts of families were often transported together to Buchenwald, family members would be separated at Buchenwald station — a process that caused indescribable distress. According to the prisoner Robert Leibbrand, children were usually sent on together with their mothers, but in some cases, fathers or older brothers managed to take their young sons or younger brothers into Buchenwald with them.[51] In other cases, however, children entered the camp alone, or at least without a father. Thus in Block 8 in Buchenwald, there were children between the years of seven and twelve whose fathers, Soviet Party and state functionaries, or "partisans," had been murdered by the Nazis.[52]

Clearly, children were at particularly great risk from the SS because they were often unable to protect themselves; they lacked the resources of experience available to adults. Hunger, disease, and psychological distress rendered them weak and susceptible. Another danger, arguably as great as any of these, was posed by some of the adult prisoners themselves. Former Buchenwald prisoner Eugen Kogon, author of *The SS State*, writes that a number of prisoners, in their sexual need, turned first to homosexuality, and then, when young boys arrived in the camp, to pederasty. This was a development typical of many camps.[53] Although there was, as of 1943, a brothel in Buchenwald, it did not, according to Kogon, put a stop to the abuse of boys. Youngsters were tempted into providing sexual services by the offer of food, or they were coerced and threatened into providing them. Such youngsters, known as "doll-boys" ("Puppenjungen"), soon became morally utterly corrupt, and Kogon even describes those Polish boys among them who had been in the camp since 1939 as hooligans and "rowdies."[54] But whatever the horror of pederasty, the ultimate threat was always the SS. One of the most distressing events remembered by Buchenwald prisoners was the deportation of children to Auschwitz in September 1944. The German prisoner Karl Barthel recounts how one morning he saw about 200 Gypsy children taking part in gymnastic exercises under the guidance of an older prisoner. The sound of cheerful children's voices made Barthel ask himself, very briefly, if fascism might be developing in a more humane direction. A few weeks later, he writes, he got an answer to his question when he found out that "today, 200 Gypsy and Jewish children were sent to Auschwitz . . . to be murdered in the gas chambers."[55] We will return to this particular transport later.

Eugen Kogon explicitly lauds those prisoners who unselfishly endeavored to protect children.[56] Indeed while some older prisoners could represent a threat, others, recognizing the various dangers facing the children, were their only hope of survival. There can be no doubt that German communist prisoners played a key part in helping children. It was Albert Kuntz, head of the illegal KPD group in Buchenwald, who had the idea of setting up a so-called "Masons' School" in 1939. Robert Siewert, another communist prisoner and Kapo of the bricklaying detail, thereupon persuaded SS camp leader Schobert to allow Polish youngsters to be trained as bricklayers, arguing that he needed more laborers if the SS's various construction plans were to be realized on schedule. In this way, the lives of hundreds of young Poles were saved.[57] The establishment of this bricklaying school led, in 1940, to the setting up by the German communists of the "School for Poles." The SS accepted this idea too because bricklaying work, clearly, would proceed more efficiently if the Poles had been taught German beforehand. In time, the school became independent of the bricklaying work detail. Polish boys were not just taught German by their Polish prisoner teachers but were introduced to the tradition of Polish patriotism and to the ideals of antifascism.[58]

Perhaps the greatest of all communist achievements for children was the setting up of a children's block, Block 8. It was the communist Camp Elder Erich Reschke who, along with other prisoners, persuaded the SS in 1943 that it would be sensible to gather the younger children inmates under one roof and teach them a sense of "German order and discipline," rather than leave them unsupervised. Behind this idea was a strategy: namely to prevent the children from wandering around the camp in search of food, entering other blocks or rummaging through rubbish-bins in the process, things that were strictly forbidden. In Block 8, moreover, the children were out of sight from the SS and could be afforded a degree of protection against transportation;[59] they were also shielded from allocation to work details. The Austrian communist Franz Leitner and, later, the German communist Wilhelm Hammann acted as Block Elders, but Soviet, Polish and Czech antifascists were also involved in looking after the children, aged between 7 and 12.[60] The number of children in the block rose from 150 in 1943 to 400 in 1944; most of them were Jewish.[61] According to the Australian Buchenwald prisoner Colin Burgess, "the inmates were even able to set up an education system using the talents of Soviet and German teachers, in particular a gentile Czech who not only taught the children but was appointed to supervise their barracks."[62] The ILK was also involved in setting up another children's block, Block 66, in the Small Camp in 1945. Elie Wiesel and Israel Lau, who later became Chief Rabbi of Israel, were in Block 66. All in all, many of the children who survived Buchenwald did so either in Block 8 or Block 66. In the words of Erich Fein and Karl Flanner: "the rescue of 328 children and adolescents in Block 8 as well as of those in Block 66 in the Small Camp was the crowning achievement of the solidarity practiced at Buchenwald."[63]

Non-communist prisoners such as Colin Burgess,[64] as well as some of the surviving children themselves, have confirmed the role played by the illegal resistance organization.[65] One should nevertheless approach the communists' own accounts with at least some caution. The Jewish prisoner Jack Werber, a Pole, who worked in Siewert's bricklaying detail, has related how he was approached by German-Jewish communist Emil Carlebach in 1942 and asked to join the international underground. He claims there were about ten Polish Jews in the underground, including Gustav Schiller, later to become deputy Block Elder of Block 66.[66] Occasionally, according to Werber, the Polish Jews in the resistance met as a group. This was the case, for instance, following the arrival of 2,000 Polish Jews, mainly from Skarzysko, in August 1944. The Polish-Jewish underground cell resolved to rescue the 700 children in this transport. "The general non-Jewish underground," Werber maintains, "did not oppose our efforts to save the children, although for them this wasn't a priority like saving politicals or those with military skills." His next sentences are even more revealing: "some even thought the children shouldn't be in Buchenwald because it was so difficult to hide them. I guess you could say that we arrived at a gentleman's agreement that they wouldn't mix into our business and that we would continue to cooperate with the underground on general problems" (96). Werber implies that the communist underground leaders needed some persuasion before they accepted the rescue plan drawn up by the Polish-Jewish cell (96). It was thanks to Werber and two other Jews, Jack Handelsmann and Elek Greenbaum, that 150 Jewish children survived Buchenwald in Block 23 — a block rarely if ever mentioned in communist accounts of Buchenwald. Werber does, though, stress the supportive role of one particular German communist, namely Karl Siegmeyer, Block Elder of Block 23 (98).

Werber also recalls that the Jewish children in Block 23 received an education in Jewish culture, and there were choir performances, plays, and poetry readings. The Jewish-Polish cell was nevertheless clearly anxious "that if we emphasised Jewish culture too much, the Underground would see it as anticommunist and against the spirit of international brotherhood" (102). In Block 8, according to Werber, the Russian communists' education program for Soviet children was dictated by communist dogma. But in Block 8 — another fact never mentioned in communist memories of Buchenwald — there were also a number of Jewish children from the Carpathians who received education in Jewish religion and Zionism. There were, then, different groups of children in Block 8 receiving different forms of education depending on their religion, background, and origin (102).

Prior to the removal of most Jews from Buchenwald in 1942, German Jews had played a significant role in the communist prisoners' struggle against the "Green" prisoners for control of functionary positions.[67] Werber's account demonstrates that there was also some (limited) cooperation between Jews and non-Jews in the underground at a later stage in Buchenwald's history. He in no way denies the success of the largely non-Jewish communist underground in saving children's lives, and where he points out that this endeavor had its limits, he does not criticize the underground for having different priorities, such as a commitment first and foremost to protecting fellow-communists. Nevertheless, the most powerful impression that emerges from Werber's story is that Jewish empathy with the fate of Jewish children could often be a stronger protective trigger precisely because it was less inhibited by such priorities. What Werber's account also shows is that, for all the ILK's leadership in matters of resistance, antifascist activities at Buchenwald could be variously inflected and motivated. Not only were disagreements in resistance policy possible, but there were also contrasting programs of education, not to mention different visions of the future, underpinned by political beliefs, ranging from various forms of Zionism, national communism, and far-left social democracy to Soviet-style international communism. In accounts of resistance at Buchenwald published in communist East Germany, while there were nods toward the achievements of communist national groups within the antifascist front, little mention is made of Jewish resistance. And rarely was it suggested that Jews or non-communist groupings took the initiative for saving lives.

The Testimony of Zacharias Zweig

The general discussion of communist conduct at Buchenwald in the first part of this chapter has demonstrated that it was ambivalent — in contrast to the view promulgated in the GDR that the communists were heroes, a view that informs Apitz's *Naked among Wolves*. The references to Werber's account, moreover, show that resistance at Buchenwald was a more complex phenomenon than post-1945 communist versions allow, versions, analyzed later in this book, that routinely marginalize Jewish involvement. The context has thus been established for the introduction into this wider narrative of the story of the rescue of Stefan Jerzy Zweig — for it too demonstrates how ambivalent communist conduct could be and the importance of Jewish resistance. The remainder of this book will illustrate how these ambivalences and the role of Stefan's father, Zacharias, in saving his son were hidden from view in an attempt to glorify the role of the communists — and how they were again hidden from view, with different emphases, after 1990.

What follows below, in summarized form and focusing above all on Buchenwald, is the testimony provided by the Polish-Jewish lawyer Dr. Zacharias Zweig to Yad Vashem in 1961 of his and his family's experiences under Nazism. Yad Vashem, Israel's official memorial and museum dedicated to the victims of the Holocaust, had approached Zweig in the late 1950s and requested this account from him.[68] Excerpts from Zweig's testimony — translated from the original Polish into German — were published for the first time in the East German newspaper *Berliner Zeitung am*

Abend in 1964. A complete translation of the testimony did not appear until 1987, when it was published as a book by the West German publishing house dipa.[69] The account, in the 1987 book, runs to about 100 pages. Zacharias's testimony concentrates largely on the story of the remarkable rescue of his young son, Stefan. I offer it here as the closest approximation to the "real" story of Zweig's rescue as we are likely to get. The gap of some sixteen years between the end of the war and Zweig's testimony will, of course, have resulted in some lapses and impreciseness of memory. But generally I see no reason not to accept Zacharias's account in its broad outline, not least because of its open confrontation with the complexities and ambiguities — as well as the harsh realities — of life, death, and survival in the Nazi camps. Nevertheless, Zacharias's testimony does raise certain questions that it leaves unanswered, or answers only incompletely, and these questions will be explored in the final section of this chapter.

Cracow and Biezanow

Stefan was born in the Cracow ghetto on 28 January 1941 to Zacharias and Helena Zweig; he had an eight-year-old sister at the time of his birth. Barely a month later, in order to avoid deportation, the Zweig family took refuge in the village of Wola Duchacka. Here, Zacharias successfully applied for the right for his family to live in the Cracow ghetto, where he worked for the Jewish Community. In 1942, the Nazis began the construction of the Plaszow concentration and labor camp; deportation to this camp would certainly have meant the separation of parents from their children, and Zacharias resolved to keep his family together by staying in the ghetto. Even when sent to do forced labor in the Biczanow concentration camp in late 1942, Zacharias was able to maintain contact with Helena and his children. On 13 March 1943, the Nazis began the third major "resettlement" action within the Cracow ghetto. Fearing this would lead to the liquidation of their families in Cracow, a number of Biezanow inmates, including Zacharias, pleaded with Biezanow's SS camp commandant, Müller, for help. Müller, after negotiations with Amon Goeth, who was in charge of the resettlement action, secured permission to enter the ghetto and gather together the families of the inmates of Biezanow and "Julag-I." But before they could leave the ghetto, all these family members were subjected to an inspection. To hide Stefan from the probing eyes of Goeth, Helena hid him in a sack. But she was unable to conceal her daughter. Goeth tore Sylwia away from her mother and ordered her to return to the ghetto. But Sylwia secretly rejoined the group at the gate before it left the ghetto and was taken to "Julag-I" with the other members of her family. From there, Zacharias and his family were sent to Biezanow. Here, new problems arose. Stefan was too young to be allowed to stay there.

Zacharias first hid Stefan, then persuaded a Pole living in the area to take Stefan in. Some Poles reported such illicit acts of concealment to the Nazis, and several times Poles who had taken Stefan in became afraid and abandoned him, leaving him lying next to the camp wire.

This psychological torture went on for some months, until the Nazis scaled down their search for hidden children and it became conceivable to bring young children into Biezanow. When Zacharias had run out of money to pay for Stefan's protection, he took him back into the camp. Still, the SS did occasionally go through the prisoners' blocks looking for children. Sometimes this happened without warning, and on such occasions Stefan had to be hidden. Thus a member of the work detail responsible for removing the garbage sometimes hid Stefan among the refuse and took him out of the camp to safety; Zacharias later would retrieve him from the garbage dump. On other occasions, Zacharias entrusted Stefan to the care of a Polish woman outside the camp — to whom he once had to throw the child over the barbed-wire fence. By now, Stefan was so well-trained that his father only needed to mention the word "SS" for him to remain completely silent.

Plaszow and Skarzysko Kamienna

On 15 November 1943, the Biezanow camp was dissolved, and the Zweig family was forced to move to Plaszow, where men and women were separated: Sylwia went with her mother, Stefan with Zacharias. The SS began to take children and older prisoners out of the camp and shoot them on a nearby hill. When a doctor in the camp by the name of Gross came to the women's barracks to register the remaining children, Helena, who knew Gross personally and knew too that he had certain obligations toward the Zweigs,[70] begged him to try to prevent any further separation of mothers from their children. Gross subsequently promised Zacharias he would do what he could to help all threatened children. He informed Zacharias of an impending transport to Skarzysko Kamienna, assuring him that Skarzysko was a labor camp, not a death camp. Zacharias resolved to join the transport with his family. Gross promised to ensure that nothing would happen to the children as they left the camp — thereby returning a favor to Zacharias, who had helped him in the past. On his way out of Plaszow, Zacharias once more hid Stefan, this time wrapping him inside his raincoat, which he then carried over his shoulder; as he passed Amon Goeth and other SS men at the gates of the camp, he struck a posture of deference. Gross followed the transport at a distance, and appeared to keep his word. Zacharias and his family arrived safely in Skarzysko.

In the new camp, the family's psychological condition improved because there was no longer any need to fight for their children's survival; in Skarzysko, children were allowed. On the other hand, sanitary conditions

Fig. 2: The entrance to Buchenwald (Gatehouse) from inside the camp. Courtesy of Gedenkstätte Buchenwald.

were appalling and hunger was severe. Both at Skarzysko and at Biezanow, children, including the two-year-old Stefan, were forced, along with the adult prisoners, to witness the hanging of Jews by the SS. Toward the end of July 1944, the Nazis decided to evacuate Skarzysko. One group of prisoners was, initially, to remain behind, one to be transported to the Czestochowa camp, and one to HASAG's armaments' factories in Germany. Zweig's family was allocated to the transport destined for Germany. In the course of the selection procedures for these transports, Zacharias tried unsuccessfully to save the life of a Jewish doctor; an SS man, Kuenemann, whipped him across the head for his pains. For the transport, the men and women were separated; Helena took Sylwia with her, while Zacharias accompanied Stefan, hiding him from the eyes of the SS before climbing into the freight car. Conditions during the transport were appalling. No light shone in, no water or food was provided, there were no toilets, and there was hardly room to lie down. The journey lasted four or five days. When the train stopped in Leipzig, Zacharias and others, through slits in the sides of the freight car, could see the women making their way to a building on which were written the letters "HASAG Leipzig Schönewald." In this way, Helena and Sylwia were separated from Zacharias and Stefan. They were never to be reunited. On 28 September 1944, as Zacharias later discovered, Helena and Sylwia were transported to Auschwitz, where they were murdered.

Arrival in Buchenwald

On 5 August 1944, the train carrying the male prisoners arrived in Buchenwald station. Zacharias had wanted to conceal Stefan in his rucksack, but was too exhausted. As news spread among the SS men that there was a child in the transport, they were astonished. News of the arrival of a child spread quickly. The prisoners wanted to see the child, and they watched it from behind the barbed wire. As Zacharias and Stefan walked toward the entrance to Buchenwald camp, Zacharias saw SS men waiting there for them, while female SS members ran out to take a look at the child. As the transport of some 2000 prisoners began to pass through the gates, it was met by the concentration camp "police," which consisted of prisoners.[71] Suddenly, Zacharias was stopped by an SS commanding officer of some sort, perhaps the head of the camp, or his deputy. This SS man asked him why he had come with a child. Zacharias answered that it had been legal in Skarzysko for children to stay with their parents; and anyhow, Stefan was registered on the transport list. In his fear he lied, claiming that the German SS authorities in the Cracow district had given permission for Stefan to remain in the camp. Zacharias begged to be allowed to keep the child with him, saying he would feed him from his own food rations, and that being able to look after the child would raise his work morale. The SS man let him through — with Stefan — saying: "Good, the child can stay here with you." But it transpired that he was not telling the truth, and it was not thanks to him that Stefan survived.

When Zacharias and Stefan reached the buildings where new arrivals had to undress for disinfection, a group of men in civilian clothing with red triangles sewn upon their shirts received them. They were obviously expecting Zacharias and Stefan, as their registration cards had already been prepared. They took them aside and one of them — who, so Zacharias later discovered, was called Willi Bleicher and was the head of the international illegal organization of prisoners at Buchenwald[72] — asked Zacharias what his profession was. At first Zacharias hesitated with his answer, until Bleicher had assured him he, Bleicher, was also a prisoner. Another prisoner, a Pole, addressed Zacharias in Polish and told him that the prisoners had taken a decision with regard to Stefan. The elite among the Czech, German, and Polish political prisoners, largely communists — surprised that so young a child should have arrived at Buchenwald, and despite the fact that this child was Jewish — had decided to rescue the child. If, so they declared, the life of this child had so far been saved, then it is a symbol of resistance against Hitler and deserves to be rescued. Only at this juncture

Fig. 3: Block 40 after liberation. The banner reads: "Block of German antifascists." Courtesy of Gedenkstätte Buchenwald.

did Zacharias resolve to trust these prisoners and divulge details of his profession and experiences.

The members of the illegal organization told Zacharias that, while he would have to go to the Small Camp for quarantine, they would take care of the child, as it would not be safe in the Small Camp. They also told him that the organization had decided to keep the child in the German political prisoners' block; for even if the SS were to kill all the other prisoners, there was a possibility that the German prisoners would survive. At first, Stefan was so distressed at the separation that those looking after him brought him to see his father the very next day. But Stefan continued to cry at night, disturbing the prisoners, and so Willi Bleicher decided it would be for the best if Zacharias *not* visit his child for one or two weeks until it got used to its new surroundings. Zacharias understood Bleicher; on the other hand he suffered, because he felt they were taking his son away from him. Three weeks were to pass before Zacharias — who in the meantime had been moved away from the appalling conditions in the Small Camp into Block 22 in the main camp — was able to visit Stefan again. When he did, he got quite a surprise. Stefan was wearing fine clothes that had been specially made for him by prisoners in the workshops, as well as specially crafted new shoes. He even had his own toys, made for him by prisoners working in the Gustloff armaments' factory; and he had his own

Fig. 4: Roll-call at Buchenwald. Courtesy of Gedenkstätte Buchenwald.

special table and chair. Zacharias was delighted for his son, but at the same time he felt a pain, because Stefan had somehow become estranged. "What are you doing here?" Stefan asked him. Zacharias told him he was his father. "Ha, ha, that's a good one, well sit down then and play with me."[73] Despite his misgivings, Zacharias was pleased that his son's condition had improved, and that he was in good hands. This gave him the strength to fight for his life despite great hunger.

Every Sunday he continued to visit his son, who soon had a complete set of winter and summer clothes, his own bed in a little curtained-off area in the German block, and silk bedclothes.[74] By way of protection, Stefan was guarded by the dog Senta, which would have torn to shreds anyone who dared to approach the child.[75] Sometimes, when Zacharias visited Stefan, the leaders of the political prisoners were holding secret meetings in the block, and he was able to listen in on discussions. Once, he was invited to relate his experiences in Poland, which he did in detail, describing the ghettos and resettlement actions, and the murder of Jews. Some of the prisoners responded by criticizing the Jews for not having defended themselves, claiming that they, the German prisoners, would break open the gates of Buchenwald. Zacharias told them he doubted they would have acted differently from the Jews.

Stefan was counted among the regular prisoners. Whenever there was a general roll call, prisoners from all blocks, even that in which the German political prisoners lived, had to appear. During these roll calls, Stefan sat on the shoulders of one of the political prisoners, who then had to try, as all inmates did, to keep in step with the rhythm of march music played by the camp orchestra — this in full view of the SS. There were, in fact, some SS men who treated Stefan like the child that he was, forgetting he was a Jew: they would bring candies and fruit, and play with him. Other SS men, however, looked askance at Stefan. One day an SS officer told Bleicher he wanted boots for his own son similar to those Stefan was wearing. Bleicher refused, saying that only if the SS man's son were himself a prisoner would he get what Stefan had. This incident almost cost Zacharias's son his life.

The Threat of Deportation

In September 1944, Stefan fell ill. The political prisoners decided to keep the illness a secret from the SS and not take the child to the sick bay. Bleicher and his friends did not want to entrust anyone other than a Jewish doctor with the treatment of the child, and they used their influence to procure one, a Dutchman. During his illness, Stefan received a special diet and was given medication. The doctor wrote out prescriptions, and the medication was obtained from private chemists in nearby Weimar — by SS men, who, however, may not have known who the medicine was for. Stefan's fever began to recede after three weeks. But he never completely recovered his health: he later suffered from lung complaints.

In late September 1944, Bleicher informed Zacharias that the SS were insisting Stefan be placed on a deportation list. Bleicher had tried to deceive the SS into thinking Stefan was no longer in Buchenwald, but the SS knew this to be untrue; a day or two before, Bleicher had been spotted driving with Stefan through the camp in a car.[76] Bleicher blamed himself for being partly responsible for this situation: was the SS man for whose son he had refused to have boots made perhaps behind the deportation order? An attempt to persuade an SS doctor to take in Stefan as a patient failed. Zacharias was to hand Stefan over to the SS at 10:00 A.M. on 2 October 1944.[77] By 9 o'clock that morning, when it seemed all hope was lost, Zacharias asked to be allowed to join his son on the transport; but the transport was for children only, and permission was denied. Bleicher, becoming increasingly desperate, began to cry and shout. With only half an hour or even less to spare, a solution was found. Zacharias took Stefan to the sick bay. He was met at the door by an SS doctor and a prisoner medic who took Stefan into the typhus department. There he was given an injection that caused an immediate fever, making him unfit to travel. The transport left Buchenwald without Stefan; apparently two or three young Gypsies were deported.[78]

The political prisoners decided Stefan could be best protected by being moved to the Small Camp.[79] He was taken to a special room occupied by the commandant of this camp, who was also a prisoner.[80] To be nearer his son, Zacharias had himself moved to another work detail where the prisoners had to transport sand, cement, or stones on carts from the Buchenwald quarry or the station to the Small Camp.[81] He was able to visit Stefan in the labor assignment office of the Small Camp, whose German Kapo was supposedly a criminal prisoner, but in fact he had never been a criminal and was an intelligent person who worked with the illegal resistance organization. One day the SS man who oversaw the labor assignment office expressed an interest in meeting Zacharias; he asked him various questions and congratulated him on his fine son. This SS man also took Stefan for walks, even taking him out of the Small Camp when he went on inspection trips. Stefan was also spotted by the women forced by the SS to work as prostitutes in the camp brothel; they asked the SS man to introduce them to Stefan. They showed him much affection, and kept sending him candies and chocolate. Once Zacharias met the SS man who was in charge of his work detail walking hand in hand with Stefan. Stefan invited his father to join them.[82] In this embarrassing situation — Zacharias felt that the SS man would have had no objection to Zacharias accompanying him but could not have allowed this — Zacharias declined, saying he had to work.

Stefan was aware that people were hungry in the camp. Whenever Zacharias visited him, Stefan asked if he had eaten anything and offered Zacharias some of his own food. Zacharias always refused. One day, in the presence of a German member of the resistance organization, Stefan drew attention to the fact that his father was not wearing underclothes; none were provided for prisoners. This prisoner immediately had a packet of undergarments sent to Zacharias's block.

Stefan was also well aware that the Jews were considered to belong to the lower class of prisoners and that they were treated badly by the Germans. Around December 1944 or January 1945, the number of prisoner transports into Buchenwald increased dramatically as camps such as Auschwitz were evacuated. Arriving prisoners were crammed into the Small Camp. They had to sleep on the ground, and many of them froze to death. Most of the people on these transports were Poles, and when they heard there was a Polish child in the camp, they wanted to see him. When Zacharias visited Stefan one Sunday, Stefan complained that one of the prisoners had called him a Jew: "I told him that you will kill him when you come."[83] Stefan insisted that his father find this prisoner and call him to account. After going through an entire block of 2,000 prisoners, Stefan recognized the prisoner. Zacharias explained why he had come looking for him. The Pole apologized. He said that when he had discovered there was a Polish child in the camp who spoke German, he had simply asked quite spontaneously if he was a Jew.[84]

Evacuation and Liberation

On 4 April 1945, all work in and around Buchenwald came to a halt. Persistent rumors about possible evacuations circulated. Zacharias had experienced these before in Poland, and so he called upon his acquaintances in the camp, including well-known German prisoners, to resist; Zacharias knew that the prisoners had access to hidden weapons. On 6 or 7 April, the SS called on all Jews to gather at the roll-call area. Zacharias decided to hide in the block in which Stefan was living. But then he found out that all Jews had returned to their blocks, and so he returned to his. At 10 o'clock that same evening, the SS ordered a general roll call for 8 o'clock the following morning. Initially, Zacharias, who had spent the night in the Small Camp with Stefan, had not intended to turn up, but the Block Elder of Stefan's block insisted that he return to the main camp. When the SS, at roll call in the main camp, ordered the inmates of the two Jewish blocks 22 and 23 to turn to the left, the prisoners fled.[85] They hid in various blocks; Zacharias hid in the Czech block. The SS went from block to block and brought out the Jews. Increasingly, they used violence, and so Zacharias came out of hiding, fearing he would be maltreated if he did not. All routes around the camp were guarded by SS men: there was no escape. The Jewish prisoners were frogmarched to a gate that opened onto a yard leading to the armaments factory. Zacharias realized that once this gate had closed behind him he would never be able to save his son. And so, as the SS began to herd the prisoners through the gate, he had the presence of mind to pretend he was on duty;[86] the SS man at the gate let him go back into the camp. With the help of two Belgian members of the Camp Police,[87] Zacharias managed to slip away and gain access to the Small Camp, where he was reunited with Stefan.

On 10 April 1945, the SS ordered the evacuation of the Small Camp. SS men stood outside its fence, while the Camp Police lined the inmates up for evacuation. In desperation, Zacharias hid himself and Stefan in the latrines for some twenty minutes. When all had gone quiet, Zacharias made his way with Stefan to the office run by the inmate camp leaders[88] — all young German prisoners — in the hope that they would be satisfied that he had succeeded in rescuing the child. Instead, some of them shouted at him that they did not want to be held responsible, and insisted he return to the main camp. Zacharias refused, taking refuge with Stefan in the now empty horse stables of the Small Camp, and in a shed.[89] When Zacharias saw a Czech prisoner walking by whom he knew, he told him everything, and complained about the German prisoners. In Zacharias's presence, the Czech then upbraided the German prisoners for the way they had treated Zacharias and his son.

Zacharias rested for half an hour. But when the prisoners saw the child again, they feared for their own safety and insisted Zacharias go to the

main camp.[90] Zacharias gave in. On his way there he met a German prisoner who was a member of the auxiliary police. On hearing how his
German comrades had pressed Zacharias into abandoning his attempts to
rescue the child, this prisoner went back to the Small Camp office with
Zacharias, where he launched a tirade against the German prisoners, telling
them that they should know that a decision had been made to save the
child, and that it was their duty to hide Zacharias and Stefan in one of the
German blocks in the main camp. The same German prisoner advised
Zacharias to go to one of the German blocks, Block 45, and say he had
come on his recommendation. The prisoners in Block 45 welcomed
Zacharias and Stefan.

The following morning, on 11 April 1945, the prisoners began to prepare for the expected evacuation. During the night there had been the
sound of cannon fire, and now this grew louder. At 10:30 A.M. the SS gave
an order that no prisoners were to leave their blocks. The prisoners were
unsure as to what this meant. Some thought the SS were going to flee and
did not want any witnesses; others feared the SS would set about mas-
sacring all remaining prisoners. The prisoners stayed in their blocks till
1:30 in the afternoon, all eyes focused on the camp wire. The news came
through that the SS had fled. At about 2:00 P.M. the prisoners noticed that
the guards were leaving the watchtowers and that the soldiers were also
fleeing. Then they heard the voice of a Camp Elder speaking to them over
the loudspeaker system: they were free! Zacharias and his fellow prisoners
waited in their block for the Americans to arrive. Half an hour later, they
heard the voice of an American tank-unit officer informing them that
they were free. Zacharias took Stefan in his arms, telling him that, now,
they would live. He cried with joy, and at the same time felt pain. He was
convinced that his wife and daughter would no longer be alive.

Other Memories of Zweig's Rescue

Zacharias Zweig's account tells a remarkable tale of paternal rescue in a
world of death — and of filial love, given Stefan's touching concern for his
father's welfare. Courage, presence of mind, persistence, imagination, and,
most of all, love were resources that Zacharias drew upon again and again
in his fight to save Stefan. Even when he was able to depend, as in
Buchenwald, on the assistance of others, he could never do so absolutely;
indeed, in the chaos of the final days there seems to have been a lack of
coordination within the network of communist prisoners that nearly
resulted in the struggle for Stefan's life being abandoned so shortly before
liberation. Nevertheless, there can be little doubt that communist prisoners did help to save Stefan's life on a number of occasions. In his testimony,
Zacharias suggests that it was the *leaders* of the resistance movement who

gave the initial order to hide Stefan. In fact, the initial decision to hide Stefan probably was taken by Bleicher himself, although the ILK may have become involved in protecting Stefan at a later stage, as Apitz's novel suggests. Certainly there is much evidence to support what can be inferred from Zacharias's testimony, namely that a considerable number of communist prisoners played their part in Stefan's rescue. This becomes clear from the postwar accounts of former Buchenwald prisoners; an element of self-glorification and exaggeration notwithstanding, such accounts serve to complement the testimony provided by Zacharias.

Thus Willi Bleicher, in a 1976 letter to Walter Bartel, has confirmed the part he played in Stefan's rescue. He states that, as Kapo of the Personal Property Room (*Effektenkammer*) in the Storage Building and after talking to others in his work detail, such as Heinz Bausch and Willi Pippig, he decided that Stefan should stay with the prisoners in his work detail, which had its sleeping berths in the cellar of the Disinfection Building (others in Bleicher's work detail included Hans Burkhard, Felix Müller, Paul Heilmann, and Richard Nagel). Bleicher recounts that not all prisoners in the work detail agreed with hiding the child; "there were . . . differences of opinion." He goes on to relate that it was the SS man in charge of Buchenwald's "garden," Dombeck, who, on spotting the child, reported it to his superiors, whereupon the SS ordered Stefan's deportation.[91] Robert Siewert's version of this is slightly different. According to Siewert, Domböck [*sic*] was the SS man who asked Bleicher to make his son a pair of shoes; as he did so, Juschu — as Stefan Jerzy was affectionately named — came into the room. Infuriated, Dombeck reported the child's presence. Both Bleicher's and Siewert's versions nevertheless agree that Dombeck was the culprit, and that it was the prisoner Otto Kipp who later had Stefan brought to the sick bay and given a fever-inducing injection, making him unfit for transport.[92] According to the testimony of Karl Huber, who looked after Stefan in the sick bay, SS doctor Schiedlausky caught sight of the child and ordered his removal, whereupon he was hurriedly concealed in the Tent Camp (part of the Small Camp).[93]

Here, Stefan was hidden in the stone barracks that had been built for the Camp Elder in the Small Camp, Eugen Waller, and the Camp's Block Elders.[94] Stefan slept between Alois Lohr — one of the Block Elders — and Walter Vielhauer, who recalled that during the day two Jewish prisoners from Vienna looked after Stefan. "If my memory serves me right, they were brothers and were called Katz."[95] The Czech political prisoner Jiri Zak, a member of the Transportation Protection work detail that was also housed in the stone barracks, confirms Stefan's presence there — as well as that of Walter Sonntag, a German communist who saved the lives of Jewish fellow prisoners and was honored as "Righteous among the nations" by Yad Vashem in 2004.[96] According to a report by former Buchenwald prisoner

Fig. 5: The "garden" at Buchenwald. Courtesy of Gedenkstätte Buchenwald.

Fritz Freudenberg, Stefan was often taken to his block in the main camp, which was also Zacharias's block. At this time — which was shortly before liberation — Stefan had been in the sick bay again, this time as a result of "eating candies" that he had been given by Danish police prisoners. The prisoners working in the sick bay allocated a medic to Stefan, who looked after him constantly and took him to see his father in the main camp.[97]

While there is therefore plenty of testimony to the participation of prisoners, particularly communists, in helping Stefan to survive, former prisoners are less forthcoming on the issue of what knowledge the SS had of Stefan's presence in the camp. Zacharias is quite clear on this point: Stefan entered in full view of the SS and was present at general roll calls (in which even members of the Personal Property Room work detail had to participate). As I shall point out below, Stefan and his father were registered prisoners, which certainly confirms that the SS knew of their presence. Even the 1960 Buchenwald documentation printed in the GDR acknowledges — in a footnote — that Stefan was in the Camp "legally," having the prisoner number 67509.[98] Willi Bleicher, moreover, wrote in one letter that "the Camp SS were shocked at the arrival of this child and it caused them considerable embarrassment." He thus confirms Zacharias's account that the SS knew of the boy when he entered Buchenwald. In the same letter, Bleicher states that he persuaded the SS man in charge of the Personal Property Room to allow him and the other prisoners working there to take Stefan under their wing — on the grounds that there would be a danger of Stefan being pampered were he to be accommodated elsewhere in the camp.[99] Bleicher is the only former prisoner apart from Zacharias, to my knowledge, to have testified to the need to collaborate with the SS. Too many others, especially those who (unlike Bleicher) lived in the GDR, were seemingly reluctant to recall this necessity.

Nor did former prisoners care to reflect on the complexity of motives behind the decision of the political prisoners to "take responsibility" for Stefan. Given that the child was registered as a prisoner, and that he was tolerated in Bleicher's work detail, it would be possible, at least, to assume that the motives for keeping him there were to "adopt" him, rather than protect him. On the other hand, the political prisoners told Zacharias that they were concerned that Stefan would not be safe in the Small Camp — where he would first have to go for quarantine purposes.[100] Bleicher later claimed that he was even concerned that the child would not be safe in the main camp.[101] In the end, motives of adoption and protection were mixed. Certainly, Bleicher and other prisoners proceeded to fuss somewhat excessively over Stefan, getting a little bed made for him and feeding him with food donated by Norwegian prisoners from their Red Cross parcels.[102] That political prisoners should want to lavish such attention on a small child is not reprehensible. Many German communists had been in Buchenwald more or less since its founding. Stefan seemed, as Bruno Apitz put it, like a sudden "gust of wind" from the outside world from which Apitz and many others had become estranged.[103] For all those communist prisoners who had a part in making shoes, toys, or items of clothing for Stefan, and especially for those who cared directly for him, he was a surrogate son, a living, fragile reminder of birth, motherhood, and fatherhood. Nevertheless, it is clear from Zacharias's testimony that the decision by Bleicher and others to take responsibility for Stefan resulted, from the father's perspective, in a painful separation of father and son, indeed almost in an act of dispossession. In seeking to overcome their own estrangement from family life, the political prisoners estranged Stefan from the only member of his family still with him — his father, the man who had proved himself more than capable of looking after his son in the bestial conditions of camp life.

Whatever the motives behind taking in Stefan, and whatever the degree of collaboration with individual SS men, there can be no doubt that it *was* necessary to hide Stefan at certain points; after all, being a registered prisoner and benefiting from the connivance of an SS man were hardly long-term guarantees of safety. That he had to be hidden frequently is evident from his father's testimony. Nor should one imagine that such concealment was in any way pleasant. A young prisoner of Block 66 in the Small Camp at the time, Thomas Geve, tells of seeing "a boy of four, the saddest character I had ever come across, abnormal in his physique, behavior and speech. He staggered along like some weak, wounded animal and uttered cries in German-Polish-Yiddish gibberish. 'That,' I was told, 'is the kid they keep hiding from the SS.' "[104] This may, or not may have been Stefan — even if it wasn't, the traumatic effects of concealment will, in his case, surely have not been dissimilar. One should also be wary of assuming that, when not being concealed, Stefan was necessarily in the best of hands. The pampering by the prisoners (and even, on occasion, by the SS, according to Zacharias) to which he was exposed was not always good for him. Fritz Freudenberg, after relating that Juschu had to be treated in the sick bay following the consumption of candies, writes: "the boy, who was very spoilt by all the attention he was getting from the adult prisoners . . . ran around like a wild thing."[105] Could this "wild thing" be the same boy as the "weak, wounded animal" described by Geve? It is quite possible. Stefan had much attention lavished on him and clearly at certain times enjoyed a degree of freedom; at other times, his life was threatened and he had to be hidden away. For a young child, this alternation between being at the center of attention one moment, only to be whisked away and concealed the next, will have been bewildering, to say the least.

Whatever the psychological stress caused by protection, it ensured Stefan's survival. The testimony by Zacharias is at its most problematic, perhaps, when he indicates that "two or three" young Gypsies were sent on the transport to Auschwitz for which his son was originally destined.[106] Zacharias does not explicitly state that they were sent as replacements for Stefan and other prisoners who, like Stefan, had been struck from the transport list. But the context of his comment invites this interpretation; otherwise there seems little point in mentioning their addition to the list. And indeed archive material provided to Buchenwald Archive in the late 1980s indicates that the names of Stefan and of *eleven* other prisoners were removed from a list of deportees who were to be sent to Auschwitz on 25 September 1944.[107] Each of these has been replaced by the name of another prisoner who was then deported instead.[108] According to the Buchenwald historian Harry Stein, eleven of the prisoners elided from the list were Sinti or Roma;[109] Stefan was the only Jew. The twelve replacements were Sinti and Roma prisoners, rendering the transport an exclusively Gypsy transport of 200 children and youths. Stefan's name was replaced by that of the Gypsy boy Willy Blum, who was sixteen. Stein considers it likely that these changes resulted from a decision taken by the SS doctor August Bender, but then adds: "that this decision did not result from the personal initiative of the SS doctor, but rather was forced through by political functionaries is highly probable."[110]

In other words, Stefan and eleven other, in this case Sinti or Roma, prisoners were fortunate enough to benefit from the protection of political prisoners, who were capable of wielding enough influence to bring about changes to the transport list. I pointed out earlier in the chapter that such influence was brought to bear particularly by communist prisoners in an attempt to protect their cadres. But it was also exercised in other cases.

Thus the Czech communist prisoner Jiri Zak, by his own account, not only saved Stefan's life in the Small Camp by aborting yet another attempt to deport him, claiming to the SS that the boy was suffering from diphtheria; he also intervened on behalf of Zacharias. Stefan's father "visited me at least 10 times, because again and again his name was on a transport list." Zak then writes that he struck Zacharias's name from the list, but he reveals nothing of any names placed on these lists to replace that of Zacharias.[111] Robert Siewert confirms Zak's role in striking out Zacharias's name — and Juschu's — "repeatedly."[112] Zacharias does not mention any such appeals to Zak in his Yad Vashem testimony. However, in an earlier, two-page account of Stefan's rescue included in the International Camp Committee's 1945 report on Buchenwald, he claims that the "German prisoner functionaries not only kept my son in the camp, they also protected me again and again from transports to other camps or external work details."[113] Zacharias does not state explicitly here that his name was removed from lists, but it is likely that protection from transport meant precisely this. The problematic issue of such alterations and of "name-swapping" ("Opfertausch") was never overtly discussed in the GDR. It was not until the 1990s, as we shall in chapter 6, that it became central to the discussion of Buchenwald's past.

So far, I have presented testimony from prisoners that appears to fill in gaps in Zacharias's account, or provide more detail on individual aspects of Stefan's protection. There are few variations of note between testimonies, or between these and Zacharias's account. Differences consist rather in what prisoners choose to leave out. In the final analysis, Zacharias's account is the most open and comprehensive. But we need to at least be aware of one significant variation, to be found in the testimonies of two prisoners who worked in the Personal Property Room, Heinz Bausch and Felix Müller.

Heinz Bausch recalls how, in 1942 or 1943, a Polish prisoner arrived at the camp with a rucksack in which he had been carrying his two-year-old son. The prisoners in the Personal Property Room work detail resolved to hide the child, making a small bed for him behind a pile of cases. The child remained hidden in the building until Buchenwald was liberated. Bausch claimed that the child was called Josef Streich.[114] Felix Müller remembers a similar incident where a Jewish prisoner entered the Personal Property Room with a three-year-old boy hidden under his raincoat. The work detail prisoners resolved to protect the child; they made a small bed for him, which they hid behind the bunks in their dormitory. Müller also recalls that the father used to visit the child there. Müller calls this prisoner Stefan Zweig. But he admits in an addendum to his testimony that he had learnt of this name *after* liberation; what name the boy had actually had in Buchenwald he was unable to remember.[115] To confuse matters more, Bausch — who produced his testimony in 1957 (Müller's dates from

Fig. 6: The Storage Building ("Kammergebäude") at Buchenwald. Courtesy of Gedenkstätte Buchenwald.

1960) — claimed later that he may, in retrospect, have mixed up the names of Streich and Zweig.[116]

The accounts by Bausch and Müller, if they describe another child or children rather than Stefan, may indicate that more than one child found refuge in the Personal Property Room, or elsewhere in the Storage Building. Second, they may indicate that some children — in contrast to Stefan Zweig — were brought into the camp without the knowledge of the SS. Third, they may provide evidence that Apitz conflated the stories of several protected children in his novel. While he certainly based it mainly on the story of Zweig, he seems to have borrowed the idea that a child was brought into the camp secretly from other stories. This was certainly the opinion of the first edition of the Buchenwald documentation published in the GDR in 1960.[117] There are even grounds for asking whether Stefan Zweig was housed in the Storage Building *at all*, or at least only there, in the initial weeks. According to Buchenwald's arrivals registration list ("Zugangsbuch"), Block 40 is the block to which Stefan was to be assigned.[118] Given that he would in all probability have been safe there, as it was a main camp block of political prisoners, why would Bleicher have felt the need to accommodate the child in the cellar of the Disinfection Building?[119] Or was Stefan in both Block 40 and the Storage Building, depending on circumstances? Zacharias's testimony makes reference both to the Storage Building and a "political prisoners' block" as the place

Fig. 7: The Personal Property Room ("Effektenkammer") inside the Storage Building. Courtesy of Gedenkstätte Buchenwald.

where Stefan was kept.[120] The matter cannot be resolved. What is clear is that the fact that Stefan was a registered prisoner, whereas Stefan Cyliak in Apitz's novel was not, led to some embarrassment when Stefan Zweig came to the GDR in 1964, as we shall see in chapter 5.

Conclusion

The point of this first chapter has been, first of all, to provide a balanced overview of the history of communist resistance at Buchenwald, and particularly of the role of the resistance in saving the lives of children at the camp. The mixture of selfishness and altruism that characterized communist resistance is then brought out by Zacharias's testimony; while he is explicit in his praise of the help provided to his son, his testimony implies again and again that the communists, in a sense, took Stefan away from him and then almost abandoned the child in the final days. That survival was dependent on a degree of collaboration with the SS, and on SS connivance in certain situations, is a point made in my overview of resistance, and it is something that can be inferred both from Zacharias's testimony and from the comments of Willi Bleicher. The prisoners' testimonies, by means of which I have sought to amplify Zacharias's testimony, not only provide evidence of the many prisoners involved in Stefan's protection, but also hint at the problematic fate of a child whose life seemed at one moment to be cocooned in almost excessive love and care, only to be hanging by a thread the next. Stefan's life at Buchenwald, then, was a complex one. What the rest of this book seeks to demonstrate is that, in the GDR, the complexity of communist resistance, and within that context the complexity of Stefan's protection, was largely obscured by a much more streamlined version of events. In the GDR version, the communist prisoners were heroic rescuers of generally flawless morality who never sought the indulgence of the SS, nor ever acted only in their own interests. This version also played down the role of Zacharias in rescuing his son, and indeed made of Stefan's survival a manifestation of the achievements of communist resistance. While it was particularly Apitz's novel *Naked among Wolves* that was responsible for disseminating this version, it predated Apitz's novel, which was in a sense its literary monumentalization. First, then, we must turn our attention to the postwar history of Buchenwald — and the place of the memory of Stefan Jerzy Zweig in that history prior to the publication of *Naked among Wolves*.

Notes

[1] This is the title of one of the earliest memoirs written by a survivor of Buchenwald: Konrad Finkelmeier, *Die braune Apokalypse* (Weimar: Thüringer Volksverlag, 1947).

[2] These prisoners, who had to wear green triangles in the camp (hence "Greens"), were officially called "Befristete Vorbeugungshäftlinge" — best translated as "prisoners taken into preventive custody for a limited period." The acronym "BV" used to refer to these prisoners was reinterpreted to stand for "Berufsverbrecher," professional criminals.

[3] See, for instance, Hanns Berke, *Buchenwald: Eine Erinnerung an Mörder* (Salzburg: Ried-Verlag, 1946), 61–68.

[4] See Gedenkstätte Buchenwald, ed., *Konzentrationslager Buchenwald, 1937–1945: Begleitband zur ständigen historischen Ausstellung* (Göttingen: Wallstein, 1999), 156–57.

[5] For a reasonably fair account of the liberation of the camp, see Gedenkstätte Buchenwald, *Konzentrationslager Buchenwald*, 232–36.

[6] The boundary between slave labor and plain murder was a fluid one. Countless numbers of Buchenwald prisoners died either from their physical exertions or through the savagery of the SS in Buchenwald's notorious quarry. See, for instance, M. Zahnwetzer, *KZ Buchenwald: Ein Erlebnisbericht* (Kassel-Sandershausen: Verlag M. Zahnwetzer, 1946), 9–11; also Berke, *Buchenwald: Eine Erinnerung an Mörder*, 45–49.

[7] On the Small Camp, see Gedenkstätte Buchenwald, *Konzentrationslager Buchenwald*, 224–25.

[8] For an account of conditions in Dora, see Nationale Mahn- und Gedenkstätte Buchenwald/Lagergemeinschaft Buchenwald-Dora beim Komitee der Antifaschistischen Widerstandskämpfer der DDR, eds., *Buchenwald: Mahnung und Verpflichtung, Dokumente und Berichte*, 4th ed. (Berlin: VEB Deutscher Verlag der Wissenschaften, 1983), 270–80.

[9] Kapos were prisoners placed in charge of their fellow inmates, typically as supervisors of work details.

[10] Wolfgang Sofsky, *Die Ordnung des Terrors: Das Konzentrationslager* (Frankfurt am Main: Fischer, 1997), 140.

[11] See, for instance, *Konzentrationslager Buchenwald: Geschildert von Buchenwalder Häftlingen* (Vienna: Stern-Verlag, 1945), 10.

[12] Ulrich Peters, *"Wer die Hoffnung verliert, hat alles verloren": Kommunistischer Widerstand in Buchenwald* (Cologne: PapyRossa, 2003), 238.

[13] Thüringisches Hauptstaatsarchiv Weimar, NS 4 Bu, Erinnerungsberichte, Akten-Nr. 44: "Liste über mir bekannte S.A. — SS-Führer und Kapos."

[14] Peters, *"Wer die Hoffnung verliert,"* 254.

[15] Harry Stein, *Juden in Buchenwald, 1937–1942* (Weimar: Weimardruck, 1992), 117.

[16] See Gedenkstätte Buchenwald, *Konzentrationslager Buchenwald*, 129.

[17] Elie Wiesel, *Night* (London: Penguin, 1981), 124–25.

[18] Such methods included both direct murder and the denunciation of prisoners to the SS, which had equally fatal effects. The most notorious example of communist machinations in this respect is their role in the death of Friedrich Wolff. Wolff was in fact not a "Green" prisoner, but a Jewish reserve officer who was "Aryanized" by the SS for his "services" to Buchenwald's administration and made Camp Elder in 1942. Wolff, it seems, began to bestow favors on a group of Jewish Poles from Auschwitz and proved resistant to the influence of the communist prisoners. As a result, the "Reds" denounced him to the SS, claiming he was planning an uprising together with Polish prisoners. He was subsequently sent to Peenemünde, where he died. The SS also set about murdering a number of Poles. For more detail on this, see Lutz Niethammer, ed., *Der "gesäuberte" Antifaschismus; Die SED und die roten Kapos von Buchenwald* (Berlin: Akademie Verlag, 1994), 46–47.

[19] For a discussion of Buchenwald's change in function and what this meant for the camp's self-administration, see Peters, *"Wer die Hoffnung verliert,"* 207–9.

[20] For more detail on communist influence in these areas of the camp, see Internationales Buchenwald-Komitee/Komitee der Antifaschistischen Widerstandskämpfer in der Deutschen Demokratischen Republik, eds., *Buchenwald: Mahnung und Verpflichtung, Dokumente und Berichte* (Berlin: Kongress-Verlag, 1960), 335–54.

[21] For Sofsky's account of the importance of certain work details for influencing chances of survival, see Sofsky, *Die Ordnung des Terrors*, 152–68.

[22] Walter Poller, *Arztschreiber in Buchenwald* (Hanover: Verlag für Literatur und Zeitgeschehen, 1960), 32.

[23] Poller, *Arztschreiber in Buchenwald*, 31.

[24] Eugene Heimler, *Night of the Mist* (London: Love & Malcomson, 1961), 94.

[25] Benedikt Kautsky, *Teufel und Verdammte* (Vienna: Verlag der Wiener Volksbuchhandlung, 1947), 156.

[26] Kautsky, *Teufel und Verdammte*, 95.

[27] Kautsky, *Teufel und Verdammte*, 156, 157.

[28] Kautsky, *Teufel und Verdammte*, 236.

[29] Christopher Burney, *The Dungeon Democracy* (New York: Duell, Sloan and Pearce, 1946), 39–40.

[30] Burney, *The Dungeon Democracy*, 156.

[31] Udo Dietmar, *"Häftling . . . X . . . in der Hölle auf Erden"* (Weimar: Thüringer Volksverlag, 1946), 119.

[32] Kautsky, *Teufel und Verdammte*, 157.

[33] This is a point conceded even by the post-unification Buchenwald Memorial Site, which is otherwise critical of the communists in the camp. See Gedenkstätte Buchenwald, *Konzentrationslager Buchenwald*, 147.

[34] See Internationales Buchenwald-Komitee/Komitee der Antifaschistischen Widerstandskämpfer, *Buchenwald: Mahnung und Verpflichtung*, 411–19.

[35] For an albeit biased account of the way the KPD fought it out with the "Greens," see Günter Kühn and Wolfgang Weber, *Stärker als die Wölfe* (Berlin: Militärverlag der Deutschen Demokratischen Republik: 1976), 69–82.

[36] For GDR accounts of the ILK's origins and activities, see Kühn and Weber, *Stärker als die Wölfe*, 93–102, and Internationales Buchenwald-Komitee/ Komitee der Antifaschistischen Widerstandskämpfer, *Buchenwald: Mahnung und Verpflichtung*, 394–97. For an overview of the KPD's structures in the camp, see Peters, *"Wer die Hoffnung verliert,"* 118–38.

[37] See Peters, *"Wer die Hoffnung verliert,"* 370–90.

[38] See Kühn and Weber, *Stärker als die Wölfe*, 142–46.

[39] See *KL Bu: Konzentrationslager Buchenwald: Bericht des internationalen Buchenwaldkomitees Buchenwald* (Weimar: Thüringer Volksverlag, 1945), 142–48.

[40] Elie Wiesel, *Night*, 124–25.

[41] Thomas Geve, *Youth in Chains* (Jerusalem: Rubin Mass, 1958), 212.

[42] Gedenkstätte Buchenwald, *Konzentrationslager Buchenwald*, 232.

[43] It was the prisoners Otto Roth and Fritz Freudenberg who succeeded in opening the gates. For their accounts of this, see Gedenkstätte Buchenwald, *Konzentrationslager Buchenwald*, 232–34. For more detail, see Freudenberg's exchange of letters with Max Mayr, published in Manfred Overesch, *Buchenwald und die DDR oder die Suche nach Selbstlegitimation* (Göttingen: Vandenhoeck & Ruprecht, 1995), 76–81. The GDR — belatedly — did come to acknowledge that the gates had been opened peacefully, but then the official story was that the communist Arthur Ullrich had switched off the electricity, and that the gate was opened by a locksmith. Despite this acknowledgement, the idea that the gates had been

"stormed" by the prisoners was never really abandoned. See Nationale Mahn- und Gedenkstätte Buchenwald/Lagergemeinschaft Buchenwald-Dora, *Buchenwald: Mahnung und Verpflichtung*, 615.

44 See Alfred Bunzol, *Erlebnisse eines politischen Gefangenen im Konzentrationslager Buchenwald* (Weimar: Thüringer Volksverlag, 1946), 44–45. See also W. A. Beckert, *Die Wahrheit über das Konzentrationslager Buchenwald* (Weimar: Rudolf Borkmann, 1946), 15. Beckert also claims that, while the resistance organization did storm the fences as soon as the first tanks were sighted, not a single shot was fired because the SS had already fled.

45 Stiftung Archiv der Parteien und Massenorganisationen im Bundesarchiv (henceforth SAPMO-BArch), DY55/V 278/2/23: "Achtung! Hier spricht Buchenwald!" Buchenwald, 11 April 1945.

46 SAPMO-BArch, DY55/V 278/2/23: Letter from the "Internationales Lagerkomitee Camp Buchenwald bei Weimar" to the "Gewerkschaftsorganisation in den USA," 1 May 1945.

47 Claims made in the GDR that the Americans did not enter the prisoner area of the camp until 13 April are false. One Jewish prisoner, S. B. Unsdorfer, describes how the first US armored car drove into the camp on 11 April: "we rushed towards it, kissing, patting, and stroking its bullet-proof body, and when the first man, an officer, thrust his steel-helmeted head out of the turret, he was pulled out by the mass of men and . . . hailed by the Buchenwald prisoners as the symbol of their freedom and victory" (S. B. Unsdorfer, *The Yellow Star* [New York and London: Thomas Yoseloff, 1961], 195).

48 Kautsky, *Teufel und Verdammte*, 237.

49 Gedenkstätte Buchenwald, *Konzentrationslager Buchenwald, 1937–1945*, 155.

50 Internationales Buchenwald-Komitee/Komitee der Antifaschistischen Widerstandskämpfer, *Buchenwald: Mahnung und Verpflichtung*, 376–78.

51 Robert Leibbrand, *Buchenwald: Ein Tatsachenbericht zur Geschichte der deutschen Widerstandsbewegung* (Stuttgart: Europa-Verlag, 1946), 44.

52 Internationales Buchenwald-Komitee/Komitee der Antifaschistischen Widerstandskämpfer, *Buchenwald: Mahnung und Verpflichtung*, 380–81.

53 See, for instance, Jakob Boulanger's memory of "Puppenjungen" in Mauthausen, recounted in Michael Tschesno-Hell, *Eine Ziffer über dem Herzen: Erlebnisbericht aus zwölf Jahren Haft von Jakob Boulanger* (Berlin: Volk & Welt, 1957), 116–17.

54 Eugen Kogon, *Der SS-Staat: Das System der deutschen Konzentrationslager* (Munich: Heyne, 2001), 288.

55 Karl Barthel, *Die Welt ohne Erbarmen* (Rudolstadt: Greifenverlag zu Rudolstadt, 1946), 136.

56 Kogon, *Der SS-Staat*, 288.

57 For an account of the "Maurerschule," see Heinz Albertus, *Verbrechen an Kindern und Jugendlichen im KZ Buchenwald und der Kampf der illegalen antifaschistischen Widerstandsorganisation um ihre Rettung*, 5th ed. (Weimar:

Druckhaus Weimar, 1989), 28–31; and Emil Carlebach, Paul Grünewald, Hellmuth Röder, Willy Schmidt and Walter Vielhauer, *Buchenwald: Ein Konzentrationslager* (Berlin: Dietz, 1986), 86. See also Siewert's report in Internationales Buchenwald-Komitee/Komitee der Antifaschistischen Widerstandskämpfer, *Buchenwald: Mahnung und Verpflichtung*, 376–78.

[58] For an account of the "Polenschule," see Albertus, *Verbrechen an Kindern und Jugendlichen*, 31–35.

[59] See Albertus, *Verbrechen an Kindern und Jugendlichen*, 36.

[60] See Albertus, *Verbrechen an Kindern und Jugendlichen*, 38.

[61] See Erich Fein and Karl Flanner, *Rot-Weiss-Rot in Buchenwald* (Vienna and Zurich: Europaverlag, 1987), 182. See also Peters, *"Wer die Hoffnung verliert,"* 75–78.

[62] Colin Burgess, *Destination: Buchenwald* (Kenthurst, Australia: Kangaroo Press, 1995), 111.

[63] Fein and Flanner, *Rot-Weiss-Rot in Buchenwald*, 182.

[64] Burgess, *Destination: Buchenwald*, 110–11.

[65] See, for instance, Thomas Geve, *Youth in Chains*, 212.

[66] Jack Werber with William B. Helmreich, *Saving Children: Diary of a Buchenwald Survivor and Rescuer* (New Brunswick and London: Transaction Publishers, 1996), 76. Further references to this work will be given in the text using page numbers alone.

[67] Peters, *"Wer die Hoffnung verliert,"* 238–60.

[68] Zacharias Zweig and Stefan Zweig, *Tränen allein genügen nicht* (Vienna: Eigenverlag, 2005); here, 379.

[69] Berthold Scheller, ed. (in cooperation with Stefan Jerzy Zweig), *"Mein Vater, was machst du hier . . . ?" Zwischen Buchenwald und Auschwitz: Der Bericht des Zacharias Zweig* (Frankfurt am Main: dipa, 1987).

[70] According to the longer version of Zacharias's report published in 2005 (see Epilogue), Dr. Gross — a Jew — was indebted to Zacharias because Zacharias had offered him legal advice earlier in the war. See Zweig and Zweig, *Tränen allein genügen nicht*, 68.

[71] This is a reference to the so-called "Lagerschutz," or camp protection force, a work detail composed of prisoners whose duty it was to keep order within the camp, and who usually accompanied new arrivals into the camp.

[72] Willi Bleicher was Kapo in the "Effektenkammer," where the prisoners' personal effects were kept. Whereas he was in the resistance at Buchenwald, he was never a member of the ILK. Zacharias took him to be more important than he actually was.

[73] Scheller, *"Mein Vater, was machst du hier . . . ?"* 46.

[74] In the version of Zacharias's report published in 2005, the word "silk bedclothes" has been replaced with "bedlinen made from material used for flags" (see Zweig and Zweig, *Tränen allein genügen nicht*, 60).

[75] When the Personal Property Room became full, the prisoners had no alternative but to store sacks of clothing and personal effects outside the building. "Senta" was an SS dog "lent" to the prisoners by the SS for the purpose of guarding these sacks

against theft. See Eugen Ochs, *Ein Arbeiter im Widerstand* (Stuttgart: Editions cordelier, 1984), 80–81.

[76] Stefan Zweig, in an interview of 29 March 2004, explained to me that he believed his father to have meant not a car but a van or small lorry. One of Bleicher's duties as Personal Property Room Kapo, according to Stefan Zweig, was to transport blankets and clothing to satellite camps of Buchenwald. See also Zweig and Zweig, *Tränen allein genügen nicht*, 68.

[77] According to Stefan Zweig, Zacharias realized after he had lodged his testimony with Yad Vashem that he had made mistakes with some of the dates. In the version of his testimony published in 2005, this date of 2 October, for instance, now appears as 25 September (see Zweig and Zweig, *Tränen allein genügen nicht*, 70).

[78] In other words, Stefan was declared too ill to travel and so was saved from deportation.

[79] Stefan was actually brought to the so-called tent camp ("Zeltlager"), which was part of the Small Camp. The tents were replaced by primitive wooden barracks in the winter of 1944/45. Stefan was fortunate in the sense that he was hidden in the Small Camp's only stone barracks, in which the Camp Elder lived together with the Block Elders. See Albertus, *Verbrechen an Kindern und Jugendlichen*, 55.

[80] This is a very confusing claim. Zacharias presumably means the "Lagerältester" or "Camp Elder" a function exercised in both the Small and main camps by prisoners. The commandant was an SS position. The Camp Elder of the Small Camp was Eugen Waller. See Hermann G. Abmayr, *Wir brauchen kein Denkmal: Willi Bleicher; Der Arbeiterführer und seine Erben* (Tübingen and Stuttgart: Silberburg-Verlag, 1992), 20.

[81] The work detail in question was one of Buchenwald's hardest. Twelve prisoners, functioning as "horses," had to pull heavily loaded carts over rough terrain and up and down slopes. Zacharias had a slightly lighter burden at the back of the cart, but will still have suffered enormously.

[82] According to Hermann G. Abmayr, this SS man was a student from Württemberg who had been compelled to serve in the SS. See Abmayr, *Wir brauchen kein Denkmal*, 19. According to the later version of Zacharias's report (see epilogue), he was a former student from Heidelberg (see Zweig and Zweig, *Tränen allein genügen nicht*, 76). If this was so, he will have had a low rank in the SS and cannot have been the same SS man, referred to a few lines earlier, who oversaw the labor assignment office of the Small Camp.

[83] Scheller, *"Mein Vater, was machst du hier . . . ?"* 73.

[84] I have included this passage because it indicates that Stefan's identity as a Jew was unclear to him. What obviously was clear to him was the hierarchical structure that existed among Buchenwald's prisoners. The Jews, most of whom perished in their thousands in the Small Camp, were at the bottom of this hierarchy, while the political prisoners, notably the Germans, were at the top. Stefan identified with the latter. Hence he felt insulted when called a Jew. According to the Soviet prisoner Juri Sapunow, the word "Jew" at Buchenwald was also used to characterize a physical condition that was even worse than that of those prisoners called "living corpses." Stefan's reaction may also be explicable as an angry denial of any sugges-

tion that he might be about to die or be murdered. For Sapunow's comments on the Small Camp, see Juri Sapunow, "Die Getreuen der Heimat," in *Kampf hinter Stacheldraht*, ed. M. Wilenski and N. Kjung (Moscow: Staatlicher Verlag für die Veröffentlichung politischer Literatur, 1960), 39–59. (A translation of this chapter can be found in the Stadtarchiv Weimar, 74 22 75/1751.)

[85] Because they feared they were about to be evacuated, or even massacred there and then.

[86] In this way, Zacharias pretended that he did not belong to the group of evacuees, but was a member of the Camp Police or "Lagerschutz," which appeared to be helping the SS escort the prisoners to the gate.

[87] Again, this is a reference to the Camp Police composed of prisoners.

[88] It is not clear which office is being referred to here. Zacharias certainly means one of the prisoner-run offices in the Small Camp.

[89] These horse stables had been used to house prisoners, who were crammed into the makeshift sleeping berths like sardines.

[90] Zacharias probably means the same German prisoners who had ordered him to go to the main camp just a few hours earlier.

[91] Archiv der Gedenkstätte Buchenwald (henceforth BwA), Nachlaß Walter Bartel, 77: Letter from Bleicher to Bartel, 6 September 1979.

[92] See BwA, V-30/1-15: Robert Siewert, "Über Juschu und über die Kinder von Buchenwald," 31 May 1948. Willi Bleicher himself later provided another slightly different version. He separates the "boots" incident from the sighting of Stefan by Dombeck — perhaps to play down his own responsibility for bringing about the situation that led to Stefan's threatened deportation. See BwA, 5211-752: Letter from Bleicher to Karl [no surname specified], 9 April 1957.

[93] Quoted in Albertus, *Verbrechen an Kindern und Jugendlichen*, 55.

[94] See Abmayr, *"Wir brauchen kein Denkmal,"* 20.

[95] Quoted in Albertus, *Verbrechen an Kindern und Jugendlichen*, 57.

[96] See BwA, Nachlaß Walter Bartel (1904–92), Bu-Häftlinge: "Stefan Zweig: Auszug aus einem Brief von Jiri Zak (Prag) vom 17.2.1963."

[97] See BwA, 5211-752: Letter from Fritz Freudenberg to Heinz Albertus, 19 July 1984.

[98] See Internationales Buchenwald-Komitee/Komitee der Antifaschistischen Widerstandskämpfer, *Buchenwald: Mahnung und Verpflichtung*, 123.

[99] BwA, 52-6-3: Letter from Willi Bleicher to Karl [no surname specified], 9 April 1957.

[100] Scheller, *"Mein Vater, was machst du hier . . . ?"* 40.

[101] According to a 1958 letter of Bleicher's on display at the Buchenwald Memorial Site's main museum.

[102] BwA, 52-6-3: Letter from Willi Bleicher to Karl [no surname specified], 9 April 1957.

[103] Bruno Apitz, "Meine Hände: Erinnerungen an das Buchenwaldkind," *Berliner Zeitung*, 27 February 1964.

[104] Thomas Geve, *Youth in Chains*, 203.

[105] See BwA, 5211-752: Letter from Fritz Freudenberg to Heinz Albertus, 19 July 1984. The Buchenwald historian Heinz Albertus corresponded with a number of former prisoners in the 1980s when putting together a new edition of his book on children at Buchenwald. He chose, however, not to include Freudenberg's testimony, presumably because it raises questions about the wisdom of the way the prisoners treated Stefan.

[106] Scheller, *"Mein Vater, was machst du hier . . . ?"* 61.

[107] Zacharias wrongly gives the date of this transport as 2 October 1944 (see Scheller, *"Mein Vater, was machst du hier . . . ?"* 61).

[108] See BwA, 52-11-752: Stefan Jerzy Zweig, 21–23.

[109] I am grateful to Nina Gladitz for passing on this information to me, which she gleaned in an interview with Harry Stein in May 2004.

[110] See Harry Stein, " 'Nackt unter Wölfen' — literarische Fiktion und Realität einer KZ-Gesellschaft," in *Sehen, Verstehen und Verarbeiten*, ed. Thüringer Institut für Lehrerfortbildung (Saalfeld: Satz & Druck, 2000), 27–40; here, 32–33.

[111] See BwA, Nachlaß Walter Bartel, Bu-Häftlinge: "Stefan Zweig: Auszug aus einem Brief von Jiri Zak (Prag) vom 17.2.1963."

[112] See BwA, Nachlaß Walter Bartel, Bu-Häftlinge: "Robert Siewert — Schreiben vom 29.5.1964: Juschu."

[113] See *KL Bu: Konzentrationslager Buchenwald*, 43–45, here 45.

[114] See Internationales Buchenwald Komitee/Komitee der Antifaschistischen Widerstandskämpfer, *Buchenwald: Mahnung und Verpflichtung*, 381.

[115] BwA, 31/1-31/30: "Aussagen und Berichte ehemaliger Häftlinge des KZ Buchenwalds," vol. 1: Report by Felix Müller, 24 May 1960.

[116] BwA, Nachlaß Walter Bartel, Bu-Häftlinge: Letter from Heinz Bausch to Walter Bartel, 12 February 1963.

[117] Internationales Buchenwald-Komitee/Komitee der Antifaschistischen Widerstandskämpfer, *Buchenwald: Mahnung und Verpflichtung*, 123.

[118] See National Archives and Records Administration Washington (NARA), RG242, Film 5: "Zugangsbuch," 1, 2808.

[119] For an overview of the composition of blocks, see Niethammer, *Der "gesäuberte" Antifaschismus*, 521–28; here, 524.

[120] See, for example, Scheller, *"Mein Vater, was machst du hier . . . ?"* 48–50.

CHAPTER TWO

BUILDING THE BUCHENWALD MYTH

Prelude: The Buchenwald Children after Liberation

ACCORDING TO THE INTERNATIONAL CAMP COMMITTEE'S report on Buchenwald produced shortly after the war, about 900 children — 85 percent of them aged between fourteen and eighteen — were among those liberated at the camp on 11 April 1945. The vast majority of these children were Hungarian, Polish, or Czech Jews; the youngest was a three-year-old Polish child.[1] While some subsequent publications claim that this latter child was Stefan Zweig,[2] others claim it was Josef Streich.[3] Klaus Drobisch, a GDR historian, claims that Zweig was the second youngest.[4] What is certain is that a number of very young children survived. One of these was the Polish-Jewish boy Joseph Schleifstein. On arrival at Buchenwald in 1943, he was hidden by his father in a sack. His father and other inmates protected him until liberation in April 1945, by which time Joseph was four. A famous photograph of Joseph shows him sitting on the running board of a United Nations Relief and Rehabilitation Agency (UNRRA) truck.[5] Schleifstein's memories of his time at Buchenwald surfaced in the American press shortly after the release of Roberto Benigni's film *Life Is Beautiful* (*La vita è bella*, 1997).[6] The most astonishing survival tale is surely that related by an American soldier, Leo Pine, who entered Buchenwald with the 183rd Engineer Combat Batallion one or two days after liberation. Pine tells of his encounter there with a three-year-old Dutch Jew by the name of Yankala. An adult Jewish prisoner told Pine that Yankala had been *born* in Buchenwald. The baby was hidden by prisoners between floorboards and fed on potato-gruel.[7] The miraculous survival of Yankala and other children should not, however, be allowed to obscure the fact of the terrible loss of their parents. Yankala's mother was murdered by the SS after she had given birth. Elie Wiesel, who was fifteen when he was brought to Buchenwald and went on to become one of the most famous of all Holocaust survivors, was scarred for life by the loss of his parents and sister. In his memoir *Night* (1958), he provides a painful description of the death of his father from dysentery and weakness at Buchenwald. At the time, his own continued survival meant little to him: "I have nothing to say of my life during this period. It no longer mattered. After my father's death, nothing could touch me any more."[8]

When the Americans liberated Buchenwald, they were surprised to find hundreds of largely Jewish children at the camp, most of them orphans.

According to Judith Hemmendinger, the commander of the American troops was totally bewildered and sent a cable to the Oeuvre de Secours aux Enfants (OSE), a children's aid organization in Geneva. " 'Have found a thousand Jewish children in Buchenwald. Take immediate measures to evacuate them.' " Hemmendinger, a refugee working at the OSE, made efforts to obtain visas for the children. "Switzerland was prepared to take 280 children, France 480, and England 250."[9] Ninety-six orphaned children who had, even more miraculously, survived the death-camp of Bergen-Belsen, were brought to Buchenwald in a convoy of cars in June 1945. Hilde Huppert, whose account of her Holocaust experience, edited by the famous novelist Arnold Zweig, was published in the GDR in 1951, describes how the Bergen-Belsen children were evacuated to Paris by train along with over 400 Buchenwald children.[10] Once in France, many of the children spent up to two years in recovery homes at Écouis, Ambloy, and Taverny.[11] From France they then moved on to a variety of countries, notably the United States. Elie Wiesel was one of those who recuperated at Ambloy and Taverny; he later moved to the USA. Hemmendinger maintains that, immediately after liberation, most of the Buchenwald children wanted to go to Palestine; this, however, was impracticable, as Palestine "was still a British mandate that refused admission to the refugees."[12] Some of the Bergen-Belsen and Buchenwald children, including Hilde Huppert, nevertheless did manage to find their way to Palestine.

The question arises as to why the children were not returned to those countries in eastern Europe from which they originated. The OSE made considerable efforts to trace surviving members of their families, in some cases successfully. Unsurprisingly, most of these were no longer living in eastern Europe, having emigrated to countries such as Canada, the United States, or Australia.[13] In other words, the murder of members of their family in the Holocaust and the emigration of any survivors meant that there was no home in eastern Europe to which the Jewish children could be repatriated. Not that the children would have wanted to return in any case. Hemmendinger writes that "communist Russia occupied their home countries, Poland and Hungary, and the children distrusted the German communists who were also prisoners at Buchenwald."[14] Clearly, then, the children had a poor impression of communism. Moreover, returning them to eastern Europe would have exposed them to the danger of anti-Semitism; the notorious pogrom at Kielce (Poland) in July 1946 was evidence of the severity of this danger. There is little evidence, by contrast, to support GDR historian Heinz Albertus's claim that American-supported exile groups (such as the Polish exile government in London) and nationalists (such as Zionists) deliberately blocked the repatriation of Buchenwald children.[15] While children at displaced-persons camps did become caught up in Cold War repatriation politics, this did not happen in the case of Buchenwald's children.[16]

Stefan Zweig was, in one respect at least, lucky: he survived Buchenwald together with his father. Before being separated from his wife Helena in 1944, Zacharias had agreed with her that, if he survived the war, he would make his way to one of his former clients in Cracow; she was to do the same in the event of her survival.[17] Although he knew there was little chance of finding his wife and daughter alive, Zacharias still resolved to return to Poland with Stefan — despite rumours that anyone doing so would not be able to leave the country again.[18] Sadly, there was to be no reunion in Cracow; returning there brought painful certainty that Helena and Sylwia had been murdered in Auschwitz. At least the new government in Poland reinstated Zacharias in his former home and legal practice; he was even offered the post of mayor of Wroclaw (Breslau), but turned the offer down on the grounds that he was not a politician.[19] Stefan, diagnosed as having a spot on his lung, was provided with medical care and sent to a recuperation home at Odowsk near Warsaw, from which he returned home to his father in May 1946.

But hopes that Zacharias and Stefan, in contrast to most Holocaust survivors, would be able to pick up the remaining pieces of their former lives were shattered by reports of anti-Semitic pogroms in Polish towns. Zacharias remained in Poland only until two of his brothers returned from the Soviet Union in early 1946; one of these, Jakob, had served in the Red Army, while the other, Leon, had been in a Gulag near Semipalatinsk (see chapter 5). Following an invitation from a surviving relative of Helena's, the Zweigs then moved to France, the plan being to emigrate at some point to Palestine.[20] Stefan was sent to a reconvalescence home at Autrans near Grenoble. But the mountain air proved detrimental to his recovery, and he was transferred to a nursing home, run by Catholic nuns, for children infected with TBC at Menton on the Riviera near Nice, where he stayed until June 1949. Later Stefan moved to a Jewish orphanage at Castle Malmaison near Paris.[21] Zacharias reports that, following a shift to the right in 1949, foreign nationals such as himself and Stefan were finding it difficult to continue living in France, and so they boarded a ship at Marseilles (the *Negba*) bound for Haifa in the newly founded state of Israel in August 1949.[22]

For a while, at least, Israel proved a hard environment for Stefan and Zacharias. On arriving, they were taken to a primitive tent camp at Atlit near Haifa mass camp, and then to an emigrés' camp at Talpijot near Jerusalem, where Zacharias found work in the administration and in road construction.[23] Stefan remembers that in the early years of Israel's existence Holocaust survivors were often regarded as "cowards" for not having staged more resistance against Hitler. There was little scope for relating their experiences.[24] But not all was negative. Zacharias, in order to adapt quickly to his new life, succeeded in learning Hebrew in a very short space of time.[25] In late 1950, he procured a job in the Finance Office, though he continued to live at a camp near Jerusalem. Stefan at this time lived in a home in Benjamina that was run by the Welfare Ministry.[26] It was not until the summer of 1952 that Zacharias was able to move into a room in Jerusalem, where Stefan soon joined him and began to attend school. In 1956, Zacharias and Stefan moved to Tel Aviv. Following the completion of his school studies in 1959, Stefan did two and a half years of military service in the Israeli army. Between February and June 1962, after leaving the army, he attended a foundation course in mathematics and physics before beginning a degree in applied mathematics at the University of Tel Aviv. In the summer of 1963, he was successful in securing a stipend that enabled him to continue his studies in France at the Institute for Applied Polytechnology in Lyon. While Stefan remembers that he was awarded this stipend very much on his own merit, he also recalls that he was supported in his application by Pierre Sudreau, a center-left politician who was the Minister of National Education in Georges Pompidou's government at the time.[27] Sudreau, a member of the French resistance, had himself been in Buchenwald (from May 1944). Here again, as in the immediate postwar period, and as in later years, the network of former Buchenwald prisoners was to play a supportive role in Stefan Zweig's post Buchenwald life.

The Beginnings of the Myth of Buchenwald

When he began his studies at Lyon, Stefan had no idea that the story of his rescue had become common knowledge in East Germany, thanks to the success of Apitz's *Naked among Wolves* (*Nackt unter Wölfen*, 1958). Nor did the East German communist survivors of Buchenwald know what had become of Stefan; all contact had broken off after liberation following Zacharias's decision to return to Poland. The East German network of former Buchenwald prisoners only reestablished contact with Stefan when he was "discovered" by the East German newspaper *Berliner Zeitung am Abend* in 1963, of which more later in the book. Toward the end of this chapter, I will examine the pre-*Naked among Wolves* reception of the theme of the Buchenwald child in East Germany. For while before 1958 it played only a marginal role within the larger narrative of communist resistance that came to dominate the image of Buchenwald in the GDR, its presence was nevertheless not without significance. By and large, it was within the context of post-1950 developments at Buchenwald — the construction of a memorial complex on the southern slopes of the Ettersberg near Buchenwald, and the establishment of a museum at the site of the camp itself — that the theme of the child's rescue was taken up. Before turning our attention to this pre-1958 reception, then, it is important to set the scene. What role did Buchenwald's communists play in the eastern zone and in the early years of the GDR? How did they seek to take control of the representation of

Buchenwald and shape the memory of the camp in the public realm? How was this memory appropriated and used by the Socialist Unity Party (SED) as a tool in what Manfred Overesch has called the GDR's "search for self-legitimation"?[28] Only within the context of the answers to these questions will the precise function of the rescue narrative become clear.

After Buchenwald was liberated by the Americans on 11 April 1945, some German communists made their way to the western parts of occupied Germany; others stayed in what was to become, as of July 1945, Soviet-occupied Thuringia, or moved to other parts of the eastern zone. Much depended, simply, on where the prisoners had been at home before their time at Buchenwald. This was certainly the case with Willi Bleicher, the communist prisoner who had played the biggest part in protecting Stefan. After the war, Bleicher eventually returned to his native Stuttgart, leaving the Communist Party (KPD) and joining the Social Democratic Party (SPD) in 1954. In 1959, he became head of the Baden-Württemberg section of the West German trade union IG Metall (IGM).[29] Other Buchenwald prisoners such as Eugen Ochs and Ludwig Becker also became West German IGM functionaries.[30] For Bleicher, his post-1945 trade union work was a chance to realize some of the aims of the Communist Party Opposition (KPO), which, set up in Germany in the late 1920s, believed in working within existing union structures rather than pursuing the more revolutionary tactics advocated by the KPD. In fact, Bleicher, Becker, and Ochs were all former KPO men (Bleicher had joined the KPO following his expulsion from the KPD in 1929). The KPO had, arguably, diagnosed the danger Hitler posed more acutely than the KPD and had advocated cooperating with the SPD in a so-called "people's front" at a time when the KPD still regarded the SPD as "social fascists." While Bleicher was readmitted into the KPD in Buchenwald, he remained true to his KPO ideals.

Other communists involved in Stefan's rescue also settled in the west of Germany, such as Eugen Waller, who worked for the Stuttgart criminal police. But Otto Kipp, who had given Stefan Zweig a fever-inducing injection to prevent his being sent on a transport, settled in the east of Germany. Generally speaking, the communists who had played an important role in resistance at Buchenwald chose to remain in the Soviet-occupied zone, where they soon found themselves occupying important positions. Thus Ernst Busse, one of the three KPD leaders in Buchenwald, was Minister of the Interior and deputy Minister-President in postwar Thuringia until 1947, while Robert Siewert became Minister of the Interior for Saxony-Anhalt until 1950.[31] Other former Buchenwald prisoners held important posts in the postwar regions of Thuringia and Saxony-Anhalt.[32] Given the influence they were therefore capable of wielding, and given too the close networking that was to remain a feature of relations between them, Buchenwald's communists were in a strong position in the postwar period.

Of all former Buchenwald communists, it was perhaps Walter Bartel who, as personal ministerial adviser to Wilhelm Pieck, was closest to the center of power; Pieck was chairman of the SED from 1946 and, from 1949, president of the GDR. Bartel was not without influence on the mightiest man of all, Walter Ulbricht. According to historian Manfred Overesch, it was as a result of discussions with Bartel that Ulbricht instigated measures leading to the removal of the first postwar head of Thuringia's regional government, the social democrat and former Buchenwald prisoner Hermann Brill, in July 1945.[33] Bartel had been one of the most powerful figures in the KPD and the International Camp Committee (ILK) at Buchenwald. After the war, as his involvement in Brill's removal demonstrates, he was able to continue the conspiratorial tactics adopted against political opponents — not least social democrats — at Buchenwald.

But the ex-Buchenwald communists soon came to realize that they themselves were not immune from attempts to oust them from their newfound positions of influence. The first fifteen years of political life in the eastern zone and the GDR were marked by a power struggle between various individuals and groups. Often the demarcation line of this struggle ran between those communists who had spent part of the Nazi years in exile in western countries and the Americas on the one hand, and those communists who had sat out the end of the Third Reich in Moscow, such as Pieck and Ulbricht. But there were also conflicts between this latter group and the so-called "Inlandkommunisten," that is, those who had spent the period of the Third Reich in Nazi prisons or concentration camps or had managed to remain "underground." Criticism of the KPD's conduct during the war, disseminated by the SPD in the western zones in its attempts to discredit the SED following the forced union of the SPD with the KPD in the eastern zone in 1946, itself came to play a part in this struggle. Added to this was the indignant reaction in the western zones to the terrible conditions of the Special Camps set up by the Soviets largely — but not exclusively — for former Nazis in Sachsenhausen and Buchenwald in 1945 (as well as elsewhere in the eastern zone). In the west it was argued, in line with the totalitarianist theory, that the communists were no better than the Nazis they had displaced. As historical evidence of this theory, it was asserted that Buchenwald's communist prisoners had effectively shared power with the SS. Soon Buchenwald's surviving communists found themselves very much on the defensive.

Shaping Memory in Self-Defense

Indeed one could contend that they were already on the defensive shortly after liberation. In April 1945, the American Psychological Warfare Division (PWD) sent a five-man intelligence team to Buchenwald under

Lieutenant Albert Rosenberg. The team commissioned Eugen Kogon, a Catholic socialist Buchenwald survivor, to oversee the production of a collective report by former prisoners on their experiences at Buchenwald. The communist-run ILK made sure that the majority of the individual statements provided were by communist camp functionaries. In seeking to prevent criticism, the communist cadre effectively continued to act as it had during the years of imprisonment at Buchenwald, when dissenting voices within the KPD or indeed criticism from fellow prisoners outside the illegal communist organization were suppressed. In fact, throughout their lives in the eastern zone and the GDR, several of Buchenwald's communists, not least Walter Bartel, continued to live as if they were still incarcerated within its barbed-wire fence. The increasingly heroic image of communist resistance at the camp that they sought to convey was but another form of resistance, only now it was the present-day critics of their past conduct who were being resisted.

While the ILK was able to preempt criticism in Kogon's report, there was nothing former Buchenwald communists living in the eastern zone could do to prevent the Americans from holding communist Buchenwald prisoners in custody at Dachau as of late summer 1945 — either because they were to be called on as witnesses at the anticipated trial in Dachau of some of Buchenwald's SS men or because they were themselves suspected of having abused prisoners, not least in their function as Kapos. Rumours began to circulate in October 1946 that even Ernst Busse was to be tried as a war criminal at Dachau.[34] The SED seized the initiative, and on 7 October 1946 the Central Committee (ZK) set up a commission to investigate Busse's conduct at Buchenwald. While this commission exonerated Busse and indeed attested to the "outstanding achievements" of the KPD functionaries at Buchenwald, it did point out that the latter had made themselves susceptible to criticism by appearing to collaborate with the SS.[35] Hardly had word come through on 9 April 1947 that the Americans did not intend to put Buchenwald prisoners on trial after all, when Buchenwald's communists found themselves facing fresh accusations. Apparently without the ILK's knowledge, the American PWD had conducted a series of interviews after Buchenwald's liberation with some of its prisoners *before* Rosenberg's team was sent there. The resulting report by Edward Tenenbaum and Eugon Fleck found its way into the hands of American military historian Donald Robinson, who published it in the *American Mercury* in October 1946 in a version that highlighted the parts that were critical of the communists. The information service of the SPD translated this version into German and republished it at the end of April 1947, whence it found its way into West German newspapers. It was not long before it had come to the attention of the eastern zone. It conveyed the impression that the communist-dominated Camp Police at Buchenwald had been guilty of atrocities; that the communist-staffed

Work Office had wielded power over life and death in putting together transport lists; that the communists had used their positions of power within the camp administration to privilege their own kind; and that they had sought to liquidate any individuals or groups perceived as a threat to their power.[36]

Certainly Robinson was manipulating the Fleck and Tenenbaum report in the interests of the intensifying Cold War. As for social democrats in the western zones, they had an axe to grind with the Soviet zone for its elimination of the SPD.[37] In the face of such criticism, the communist ex-prisoners of Buchenwald set about reinforcing and expanding the myth of resistance. In the case of Kogon's 1945 report, the onus had been on preventing criticism; gradually, the focus shifted onto an aggressively marketed heroic self-image. Fearing the prosecution of former communists at Dachau, Walter Bartel insisted that press reporting on the Dachau trials should be given a particular slant, adding that the time had come to highlight the role of resistance groups at Buchenwald.[38] Ernst Busse, as Thuringian Minister of the Interior, then sent round an astonishing circular calling on Buchenwald's former prisoners to answer five questions, one of which was "what was your finest experience in Buchenwald," and all of which basically asked for a confirmation that political prisoners had acted with superhuman qualities.[39] The foundation of the Buchenwald Committee in April 1947 as part of the Association of Those Persecuted by the Nazi Regime (VVN) very much aided the organization of protests against the perceived defamation of Buchenwald's communists. At the first meeting of this committee in July 1947, Walter Bartel presented a list of tasks, the first of which was to continue to fight, as at Buchenwald, against "reactionary" forces at home and abroad. The striking thing about Bartel's list is that the task of supporting the process of bringing Buchenwald's SS to justice only comes second. The first priority is antiwestern agitation. The interest in the projection of an image of heroic communist resistance at Buchenwald was motivated not merely by the wish to establish a total counter-image to that presented by Robinson. At the same time this image was to symbolize the historical dimension to an ongoing struggle against fascism, now believed to be endemic in the west of Germany.[40]

The more communism at Buchenwald was criticized, the more the communists strove to depict the KPD as the source of most resistance at the camp. To be sure, the Buchenwald Committee at first appeared committed to emphasizing the entire range of antifascist resistance. Thus the statement issued by the committee on 2 January 1948 in response to Robinson's version of the Fleck/Tenenbaum report declared that this constituted an attack, not just on Buchenwald's communists, but also on the whole antifascist resistance movement within Buchenwald, to which social democrats, Christian democrats, and others without party affiliation had contributed.[41] The motives behind the statement, however, are not free of self-interest. For by implying that Robinson had attacked a politically broad-based antifascism, the communists could hope to set the western CDU and SPD against him. At the same time they could as it were hide behind the untarnished reputation of non-communist political prisoners. This end was surely served by the fact that the above-mentioned statement was also signed by non-communists such as Brill (SPD) and Werner Hilpert (CDU).

Certainly, by the late 1940s, the Buchenwald communists had lost any residual doubts they might have had as to whether they were the real heroes. On 11 April 1948, at the third anniversary commemoration of the liberation of Buchenwald in Weimar, Walter Bartel interpreted the American liberation of Buchenwald as an act of self-liberation by the prisoners organized by the ILK.[42] This was hardly a new claim; it began to take root soon after 11 April 1945. But Bartel sought to promulgate it with increasing intensity as the Cold War itself began to intensify. In doing so, he attempted simultaneously to dispossess the Americans of part of their own liberation history, to undermine their right to pass judgment on Buchenwald's communists, and to make heroes of the latter. The integration of the self-liberation topos into the existing narrative of communist resistance — one that emphasized the communists' contribution to sabotage and the protection of prisoners — gave the latter shape and direction, providing a victorious conclusion, and legitimated the self-appointed role of Buchenwald's communists as key ideological players in the struggle against the perceived renascence of fascism in what was to become West Germany. With the division of Germany in 1949, the Buchenwald Committee continued as an East German organization dedicated to the promotion of the view that Buchenwald's (German) communists had staged a hugely effective and selfless resistance at the camp.[43]

The Memorial Complex on the Ettersberg

Communist former prisoners took advantage of several media in their attempt to promote awareness of the resistance they undertook at Buchenwald: book publications; press articles; declarations; carefully stage-managed acts of commemoration; and, last but not least, memorials. Yet initial endeavors in the area of memorialization were not exactly crowned with success. At the behest of the KPD, architect Hermann Henselmann drew up plans in 1945/46 to transform a complex of former Nazi Party buildings, the so-called "Gauforum" on Karl Marx Square in Weimar, into a massive Buchenwald memorial. But this project collapsed in 1946 when the Soviet military administration in Weimar took over the "Gauforum" and sealed off the Karl Marx Square.[44] The local VVN in Weimar also hoped to erect a memorial on Weimar's former Watzdorf Square, renamed

Square of the 51,000 in honor of those killed at Buchenwald by the Nazis (later, the actual number was established as 56,000). This idea also failed to come to fruition. What is important to stress is that, had it been built, it would have promoted a view of Buchenwald's prisoners as divided into "victims" and "fighters," with the "fighters" showing the way to the future.[45]

That plans for a memorial focused initially on Weimar rather than Buchenwald had to do with the fact that Buchenwald was still in use in the 1945 to 1950 period as a Soviet Special Camp with German prisoners. There was, however, another possible location near to the camp on the southern slopes of the Ettersberg, namely, the site of the Bismarck Tower, not far from which the SS had buried hundreds of Buchenwald's prisoners shortly before the camp was liberated. It was on 22 April 1949 that Walter Ulbricht, at the time deputy chairman of the SED, wrote to Walter Bartel informing him that the Bismarck Tower on the Ettersberg was to be demolished. Ulbricht also told Bartel that he expected the VVN to come up with a draft plan for a memorial to replace the tower.[46] Manfred Overesch has argued that Ulbricht's interest in the construction of such a memorial indicates that the soon-to-be-founded GDR was preparing the "monumentalization of its self-legitimation."[47] The state-to-be, in other words, was seeking to found itself on a myth of heroic and victorious resistance. But while the SED did come to steer the course of memorialization on the Ettersberg for purposes of state legitimation, this happened somewhat later than Overesch suggests. Ulbricht, after all, refers in his letter to Bartel to a memorial for *victims*, not resistance heroes. Besides, when Thuringia's Minister-President Werner Eggerath turned to the Minister-President of the GDR, Otto Grotewohl, in December 1949 asking for one and a half million marks for the building of a memorial by Siegfried Tschiersky at the site of the Bismarck Tower, he was sharply rebuffed. Grotewohl thought the money would be better spent on building accommodation for the victims of fascism.[48]

Nevertheless, the idea of constructing a memorial at the site of the former Bismarck Tower gathered momentum. In November 1951, a Planning Commission for Memorial Sites was set up, consisting not just of VVN and Buchenwald Committee members but also of representatives of art and architecture academies. One month later, this Planning Commission announced a closed competition for the design of a memorial complex on the Ettersberg.[49] What was envisaged was not simply the construction of a memorial or memorial hall. The two mass graves also had to be integrated into the final design; later, a third mass grave was discovered and also integrated. The competition's brief, possibly as a result of the diversity of the Planning Commission's membership, was ambivalent. It made reference to the victims of the camp, but it also encouraged participants to design a complex that would honor "the unwavering of many nations." The term "grove of honor" ("Ehrenhain"), moreover, seemed to imply that Buchenwald's inmates had died in battle, rather than in an act of calculated murder. This somewhat contradictory message, not surprisingly, was reflected in the proposed designs.

On 28 March 1952 the Planning Commission awarded prizes to two of the participating groups of competitors. One of the groups consisted of the famous sculptor Fritz Cremer, the even more famous dramatist Bertolt Brecht, and the landscape gardener Reinhold Lingner; the second of the groups, the so-called Makarenko Brigade, was made up of three architects, two sculptors, and a landscape gardener. Both groups, as is clear from their proposals, grappled with the conundrum posed by the Planning Commission. Cremer and Lingner asserted that Buchenwald was the symbol of consciously organized resistance staged by heroes against fascism — heroes who were exposed the most to fascist brutality. But the German term here for exposed, "preisgegeben," suggests helplessness in the face of exposure, in contrast to ideas of heroism. The Makarenko Brigade, for its part, emphasized the need for any memorial to represent the "appalling suffering of all prisoners," "the mass of people tortured to death," and the "passionate will of all peoples to extirpate fascism by its roots." Their proposal lists these representational features in one sentence, separating them by oblique strokes as if they were compatible.

In the sculpture he planned for the Ettersberg, Cremer tried to get round the dilemma by depicting eight prisoners in simultaneously defiant and threatened posture. They stand in a line, some with clenched fists, one with the right arm raised as if swearing an oath, another with both arms raised and bent at the elbow in a show of angry refusal. Most of the figures are leaning forward, suggesting that, for all their defiance, they are bracing themselves for the impact of blows or bullets. All in all, Cremer suggests in the sculpture that, while the prisoners put up a brave show of self-assertion, they were ultimately doomed. As Cremer's sculpture was to be the centerpiece of the memorial complex, it came in for much critical scrutiny — not least from Wilhelm Girnus, head of the Literature Department of the State Commission for Artistic Matters, and editor of the Party newspaper *Neues Deutschland* (*ND*). In a *Neues Deutschland* article of 2 July 1952, Girnus stressed that the heroes of Buchenwald were positive heroes, whose cause was a just and therefore indomitable one. Consequently, their artistic representation should reflect this victoriousness. Girnus took Cremer to task for focusing on what Girnus adjudged to be the inessential — namely the external appearance of the prisoners, their ragged clothes, their shorn hair, and the distorted features of the dying and starving — and overlooking the essential: "the struggle, and the victory."[50] Girnus also lamented the fact that no attempt had been made to depict the "indissoluble friendship," a friendship characterized by mutual struggle, between the Soviet and German prisoners. Girnus demanded a new conception that expressed the following idea: "here, German people, you see people who held high the flag of peace, progress, and humanism and were victorious as a result." And the German people, Girnus concluded, should follow their example.

This criticism was amplified in a 9 October 1952 meeting with Girnus, Bartel, and others in Cremer's atelier. Cremer, according to artist René Graetz, was "shattered" by Girnus's dismissal of his plans.[51] Nevertheless, he subsequently produced a new draft which, as Volkhard Knigge has argued, corresponded both artistically and politically to Girnus's wishes.[52] In the new version, the prisoners are standing in a group rather than a line; they have formed a collective. The group is wedge-shaped and has a forward-moving dynamic. Some prisoners are holding rifles, and the prisoner with his arm held high now bears the features of Ernst Thälmann. The inclusion of a Thälmann-like figure creates a cross-reference, given that plans were by now under way to transform the camp crematorium into a shrine to the former KPD leader. This new model clearly refers to the supposed self-liberation by the prisoners on 11 April 1945. It emphasizes resistance, not in the form of defiance in the face of death, but of triumph over the SS. And this victory, so the inclusion of the Thälmann figure suggests, is at the same time symbolic of the long-anticipated triumph of the KPD as a whole over reactionary political forces.

Following Cremer's presentation of the new draft, he, Lingner, and the former members of the Makarenko Brigade formed a new architectural collective in late 1953 (Brecht, following the rejection by the Memorial Commission of his idea for an amphitheatre on the Ettersberg, was no longer involved). This collective set about drawing up plans for a merger of both prize-winning designs. The artistically most impressive feature of the final memorial complex as completed in the late 1950s was Cremer's group of figures, which he changed once more before it was cast and mounted. The third version retains the forward-moving dynamic of the second version. More of the figures bear the features of Ernst Thälmann, and all are now more sharply drawn. Far from looking emaciated, they are characterized by muscularity, and the shirts, coats, or robes with which they have been fitted out are anything but ragged. A flag has been introduced, surely representing the red communist flag. In deference to calls for a more international dimension to the sculpture, Cremer has added a figure with a beret whose presence evokes the Spanish Civil War. But this remains a very "German" sculpture in its implicit focus. It even features a reference to the Faust story. On the far right, a Mephisto-like figure with slanted eyebrows, "The Cynic," has been included; his marginal position, and the fact that he appears dwarfed by the more robust figure of "The Caller" who summons him to join the struggle, render him weak.

The complex of which Cremer's sculpture formed a part represents, essentially, a journey from pain to triumph that transcends any victimhood.

Fig. 8: Cremer's statue showing the prisoners' uprising against the SS. Courtesy of Gedenkstätte Buchenwald.

Visitors make their way down a set of steps past a series of seven upright stelae depicting scenes from the camp, designed variously by sculptors René Graetz, Waldemar Grzimek, and Hans Kies; on the back of each of the stelae is one of the strophes of a specially commissioned seven-verse poem by GDR poet and Minister for Culture Johannes R. Becher. The scenes on the first four stelae and the accompanying strophes describe the construction of the camp, the arrival of the prisoners, the agony of prisoners forced to work in Buchenwald's quarry, and the exploitation of prisoners by the SS. But the last three stelae focus on solidarity, the illegal commemoration of Thälmann's murder, and liberation, where liberation is presented as self-liberation, in the form of a towering figure holding a rifle. The visitor, passing one of the mass ring graves on the right, then turns to the left along the "Street of Nations," which features a series of pylons dedicated to the nations whose citizens were incarcerated at Buchenwald. Reaching another wall-enclosed ring grave at the end of the street, the visitor turns again to the left and walks up a wide set of steps, proceeding to the Cremer memorial and, behind it, an enormous bell tower affording a view of Weimar and beyond.

In a description of the memorial complex as planned in 1954, Buchenwald's architectural collective referred to the tower with its "upward-striving architecture" and its "light-filled structure" as a symbol of the freedom for which Buchenwald's antifascists had fought. The whole memorial complex, in fact, stresses the success of the prisoners' struggle against death and fascism. The prisoners are to be understood as men who threw off their yoke to become shapers of their own destiny. It is as actors in the war against fascism, not as its victims, that they are to be remembered. One might argue that the massive falling figure in Cremer's memorial, who clearly is *not* going to survive, is a victim: but he symbolizes an ennobled image of victimhood, as a soldier dying in the moment of victory, for a successful cause. The victimhood of those who were butchered and starved by the SS as a matter of course, which the initial competition brief had albeit very awkwardly sought to include, is given little attention in the final memorial. And certainly there is no reference anywhere in the memorial complex to the Jewish victims of racial persecution, thousands of whom were killed at Buchenwald.

The Involvement of the SED

Girnus's significant intervention, which certainly encouraged the development of the memorial complex in a direction that will have pleased communist survivors of Buchenwald, was not undertaken on their behalf. It was the first hint of that strong, official state interest in Buchenwald's symbolic potential that was to develop throughout the mid-1950s. With the end of hopes of unification in 1952/53, the massive loss of trust in the SED manifested in the GDR-wide strikes and protests of 17 June 1953, the embedment of the FRG and the GDR within their respective western and eastern blocs in 1954/55, and the introduction of the Hallstein Doctrine in 1955, the SED was desperate to provide for its citizens a point of identification that could at the same time be emphasized in the struggle for international recognition. In danger of being perceived as a "rump," even an artificial state, the GDR had to be cast as a legitimate entity with its own national history. Buchenwald came to play a key part in this process of building a national identity. Resistance at the camp was to be presented as an exemplary act of humanist German patriotism — a patriotism visible in the history of the KPD and embodied particularly in its leader Ernst Thälmann. This patriotism had as its goal the construction of a socialist fatherland, achieved with the founding of the GDR. At the same time, this resistance history was to be related as a narrative of positive international cooperation and solidarity between nationals of different countries — a narrative in which the Germans were key protagonists, thus underpinning the GDR's right to its place among nations in the present. Moreover, by contrasting the antifascist prehistory and traditions of the GDR with supposed fascist continuities in the west, the SED could argue that the GDR had more right to be recognized as the "true" Germany than the FRG.

In the same measure as the SED recognized the propagandistic potential of antifascism as a whole and of Buchenwald in particular, it began to
marginalize the prisoners' organizations. In 1953, the politburo ordered
the dissolution of the VVN. Encompassing as it did a whole range of former Nazi victims, it was too broad a church for Ulbricht's liking. Anti-
Semitism, a central pillar in the Stalinist purges, which began in the early
1950s, led to an obeissant self-purge by the VVN of some of its Jewish
members in 1952, but this did not save it from the anti-Zionism of the
SED. Another reason for its dissolution was the SED's wish to wrest control from the VVN of the representation of antifascism. From now on it
would be the task of state organizations such as the National Front, the
Free German Youth, and the Ministry of Education to cultivate the memory of antifascist traditions — albeit together with the Committee of
Antifascist Resistance Fighters (KdAW), a streamlined and at the time of
its founding somewhat impotent successor to the VVN.[53] The disbanding
of the VVN was followed later in 1953 by the downfall of Walter Bartel,
who lost his position as spokesman for Wilhelm Pieck because he had
ostensibly engineered a meeting in his flat of Franz Dahlem with the supposed American spy Noel Field shortly after the war.[54] The Central Party
Control Commission (ZPKK), which subjected Bartel to grueling interviews in late May 1953, also questioned him on the role of the communists at Buchenwald (in relation to the compilation of transport lists, for
instance). Bartel was not the only ex-Buchenwald prisoner to suffer demo-
tion of one sort or another in the early 1950s. He became caught up in
Ulbricht's power struggle against Franz Dahlem, which was simultaneously a struggle between exile communists and "Inlandkommunisten"
(Dahlem had been incarcerated in Mauthausen).

The dissolution of the VVN and the sidelining of Bartel led to the
temporary stagnation of the Buchenwald memorial complex project. But
when the SED Central Committee Secretariat passed a resolution on
2 December 1953 concerning the setting up of "Buchenwald National
Memorial Site," it signaled the SED's intention to take control of all further developments toward the building of the memorial complex. Overall
responsibility for overseeing its construction passed to the State
Commission for Artistic Matters, which became the Ministry for Culture
in 1954. On 28 April 1954, the Ministry for Culture set up a Scientific-
Artistic Advisory Committee, under Deputy Minister for Culture Alexander
Abusch, to advise on the memorial complex. To help procure funds for its
construction and the construction of memorial sites at other former
camps, a Curatorium for the Construction of National Memorial Sites was
constituted under the chairmanship of GDR Minister-President Otto
Grotewohl. The Curatorium agreed that over 1.3 million certificates
would be issued, worth a total of nearly 5 million marks, which the population was to be encouraged to buy. The motif on the certificates, which

were priced at between 1 and 1,000 marks, was the Cremer memorial, with the tower in the background.[55]

A degree of pressure was brought to bear on state organizations, ministries, political parties, and industry to sell a certain quota to their members or employees; photographs, stamps, and even porcelain plaquettes of Ernst Thälmann were also sold, proving that no level of kitsch was ruled out in the attempt to drum up 18 million marks for the construction of Buchenwald, Sachsenhausen, and Ravensbrück memorial sites. On 1 April 1957, Ernst Saemerow, the Curatorium's secretary, was able to announce that the total income by the end of December 1956 was 11,345,639 marks.[56] As the memorial complex on the Ettersberg neared completion, another committee, again with Grotewohl as chairman, was set up to stage-manage the opening in 1958 of what was now to be called the National Site of Warning and Commemoration at Buchenwald (henceforth NMGB). Otto Grotewohl, who as we have seen had opined in 1949 that it would be more sensible to spend 1.5 million marks on housing, had by October 1956 radically changed his mind. Now he was convinced that erecting houses in preference to memorial sites was not a good idea. The ashes and other remains of the dead on the Ettersberg, he implied in an extremely tasteless remark, would exercise a stronger attraction than housing blocks.[57]

While this all sounds forcefully streamlined, one should nevertheless be wary of envisaging the development of the memorial complex between 1953 and 1958 as unproblematic. As is not uncommon even today in German memorial projects, there were simply too many departments involved, at state, regional, and local levels, and too many contracted and subcontracted parties. Tensions and rivalries, as well as a lack of coordination and inadequate delineation of responsibilities, were an inevitable result. It seems too that not everyone took the project as seriously as was hoped. A June 1954 report by a control commission established that those carrying out the project had not fully recognized its political significance.[58] This is putting it mildly; the firm responsible for building at the site, VEB Bau-Union (Erfurt), initially provided a woefully inadequate number of builders.[59] And while the Curatorium did raise the cash it required, at working committee meetings there were frequent complaints that various organizations, not least the Free German Youth (FDJ) and the CDU, were not selling as many certificates as had been expected. Even when the memorial was dedicated with much pomp and ceremony in September 1958, it was not really finished; while the Cremer sculpture was displayed, only two of the figures were actually cast in bronze. After the inauguration, the figures had to be taken down again so that the casting process could be completed.[60]

But whatever these practical difficulties, there can be no doubt that the SED was keen to present Buchenwald as a center of national memory. The

Fig. 9: Opening of Buchenwald's National Site of Warning and Commemoration in 1958, with Cremer's statue in the foreground. Courtesy of Gedenkstätte Buchenwald.

Curatorium's sales program was at the same time a massive propaganda drive seeking to popularize this view. In his speech celebrating the foundation of the Curatorium in mid-1955, Grotewohl described the struggle and death of the resistance fighters as an expression of "the highest patriotism."[61] Grotewohl's speech at the opening of the NMGB in September 1958 made similar claims, although here — given his audience of guests from western and eastern countries — he emphasized more the international dimension to antifascist resistance. Buchenwald, then, was to enshrine the historical legacy of German socialist patriotism *and* international antifascist solidarity. In ritually evoking Buchenwald's history of resistance, GDR politicians simultaneously stressed the GDR's continuation of this tradition in the present. Now, as Grotewohl's inaugural speech made clear, it was West Germany that was the fascist enemy, and East Germany was the country that embodied the best German traditions and the spirit of internationalism.[62]

The SED wanted Buchenwald's "self-liberation" to symbolize, as it were, the outcome of the trajectory of the KPD's history as a whole, and therefore stressed its association with Thälmann in their commemorations, while repeatedly pointing out that the ILK's resistance was an admittedly important example of communist resistance generally. Afraid that Buchenwald's former prisoners in the GDR might seek to hijack memorialization in the interests of their own self-glorification, the SED ensured that they played only an accompanying role in developments between 1955 and 1958. Had they operated too much in the foreground, there was a risk they would seek to present their struggle at Buchenwald as exactly what it was not to be represented as, namely, unique. Not that the downgraded Buchenwald communists were completely without influence in the wake of the dissolution of the VVN; Robert Siewert, for instance, was a member of the Scientific-Artistic Advisory Committee for the memorial complex. As for Bartel, he reemerged in 1956, making suggestions along with other ex-prisoners of Buchenwald for the Buchenwald Museum (see next section). He was also a member of the committee set up in 1957 to plan the opening of the NMGB in 1958. After 1958, moreover, the Buchenwald Committee did begin to reassert its influence. But by then control of the legacy of the camp had by and large passed into state hands. It had, effectively, been nationalized.

The Museum at Buchenwald

If this was the situation as regards the memorial complex, what of the former camp itself? When the Soviets, having dissolved the Special Camp at Buchenwald in February 1950, passed the site over to the Thuringian Ministry of the Interior in December of 1951, the issue of what was to

Fig. 10: Rosa Thälmann, Walter Ulbricht (third from left) and Otto Grotewohl (speaker) at the opening of the NMGB in 1958. Courtesy of Gedenkstätte Buchenwald.

happen with it already seemed to have been decided. On 9 October 1950, the politburo had passed a resolution stating that, of the former camp, the gatehouse building with its central tower and two wings, the two watchtowers to the right and left, together with the barbed-wire fence connecting them to the gatehouse, and the crematorium should be left standing.[63] The resolution was directed at the Soviet Control Commission. Was it born of a concern that the Soviets would set about dismantling the camp? If so, the resolution outlined the *minimum* the politburo hoped to preserve.[64] Or was it rather a procedural recommendation, an invitation to take what they wanted, as long as the gatehouse, watchtowers, and crematorium were left standing, as Volkhard Knigge implies?[65] In the event, the Soviets dismantled some parts of the camp, such as windows and gutters. And locals of the Weimar area also helped themselves to what they could get their hands on — including zinc plating from the carts used to transport corpses, and wood from the gallows. They showed little respect for what was evidence of murder.[66] But it was Weimar's local authorities who, as of May 1952, were officially commissioned with the demontage of the camp site, a demontage which proceeded despite protests. Knigge's reading of the politburo ruling would, then, seem to be the correct one.

If dismantling the relics seems bad enough, selling them off to local industry and other organizations was certainly tasteless.[67] The motivation for this deconstruction was, first, to remove the traces of suffering and crime. In both the GDR and the FRG, state and regional authorities were keen to cover over such traces at concentration camp sites — in the vain hope, no doubt, that guilt and responsibility could be just as easily erased. In the case of Buchenwald, of course, there was a second past to be erased: that of the Soviet internment camp, in which human rights had been flagrantly violated. But it was also possible to put a positive spin on this process. For example, Fritz Beyling, general secretary of the VVN, stated in November 1951 that those areas of the camp from which parts had been removed should be explicitly marked to demonstrate that "here a quite conscious destruction of fascist horror has taken place."[68] The removal of the traces was to symbolize the triumph of communism over fascism. And the wish to preserve selected parts of the camp was similarly motivated.

Removal and preservation, in fact, went hand in hand. With all remains of the prisoner huts expunged, the gatehouse opened out, not onto vestiges of horror, but onto a vast open space. As Knigge writes, the camp-gate was transformed from a Dante-like gate to hell into a triumphal arch.[69] The 9 October 1950 politburo resolution also specified that the death of Thälmann was to be memorialized in some form at the former crematorium building. This too was a transformation. The crematorium was to be associated not with mass incineration and murder but with one individual who was given martyr-like status. In this way, Thälmann became a symbol and indeed the agent of an alchemistic inversion of history. Buchenwald was not the extreme dystopia but the origin of the utopia realized, according to official propaganda, in the GDR. As Knigge has pointed out, two former Buchenwald prisoners, Walter Bartel and Robert Siewert, and the chairman of the Thuringian branch of the VVN, Willy Kalinke, prepared the politburo resolution.[70] It thus expressed their vision of what Buchenwald was to become. Bartel, for instance, seemed particularly keen on a triumphalist expurgation of traces, and he was one of those who recommended allowing the former site to become overgrown (and indeed it was constantly covered in masses of weeds).[71] The politburo's interest was more in the veneration of Thälmann.

Initially, then, the politburo, former Buchenwald prisoners, and the VVN collaborated as equal partners. But here too, as in the case of the Ettersberg memorial complex, the year 1953 brought a significant shift. Following the dissolution of the VVN in February 1953, responsibility for the construction of memorial sites passed to the State Commission for Artistic Matters. In May 1953, the Commission decided among other things on the renovation of the gatehouse, crematorium, and camp shop ("Lagerkantine"). The latter building was to become the site of the new camp museum. The Commission passed its plans to Ulbricht on the occasion of the latter's sixtieth birthday (30 June).[72] Some three weeks later, on 18 July 1953, the politburo passed a resolution confirming the creation

Fig. 11: An exhibit at Buchenwald showing a model of the former camp (1954). The text on the wall reads: "Forward in the spirit of the antifascist heroes for peace and friendship between peoples." Courtesy of Gedenkstätte Buchenwald.

of a shrine to Ernst Thälmann at the crematorium, and the setting up of a museum in which Ernst Thälmann was also to feature.[73] The resolution stressed that the permanent exhibition should honor "the patriotic character of antifascist resistance." Here again, as in the case of the Ettersberg memorial complex, the disempowerment of the VVN was followed by an increasing emphasis on the association of Buchenwald and of its resistance tradition with Thälmann and the history of the KPD. Buchenwald's museums were to help with the construction of a socialist national identity in the present.

In line with the SED's ideological investment in memorialization at Buchenwald, it was the Museum for German History that officially took control of planning the exhibition, with the KdAW (and the Marx-Engels-Lenin-Stalin Institute (MELS)) having a purely advisory function.[74] A provisional exhibition was opened on 18 August 1954. It placed central emphasis on Thälmann and was effectively a history of the KPD from its founding through to the Second World War. This history was presented as a history of resistance — hence the title "Museum of the Resistance Movement." Thus the KPD's role in the Weimar Republic was depicted as one of resistance to imperialism and the approach of fascism, with no mention being made of course of the communist contribution to the collapse of democratic values, be this in the form of street-fighting, anti-parliamentarianism, or occasional collaboration with the Nazis (as during the November 1932 Berlin transport strike). The description of the post-1933 period focused to a considerable degree on German communist resistance within Germany and in the Soviet Union (National Committee for a Free Germany). In a Manichaean and teleological master-narrative, the 1919 to 1945 period was presented as one of conflict between good (communism) and evil (monopoly capitalism and imperialism), a conflict that had been won, as it were, by the GDR.

The marginalization of the KdAW in the organization of the exhibition led to only a small portion of it being dedicated to Buchenwald. While this was certainly what the SED had intended, the MfDG came in for criticism in mid-1954 for not including the whole spectrum of antifascist resistance.[75] For all the desirability of the emphasis on the history of the KPD, it was now felt to be equally desirable for the museum to demonstrate the patriotism of the communists by showing how they had spearheaded a truly *national* resistance movement to which groups of various political, ideological, and religious persuasions had contributed. The lack of adequate references to the *international* character of resistance was also a bone of contention, triggering objections from both the KdAW and the National Front.[76] These complaints reflect a quite basic dilemma that the GDR often faced. It was hard to find a balance between presenting the KPD as patriotic in a national sense and embedding its struggle within a narrative of international communist struggle in the name of "world patriotism." The MfDG did revise the exhibition plans in 1955 to include a greater emphasis on non-communist and international resistance,[77] but this did not mollify the critics. The most strident of these was a Russian, General Kotow, the General Secretary of the Soviet Peace Committee. In 1956 he took issue with the underrepresentation of the contribution of Soviets and other foreign nationals to antifascist resistance at Buchenwald, as well as criticizing the enormous focus on the German Workers' movement. In short, Buchenwald was "too national in character."[78]

In 1955, following meetings between the MfDG, the KdAW, and the Institute for Marxism-Leninism (IML) to discuss the future development of the Buchenwald museum, agreement was reached that it should be redesigned to incorporate more of the history of the camp itself, not least the international character of resistance there. However, the MfDG resisted attempts to excise or reduce the broad historical overview of the KPD's activities before 1933. Various plans were mooted that envisaged separating out the pre-1933 section of the exhibition from the main museum, and fitting out a special room dedicated to Thälmann; but these first steps toward disaggregation at first encountered insuperable practical problems, which need not concern us here. In the course of discussions, members of the Buchenwald Committee and the KdAW began to assert themselves more and more vis-à-vis the MfDG. Kotow's criticism, after all, was that the museum should focus more on Buchenwald itself, which is precisely what Buchenwald's communist ex-prisoners wanted. Former Buchenwald prisoners such as Otto Halle, Bruno Apitz, and Robert Siewert were involved in the evolution of drafts for a new museum in 1956/57,[79] and Walter Bartel also began to venture forth again, expressing his views on the museum.[80] There had been hopes of creating a new-look museum in time for the dedication of the memorial complex on the Ettersberg in September 1958. But at a meeting of the Buchenwald Committee, the KdAW, the MfDG, and the Buchenwald architectural collective in March 1958, a decision was taken not to make any major changes to the current museum in the Camp Shop, but rather to invest directly in a new museum in the Disinfection Building.[81] This new museum was not completed until 1964.

The endless discussions on possible relocations and changes of emphasis were symptomatic of an underlying dispute over priorities of representation. It was surely no coincidence that it was particularly Sepp Miller of the MfDG who resisted a much stronger focus in the museum on the history of the camp itself. Miller had been on the committee that, in 1946, had investigated Ernst Busse's conduct at Buchenwald. He had little interest in or sympathy for the former Buchenwald prisoners. The new exhibition of 1964 was much more of a "Lagermuseum"; Buchenwald's former prisoners were to get their way to a degree, although Ernst Thälmann was always to loom large with his own special exhibition. That they were to get their way had much to do with the huge success of *Naked among Wolves*. But it is also the case that the dispute in the GDR over priorities of representation at Buchenwald more or less petered out in the course of the 1960s. For those who cared to look at things this way, Buchenwald came to represent Thälmann and the history of the KPD. Those who wished to remember Buchenwald as a site of international solidarity and resistance would surely have been able to do so in the 1964 museum,[82] or when walking down the Street of Nations on the Ettersberg. Those German ex-prisoners of Buchenwald who saw their resistance as unique, special, rather than exemplary could gaze up at Cremer's figures and "remember" how they "self-liberated" Buchenwald in 1945. Yet Cremer's memorial surely also catered for all tastes: it celebrated the KPD (because the figures resembled Thälmann), the International Camp Committee (who had orchestrated the "self-liberation"), and international antifascist resistance as a whole.

On one thing, Sepp Miller, Walter Bartel, and Walter Ulbricht would all have agreed: Buchenwald, with its memorial complex and exhibitions, was more than a site of memory. It was a weapon with which to beat the supposedly corrupt and renazified West Germany. And this is precisely how

Fig. 12: Thälmann exhibition at Buchenwald in 1960. The text reads: "The people that I belong to and love are the German people and my nation." Courtesy of Gedenkstätte Buchenwald.

it was used. Indeed one of the earliest exhibitions to be set up, in the gate-house in 1954, juxtaposed the progressive GDR, which had realized the Buchenwald oath to extirpate fascism, with the regressive FRG, which, supposedly, had not. Throughout the GDR's existence, Buchenwald was to be the site of moral self-congratulation and antiwestern sentiment. And there would surely have been agreement between the SED, the MfDG, and the KdAW or Buchenwald Committee on another matter: memorialization at Buchenwald was not to foreground the facts of death or suffering, at least not of the kind that could not be reframed as political martyrdom.[83] On the Street of Nations, there was no Israeli flag, much to the regret of Arnold Zweig.[84] This smacked of anti-Semitism, but it also had to do with dissociating Buchenwald from the Holocaust — a dissociation, as we shall see, also characteristic of Apitz's *Naked among Wolves*.

Representations of the Rescued Boy before *Naked among Wolves*

One seminal publication on Buchenwald, dating from 1945, that appeared in eastern Germany includes a short, one-page testimony by Zacharias

Zweig. It contains, *in nuce*, elements that were to be central to his 1961 Yad Vashem testimony, focusing as it does on his role in rescuing Stefan in Cracow, Biezanow, Plaszow, and Buchenwald. Here, while he mentions (somewhat self-deprecatingly) his own considerable role in rescuing Stefan from the Small Camp in the final days, he also makes uncomplicated reference to the solidarity of German prisoners, who helped him "to hide my boy and protect him from deportation."[85] The only critical comment made in the short testimony relates to the "very bad reputation" of the Jewish Camp Police in Biezanow.[86] Certainly it was this early testimony that formed a concrete reference point for the "Buchenwald Child" rescue story in the GDR, and that formed one important source for Apitz's *Naked among Wolves*. But was it a true rendering of what Zacharias had testified? Years later, the former Buchenwald communist prisoner Stefan Heymann identified himself in a letter as the person who had written down this testimony, based on what Zacharias had told him.[87] Did he make any alterations? Omit anything? From 1945 on already, then, there are doubts as to the honesty of the reception of the Zweig rescue story in the eastern zone and the GDR.

The context for the reception of this story is visible in a radio play by Ruth Schulkow, broadcast on 11 April 1946. Schulkow's play, *Children in Buchenwald* (*Kinder in Buchenwald*), describes the rescue of children by prisoners, the supposed self-liberation, and the achievements of the illegal International Camp Committee; it also appeals to listeners to take the hands stretched out toward them by those who had been in the camp "to create together with you a new life, a new Germany, on whose flags are written freedom and truth, humanity and reconciliation."[88] The rescue of children, then — implicitly at the very least — was an achievement of the ILK. In 1948, Walter Bartel spoke on east German radio of children at Buchenwald, mentioning Stefan Jerzy Zweig by name and praising the resistance movement: "In Buchenwald we succeeded in saving the lives of 905 children." Bartel goes on to lambaste the Americans for passing too mild a sentence against the industrialist Friedrich Flick and insists that judicial proceedings would be better administered by "German democratic judges and prosecutors." Here the protection of children at Buchenwald is offered as evidence that the democratic German tradition survived even under National Socialism, and that the proponents of this democratic tradition are better placed to pass judgment than the capitalist Americans. Neither in Bartel's radio address nor in Schulkow's radio play is it made clear that most of the children at Buchenwald were Jewish. The background of the Holocaust was played down in the interests of an affirmative, forward-looking narrative.

In the history of memorialization and commemoration at postwar Buchenwald, as well as in the various guidebooks, the story of the rescue of Stefan Jerzy Zweig may have played a minor role before 1958. But the use of it warrants attention nevertheless, not least because the way his story was told was exemplary of precisely that kind of manipulation visible in Bartel's address. In a draft version of an early guide to the memorial site, we read that the three-year-old child Stefan Zweig was hidden by prisoners at the risk of their own lives. The rescue is presented as an example of courage and solidarity in the face of the brutality of the SS — in short, as a triumph over death.[89] A 1956 brochure-cum-guidebook produced by the Museum for German History features a photograph of Zweig. The text stresses that while Buchenwald was the expression of murderous bestiality, its history also bore witness above all to the strength of the solidarity of the resistance fighters, who rose above fascist atrocities. The guidebook states that an example of such fighters were the prisoners in the Storage Building, where comrades saved the three-year-old Stefan Zweig from death, hiding him between articles of clothing at the risk of their own lives. Strikingly, the story of Stefan's rescue is positioned within the guidebook at the point where the narrative first turns away from telling of the horrors of Buchenwald to consider more uplifting aspects. Up to that point, the brochure largely features photographs and drawings of suffering and dead bodies. Suddenly, the reader is confronted with an image of a healthy looking, relatively well-dressed boy wearing boots.[90] Stefan symbolizes survival, life, and above all the triumph of solidarity over murder. His rescue becomes a pivotal moment in a narrative of death and transcendence.

A similar positioning of the Zweig rescue story was characteristic of its treatment in the museum at Buchenwald. In the 1955 exhibition drafted by the MfDG, the same photograph of Stefan was shown as in the guidebook, together with Zacharias's brief 1945 account of his son's rescue as noted down by Stefan Heymann.[91] The reference to Zweig follows sections on mass murder and slave labor.[92] According to a 1958 draft for the new museum finally realized in 1964, there was to be a display board on women and children at Buchenwald, including Zacharias's early postwar account of Stefan's rescue. It was to be situated between display boards on the mass murder of Soviets, Poles, and Jews, and on the murderous conditions at Buchenwald-Dora on the one hand, and murder of Thälmann and the prisoners' uprising of April 1945 on the other.[93] Interestingly, the former Buchenwald prisoner Willi Seifert objected to the over-concentration on Zweig;[94] a revised draft features more detail on other children saved by the communist resistance movement.[95]

In the mid-1950s, a plaque commemorating Stefan's rescue was mounted on the outside wall of the Storage Building. It informs the visitor that "prisoners took care of the three-year-old Stefan Zweig, hiding him between sacks," and that they risked their lives to save him from annihilation.[96] The Storage Building itself had only survived the demolition process described earlier because it was in use as a grain store by a supply firm. In 1953, following attempts by Erfurt's Regional Council to get permission to tear it down,[97] the GDR's Institute for the Maintenance of Monuments stepped in to insist on its preservation.[98] Gradually, the idea took root that the Storage Building would be an ideal site for a new museum. Sepp Miller suggested this in 1956,[99] as did Walter Bartel[100] and the Soviet general Kotow.[101] But the necessary refurbishment proved too expensive. In January 1958, representatives of the Buchenwald-Dora Committee, the NMGB, and Weimar's SED rejected the idea of using the Storage Building as a museum in favor of the Disinfection Building.[102] But, as we shall see, the Storage Building did finally become home to the museum in 1985, thus creating a physical and symbolic link between the exhibition and the story of Zweig's rescue by the communists.

As far as representations of Stefan Jerzy Zweig in the memorial complex on the Ettersberg are concerned, the situation is less clear. The political scientist Peter Reichel has claimed that the Buchenwald child Stefan Zweig became the symbol of liberation and a central element of public memory in the GDR before Apitz's novel.[103] The photograph to which Reichel refers as evidence of this contention — it shows Stefan walking ahead of a group of prisoners at the 1 May 1945 celebrations at Buchenwald — did not feature, to my knowledge, in pre-1958 East German publications on Buchenwald. Nor is there any unambiguous evidence for Reichel's assertion that one of the figures in Cremer's group on the Ettersberg represents Stefan. Cremer himself never said as much, nor did any of those involved in the memorial complex project. Reichel's claim that Stefan was central to Buchenwald memory before 1958 is therefore overstated. It reflects a general tendency since the publication of *Naked among Wolves* to assume without qualification that Cremer's figure of "The Boy" ("der Junge") must be based on Zweig.

What we can say with certainty is that, following criticism of his sculpture by Wilhelm Girnus, Cremer read up on Buchenwald. In fact Peter Edel, a former Sachsenhausen prisoner, claims that Cremer was still gathering information on Buchenwald shortly before finishing his sculpture.[104] It was this self-education programme (and not a little pressure from the cultural authorities) that inspired him to place the emphasis in his second and third draft on the heroic self-liberation of the prisoners.[105] That Cremer included a boy in the second draft surely also resulted from his information-gathering. He will have read about Stefan in the ILK's report on Buchenwald published in 1945 and republished in 1949. But this report also mentions the protection of other children (for example, in Block 8), and cites the number of children still alive at the camp on liberation. So while "The Boy" *could* be Stefan, he could also be representative of *all* of Buchenwald's children. If anything, the apparent age of "The Boy," who looks to be nine or ten despite the fact that Cremer has fitted him out with an oversized, adult head, should discourage us from seeing him as absolutely identical to the three-year-old Stefan Zweig.

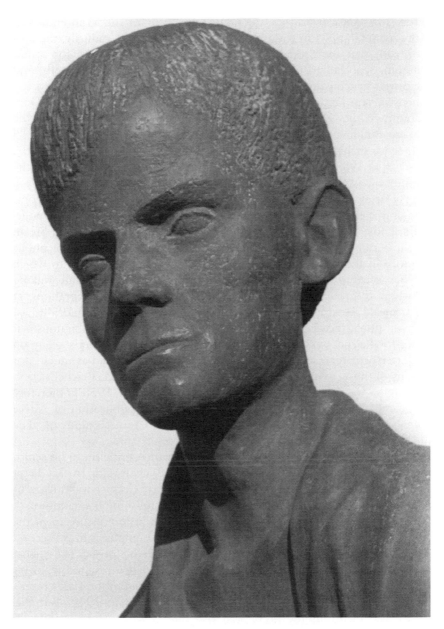

*Fig. 13: The figure of "The Boy" in Cremer's statue. Courtesy of
Gedenkstätte Buchenwald.*

Whatever the inspiration for Cremer's boy figure, its presence in the sculpture is significant, because, standing as it does at the far left next to the most dynamic-looking prisoners, it provides a contrapuntal contrast to the figures of "The Cynic" and "The Doubter" positioned at the far right. "The Boy," his features set in an expression of grim determination, his left hand clenched across his chest, is every bit as resolute as the prisoners to his immediate right. He is thus associated with resistance, heroism, and progress. He is the future, in contrast to the figures of "The Doubter" and "The Cynic." By including this sculptural reference to subsequent generations, moreover, Cremer overcomes the impression of pessimism conveyed by his first draft. Interesting too is that, in his right hand, "The Boy" is holding what looks like a metallic mug, not a rifle. This stresses his right, as youth, to life, but it places him in a relation of dependence to the rifle-holding, flag-carrying adults, as does his rather vulnerable and exposed position at the periphery of the sculpture. Rather than surmising that "The Boy" is supposed to be Stefan, it would seem more fruitful to surmise that Apitz's novel represents a narrative response to Cremer's sculpture (see chapter 3).

There is one other possible reference to Stefan on the Ettersberg. In the relief on the second of the stelae leading down to the Street of Nations, in the bottom right-hand corner, the sculptor Waldemar Grzimek has included the figure of a man reaching out to a small boy. The man has clasped the boy's hands and appears to be about to pull him upward and away from danger. On the back of the second stela is the second strophe of Becher's accompanying poem. The strophe carries the heading "Arrival in the Camp," and indeed the relief as a whole shows the abuse and torture to which prisoners were exposed on arrival at Buchenwald. The portrait of the man and boy is one of two positive moments of prisoner solidarity on the relief. Whereas Cremer's memorial shows this solidarity at the moment of liberation, here we see prisoner solidarity at the very moment of incarceration, often the time of greatest despair and greatest danger. "Oh power of suffering — what creative power!" writes Becher in his strophe. Here again, the rescue of a child symbolizes a positive turn. As with Cremer, we do not know what inspired Grzimek's motif of the man and child, but it is certainly possible that it was inspired by Zacharias's 1945 report, in which it is claimed that the prisoners did everything they could for Stefan on the very first day of his arrival in the camp.[106] One should not forget, either, that both Cremer and Grzimek will have conversed with former Buchenwald prisoners, who may well have related this rescue story to them. Certainly the child on Grzimek's relief looks to be of Stefan's age. A GDR guide to the Ettersberg memorial complex from 1960 assures the reader that Grzimek is referring quite specifically to the same "true occurrence" that formed the basis for Apitz's *Naked among Wolves*.[107] On balance, the evidence that the motif on Grzimek's relief is based on Stefan's rescue is stronger than in the case of Cremer's sculpture.

Fig. 14: Waldemar Grzimek's relief showing prisoners arriving at Buchenwald. Courtesy of Gedenkstätte Buchenwald.

Conclusion

This chapter has shown how a view of Buchenwald as a site of untarnished communist resistance gradually took root in the GDR, a development reflected particularly in the building of the memorial complex on the Ettersberg and in the exhibition landscape at the site of the former camp itself. The theme of the rescue of a child was perhaps not a central feature of this heroicization before Apitz's novel, but it was not insignificant either. Indeed its *pedagogical function* was important. Particularly in Cremer's sculpture, the inclusion of a young boy implies the necessity of integrating youth into any movement toward a better future — a message of some educational value in the paternalistic GDR. In fact Cremer's boy-figure seems to embody both youthful dynamism and vulnerability, both power and the need for guidance. As pointed out earlier, Cremer's group of figures caters for every taste in celebrating Ernst Thälmann, the KPD, international antifascism, and resistance at Buchenwald. There can be no more potent symbol of the synthesis of foci that Buchenwald, following the struggles outlined in this chapter, came to represent as of 1958. From the point of view of East German identity-building, Cremer's memorial was a masterpiece. In presenting *Germans* as (self-)liberators, Cremer seeks to nationalize the liberation narrative, without removing it from the context of international antifascist resistance. While J. W. Wutschetitsch's massive figure of a Soviet soldier in the Berlin-Treptow memorial complex built between 1946 and 1949 presents liberation as something *coming from outside*, Cremer presents it *pars pro toto* as something *coming from the inside*:[108] thus the resistance and liberation narrative becomes one with which East Germans can proudly identify. They were not only liberated, they also liberated themselves. This idea, as well as others by Cremer, was to be taken up by Apitz in *Naked among Wolves*.

Notes

[1] Walter Bartel and Stefan Heymann, eds., *Konzentrationslager Buchenwald, Band 1: Bericht des Internationalen Lagerkomitees* (Weimar: Thüringer Volksverlag, 1949), 43.

[2] See Karl Barthel, *Die Welt ohne Erbarmen* (Rudolstadt: Greifenverlag zu Rudolstadt, 1946), 150; and Colin Burgess, *Destination: Buchenwald* (Kenthurst, Australia: Kangaroo Press, 1995), 111.

[3] Internationales Buchenwald-Komitee/Komitee der Antifaschistischen Widerstandskämpfer in der Deutschen Demokratischen Republik, eds., *Buchenwald: Mahnung und Verpflichtung, Dokumente und Berichte* (Berlin: Kongress-Verlag, 1960), 123.

[4] Klaus Drobisch, *Widerstand in Buchenwald*, 4th ed. (Berlin: Dietz, 1989), 133.

[5] See http://www.shoah.dk/Courage/Schleifstein.htm for the photograph.

[6] See Stewart Ain, " 'Life is Beautiful': Real-Life Parallel," *New York Jewish Week*, 9 April 1999.

[7] United States Holocaust Memorial Museum Archives (henceforth USHMM), RG-09.005*08 (Fiche 4): "Transcription of the Tape of Dr. Leo Pine" (interviewer: Kaethe Solomon), 7 September 1978 (10:00–11:30).

[8] Elie Wiesel, *Night* (London: Penguin, 1981), 115–26.

[9] Judith Hemmendinger and Robert Krell, *The Children of Buchenwald* (Jerusalem and New York: Gefen, 2000), 21.

[10] Arnold Zweig, *Fahrt zum Acheron* (Berlin: VVN Verlag, 1951), 100–104.

[11] Some 500 to 600 Buchenwald survivors, many of them children, were taken to Switzerland by the Jewish chaplain Rabbi Herschel Schacter in 1945. After problems crossing the border, they were settled into camps around Berne. For an account of Schacter's endeavors on behalf of Buchenwald children, see Lorraine B. Meyer, "Rabbi Herschel Schacter, Former Army Chaplain, Recounts Liberation of Buchenwald," undated newspaper article (USHMM, RG-09.005*08, Fiche 6).

[12] Hemmendinger and Krell, *The Children of Buchenwald*, 25.

[13] See Union OSE, eds., *Les enfants de Buchenwald* (Geneva: OSE, 1946), 66–71.

[14] Hemmendinger and Krell, *The Children of Buchenwald*, 25.

[15] Heinz Albertus, *Verbrechen an Kindern und Jugendlichen im KZ Buchenwald und der Kampf der illegalen antifaschistischen Widerstandsorganisation um ihre Rettung*, 5th ed. (Weimar-Buchenwald: Druckhaus Weimar: 1989), 81.

[16] For more on such repatriation disputes, see Gitta Sereny, *The German Trauma: Experiences and Reflections, 1938–2001* (London: Penguin, 2000), 49.

[17] Berthold Scheller, ed. (in cooperation with Stefan Jerzy Zweig), *"Mein Vater, was machst du hier . . . ?" Zwischen Buchenwald und Auschwitz: Der Bericht des Zacharias Zweig* (Frankfurt am Main: dipa, 1987), 98.

[18] Berthold Scheller, ed., *"Mein Vater, was machst du hier . . . ?"* 106.

[19] Zacharias Zweig and Stefan Zweig, *Tränen allein genügen nicht* (Vienna: Eigenverlag, 2005), 108.

[20] See Zweig and Zweig, *Tränen allein genügen nicht*, 108–9.

[21] See Zweig and Zweig, *Tränen allein genügen nicht*, 171.

[22] "Was nach Buchenwald kam . . .," *Lausitzer Rundschau*, 21 March 1964. See also Zweig and Zweig, *Tränen allein genügen nicht*, 109.

[23] Zweig and Zweig, *Tränen allein genügen nicht*, 158 and 161.

[24] Interview with Stefan Zweig, 29 March 2004.

[25] Zweig and Zweig, *Tränen allein genügen nicht*, 161.

[26] Zweig and Zweig, *Tränen allein genügen nicht*, 162.

[27] Interview with Stefan Zweig, 29 March 2004.

[28] Manfred Overesch, *Buchenwald und die DDR oder die Suche nach Selbstlegitimation* (Göttingen: Vandenhoeck & Ruprecht, 1995).

[29] For a good account of Bleicher's time at Buchenwald and his life afterwards, see Hermann G. Abmayr, *Wir brauchen kein Denkmal: Willi Bleicher; Der Arbeiterführer und seine Erben* (Stuttgart: Silberburg Verlag, 1992).

[30] Ochs has provided an interesting autobiography in which he describes his imprisonment at Buchenwald. See Eugen Ochs, *Ein Arbeiter im Widerstand* (Stuttgart: Editions Cordelier, 1984).

[31] In 1950, Siewert was removed from office by order of the Central Committee and demoted to the position of deputy head of the Building Department within the Ministry for Construction. The reason was his former membership of the KPO.

[32] For an overview of the biographies of former Buchenwald prisoners, see Lutz Niethammer, ed., *Der "gesäuberte" Antifaschismus: Die SED und die roten Kapos von Buchenwald* (Berlin: Akademie Verlag, 1994), 493–519.

[33] Manfred Overesch, *Buchenwald und die DDR*, 234–35.

[34] Niethammer, *Der "gesäuberte" Antifaschismus*, 348–49.

[35] Stiftung Archiv der Parteien und Massenorganisationen im Bundesarchiv (henceforth SAPMO-BArch), DY30/IV 2/4/375 [Fiche 1]: "Untersuchungsergebnis in der Angelegenheit des Gen. Busse," 7 November 1946.

[36] Niethammer, *Der "gesäuberte" Antifaschismus*, 360–65.

[37] As it happened, the SPD's publication of the Robinson report backfired somewhat. In a letter to Fritz Heine (SPD), Hermann Brill expressed the fear that it

would merely encourage the tendency to ignore the resistance struggle that had taken place before 20 July 1944 (the date of Stauffenberg's attempt on Hitler's life) and lead to a campaign against those involved in this struggle. Brill himself suspected that some in the SPD were actively gathering information on his conduct at Buchenwald. He refers to tensions between exile SPD members and those who had fought fascism from within Germany, tensions that mirrored those between KPD (and, as of 1946, SED) members in the Soviet zone (see Bundesarchiv Koblenz, N1086/336: Letter from Brill to Heine, undated [probably January 1948]).

[38] Niethammer, *Der "gesäuberte" Antifaschismus*, 351.

[39] Niethammer, *Der "gesäuberte" Antifaschismus*, 75.

[40] Thüringisches Hauptstaatsarchiv Weimar, KZ und Haftanstalten Buchenwald Nr. 23: "Bericht von der 1. Tagung des Buchenwald-Komitees am 12. und 13. Juli 1947 in Ballenstedt."

[41] Bundesarchiv Koblenz, N1086/336: "Eine Erklärung des Buchenwald-Komitees," 2 January 1948.

[42] See Overesch, *Buchenwald und die DDR*, 254. That Bartel knew he was creating a myth becomes clear from a statement he made during a meeting of the Committee of Antifascist Resistance Fighters in 1958, when he conceded to Erich Mückenberger that there are "Buchenwald mythologies," and that it is difficult "not only for him" to say exactly what happened on 11 April 1945 in Buchenwald (see SAPMO-BArch, DY57/37: "Protokoll der Komiteesitzung am 23. Juni 1958").

[43] In 1964, the Buchenwald-Dora Working Group ("Arbeitsgruppe Buchenwald-Dora") was formed, replacing the Buchenwald Committee.

[44] See Volkhard Knigge, "Opfer, Tat, Aufstieg: Vom Konzentrationslager Buchenwald zur Nationalen Mahn- und Gedenkstätte der DDR," in *Versteinertes Gedenken: Das Buchenwalder Mahnmal von 1958*, ed. Volkhard Knigge (Spröda: Edition Schwarz Weiss, 1997), 5–95; here, 17–18.

[45] See Knigge, "Opfer, Tat, Aufstieg," 23.

[46] Overesch, *Buchenwald und die DDR*, 261.

[47] Overesch, *Buchenwald und die DDR*, 265.

[48] Knigge, "Opfer, Tat, Aufstieg," 31.

[49] SAPMO-BArch, DR1/6166: "Beschränkter Wettbewerb zur Erlangung von Entwürfen für die architektonische, bildhauerische und landschaftsgärtnerische Gestaltung des Ehrenhains zum Gedenken der Opfer des faschistischen Terrors in Buchenwald," 14 December 1951.

[50] Wilhelm Girnus, "Die Entwürfe zum Buchenwald-Ehrenmal," *Neues Deutschland*, 2 July 1952 (for selected quotations from this article, see Knigge, "Opfer, Tat, Aufstieg," 62–63).

[51] Graetz, in a report on a trip to Moscow, claims that he, Grzimek, and Cremer were presenting Cremer's original draft in Moscow — where it was praised by members of Moscow's Academy of Arts — when they heard about Girnus's comments. Graetz is scathingly critical of the SED's cultural policy in his report (see Stiftung Archiv Akademie der Künste (henceforth SAdK), René-Graetz-Archiv, Varia: Text of report of 25 August 1952). According to the *Stasi*, who spied on

Graetz, Graetz sympathized with the 1956 Hungarian revolution and nearly stopped working on the Buchenwald project, but continued at Cremer's insistence (a copy of this *Stasi* report can be found in SAdK, René-Graetz-Archiv, Varia: Hauptabteilung XX/7/II, Berlin: Zusammenfassender Bericht, 5 March 1970). Graetz, Grzimek, and Cremer were frequently in conflict with GDR cultural policy, despite their collaboration on the Buchenwald memorial complex.

[52] Knigge, "Opfer, Tat, Aufstieg," 66.

[53] For a detailed account of the VVN's short history in the GDR, see Elke Reuter and Detlef Hansel, *Das kurze Leben der VVN von 1947 bis 1953* (Berlin: edition ost, 1997).

[54] For more on the Noel Field affair and the GDR's Stalinist show-trials, see Jeffrey Herf, *Divided Memory: The Nazi Past in the Two Germanys* (Cambridge, MA, and London: Harvard UP, 1997), esp. chapter 5.

[55] SAPMO-BArch, DY57/950: "Protokoll über die Besprechung des Arbeitsausschusses des Kuratoriums für die Schaffung nationaler Gedenkstätten Buchenwald, Sachsenhausen und Ravensbrück im Arbeitszimmer des Ministerpräsidenten Otto Grotewohl am 4. April 1955."

[56] SAPMO-BArch, DR1/7521: "Protokoll über die Tagung des Kuratoriums für den Aufbau Nationaler Gedenkstätten in Buchenwald, Sachsenhausen und Ravensbrück am 1. April 1957, 11.00 Uhr."

[57] SAPMO-BArch, DY57/950: "Protokoll über die Sitzung des Arbeitsausschusses des Kuratoriums für den Aufbau nationaler Gedenkstätten am 10.10.56, 10.00 Uhr."

[58] SAPMO-BArch, DR1/7515: "Kontrollstelle: Abschließender Bericht," Berlin, 4 June 1954.

[59] SAPMO-BArch, DR1/7518: Letter from Mattheus to VEB Bau-Union Erfurt, 14 September 1954.

[60] SAPMO-BArch, DR1/7524: "Vermerk über ein Gespräch mit Herrn Professor Cremer am 7.1.1959 in seinem Atelier," 7 January 1959.

[61] SAPMO-BArch, NY4090/550: Otto Grotewohl, "Ansprache zur Gründung eines Buchenwald-Kuratoriums," no date.

[62] See Archiv der Gedenkstätte Buchenwald (henceforth BwA), Handapparat, Bu 48,1: "Rede des Ministerpräsidenten Otto Grotewohl zur Weihe der Nationalen Mahn- und Gedenkstätte Buchenwald am 14. September 1958."

[63] Overesch, *Buchenwald und die DDR*, 277–78.

[64] Overesch, *Buchenwald und die DDR*, 278.

[65] Knigge, "Opfer, Tat, Aufstieg," 34.

[66] See the report on plunderings by the caretaker of Buchenwald, Karl Straub (BwA, Nachlaß Karl Straub, 2/5: Karl Straub, "Bericht über den Zustand des früheren KZ-Lagers Buchenwald," 30 January 1952).

[67] For examples of such sales, see the material in Stadtarchiv Weimar (henceforth StadtA Weimar), 77 60 05/1310, Band II: Rechnungen betr. Enttrümmerung Buchenwald 1952.

68 SAPMO-BArch, vorl. DY57/248 AG, Bd. 1: "Bericht von der Tagung der Kommission für Gedenkstätten für die Opfer des faschistischen Terrors im Generalsekretariat der VVN am 24.11.51," Berlin, 27 November 1951.

69 Knigge, "Opfer, Tat, Aufstieg," 45.

70 Knigge, "Opfer, Tat, Aufstieg," 36.

71 Knigge, "Opfer, Tat, Aufstieg," 36.

72 StadtA Weimar, 13/776005/2228: Memo from "Abt. Kunst u. kult. Massenarbeit" to "Staatliche Kommission für Kunstangelegenheiten," 30 May 1953.

73 SAPMO-BArch, DY30/J IV 2/2/307: "Reinschriftenprotokoll" 53/53 of meeting on 18 July 1953.

74 On 2 December 1953, the Central Committee passed a resolution entrusting the MfDG with the construction of the museum in accordance with a draft plan submitted by the latter. See SAPMO-BArch, DR1/7523: "Entwurf: Bericht über Stand der Arbeiten zur Errichtung der Nationalen Gedenkstätte Buchenwald (Ehrenhain) bei Weimar."

75 Overesch, *Buchenwald und die DDR*, 306.

76 See, for instance, Deutsches Historisches Museum (henceforth DHM), Bestand MfdG, Abt. Gedenkstätten: Schriftwechsel der Abt. mit Universitäten, Akademien und Baubetrieben zur Ausgestaltung, baulichen Maßnahmen [sic] und Errichtung der Gedenkstätte Buchenwald, 1954–1958: "Niederschrift der Besprechung in Buchenwald am Sonnabend, dem 23.10.1954."

77 BwA, Drehbuch Widerstandsmuseum Buchenwald (Kantine), Letzte Fassung, 1955.

78 DHM, Bestand MfdG, Abt. Gedenkstätten: Schriftwechsel der Abt. mit Universitäten, Hochschulen, Akademien und Baubetrieben zur Ausgestaltung, baulichen Maßnahmen und Errichtung der Gedenkstätte Buchenwald, 1954–1958: Letter from Rudi Jahn to Sepp Miller, 1 October 1956.

79 DHM, Bestand MfdG, Abt. Gedenkstätten: Veränderungen in Buchenwald 1958: Letter from Sawadzki to Schlaack [sic], 15 January 1958.

80 BwA, Nachlaß Otto Halle, Korrespondenz: Walter Bartel, "Buchenwald — Dokumentation," December 1956.

81 SAPMO-BArch, DR1/7518: "Protokoll der Besprechung über bauliche und museale Massnahmen im Bereich des ehemaligen Konzentrationslagers Buchenwald am 20.3.1958," 28 March 1958.

82 Strictly speaking, according to Buchenwald's later director Klaus Trostorff writing in 1974, only one of the ten rooms of the 1964 exhibition was given over to the representation of the "antifascist resistance struggle" — but this rather overlooks the fact that this theme was not absent from the other rooms (see SAPMO-Barch, DR1/6297: Letter from Trostorff to Thiele, 15 October 1974).

83 In 1956, Sepp Miller did suggest using the second floor of the Storage Building to exhibit all the instruments of torture used in concentration camps. But the Museum of Resistance was to be placed on the ground floor, thus separating out the two spheres of experience. See BwA, Nachlaß Otto Halle, Korrespondenz: Sepp Miller, "Vorschläge für die weitere Ausgestaltung der nationalen Gedenkstätte Buchenwald," 22 September 1956.

84 See Arnold Zweig, *Im Feuer vergangen: Tagebücher aus dem Ghetto* (Berlin: Rütten & Loening, 1968), 9.

85 See Bartel and Heymann, *Konzentrationslager Buchenwald*, 43–45; here, 44.

86 Bartel and Heymann, *Konzentrationslager Buchenwald*, 44.

87 See BwA, Nachlaß Otto Halle, Korrespondenz: Letter from Stefan Heymann to Walter Bartel, 3 January 1961.

88 See Deutsches Rundfunkarchiv, ANR 3000015: Ruth Schulkow, "Kinder in Buchenwald," broadcast 11 April 1946.

89 DHM, Bestand MfdG, Abt. Gedenkstätten: Schriftwechsel der Abt. mit Universitäten, Akademien und Baubetrieben zur Ausgestaltung, baulichen Maßnahmen und Errichtung der Gedenkstätte Buchenwald, 1954–1958: "Buchenwald-Führung," undated, probably 1955.

90 Kuratorium für den Aufbau Nationaler Gedenkstätten in Buchenwald, Sachsenhausen, Ravensbrück, ed., *Buchenwald: Aus Vergangenheit und Gegenwart des Ettersberges bei Weimar* (Reichenbach: VEB Volkskunstverlag, 1956), 26.

91 See *KL Bu: Konzentrationslager Buchenwald: Bericht des Internationalen Lagerkomitees Buchenwald* (Weimar: Thüringer Volksverlag, 1945), 43–45.

92 BwA, Drehbuch Widerstandsmuseum Buchenwald (Kantine), Letzte Fassung, 1955.

93 DHM, Bestand MfdG, Drehbuch-Entwurf für die Gestaltung des Buchenwald-Museums und einzelner Gedenkräume, February 1958.

94 DHM, Bestand MfdG, Abt. Gedenkstätten: Ausstellungsdrehbücher für die Präsentation im Buchenwald-Museum 1958: "Abschrift: Bemerkungen zu dem Drehbuch über das Museum I. Teil," signed Seifert (undated).

95 DHM, Bestand MfdG, Abt. Gedenkstätten: Ausstellungsdrehbücher für die Präsentation im Buchenwald-Museum 1958: "Drehbuch für die Gestaltung des Buchenwald-Museums und der einzelnen Gedenkstätten. B: Widerstandsmuseum (Kantine)," 8 April 1958.

96 This plaque, according to a 1955 plan of the Buchenwald National Memorial Site, was designed as the thirty-second of forty-three texts displayed around the former camp as orientation for visitors. See DHM, Bestand MfdG, Abt. Gedenkstätten: Schriftwechsel der Abt. mit Universitäten, Hochschulen, Akademien und Baubetrieben zur Ausgestaltung, baulichen Maßnahmen und Errichtung der Gedenkstätte Buchenwald, 1954–1958: "Lageplan der Nationalen Gedenkstätte Buchenwald," 31 January 1956.

97 BwA, Nachlaß Karl Straub, 2/3: Letter from Karl Straub to Eduard Ullmann, 24 November 1953.

98 SAPMO-BArch, DR1/7520: "Protokoll über die Sitzung vom 9.12.1953 im Museum für Deutsche Geschichte," and "Genehmigung des Stellenplanes der Nationalen Gedenkstätte Buchenwald," 4 February 1954.

99 See, for instance, BwA, Nachlaß Otto Halle, Korrespondenz: Sepp Miller, "Vorschläge für die weitere Ausgestaltung der nationalen Gedenkstätte Buchenwald," 22 September 1956.

100 BwA, Nachlaß Otto Halle, Korrespondenz: Walter Bartel, "Gedanken für die Ausgestaltung des Museums in Buchenwald," December 1960.

[101] BwA, Nachlaß Otto Halle, Korrespondenz: "Abschrift" [signed Breitmann], 17 December 1956.

[102] DHM, Bestand MfdG, Abt. Gedenkstätten: Veränderungen in Buchenwald 1958: Sawadzki, "Bericht: Betrifft: Umbau Buchenwald-Museum (24.1.58)," Berlin, 27 January 1958.

[103] Peter Reichel, *Erfundene Erinnerung: Weltkrieg und Judenmord in Film und Theater* (Munich and Vienna: Carl Hanser, 2004), 199.

[104] Peter Edel, *Wenn es ans Leben geht*, 5th ed. (Berlin: Verlag der Nation, 1979), 84–85.

[105] Fritz Cremer, "Über die Arbeit an den plastischen Entwürfen meiner Buchenwald-Gruppe," *Das Blatt des Verbandes Bildender Künstler Deutschlands* 7 (July 1954).

[106] *Kl Bu: Konzentrationslager Buchenwald*, 44.

[107] Ullrich Kuhirt, "Die Stelen," in *Das Buchenwald Denkmal*, ed. Deutsche Akademie der Künste (Dresden: Verlag der Kunst, 1960), 37–49; here, 42–43.

[108] For an account of the building of the Treptow "Ehrenmal," see Arbeitsgemeinschaft Junge Historiker, *Das Treptower Ehrenmal: Geschichte und Gegenwart* (Berlin: Staatsverlag der Deutschen Demokratischen Republik, 1980).

CHAPTER THREE

—————

THE GENESIS AND IMPACT OF *NAKED AMONG WOLVES*

Introduction

A FEW MONTHS BEFORE the opening of the National Site of Warning and Commemoration at Buchenwald in 1958, a novel appeared in East Germany that in many ways corresponded, in its overall aesthetic, shape, and message, to Cremer's memorial on the Ettersberg. This was Bruno Apitz's *Naked among Wolves* (*Nackt unter Wölfen*). Just as Cremer linked the motif of a young boy with self-liberation, so Apitz integrated the narrative of a child's rescue into a wider self-liberation narrative. The albeit peripheral tension implied in Cremer's sculpture between dynamism and doubt, conclusively resolved in favor of the former, is a tension that also characterizes Apitz's novel. The conflict between prisoners and the SS implicit in Cremer's memorial is an explicit and fundamental theme of *Naked among Wolves*. And Apitz's novel heroicizes an international antifascist resistance collective under German leadership in very much the same way as Cremer's sculpture. It should also be pointed out that Apitz's novel encountered as many difficulties and went through as many stages of development as Cremer's group of figures. For here too there were those who found Apitz's view of camp life not positive enough, in terms of either his view of relations between prisoners, or his depiction of the role of the International Camp Committee (ILK). In retrospect, these objections seem founded in an oversensitivity. But they are important nevertheless.

In this chapter I will examine the genesis of *Naked among Wolves*. I will argue that, in many ways, Bruno Apitz was almost predestined to be the author of the most famous communist novel about Buchenwald. After an overview of his life before, during, and after Nazism, I will explore how he came to write his novel. Its underlying concept and the decision to write it when he did are an expression of the politicization of Buchenwald in the mid-1950s, and at the same time a response to the criticism of Buchenwald's communist prisoners outlined in the previous chapter. The novel's long genesis also reflects shifts in attitudes to Buchenwald in the GDR as well as the influence of former Buchenwald prisoners and of interference from a number of other sources. But I could trace no evidence that the SED's politburo intervened to block publication or demand changes, as is sometimes claimed.[1] Apitz undertook the changes that he did in response to suggestions and criticisms from former Buchenwald inmates, and also in response to suggestions from his publishing house itself. I will then provide a detailed overview of the action of the novel so that those readers who do not know it can gain an impression of its content. The overview, as well, makes clear the differences between the novel and Zacharias's 1961 testimony. Following this, I will consider the enormous success of *Naked among Wolves*, which was soon enthusiastically embraced by the GDR's political and cultural establishment. Finally, I will examine the way Apitz portrayed the figure of the rescued child, arguing that the novel plays down his Jewishness and marginalizes the theme of the Holocaust. In the final analysis, Apitz reinfantilizes the child figure, which in Cremer's sculpture was at least able to stand on its own two feet. Where Cremer acknowledges the dynamism of youth, Apitz reduces it to absolute helplessness, thereby reinforcing the rights of the adults in what is effectively an inversion of the feral myth of Romulus and Remus.

Bruno Apitz at Buchenwald

Bruno Apitz was born into a working-class family in Leipzig on 28 April 1900 (he was Marie Apitz's twelfth child) and left school at fourteen to take up an apprenticeship as punch cutter. In the same year, 1914, he joined the SPD's workers' youth organization, where one of his teachers was Walter Ulbricht. His active political career began on 16 August 1917, when he gave an antiwar speech to 1,500 workers during the munitions workers' strike. As a result, he was held in custody for nine months for disseminating antiwar propaganda and then sentenced to nineteen months in prison for treason. He had no sooner been amnestied and released in October 1918 than he participated in the November revolution (becoming a member of the newly-founded KPD's youth organization in 1919) and in the strikes that led to the collapse of the Kapp putsch in 1920. In 1920 he began working in the bookselling trade, and between then and 1925 he wrote and published his first, rather wooden and completely unsuccessful, poems and dramas, most in a socialist mode. Joining the long-term unemployed in 1925, just as the Weimar Republic was entering a period of short-lived stability, Apitz turned his hand to acting. From 1927, he was involved in the activities of the KPD's agitprop group in Leipzig — under Rudi Jahn, later to become a leading figure in Buchenwald's resistance organization. Between 1930 and 1933, Apitz was a member and then chairman of the Leipzig branch of the League of Proletarian and Revolutionary Writers in Germany. In 1932 he completed his first novel (about espionage within industry), but his rather tentative literary career was cut short when Hitler became Reich Chancellor in January 1933.

Within months of the Nazi takeover, in May 1933, he was back in prison again under the "protective custody" terms of the Reichstag Fire Decree, first in Colditz and then in Sachsenburg. Yet he renewed his now illegal political activities on behalf of communism after his release in August 1933 — only to be arrested again in November 1934 and sentenced to almost three further years in prison. He was not to see freedom until after the collapse of the Third Reich. After more than two years in Waldheim prison, he was transferred on 4 November 1937 to Buchenwald. The Nazis classified Apitz not just as a political prisoner but also as a "recidivist." Certainly there was no doubt that, were he to be released, he would "relapse" into undesirable political activities. Thus he remained at Buchenwald until liberation — or "self-liberation," in *Naked among Wolves* — in April 1945.

Apitz has testified to the horrific conditions at Buchenwald. Shortly after liberation, Rudi Jahn compiled a brochure in which a number of ex-Buchenwald prisoners from Leipzig, including Bruno Apitz, wrote of their concentration-camp experiences.[2] Apitz describes how one of his first impressions on entering the camp was of men hanging from trees by their arms, and of their groans and whimpering.[3] To the new arrival, Buchenwald seemed like the "forecourt to a realm of death and dissolution."[4] He was overcome by a sense of hopelessness, as is clear from his graphic description of the lack of water, the dampness, the constant hunger, and the omnipresent filth of those early days as prisoners struggled to construct the camp.[5] Particularly striking is his frank depiction of the prisoners in the Small Camp, many with suppurating wounds, many little more than walking corpses who, on 11 April 1945, were unable to register that they had been liberated.[6] In the months before liberation, as the mortality rate increased dramatically, Apitz was among those who had to transport corpses from Buchenwald station to the crematorium. Under the eyes of the impatient SS, prisoners literally tossed the bodies onto and off the carts. Apitz's portrayal of this process registers precisely the degree to which death had lost meaning, gravity, and individuality. "When you deal with corpses on a daily basis, they become objects, things," he writes.[7]

That Apitz survived, and that he managed to find hope, can be put down not least to his artistic endeavors at Buchenwald. In the confines of Buchenwald, he was an artistic multitalent — musician, cabaret-performer, poet, author, and sculptor. His cabaret sketches, sometimes performed in full view of the SS, attempted the almost impossible task of providing the prisoners in the audience with light-hearted encouragement while appearing to expose them to ridicule so as to satisfy the SS.[8] He also took part in illegal cultural evenings such as one in the Pathology Building, where he read out his political poems;[9] and on 1 May 1944, he played the violin during a clandestine celebration in the Storage Building of the traditional day of the workers.[10] Apitz was not involved in the underground activities organized by the ILK, although the SS may have thought he was.[11] Nevertheless, given that he participated in performances that were illegal and had a strongly political, antifascist character, his cultural activity can be classified as a form of resistance. As his contribution to the Kogon report of April 1945 indicates, this was certainly his view of things.[12] Generally, too, whether legal or illegal, his performances surely did much to shore up morale in a hostile environment, while providing for himself and his fellow performers an important creative outlet.

In one particular instance, Apitz's artistic skills did more than provide an outlet. The digging work he was forced to do on his arrival at Buchenwald, as well as the constant harassment by the SS, proved life-threatening. He nevertheless managed to sculpt from muschelkalk an astonishingly cheerful figurine, "The Worker." This drew attention to his abilities, and he was moved to the "Artists' Workshop" work detail in Block 12, which probably saved his life. Here he had to sculpt everything from life-sized figures through to decorative corks for the SS. He also had the dubious pleasure of making a crib for the tenth child of the wife of Thuringia's Gauleiter, Fritz Sauckel. Apitz was moved to the Pathology Building work detail in December 1942. Here he found time to sculpt secretly the one sculpture for which he was to become well-known, "The Last Face" ("Das letzte Gesicht"), modeled from the wood of an oak-tree.[13] This was the only tree within the prisoners' camp at Buchenwald. According to legend, Goethe and Frau von Stein had sat under the shadow of its boughs on their visits to the Ettersberg — which is why the SS left it standing. When the camp was bombed in August 1944, it was so badly charred the SS ordered it be felled and chopped up for firewood. Apitz got hold of part of the trunk and sculpted from it a death mask, taking plaster-cast death-masks of prisoners kept in the Pathology Building as his model. The resulting sculpture had to be smuggled out of the camp; it was taken to the town of Apolda, where Apitz was able to retrieve it after the war.

This remarkable sculpture is redolent with a symbolism both tragic and defiant. By imprinting the face of death upon the remnant of an oak associated with Goethe, Apitz could be poignantly gesturing toward the collapse of the humanist legacy of Weimar Classicism under the impact of Nazism. Yet, at the same time, what Apitz forms from this remnant is itself *art*, in humanist terms the highest expression of human endeavor. Without the will to create art, moreover, there would have been no remnant. Thus the survival of a fragment rescued from a famous, if apocryphal, Goethe landmark comes to signify the determined survival, under the most inhumane conditions, of that artistic spirit embodied by Goethe himself. The inherent and unresolved ambivalence of "The Last Face" is its greatest strength. In the early years of the GDR, the proximity of Classical Weimar to a Nazi concentration camp was also presented as an unresolved contradiction;[14]

but by 1960, Buchenwald had come to symbolize the resolution of such contradiction, representing as it now did the "strength, solidarity, and resistance of the antifascists, who embodied a new, combative humanism."[15] Thus a continuity was constructed between Goethean humanism and socialist humanism, helping to underpin the attempt to reinvent Buchenwald as a potent national symbol. Apitz's "The Last Face" is free of any such gesture toward ideological transcendence, whatever the attempts in the GDR to present it as a straightforward example of socialist humanism (for instance in the Museum for German History in Berlin, where it was on display).

Apitz's artistic endeavors at Buchenwald also included secretly writing prose, most notably the story "Esther" (composed in 1944), a story about a tragically brief love affair between the German political prisoner Oswald and a beautiful Greek Jew at Natzweiler concentration camp. Rather than take poison and die together with her lover, Esther opts to die with her fellow Jews in the gas-chamber. This story was not published in the GDR until 1959, and it was not until 1988 that it appeared as a separate volume. The story highlights the fate of Jews, the racism and racial experiments of the SS, and the contrast between the lot of Jews and that of the more privileged political prisoners. At one point, Esther even mentally associates the politicals with the SS, asking Oswald, "What do you intend to do with us [the Jewish female prisoners]?"[16] Somewhat problematically, Esther's self-sacrifice, indeed the death of Jews in the gas chambers, is valorized as a fructification of the soil in the interests of a better future.[17] Nevertheless, the world of "Esther" is far away from that of *Naked among Wolves*, where the Holocaust is marginalized, the prisoners are all male, and the conclusion is one of victorious communist triumph, not Jewish death.[18]

If "The Last Face" and "Esther" seem shot through with uncertainty and moments of pessimism, then this is because Apitz at Buchenwald was a different man from Apitz in the mid-1950s, when he came to write *Naked among Wolves*. In fact, immediately after the war Apitz set about constructing a more heroic view of Buchenwald. Certainly, in Rudi Jahn's 1945 compilation referred to above, it is left to other contributors such as Jahn himself and Harry Kuhn to sing the praises of the antifascist resistance group at Buchenwald.[19] Elsewhere, however, Apitz showed himself no less capable of post-liberation eulogy. In his appellative poem "Last Roll Call," composed for the last conference of Buchenwald's communists on 14 May 1945, Apitz ecstatically claims that a front has been formed from the thousands of dead and murdered prisoners, from blood and sweat and tears, and that the "free army" of former prisoners should now march out into all countries, villages, and towns, sowing the seeds "that flourished here" and forcing the last enemy to his knees. "But we are stronger than death," we read in the last verse. "Come, comrades! Our gate is open, red glows the morning and the sun . . . red!"[20]

Bruno Apitz after 1945: The Failed
DEFA Experiment

Given Apitz's artistic talents, one might have expected him to seek to give creative expression to his experiences in Buchenwald when he returned to Leipzig in 1945. But he did not. In later years, after the huge success of *Naked among Wolves*, he claimed that he had already formed the intention at Buchenwald of writing about the rescue of Stefan Zweig: Apitz had witnessed Stefan's arrival in the camp and knew of the events surrounding his rescue, although he was not personally involved.[21] That it took him until the mid-1950s to begin to realize this intention can be put down partly to the exigencies of making a living; but it also has much, and perhaps more, to do with his commitment in the immediate postwar period to helping with the construction of a socialist society in eastern Germany. From the moment the SED was founded in 1946, Apitz was a member. He was active in various capacities. In postwar Leizpig, he worked as an editor and journalist for the *Leipziger Volkszeitung* and served as administrative director to Leipzig's Municipal Theatre. Between 1946 and 1950, he wrote a number of short contributions for radio as well as radio plays. These demonstrate a pedagogical commitment to the popularization of socialism through a focus on iconic figures such as Karl Marx and Carl von Ossietzky. In addition, he wrote a number of playlets on industrial themes, which were staged in workers' theatres. In 1948, he even worked for VESTA, a nationally owned iron and steel firm, where he had the job of organizing cultural events to help raise productivity.

But soon his life took a new direction. When the author Jan Koplowitz told Helmut Spiess, at the time head dramaturgist at DEFA, that Apitz was a raconteur of amusing and interesting stories taken from the life of activists in East German industry, Spiess wrote to Apitz in September 1950 expressing interest in these stories, which he hoped might form the basis for "cheerful contemporary films."[22] This letter marked the beginning of a five-year partnership between Apitz and DEFA — one that was far from easy, as Apitz proved incapable of working together with others. Thus when DEFA brought in the scriptwriter Erich Conradi to help Apitz turn one of his film outlines into a script, the two men fell out, and Apitz eventually left Conradi to do the scriptwriting. Apitz and Conradi also argued over the payment of a secretary.[23] In July 1952, DEFA offered Apitz a contract as film dramaturgist. But he proved no better at working with authors than with scriptwriters. Appointed to assist Wolfgang Luderer with writing the filmscript from the latter's outline for a film about football, Apitz was soon being accused by DEFA of having "taken possession of Luderer's material and thrown him out."[24] The dramaturgist contract was changed into a one-year author's contract on 1 November 1953.

None of Apitz's envisaged projects was ever turned into a film. By the time the filmscript for *That's Habenack for You* (*So einer ist Habenack*) was complete in 1952, it was considered out of date.[25] *Thief in His Own House* (*Dieb im eigenen Hause*) was vetoed by the head of the Main Department for Film in the Ministry for Culture, Anton Ackermann, because "it could awaken certain associations in our population."[26] While Apitz's focus here is on the forced occupation by the American army of houses in West Germany, Ackermann presumably feared that some GDR citizens might be reminded of similar actions on the part of the Soviets in eastern Germany — and of course the GDR had itself carried out forced evacuations on the German-German border in May 1952 (in the interests of "security"), and on the islands of Usedom and Rügen between February and March 1953 (in the interests of "nationalizing" the tourist trade). Another of Apitz's more hopeful outlines, *How Do I Tell My Husband?* (*Wie sag ich's meinem Mann?*), was finally rejected in May 1955 because, according to DEFA dramaturgist Willi Brückner, its central theme, namely equal rights for women, did not sit easily with other narrative elements in the plot.[27] It is not inconceivable that there was also an ideological objection here. In the film outline, Irma Raunack wants her husband to work so that he can pay off the house. Private interests are the stimulus, not commitment to building socialism.

Not that Apitz was anything other than the most loyal of SED members: but sometimes he seems to have lacked the necessary intuition for the often paranoid, prescriptive, and rigid forms that ideology, in the GDR, could assume. In one particular instance, however, he appears to have had greater ideological prescience than DEFA. In late 1954, he submitted an outline for a planned film about the last days of Buchenwald and the rescue there of a young child. This film, he wrote, would be directed particularly at people in West Germany, "who are witnessing the renascence of fascism." After relating the essential ingredients of the rescue story, he states: "since the Paris Treaties and the Moscow Conference, and since the trial in Karlsruhe, I just can't get this story out of my mind." For Apitz, then, "the history of the struggle of international solidarity of antifascist fighters" was very topical:[28] West Germany's integration into NATO, its commitment to rearmament, and the attempts to ban the KPD in Karlsruhe were, in his opinion, symptomatic of a development that called for an antifascist resistance front comparable to that at Buchenwald. This all sounded ideologically robust, but DEFA rejected the idea because "we believe," as Eva Seemann told Apitz, "that the struggle against West German refascistisization can be more effectively treated in a contemporary subject." Moreover, "a film set exclusively in a concentration camp, seen from the perspective of its effect on today's viewers, is problematic." Finally, Seemann informed Apitz that DEFA found it inappropriate to place a three-year-old child at the center of the film plot, "even if the facts in themselves are very moving."[29]

These reasons could be reformulated more explicitly as follows: first, a film set in a concentration camp cannot be deployed to demonstrate supposed fascist continuities in the West, and is therefore of limited use as antiwestern propaganda; second, today's East Germans need uplifting, forward-looking socialist films, not depressing ones about Buchenwald; and third, a three-year-old child can hardly function as a positive and active hero. It might seem that DEFA had failed to understand Buchenwald's ideological significance. But in late 1954 and early 1955, the propagandistic exploitation of this significance had not yet become state policy. It was only in April 1955 that the official SED drive to *popularize* Buchenwald really set in in earnest. The dissolution of the VVN in 1953 and the marginalization of former Buchenwald prisoners such as Walter Bartel (see chapter two) lay in the past, but this past was not too distant, its effects were still being felt, and there were those in DEFA who surely knew of the problematic status of communist ex-prisoners of Buchenwald. In fact DEFA may well have rejected Apitz's film outline for precisely the reason that he conceived it — because it sought to rehabilitate Buchenwald's communists by lauding their achievements at Buchenwald and indeed reinterpreting them as visionaries. Apitz will have been following events closely in the early 1950s, not least because of his association with the memorial site at Buchenwald.[30] Years later, he said he was glad he had not written his novel immediately after liberation, because then he would only have described the rescue of the child; "I felt there was more to say here."[31] It was the criticism of Buchenwald's communists in the 1948 to 1953 period that drove Apitz to put pen to paper. The "more" he added, was the celebratory story of communist resistance at Buchenwald, with the child's role still central, but now emblematic rather than interesting in itself.

That this agenda, differently inflected, was to become that of the SED as a whole was surely not clear to all in late 1954. Certainly by 1958, when Apitz's *Naked among Wolves* appeared, the official image of Buchenwald was exactly contrary to that conveyed by Seemann a few years earlier. Buchenwald had now become a key symbolic site in the struggle against the "refascistisization" — to use Seemann's term — in West Germany. It had at the same time evolved into a symbol of just how uplifting and inspiring socialism could be even under the most difficult conditions, and a manifestation of the GDR's loyalty to the spirit of the resistance legacy. And the story of the rescue of a child had become representative of the larger narrative of communist-led antifascist solidarity and humanism. According to the author Peter Edel, the GDR's Minister for Culture Johannes R. Becher had also recognized the significance of Stefan's rescue as early as the mid-1950s. In 1955, standing in front of the exhibit pertaining to Stefan in Buchenwald's museum, Becher had said that the rescue was more than a small episode: it symbolized the "greatness of that other Buchenwald."[32]

Fig. 15: Bruno Apitz (left) in Weimar in 1965. Courtesy of Gedenkstätte Buchenwald.

The Evolution of *Naked among Wolves*

In her note on her meeting with Apitz, Seemann wrote that the failure to interest DEFA in the project had prompted Apitz to consider writing a story ("Erzählung") about Buchenwald. He set about writing what was soon to become a novel in early 1955, his work for DEFA effectively petering out by May of that year. Not that his initial attempts to generate interest in a literary adaptation of the theme met with any greater success. Indeed, in May 1955, the Berlin executive committee of the German Writers' Union rejected Apitz's application for a loan to enable him to undertake his project. This time the reason was lack of confidence in Apitz's literary abilities. While the committee adjudged both the theme and the material to be interesting, it felt there was no guarantee "the author could create a novel from the material presented" (Apitz had submitted some sixty pages).[33] According to the author Eva Lippold, Apitz also sent this first draft of part of the planned novel to various publishers, but without success.[34] Only when he followed the advice of the Writer's Union Party Secretary Jürgen Lenz and approached Mitteldeutscher Verlag (MDV), a publishing house in Halle, did he awaken interest. In his

13 May 1955 letter to Hans Holm of MDV, Apitz wrote laconically that he "want[s] to write about the resistance struggle and the liberation of Buchenwald concentration camp."[35] Fritz Bressau of MDV visited Apitz in Berlin on 18/19 May 1955 and took the manuscript away with him for his editorial team to read. They were impressed. Bressau wrote to Apitz on 20 October, returning the manuscript with the encouraging words: "under all circumstances keep on writing!"[36]

Apitz had now found a home for his burgeoning novel, and he did keep on writing under all circumstances, living very much from hand to mouth as it progressed. And it progressed slowly. Instead of the six months he had originally envisaged,[37] he needed over three years. How can this delay be explained? In later years, Apitz claimed that, apart from beginning the novel again when the first hundred pages seemed to him too documentary in character, he made no further changes.[38] As we shall see, this claim is quite false; why Apitz chose to make it is difficult to establish, though he may have been wary of giving too much away about the novel's difficult birth. Certainly it was the constant changes to the novel, both substantive and stylistic, that delayed its completion. In the following, I examine these changes, seeking to explain them and the background against which they were made. It will become clear that *Naked among Wolves*, while of course Apitz's own work, evolved to a degree in accordance with the views of other ex-prisoners of Buchenwald, the Committee of Antifascist Resistance Fighters (KdAW), and the Mitteldeutscher Verlag. While these views were varied, there is one that recurs — namely concern that Apitz's novel, for all its glorification of communism at Buchenwald, risked exposing those very aspects of its conduct that it sought to justify and explain away.

What changes did Apitz make? A version of part of the novel contained in the Bruno Apitz archive in Berlin — a version that could in fact be the earliest one, which Apitz admitted to casting aside — features a character called Papa Berthold, who delights in killing prisoners with lethal injections.[39] This figure was omitted in subsequent drafts. Moreover, between mid-November 1956 and mid-February 1957, Apitz partly rewrote what he had written in order to *include* a character, Herbert Bochow. Before this major rewrite, the character Walter Krämer was both Camp Elder *and* the driving force behind the ILK. But in the final draft as submitted to MDV, Krämer's ILK role has been transferred to Bochow. The MDV typescript — MDV's typed-up version of Apitz's final draft — was also subjected to changes prior to being set for printing, changes that went far beyond those made in the interests of good style, grammar, and punctuation. For example, a significant alteration has been made to a scene describing the relationship between the SS and the ILK, while scenes of conflict between prisoners have been toned down. Even at the proof stage there was at least one significant change, namely to those sentences and phrases referring to the possible deportation of the child out of the camp. Why were these changes made?

In the case of the sadistic Papa Berthold, we can only surmise, as the archives do not provide an answer. The most likely explanation for Berthold's excision is that he stands for gratuitous violence; the prisoners he kills die only because he likes killing them. Elsewhere in the novel, the SS are seen torturing antifascist prisoners with the aim of extracting information. They are sadists, but deploy their sadism to a particular end. Their victims, such as Pippig and Höfel, are also victims with a purpose, namely, protecting the child and the ILK. In removing Berthold, Apitz keeps suffering almost entirely within the context of the conflict between SS and antifascist resistance. Victimhood is seen in near-exclusive relation to its heroic transcendence and is given meaning. The elision of Berthold can perhaps be compared to the changes Cremer made to his plans for the sculpture on the Ettersberg. Apitz and Cremer had always intended the transcendence of suffering to be the essence of their representations, but they had not necessarily wanted to avoid conveying any impression that suffering might also, to a degree, have been senseless.

We are better informed of the reasons for the most significant structural change to the novel, namely, the decision to incorporate the figure of Herbert Bochow as German ILK representative. On 15 February 1957, Apitz wrote to MDV saying that he had had to completely overhaul what he had so far written "for compelling reasons." Friends from his time at Buchenwald, Apitz continued, were of the opinion that the figure of Krämer should not function as both Camp Elder and the leading member of the illegal camp resistance movement. This, so his friends thought, would contradict historical reality. Apitz claims he had been aware of this contradiction, but had conflated the two roles in an act of "personal union" because he felt it was in the interests of his dramaturgical concept. After long consideration, Apitz came to the conclusion he could not ignore his friends' arguments, and introduced the character Bochow. He anticipated he would now not finish the novel until June or July 1957. In the event, it took him longer.[40] Dividing up one character over two roles was not easy, for more was required than substituting Krämer's name at apposite points in the text. Apitz also had to create exchanges between Krämer and Bochow, as Krämer could not take certain decisions without consulting Bochow, who then had to consult the whole ILK.

Were Apitz's Buchenwald friends merely concerned about authenticity? Perhaps. At Buchenwald, communists in administrative positions were well-known to the SS and therefore not leading members of the resistance organization. Apitz's conflation of roles might have implied a certain conspiratorial laxness on the part of the ILK, suggesting they had their members in exposed positions. Apitz's friends may also have been worried that

Apitz's "personal union" implied that the ILK had had a direct influence on the compilation of transport lists. Of course, the ILK *had* had an influence — after all, the ZPKK had cross-examined Walter Bartel on this very point in 1953. The opinion of some in the SED was that the resistance organization should never have got involved in this questionable practice.[41] Bartel had defended it as unavoidable, and as the only way to protect antifascists from probable liquidation. Apitz's novel, as I shall discuss later, also defends the practice, suggesting that even an ILK member's order to deport a young child could, in circumstances where the child's presence in the camp represents a threat to the resistance organization, be understandable. No doubt there will nevertheless have been former Buchenwald prisoners who wished Apitz had never addressed the deportation issue in the first place. In splitting Krämer's role over two characters, however, Apitz hardly rectified the situation, for he now transferred sole responsibility for the order to deport the child to ILK leader Bochow; Krämer in fact initially distances himself from Bochow's decision. As we shall see later, Bochow's role was not to the liking of Walter Bartel.

In March 1957, Apitz began sending MDV parts of the novel for typing up; the last batch of pages he despatched on 4 October 1957 with the words, "now my book is finally complete."[42] Unfortunately, it was not. Apitz and MDV's editors soon found themselves engaged in pruning and adjusting Apitz's wordy, stylistically rough-hewn prose. Even after Apitz returned his copy of the typescript with his changes on 7 January 1958, claiming he had freed it of "weeds" as far as possible,[43] MDV was not happy. At a meeting on 2 February 1958, MDV entrusted one of its editors, Feudel, with further stylistic changes.[44] The typescript containing Apitz's and MDV's changes, set for printing, has survived.[45] A study of it reveals that it was not just the style that was altered: a passage describing how Krämer came to be Camp Elder has been deleted. The passage stated that Camp Commandant Schwahl had a preference for using political prisoners in administrative roles, while Deputy Camp Commandant Kluttig preferred to use criminal elements; in allocating the role of Camp Elder to Krämer, a communist, Schwahl is seeking to assert his supremacy over Kluttig.[46] This deletion has been replaced in the typescript with the version as it stands in the published novel. Here, rather than Schwahl using the political prisoners for his ends, it is the ILK who exploit the differences between Kluttig and Schwahl in order to hoist Krämer, described in the text as a "reliable comrade" into the role of Camp Elder.[47] Thus while the original version could be taken to imply that the political prisoners could sometimes be the object of an SS power game, the substituted version makes the SS the object of a power game controlled by the ILK.

Before discussing this change further, we should look at a number of other modifications to the MDV typescript, modifications that have the effect of softening the impression of conflict between prisoners. The most significant example of this occurs in a passage describing an argument between Höfel and Krämer. This ensues when Höfel informs Krämer that he, Höfel, has not passed the child on for deportation as instructed. On the MDV typescript, many alterations to this altercation have been made. Thus a sentence describing Krämer's "threatening silence" has been crossed out,[48] as has the sentence "their dark silence opened up between them like a rift."[49] True, this is hardly elegant prose, but the altercation has been too systematically pruned for this to be classified merely as a stylistic measure. Moreover, scenes involving disputes between August Rose, the one Personal Property Room prisoner who disapproves of hiding the child, and the other prisoners in the work detail have been all but excised. Among the excisions is a section where the prisoners pour insults on Rose, calling him an "old shitbag" and threatening to beat him up if he utters a word about the child to anyone outside the Storage Building.[50] A final key example of a change that reduces the impression of intense conflict can be found in the scene in which Krämer and Bochow discuss the disappearance of the child from Block 61. In the original version, Bochow is angry at the ILK member who took the child out of Block 61 without ILK permission. Changes to the typescript include the deletion of Bochow's reaction and its replacement with a passage in which Bochow expresses approval of the ILK member's action. His deed Bochow now describes as "good" and "deeply humane."[51]

The changes outlined above seek to iron out any implication that there might have been (ultimately unsuccessful) attempts by the SS to exploit the communists, or that solidarity within this collective was on occasion strained to the limit. Apitz certainly had not wanted to suggest that political prisoners were tools of the SS; he had merely sought to acknowledge internal SS squabbles and their impact on political prisoners, who, however they came to be in the positions they were, then did what they could to turn them to their advantage — witness Krämer's attempts in the novel to hinder the evacuation of Buchenwald. Nor had Apitz wished to imply that prisoner solidarity was anything other than triumphant. But he had seen no reason to deny moments of dispute. Moreover, he intended the figure of Rose, who was modeled on a real-life social democrat of the same name, to symbolize what Apitz perceived to be the treacherousness and subservience to authority of social democracy.[52] Why, then, did he make the changes? Under pressure from other former Buchenwald prisoners? Perhaps. Perhaps, also, as a result of his own fear of criticism. Apitz was not the most robust of individuals. In the end, the neuroticism of those with whom Apitz consulted led him to defuse those tensions in the novel whose overcoming Apitz wished to celebrate — I stress "defuse," because they were not absolutely expunged.

But were former Buchenwald prisoners the only source of pressure here? What of the influence of MDV itself? On 5 April 1958, Apitz wrote to his editor, Martin Gregor Schmidt, assuring him that changes to the novel suggested by MDV had now "almost entirely" been incorporated.[53] While it is not possible to reconstruct what changes were meant, they may well have gone beyond the purely stylistic. Was MDV, and above all Schmidt, worried that Apitz's novel might get the publishing company into trouble with the authorities because of scenes they believed could be misconstrued? This cannot be ruled out. MDV was a courageous publisher, pioneering the works of young, sometimes controversial writers. But in 1957 MDV had fallen foul of the SED. In the same month in which Apitz began his changes, November 1957, Erich Loest, an MDV author, was arrested; a 1956 manuscript depicting the neurotic suspiciousness of Department K5 of the Criminal Police was found in his house.[54] It was also in 1957 that MDV produced a series of short volumes in a series entitled "tangenten." This series, to which Schmidt himself contributed, came in for criticism on the grounds of supposed experimentation, modernism, and western "decadence."[55] The notorious *Stasi* even began to spy on Schmidt — and solicited Apitz's services for a short period. Given the code name "Brendel," Apitz was hired because the *Stasi* was interested in his mail — which would suggest that his communications with Schmidt were the focus of the *Stasi*'s interest.[56] In mid-May 1958, Schmidt, who according to one of Apitz's *Stasi* reports had been under increasing pressure, fled the GDR.[57] It is quite possible that he passed some of this ideological pressure on to Apitz.

One person who certainly had a hand in content changes made by Apitz was Walter Bartel. Apitz lent him a copy of the MDV typescript, perhaps to seek his advice, perhaps because Bartel had expressed an interest.[58] A number of changes at the proof stage of the novel's production are directly traceable to Bartel. According to Apitz, Bartel objected that the Party organization in the novel was pursuing the "wrong political line" because Bochow demands that the child be sent on a transport to Bergen-Belsen and therefore to his possible death: "the Party sacrifices the child."[59] Apitz wrote to Schmidt that he intended to go over the text again and make changes in order to "defuse the danger of Herbert Bochow's attitude being misunderstood." Given that no copies of the proofs have survived, the only way to establish which passages he modified is by comparing the MDV typescript in its copy-edited form with the published version of the novel.[60] Such a comparison reveals that Apitz elided all references to Bergen-Belsen as the destination of the transport. Thus whereas Krämer says to Bochow in the copy-edited MDV typescript, "the transport is going to Bergen-Belsen,"[61] in the published version of the novel this has been changed to "the transport is going into the unknown."[62] In the typescript, Höfel expresses his horror that Jankowski has rescued the child from Auschwitz "only for him to accompany it all the more surely to its death at Bergen-Belsen."[63] In the published version, this clause has been changed to "only to take it toward new, unknown dangers."[64] Overall, Apitz deleted at least twelve references to Bergen-Belsen,[65] sometimes introducing phrases that suggest that Stefan's deportation will not necessarily lead to his death. One or two other changes had a similar function. Thus the second Camp Elder Pröll's comment on the approaching transport in the MDV typescript, " 'that's another thousand corpses off on a journey' "[66] has been replaced in the published novel with " 'that's another thousand we have to send out into the unknown' "[67]

In his letter of 5 February 1958 to Schmidt, Apitz wrote that he had wanted to illustrate "the law of the jungle under which, ultimately, we all lived and which forced us to do things we would have avoided under normal circumstances."[68] In *Naked among Wolves*, Bochow is faced with the choice between accepting the protection of one child from the SS and putting the members of the resistance organization at risk on the one hand, and, on the other, ordering the deportation of the child. It is the SS who create the conditions under which such choices have to be made; at no point does Apitz suggest that Bochow is in any way to blame for making the decision he does, or that his decision is wrong. Indeed he makes it clear that the lives of 51,000 prisoners depend on the ILK, whose interests Bochow represents. Nevertheless, because the reader is likely to feel empathy with the child, he or she is likely to identify less with Bochow than with Höfel, who refuses to hand over the child for deportation. Bressau, in a 1955 exchange of letters with Apitz, had expressed concern that Höfel appeared to occupy the higher moral ground.[69] This, clearly, was also Bartel's concern. The Party, in the figure of Bochow, might come across as heartless. And hard-heartedness in the name of protecting the communist cadre was precisely one of the things for which Bartel, of whom Bochow is the literary equivalent, was upbraided by the ZPKK in 1953. Bartel may have feared a new bout of criticism. To allay his fears, Apitz tried to blur the issue of what would happen to the child if deported, so that Bochow's decision with regard to the child is no longer *necessarily* one between life and death. In the event, the changes had little effect, as reviewers still assumed deportation to mean death. In the event, too, Bartel's objections were overstated. We shall come back to this point later.

There was one other actor in the pre-publication drama: the Committee of Antifascist Resistance Fighters. At the end of January 1958, the KdAW procured from the Ministry for Culture the right to evaluate prior to publication all books pertaining to the history of communist resistance. The committee felt bound to intercede in this way because of a number of "misrepresentations" and "mistakes" in GDR novels and other publications dealing with this theme.[70] When MDV applied to the Ministry for Culture in February 1958 for permission to publish Apitz's novel, Schmidt and Bressau in their joint report pledged to pass on proofs to the committee.[71] The KdAW had these read by two former Buchenwald

Fig. 16: Robert Siewert (left, in foreground) and Walter Bartel (far right) at Buchenwald in 1959. Courtesy of Gedenkstätte Buchenwald.

prisoners, Robert Siewert and Richard Großkopf. Großkopf, like Siewert, had also been active in Buchenwald's resistance movement, where he had responsibility for military-political matters and counterintelligence. Apitz also met with representatives of the KdAW at the end of April 1958 to discuss his novel. Finally, on 12 May Rudolf Wunderlich of the KdAW wrote to him to say that both Robert Siewert and Richard Großkopf had provided positive assessments.[72] Given that the Ministry for Culture had already confirmed the granting of printing permission for the novel on 3 April 1958, the KdAW's agreement represented the last obstacle to publication.[73] Once this was overcome, printing began.

In the course of 1957 and 1958, a number of publications relating to Buchenwald were vetted by either the Ministry for Culture, the KdAW, or the Institute for Marxism-Leninism, with which the KdAW also cooperated in evaluating manuscripts. Apitz's novel was not the only subject of concern. In the run-up to the opening of the National Site of Warning and Commemoration at Buchenwald in September 1958, tighter ideological controls were put in place to ensure that publications would help disseminate the desired image of Buchenwald. There was total agreement among all constituencies that this desired image should be one that focused on communist resistance at Buchenwald and its achievements. Nevertheless, the SED Party Group within the KdAW's presiding committee, as well as the SED's Central Committee, became reluctant to allow former Buchenwald prisoners to promote this image without supervision and control. When Bartel and other ex-prisoners of Buchenwald organized commemorative ceremonies in April 1958 without consulting the KdAW, they were severely reprimanded.[74] Deeply suspicious of the tendency of former Buchenwald prisoners to exercise commemorative autonomy and indulge in self-glorification, the politburo on 28 April 1958 passed a resolution drafted by KdAW Party stalwarts that stated that all publications and events related to the opening ceremony in September had to stress that "the 14th of September is not an occasion for former Buchenwald prisoners, but for all antifascist resistance fighters."[75]

The official SED policy toward Buchenwald was committed to making of Buchenwald a shrine to antifascist resistance as a whole. The achievements of Buchenwald's communists had to be seen to redound to the greater glory of the KPD inside and outside the concentration camps, inside and outside Germany. On no account was the impression to be conveyed that Buchenwald's ILK and the resistance it organized were somehow unique, or that Buchenwald's brand of communism was somehow different, superior, more dynamic, more effective than that outside the camp. The guiding light of the KPD had to be made visible. It was clearly with this in mind that Siewert and Großkopf were asked to scrutinize Apitz's text. Thus Siewert states that "the planned corrections on the role of the Party do justice to the situation as it was in Buchenwald."[76] Given that no further corrections were made at proof stage beyond the alteration of the Bergen-Belsen passages, Siewert must be referring to these, or to other passages that were then not altered after all. Großkopf's whole report focuses on Apitz's depiction of the role of the Party. He takes issue with the impression conveyed by the novel that the Storage Building was the center of resistance, and with the fact that Apitz did not provide examples of resistance in other work details or depict the regional and national organization of the Party throughout the camp. "Leninist principles should have been brought out more," he remarks, suggesting that the political role of the ILK should have been foregrounded to a greater extent.[77] Großkopf's report shows that, as a *Stasi* man, he could be relied upon to sound out whether or not Apitz's portrayal of resistance was ideologically sound. Despite the above caveats, he was basically of the opinion that it was.

I was unable to trace evidence of further interventions in the evolution of Apitz's novel. Martin Gregor-Dellin — as Martin Schmidt later came to call himself — claimed years later that the SED's Central Committee asked MDV for seven copies of the proofs and slowed down the publication process by some months.[78] According to Gregor-Dellin, the fact that the initiative for the rescue of the child in the novel was taken by someone outside the "Party group" may have caused a problem. But Höfel, while not a member of the ILK, is an important Party figure in the military resistance. Gregor-Dellin appears to misunderstand the novel, though certainly it is true that the ILK leader Bochow is initially against keeping the child in the camp. While the possibility cannot be ruled out that the Central Committee did approach MDV, there is no archival evidence that it did, or that MDV sent out proofs to the Central Committee. Besides, what archival evidence we do have suggests that Apitz's novel, submitted for scrutiny to the Ministry for Culture on 24 February 1958, went through the often laborious vetting procedure very swiftly. On 19 March 1958, Helmut Elsholz of the Main Publishing Department granted typesetting permission *although* the external evaluation of the novel commissioned by his Department was still outstanding. The reason for this unusual step was that "the book is to appear in time for the fifth Party Congress" (10–16 July 1958). The slogan for this Congress — during which Ulbricht famously promulgated his ten commandments of socialist morality and ethics — was "Socialism Triumphs!" Given that Apitz's novel ends with an uprising of the prisoners under the guidance of the communist ILK, it was a very suitable literary accompaniment indeed to the Congress.

Written in bright red crayon across MDV's printing application are the words "Urgent!" and "For the fifth Party Congress." This is hardly the language of delay. When Elsholz received the external evaluation — of which I could trace no surviving copy in the archives — it was clearly positive, because Elsholz, referring to it, stated he had "no reservations" and then proceeded to grant printing permission. As early as 1 April the manuscript was returned to Apitz and a decision taken to raise the print-run from 8,000 to 10,000 copies (the original number MDV had envisaged was 7,000; the novel was not expected to be a success).[79] The only slight delay to publication was caused by the KdAW's scrutiny of the proofs, the result of which only became known in early May. Quite why, therefore, Gregor-Dellin should suggest that there was significant, time-consuming, top-level intervention is hard to fathom. Nevertheless, as I have shown above, there certainly was interference from other quarters, interference that came, basically, from two directions: there were those, such as Bartel, who were concerned that Apitz's novel might expose the ILK to criticism; and then there were those, such as the SED group within the KdAW, who, while sharing Bartel's concerns to an extent, also wished to be reassured that the novel in no way implied that Buchenwald's communists, or some of them, were operating in isolation from the structuring hand of international communism in Moscow. In short: had Apitz not celebrated the ILK enough, or had he done so too much?

In many ways, the answer was provided by the huge success of Apitz's novel with public, critics, and SED stalwarts alike. Just as Cremer's monument on the Ettersberg extends its celebration of Buchenwald's communists to include the KPD and international antifascism, so Apitz's novel, despite the anxieties discussed above, can be seen as striking a similarly perfect balance — a balance that it was always Apitz's intention to strike. Apitz was involved in draft plans by former Buchenwald prisoners for the new museum as of 1956/1957.[80] His name, along with those of Anna Seghers and Kuba, was mentioned when considering who might be asked to provide the strophes for the back of the stelae in the memorial complex.[81] He was thus well acquainted with the debates surrounding Buchenwald, and, as a man who always preferred harmony to conflict, attempted to bridge all the differences of opinion in his novel. Before turning to a discussion of the reception and message(s) of Apitz's novel, however, it seems apposite to provide the reader with an overview of its contents — not least because it will become clear that Apitz's "take" on the rescue is quite different from that of Zacharias Zweig in his testimony for Yad Vashem.

Naked among Wolves: The Story

Set in Buchenwald in March and April 1945, the novel depicts both the events leading up to "self-liberation" on 11 April and the events surrounding the attempts to save the life of a young Polish Jew, Stefan Cyliak. While the "rescue narrative" predominates in the first part of the novel, the "liberation narrative" is foregrounded more and more as 11 April approaches. But the two narratives are frequently interconnected, and indeed are brought together in the final scene, when the prisoners hold the child up high as they storm through the camp's gate.

At the outset of the novel, a goods train arrives at Buchenwald station, packed with prisoners from Auschwitz. One of these, Zacharias Jankowski, is carrying a heavy suitcase. A member of the Personal Property Room work detail, Rudi Pippig, opens the case and sees a small boy curled up inside. André Höfel, Kapo in the Storage Building, orders Pippig to hide the child, and then informs Herbert Bochow, leader of the illegal International Camp Committee (ILK), of the child's concealment. Bochow reacts angrily. If the child should be discovered by the SS, Höfel's role in hiding it may also come to light. Höfel, a military instructor within the resistance organization, would then be interrogated by the SS; the child is thus a danger to the ILK, indeed to all the prisoners, whose interests are protected as far as possible by the ILK. Bochow tells Höfel that Jankowski and the child must be sent out of the camp on the next transport, and informs Walter Krämer, the communist Camp Elder with responsibility for the camp's self-administration, of the addition to the transport list.

Meanwhile, the camp's SS leadership is beginning to panic because of the rapid advance of the Allies. Camp commandant Schwahl plans to set up a "sanitary troop" of prisoners whose job it will be to provide medical help to any SS members injured during Allied bombing raids on

Buchenwald. As the sanitary troop will operate outside the camp, this is a sensitive work detail. While Schwahl advocates using political prisoners, his deputy Kluttig fears that the communist resistance organization, which he passionately hates, will exploit the sanitary troop to extend its activities. But he has to back down, and Krämer is ordered to set up the sanitary troop. Krämer, although not a member of the ILK and kept in the dark about its innermost workings, suggests to Bochow that he, Krämer, put together the troop using reliable comrades who can gather useful information about the SS area of the camp. Krämer and Bochow also discuss the child; Krämer wants to take him under his wing, but Bochow insists he be deported. Before Bochow can accept Krämer's sanitary troop suggestion, he has to consult with the other ILK members, who approve the plan.

The following morning, Pippig and the Polish prisoner Kropinski protest so vigorously against Stefan's deportation that Höfel allows him to remain where he is for the time being. This moment of hesitation proves significant, because shortly afterward Zweiling, the SS man in charge of the Storage Building, discovers the prisoners' secret. However, Zweiling gives Höfel to understand that he will tolerate the concealment of the child (so that he can curry favor with the Americans when they arrive). Höfel, sensing he has Zweiling where he wants him, decides not to hand over the child for deportation. Only Jankowski, the man who smuggled Stefan into the camp, is deported. When Höfel tells Krämer he has defied his order, Krämer is dismayed. He regards Zweiling as a rascal who, should the Allied advance be repelled, will change his tactics and hand Höfel and the child over to his superiors. Krämer realizes that there is now no alternative to keeping the child in the camp, but it must be put beyond Zweiling's reach. He suggests hiding it in the Small Camp, in the so-called "epidemic barracks" (Block 61), where two Polish prisoners are doing their best to alleviate the pain of prisoners suffering from typhus and other diseases. Krämer is convinced it is the safest option given that the SS never enter Block 61; the Polish medics, moreover, will be able to protect Stefan from infection.

Krämer's eagerness to move the child proves well-founded. Zweiling's wife, Hortense, convinces him that colluding with prisoners could lead to his execution should the SS find out. He writes a note, purporting to come from a prisoner, to Reineboth informing him that Höfel and Kropinski have hidden a child in the Storage Building. Just before Reineboth receives this note, however, Höfel, Pippig, and Kropinski smuggle Stefan into the Small Camp, so that when the SS search the Storage Building, the child is no longer there. Höfel and Kropinski are taken to the Bunker Building, where they are tortured by Mandrak, Kluttig, and Reineboth in the hope they will reveal the whereabouts of the child. Bochow, on finding out that the child has not been deported, is angry, but also realizes he was mistaken not to have informed Krämer about the sensitivity of Höfel's position.

Bochow now informs Krämer about the activities of the ILK and orders him to find out how well Höfel is standing up to interrogation. There follows a famous scene between ILK member Bogorski (a Russian) and Bochow, where Bogorski reproaches Bochow for having acted purely rationally in insisting on the child's deportation, and criticizes Höfel for having acted purely emotionally.

Krämer instructs the prisoner Heinrich Schüpp, who as camp electrician has access to SS areas, to find out what is happening to Höfel. Schüpp establishes that Höfel has not given anything away, and that the SS regard him as a key to finding out more about the ILK. Schüpp suggests to Krämer that Zweiling be used as a lever to secure Höfel's and Kropinski's release. Krämer agrees, and Pippig is given the task of suggesting to Zweiling that, if he helps, the prisoners will put in a good word for him later. The ILK subsequently assents to Schüpp's plan; at the same ILK meeting, Bochow reproaches himself for having given Höfel the cold shoulder when Höfel came to him for advice about the child.

What the ILK do not know, however, is that Reineboth suspects Zweiling of having written the note about the child's concealment himself. Zweiling is thus in no position to engineer Höfel's release. Reineboth makes it clear to Zweiling that, in order to rehabilitate himself, he will have to find out who the members of the resistance are. Zweiling plants a spy, Wurach, in the Personal Property Room work detail. Meanwhile Höfel, delirious with pain after having been subjected to torture, makes some confused remarks that lead Reineboth to assume that the resistance organization as a whole is responsible for hiding the child. At the same time Reineboth, realizing that neither Höfel nor Kropinski is likely to divulge any really valuable information, hands over ten of the prisoners working in the Storage Building, including Pippig and Rose, to the Gestapo in Weimar. At the same time, Zweiling passes on a list of names of individuals suspected of belonging to the resistance organization to Reineboth. The SS appears to be coordinating its "attack" on the ILK.

In Weimar, Rochus Gay of the Gestapo tortures Pippig, but Pippig reveals nothing. Back in Buchenwald, Bochow hears that the SS will evacuate the camp before the Americans reach Buchenwald, which could result in the death of the entire prisoner population. The ILK meets and agrees that an armed revolt against the SS at the current point in time would probably be crushed, and that the best that can be done is to obstruct the evacuations. The ILK also discusses what to do about the child. Bochow suggests moving him again, this time to a hiding place beneath the sick-bay building. Eventually there is agreement on this, and that Krämer is the one who should move the child.

Meanwhile, camp commandant Schwahl informs Kluttig that he intends to carry out Himmler's orders to evacuate Buchenwald. Kluttig, clearly, would prefer to massacre all the prisoners on the spot. For the diplomat Schwahl, this is a not a good idea. Leaving piles of corpses behind for the Americans to find would incriminate Buchenwald's SS leaders. As a sop to Kluttig, Schwahl gives him permission to execute all the prisoners on the list of suspect prisoners compiled by Zweiling — with the exception of Krämer, whom Schwahl needs to help coordinate the evacuation process. In Weimar, August Rose gives in to Gestapo torture and betrays the whereabouts of the child. But when Kluttig, given the tip-off by Gay, rushes to Block 61, there is no sign of Stefan. Kluttig informs Gay of this, whereupon Gay angrily assaults Rose, who in his panic insists that Pippig is the one who knows where the child really is. In frustration at Pippig's intransigence, Gay kicks him to death.

Bochow is mystified at the child's disappearance — it was moved before Krämer could be entrusted with the task of hiding it. He is also annoyed, because he has now lost track of the child's whereabouts. He suspects that it may have been another member of the ILK who moved the child — in contravention of what was agreed at the meeting. At the same time Bochow realizes that whoever moved it acted with great presence of mind and in the best interests of Stefan. As Krämer, on Bochow's orders, tries to locate Stefan, Reineboth calls on the prisoner administration to summon the forty-six prisoners on Zweiling's list, claiming they are to be set free. As it happens, while the list contains the names of proved antifascists, none of the ILK members is on it; Zweiling and Wurach have, in essence, got it wrong. The ILK, guessing what the SS really wants to do with the men on the list, orders that they be hidden throughout the camp. Schwahl gives his word of honor to Krämer that the camp will not be evacuated: the prisoners will merely be sent out of the camp to help clear away war damage in the area. Höfel and Kropinski, whom Reineboth has now turned over to Mandrill to do with as he sees fit, overhear Schwahl's pledge and are hopeful that they might survive after all. But Krämer knows Schwahl is lying.

When the forty-six prisoners fail to turn up to roll-call, the Camp Police are called in, but, being a prisoner organization, they only make a pretense of looking for them. At the next ILK meeting, Bochow and Bogorski argue that it is still too early to start a revolt. When the SS sets about evacuating thousands of Jews, Bochow instructs Krämer to hinder this process. The Jews, in any case, panic and seek refuge where they can. Reineboth sends in SS men, who use violence to drive the Jews up to the roll-call square, where the Camp Police are given the task of cordoning them off. The Camp Police, however, allow the Jews to escape back into the camp. On the following day, Reineboth orders all the prisoners to assemble in the roll-call area, whereupon the SS men seize as many Jews as they can. But at the following ILK meeting it is still deemed too early to launch a rebellion. As more and more prisoners are brutally driven toward Buchenwald from other camps, Reineboth orders Krämer to prepare 10,000 prisoners for transport. Bochow and Bogorski ask the resistance groups to recruit volunteers equipped with hidden weapons to accompany the transports and, if possible, liberate them.

Even if everyone else seems to have forgotten the child, Krämer has not, and he insists that Bochow find out where he is. But Bogorski, whom Bochow suspects of hiding Stefan, refuses to admit anything. Contradictory rumors about the advance of the Americans are causing conflicting feelings among the prisoners. The decision is taken to let the forty-six out of hiding: the SS has other worries and appears to have lost interest in them. Frustrated by further delaying tactics on the part of Krämer, the SS men storm the camp and seize prisoners for transport. Following a heated meeting of the ILK with the heads of the resistance subgroups, the delaying tactics are confirmed. On 7 April, the SS orders the evacuation of another 20,000 prisoners and 800 Soviet POWs. Krämer decides he will not put together the second transport of 10,000 prisoners. Bogorski and a number of others in the Soviet resistance group resolve to accompany the 800 POWs and try to liberate them. Only now does Bogorski admit that he is behind the hiding of the child — acting on his orders, a Soviet POW had removed Stefan from Block 61. Stefan's new hideout is a pigsty, where he shares a covered run with a pregnant sow. The child, stinking from its own excrement, is duly fetched, taken to Block 38 (Bochow's block) and cleaned thoroughly. Meanwhile, over the next days, the evacuations continue; of 50,000, only 21,000 prisoners now remain in the camp.

In case the SS should decide to try to liquidate these remaining prisoners before fleeing, the ILK prepares a contingency plan. On 10 April, the situation is dramatically exacerbated when Reineboth informs Krämer that the camp is to be evacuated by 12 noon; yet there is also hope, for it is clear that the Americans must now be very near, so that a further delay could save the prisoners. When no prisoners appear at the appointed time, a few hundred SS men are brought into position around the blocks, with machine guns. By chance, Kluttig discovers the child in Block 38. He draws his gun, but the prisoners form a threatening ring around him, and he is forced to withdraw — but not before he has shot Krämer, who is badly, but not mortally, wounded. After further disputes among the SS leaders, Kluttig flees, taking Hortense, Zweiling's wife, with him. In the morning of 11 April, Reineboth and Mandrill also depart, though not before Mandrill, Brauer, and Meisgeier have slaughtered most of the Bunker Building prisoners. Luckily, Höfel and Kropinski survive. Zweiling, caught trying to forge a new identity for himself with false papers, is seized by two members of the Camp Police. Schwahl flees. As the sound of fighting near Buchenwald grows louder by the minute, Bochow gives the order for the uprising to begin. The resistance groups fan out through the camp, exchanging fire with the SS before occupying the watchtowers; the SS men flee or are captured. Krämer runs out to join the celebrating masses, holding the child under his arm. He sees Höfel and Kropinski. In his joy, Höfel clutches the child away from Krämer; Kropinski then takes Stefan as Höfel appears to stumble, and runs, the child held above his head, in the midst of the throng of prisoners, through the opened gate.

The Success of *Naked among Wolves*

Apitz's *Naked among Wolves*, as this brief summary demonstrates, is certainly an action-packed novel. The narrative is full of twists and turns, and the conflict between the SS and the communist prisoners dominates throughout. The rescue story provides a sentimental focus for those readers less interested in this grander struggle. Not surprisingly, then, the novel became a bestseller almost as soon as it appeared. Overwhelmed by the novel's huge success, MDV found itself rushing to catch up with demand: in the second half of 1958, five editions of the novel were published (61,032 copies), and another four followed in 1959 (179,920 copies).[82] Sales of the novel continued at a high level. By 1976, MDV had published thirty-eight editions — 925,000 copies all in all. A further fourteen editions, 585,000 copies, had appeared by 1976 with Reclam publishing house in Leipzig, while throughout the rest of the world another million copies of the novel had sold in translation.[83] *Naked among Wolves* had been translated into seventeen languages by 1962: its popularity was not restricted to the GDR. Within the first year or so of publication, Apitz, from living on the breadline, had become a reasonably wealthy man: the first eleven editions earned him about 230,000 marks in royalties, and he received additional royalties for the publication of parts of his novel in newspapers. Until his death, Apitz was able to live more than comfortably on a continuous flow of cash from new editions and translations of one book. His later novels, set in the Weimar Republic — *The Rainbow* (*Der Regenbogen*, 1976) and *Smoldering Fire* (*Schwelbrand*, 1984) — sank into immediate obscurity.

Naked among Wolves was not only a success with the general public; it also met with the approval of the state. Indeed it soon achieved cult status. It was widely on display in bookshops in September 1958, when the National Site of Warning and Commemoration was dedicated at Buchenwald. In 1960, it was introduced into the school curriculum.[84] It remained a staple of the curriculum right up until 1989/90. Also in 1960, at the prompting of the Ministry for Culture, the novel was officially recommended for all public libraries as one of the novels ideally suited for readings to celebrate the fifteenth anniversary of liberation on 8 May.[85] Readings of the novel were integrated into the various courses held at the NMGB for teachers (of history and civic studies) and Pioneer Leaders as of 1962.[86] And it was soon turned into a radio play (broadcast on 14

September 1958), a television drama (broadcast on 12 April 1960), and then a DEFA film (1963). Not surprisingly, given the official backing for book and film, Apitz was heaped with accolades and medals. In September 1958, for instance, he was awarded the "Medal for Fighters against Fascism," and in October he received the "German National Prize for Art and Culture."

The literary historian Wolfgang Emmerich has claimed that *Naked among Wolves* was viewed in the GDR as the very quintessence of socialist realism.[87] Emmerich's judgment can be corroborated by reference to statements by GDR cultural functionaries. Thus Alexander Abusch, the GDR's Minister for Culture between 1958 and 1961, maintained that the novel "corresponds in every respect to the very best one can expect of a work of socialist realism."[88] This was one important reason for the official approval of *Naked among Wolves*. More than any other work of GDR antifascist literature, it exemplified both a Hegelian and Marxist view of history. First, the novel shows within the resistance group the existence of a thesis and antithesis. Bochow appears to represent the rational, Höfel and Pippig the emotional. It is the Russian Bogorski who pleads for a synthesis of these faculties: Apitz makes an appropriate nod in the direction of the Soviet Union and the GDR doctrine "learning from the Soviet Union means learning to be victorious." In the end, the communist resistance group achieves the superhuman feat of combining concern for the whole prisoner collective with concern for the individual — superhuman because the objective circumstances appear to militate against such a synthesis. Second, the novel shows a progressive conflict between the SS and the communist prisoners. The self-liberation at the end represents a revolutionary triumph as capitalist imperialism as embodied by the SS is overcome in the name of an impending socialist order.

One might summarize the above by claiming that a key facet of the novel's socialist realism is its championship of socialist humanism. While the disputes between the SS leaders in the camp lead to internecine strife, increased brutality toward the prisoners, and utter selfishness, the prisoners move closer together in a learning and bonding process, their increased unity finding powerful expression in the final pages. Integrity, altruism, loyalty, courage, and infinite resourcefulness are the hallmark of the ILK and its dependent groups. Apitz's novel thus gave literary form to the purported link established in the GDR between the classical humanism of Weimar (Goethe and Schiller), and the communist humanism of Buchenwald. In fact *Naked among Wolves* is in a sense of piece of tendentious socialist historiography. Through the prism of Buchenwald, it interprets the National Socialist period as that era when the morally bankrupt bourgeoisie finally abandoned all pretense to humanism and when it became the turn of the communists to hold up and carry forward the torch of enlightenment — symbolized in the rescue of a child, whose survival testifies to the victory of humanism over death and destruction.

But it was not just the novel's view of history that rendered it so appealing to the GDR's political and cultural establishment. In a statement in 1960 celebrating Apitz's sixtieth birthday, Abusch congratulated him on having created "a literary memorial to antifascist resistance that fires hundreds of thousands of people with enthusiasm for . . . the active struggle against renascent fascism and militarism in West Germany."[89] The term "literary memorial" aligns Apitz's novel with the physical memorial on the Ettersberg and the memorialization of Thälmann and communist resistance at the former camp site itself. But the NMGB was also a *site of warning*: remembering the past simultaneously meant drawing attention to dangerous continuities in the present. Likewise, Apitz's novel was understood in the GDR as a protest against the supposed recrudescence of fascism on the other side of the border. Its message was seen as a contemporary one. Abusch's view of *Naked among Wolves* was shared by none other than the General Secretary of the SED, Walter Ulbricht himself. On the occasion of Apitz's sixty-fifth birthday, Ulbricht declared crisply in the SED newspaper *Neues Deutschland* that *Naked among Wolves* had become a "sharp weapon in the fight against fascism and dark, reactionary elements."[90] In essence then, the GDR, a liberated country, was engaged in a struggle for liberation on behalf of the citizens of the FRG comparable to that waged by the prisoners of Buchenwald against the SS.

Small wonder that Abusch, in his 1960 message of congratulation, claimed that Apitz's novel had "enriched our socialist German national culture." One year later, in similar vein, the town of Weimar decided to make Apitz an honorary citizen because of his contribution to "socialist German national literature."[91] The SED was forever attempting to build a "combative" and "humanist" *German* socialist identity in the present by inviting its citizens to identify with German socialist achievements in the immediate past. It was an attractive invitation because it offered the prospect of self-exculpation. Apitz's novel appeared to be the ideal vehicle for promoting this policy. Nazism in *Naked among Wolves* is presented as the instrument of a somehow alien bourgeois class that had manipulated the hapless Germans in its interests. Communism, by contrast, is presented both as the expression of the international working class *and* as the true political home of the German people. *Naked among Wolves*, then, shows the Germans to be victims of Hitler, or antifascists who had even thrown off the fascist yoke themselves (by liberating Buchenwald) — whereas the perpetrators had been *petit-bourgeois*. It is important to bear this in mind when seeking to understand why Klaus Höpcke, deputy Minister for Culture at the time (1979), could declare that *Naked among Wolves* is "one of the foundational texts for the education of the people in the GDR and for the socialist nation developing in our country."[92]

Stefan Cyliak: The Figure of the Child

Apitz's novel was indeed a foundational text, suggesting as it did that the GDR was founded on the humanist, combative, and liberating achievements of German communists. With critical hindsight, *Naked among Wolves* can also be described as a foundation *myth*, given that it can only create the image it does by ignoring the negative and questionable aspects of communist resistance at Buchenwald and by exaggerating its importance (see chapter 1). In one particular respect, Apitz's foundation myth is more rooted in traditional cultural heritage than might at first appear to be the case. Its mythopoeic lineage stretches back to the child-rescue foundation myths of classical antiquity and the Bible, notably (but not exclusively) those of Romulus and Remus and of the infant Moses. As the reader will surely recall, baby Romulus, together with his brother Remus, was put into a basket and placed in the river Tiber; Moses was placed in an ark made of bulrushes and hidden on the banks of the river Nile. Both Romulus and Remus were rescued and survived, not least thanks to being suckled by a she-wolf; and of course Moses also survived. Without Romulus, at least in myth, there would have been no Roman Empire. While Abraham is regarded as the father of Israel, it was Moses who freed the Hebrew people from servitude and who is often seen as the lawgiver and founder of the nation. The similarities to *Naked among Wolves* are striking. Stefan Cyliak, momentarily abandoned by his protector Zacharias as the latter enters the Disinfection Building, is "found" in a suitcase, the modern equivalent of the basket or ark, by the prisoner Höfel. The communists rescue the child from the SS, as great a threat as the Tiber or the Pharaoh. And the story also ends with the foundation of a new and better order.

Yet Apitz's novel also represents a significant departure from previous child-rescue foundation myths. Both the Romulus and Remus and the *Naked among Wolves* myths are feral myths. But in the latter story, milk is not provided by a she-wolf; rather cow's milk has to be stolen from human wolves (the SS) and passed on to Stefan through the antifascist prisoner Pippig. In both the Moses and Romulus myths, the maternal element is lifesaving. In *Naked among Wolves*, the communist patriarchy assumes maternal and paternal responsibilities. It is replete with a potent and life-generating masculinity. Furthermore, while Romulus goes on to found a state, Stefan does not. Throughout the novel he remains utterly passive. It is his rescuers, the communists, who penetrate the gates of Buchenwald and generate a new world. Apitz's myth appears to be characterized by the same world-changing dynamic typical of its classical forebears, but in essence it is a deeply conservative, even reactionary work. It implicitly confirms the right of the older generation to positions of power in the present, a right derived from their resistance to Hitler. It reduces youth to helpless dependency, and underpins the marginalization of women from GDR political life by celebrating the masculine self-sufficiency of Buchenwald's resistance collective.

In order to narrate Stefan's rescue as a conservative, antifascist variation on traditional child-foundation myths, Apitz makes fundamental changes to the rescue story as told by Zacharias Zweig in his 1945 account — an account that he must have known, as his adoption of the names of Zacharias and Stefan surely demonstrates. First, he alters the status of Zacharias. In *Naked among Wolves*, he is not the boy's father but a prisoner who has taken responsibility for Stefan following the death of the latter's parents at Auschwitz. Second, while Zacharias Zweig describes his and his son's experiences in Polish ghettos and camps prior to Buchenwald, Apitz focuses entirely on Buchenwald. Third, while, in Zacharias's account, he and Stefan arrive at Buchenwald in August 1944, the novel has Stefan and his guardian Zacharias arrive in March 1945. Fourth, in his report Zacharias describes how both he and his son survived Buchenwald; in Apitz's novel, by contrast, the prisoner Zacharias is transported out of the camp soon after his arrival. Finally, on a related note, Zacharias Zweig describes how he was himself involved before and at Buchenwald in his son's rescue, especially during the evacuation period.[93] But in *Naked among Wolves*, the child is protected solely by other prisoners. None of these differences is without significance.

By making of Zacharias a guardian rather than a father figure, Apitz reduces his claim on Stefan. This, together with the fact that Zacharias in the novel is something of a weak character, makes it easier for the reader to accept his subsequent deportation and the transference of paternal responsibility to the camp resistance. The same purpose is served by downplaying the importance of Zacharias's role in the protection of Stefan prior to and at Buchenwald. Had Zacharias remained in Buchenwald in the novel and retained even a guardian's claim on Stefan, this would have called into question the right of the resistance to "adopt" Stefan; and had he remained in Buchenwald and continued to fight for his protégé's survival, the communists would have had to share their courageous deeds with a Jew. Thus the degradation of the father to a dispensable role serves to concentrate the focus more completely on the courage of Buchenwald's communists. So does the shifting of the time frame from 1944 to 1945, a shift that enables the rescue to be intimately bound up with preparations for self-liberation. The differences between Zacharias's 1945 account and Apitz's novel, moreover, are differences between a Holocaust narrative and a communist-resistance narrative.

Zacharias's brief post-liberation account throws into relief the suffering and persecution of Jews against the background of the Holocaust. In Apitz's novel, Jewish suffering is not a theme. Certainly, on the surface of it, *Naked among Wolves* appears to be a book about the rescue of a Jewish child. The SS men (and Hortense) in the novel constantly use the term

"Jewish brat" in reference to Stefan.[94] But the prisoners involved in Stefan's protection rarely refer to him as a "Jew" or as "Jewish." By and large, they describe him simply as a child, or, occasionally, a Polish child. The reader thus gains the impression that it is more Stefan's youth or perhaps his Polishness which puts him at risk, rather than his Jewishness. To understand Apitz's very slight portrayal of Stefan's Jewishness, we need to understand the socialist view on which it is predicated. According to this view, Nazism was a mechanism of capitalist exploitation and imperialism. The fundamental tension and conflict lines, therefore, ran between Nazis and communists, not between Nazis and Jews. In his novel, Apitz adapts the story of Stefan's rescue to fit this paradigmatic reading of recent history. While the SS men are pursuing the child, they are simultaneously pursuing the resistance organization and its leadership, the ILK; whatever their anti-Semitism, it is essentially anticommunism that is driving them. Similarly, the communist prisoners are protecting the child not out of sympathy for his persecuted Jewishness, but because he symbolizes values that, as socialists, they are bound to defend, such as innocence, purity, human fragility, the future, and the right to life. Through and across the child, Nazism and communism lock horns in an essential moral conflict of systems.

The novel does not entirely obscure the facts of racial persecution; rather it pushes them into the background. They remain visible enough to enable us to read the novel as representing the transcendence of the positive narrative of socialist humanism over the negative narrative of destruction in the Holocaust; this transcendence is certainly implicit in the triumph of communist-directed prisoner solidarity and courage over the evil of National Socialism. It is quite conceivable that Apitz designed his novel as a counternarrative to the diary of Anne Frank. The (subsequently deleted) references to Bergen-Belsen would suggest that he had wanted to stress that Stefan's life does *not* end there after all, unlike Frank's. *Naked among Wolves* invites millions of readers to cross over the Nazi period on a bridge constructed from the courageous deeds of antifascism; there is no real need to look down into the abyss of the Holocaust, which, ultimately, is consigned to the margins of history. Not only that: the novel also implicitly consigns the "Jewish question" to history. At the end, the child, having lived among antifascist prisoners prior to liberation, has effectively become a *political* prisoner. He has been absorbed into a "combative" socialist collective, which proves far more capable of protecting him than the "victim" Jewish collective from which he was plucked. The best way forward for a Jew, in other words, is to be shed of his Jewishness and become assimilated. There is a bitter irony in this implication: there were good socialists among the GDR's Jews, but this did not protect them against anti-Semitic persecution in the 1950s.

While Stefan Cyliak in *Naked among Wolves*, then, becomes a symbolic focus in the struggle between capitalist imperialism and communism, we should not overlook the fact that he also becomes a focus of disagreement between the prisoners themselves. Thus Höfel defies Bochow by not passing the child over for deportation. Not surprisingly, it was West German critics, chief among them Marcel Reich-Ranicki, who picked up on this. In his review of the novel — which appeared in West Germany with Rowohlt publishing house in 1961 — Reich-Ranicki provided an interesting explanation of its success in the GDR. "In a country where a song is sung that begins with the words 'The Party, the Party is always right . . .,' people are grateful for a novel that praises an action that was only possible because a comrade disobeyed the Party."[95] In fact, the Party is defied twice. The Russian ILK member Bogorksi ignores the conspiratorial concerns of the ILK by personally organizing Stefan's removal from Block 61.

It might be tempting to read *Naked among Wolves* as a defense of individual rights against the claims of the Party, but this does limited justice to its intentions. Apitz may not explicitly criticize breaches of Party discipline, but he does not condone them either: Höfel should have listened to Bochow, and Bochow should have listened to Höfel. Besides, it is the SS that creates the circumstances in which Bochow has to make life-and-death choices. One should be wary, moreover, of too over-determined a view of prisoner differences. Bochow is not really the personification of cold reasoning; reason is merely another term for generic responsibility toward all the camp's prisoners, one that appears more "rational" because it is based on a principle rather than on a concrete concern for one individual. Certainly Bochow's preoccupation with the rules of conspiracy borders on the obsessive; it is the Russian Bogorski — again demonstrating that it is important to learn from the Soviets — who shows that rules sometimes have to be bent to save individual lives. But Bochow, in the novel, is always objectively right; Bogorski and Höfel take enormous risks.

In the final analysis, the tension between the prisoners is caused by Nazism; it is not at all symptomatic of the moral, political, and ideological mechanics of socialism. And any tensions are resolved in a quite heroic manner. The ILK is able to protect both the individual *and* the collective. The real moral question raised by the ILK's conduct at Buchenwald — did it allow itself to become embroiled in SS practices to save its own cadre — is ultimately circumnavigated by Apitz in Stefan's case, as the child is not deported after all.[96] The rationale for his near-deportation, in any case, is iron-cast: he appears to represent a threat to the ILK's prospects of protecting 51,000 prisoners against the SS. Moreover, while Apitz defends placing individuals on transport lists where they represent a risk, he does not seek to provide a justification for the much more common scenario, namely, the striking off of the names of valued prisoners and their replacement by individuals who represent no threat whatsoever. Yet this was precisely what had happened in the case of the real Stefan Zweig (see chapters 1 and 6). Apitz may not have known this, of course, at the time of writing his novel — although he will certainly have known it after reading Zacharias's 1961 Yad Vashem testimony (chapter 5).

Naked among Wolves, whatever the concerns of Bartel, is in essence a panegyric of communist resistance. And the child, devoid of personality and robbed by Apitz of the power of speech, remains a blank surface onto which the greater glory of adult male communist achievements can be projected. That the novel is really about the communists, and that it only requires the child for its symbolic potential, is clear from the second half of the book. As the self-liberation narrative gathers pace, the child is left to gather dirt in a pigsty. Toward the end, he is brought out, washed and, his symbolism reinvigorated, carried aloft through the opened gates. In this final scene, he becomes an icon and indeed a trophy of the magnificent triumph of communist resistance over fascist adversity.

Notes

[1] See, for instance, Ulf Heise, "Leben hinter Stacheldraht: Heute vor 100 Jahren wurde Bruno Apitz in Leipzig geboren," *Thüringische Landeszeitung*, 28 April 2000.

[2] Kommunistische Partei Deutschlands Stadt und Kreis Leipzig, ed., *Das war Buchenwald! Ein Tatsachenbericht* (Leipzig: Verlag für Wissenschaft und Literatur, 1945).

[3] KPD Stadt und Kreis Leipzig, *Das war Buchenwald!* 40–42.

[4] KPD Stadt und Kreis Leipzig, *Das war Buchenwald!* 42.

[5] KPD Stadt und Kreis Leipzig, *Das war Buchenwald!* 42–45.

[6] KPD Stadt und Kreis Leipzig, *Das war Buchenwald!* 57–63.

[7] KPD Stadt und Kreis Leipzig, *Das war Buchenwald!* 84–87; here, 87.

[8] For Apitz's own description of the contents of some of these sketches, see Wolfgang Schneider, *Kunst hinter Stacheldraht: Ein Beitrag zur Geschichte des antifaschistischen Widerstandskampfes* (Weimar: Buchdruckerei Weimar, 1973), 126–28.

[9] According to Otto Halle. See Internationales Buchenwald-Komitee/Komitee der Antifaschistischen Widerstandskämpfer in der Deutschen Demokratischen Republik, eds., *Buchenwald: Mahnung und Verpflichtung, Dokumente und Berichte* (Berlin: Kongress-Verlag, 1960), 443.

[10] According to Walter Laue. See Internationales Buchenwald-Komitee/Komitee der Antifaschistischen Widerstandskämpfer, *Buchenwald: Mahnung und Verpflichtung*, 368.

[11] Thus Apitz's name featured on a list drawn up on 5 April 1944 of forty-six antifascist prisoners whom the SS targeted for liquidation, either because they

presumed them to be prominent figures in the organization of resistance (which they were not) or because they feared that these were the prisoners best informed about the camp and the crimes of the SS who would be able to pass on information to the Americans after liberation. Along with the others on the list, Apitz was hidden on the orders of the ILK until the danger had passed. See Internationales Buchenwald-Komitee/Komitee der Antifaschistischen Widerstandskämpfer, *Buchenwald: Mahnung und Verpflichtung*, 540–43.

[12] See David Hackett, trans. and ed., *The Buchenwald Report* (Boulder, San Francisco, and Oxford, UK: Westview Press, 1995), 263–65, and the slightly amplified version of Apitz's report in *KL Bu: Konzentrationslager Buchenwald: Bericht des Internationalen Lagerkomitees Buchenwald* (Weimar: Thüringer Volksverlag, 1945), 140–42.

[13] For more on Apitz's "The Last Face," see Schneider, *Kunst hinter Stacheldraht*, 24–27.

[14] See Kuratorium für den Aufbau Nationaler Gedenkstätten, ed., *Buchenwald: Aus Vergangenheit und Gegenwart des Ettersbergs bei Weimar* (Reichenbach: VEB Volkskunstverlag, 1956), 3–4.

[15] Internationales Buchenwald-Komitee/Komitee der Antifaschistischen Widerstandskämpfer, *Buchenwald: Mahnung und Verpflichtung*, 17.

[16] Bruno Apitz, "Esther," in *Die verwischte Photographie: Sozialistische Erzähler über den Widerstand in Deutschland, 1933–1945*, ed. Gerda Zschocke (Berlin: Militärverlag der DDR, 1983), 120–39; here, 123.

[17] Apitz, "Esther," 139.

[18] In the early 1960s, GDR television set out to make a TV film of *Esther*, but Apitz took virulent exception to the screenplay — for reasons that are not clearly documented. *Esther* was not shown on East German television until 1980. See Thomas Heimann, *Bilder von Buchenwald: Die Visualisierung des Antifaschismus in der DDR (1945–1990)* (Cologne, Weimar, and Vienna: Böhlau, 2005), 128–35.

[19] KPD Stadt und Kreis Leipzig, *Das war Buchenwald!* 120–30.

[20] Internationales Buchenwald-Komitee/Komitee der Antifaschistischen Widerstandskämpfer, *Buchenwald: Mahnung und Verpflichtung*, 481.

[21] See, for instance, "Bruno Apitz: Fragen zur Person," *Wochenpost* (Berlin), 24 April 1970.

[22] Stiftung Archiv der Parteien und Massenorganisationen der DDR im Bundesarchiv (henceforth SAPMO-BArch), DR117/20.013: Letter from Spiess to Apitz, 5 September 1950.

[23] Stiftung Archiv Akademie der Künste (henceforth SAdK), Bruno-Apitz-Archiv 7: Letter from Spiess to Apitz, 25 July 1951.

[24] SAPMO-BArch DR117/20.013: Letter from Horst Reinecke and Karl-Georg Egel (DEFA) to Apitz, 15 September 1953.

[25] See SAPMO-BArch, DR117/20.013: Karl-Georg Egel, "Umwandlung des Dramaturgenvertrages des Koll. Apitz in einen Autorenvertrag," 25 November 1953.

[26] SAPMO-BArch, DR117/20.013: Letter from Karl-Georg Egel to Apitz, 19 October 1954.

[27] SAPMO-BArch, DR117/20.013: Letter from Willi Brückner to Apitz, 10 May 1955.

[28] See SAPMO-BArch, DR1/8745: Letter from Apitz to Hans Rodenberg, undated, probably December 1954.

[29] SAPMO-BArch, DR117/20.013: Eva Seemann, "Aktenvermerk," 5 January 1955.

[30] Apitz acted as a guide to the former camp, and he was actively involved in the plan for the earliest exhibition to be shown there in 1952. See Thüringisches Hauptstaatsarchiv Weimar, KZ und Haftanstalten Buchenwald Nr. 23: "Sitzung der Agit.-Prop.-Kommission für den Buchenwaldtag am 11. April 1952 in Weimar-Buchenwald."

[31] "Bruno Apitz: Fragen zur Person."

[32] Peter Edel, "Das Kind vom Ettersberg: Gedanken über ein kleines Bild und einen großen Film," *Die Weltbühne* XVIII (8 May 1963): 595–601.

[33] SAdK, Bruno-Apitz-Archiv 15: Letter from the Secretariat of the German Writers' Union to Apitz, 13 May 1955.

[34] See Eva Lippold, "Weggenosse und Freund," *Wochenpost*, 20 April 1979.

[35] Landeshauptarchiv Sachsen-Anhalt (henceforth LHASA), Bestand Mitteldeutscher Verlag Halle, VHSt 140: Letter from Apitz to Hans Holm, 13 May 1955.

[36] LHASA, Bestand Mitteldeutscher Verlag Halle, VHSt 140: Letter from Bressau to Apitz, 20 October 1955.

[37] "Bruno Apitz: Fragen zur Person."

[38] "Bruno Apitz: Fragen zur Person."

[39] SAdK, Bruno-Apitz-Archiv 6, Mappe B1: 31–32.

[40] LHASA, Bestand Mitteldeutscher Verlag Halle, VHSt 140: Letter from Apitz to Schmidt, 15 February 1957.

[41] See Lutz Niethammer, ed., *Der "gesäuberte" Antifaschismus: Die SED und die roten Kapos von Buchenwald* (Berlin: Akademie Verlag, 1994), 425–26.

[42] LHASA, Bestand Mitteldeutscher Verlag Halle, VHSt 140: Letter from Apitz to Schmidt, 4 October 1957.

[43] LHASA, Bestand Mitteldeutscher Verlag Halle, VHSt 140: Letter from Apitz to Schmidt, 7 January 1958.

[44] LHASA, Bestand Mitteldeutscher Verlag Halle, VHSt 15: "Protokoll über die Generaldiskussion zu Bruno Apitz 'Wall der Herzen,'" 3 February 1958.

[45] SAdK, Bruno-Apitz-Archiv 7, Mappe 2.

[46] See SAdK, Bruno-Apitz-Archiv 7, Mappe 2: 34. The key deletion in German is: "die Einsetzung Krämers als 'LA-I' war der Ausdruck von Gegensätzen zwischen Kluttig und Schwahl. Kluttig benutzte mit Vorliebe kriminelle Elemente für die Posten im Lager, und machte die Verbrecher zu Spitzeln und Zuträgern. Schwahl nutzte lieber Intelligenz und Korrektheit der Politischen aus."

[47] See Bruno Apitz, *Nackt unter Wölfen* (Berlin: Aufbau, 2001), 34. The key addition in German here is: "unter geschickter Ausnutzung der Gegensätze zwischen

Kluttig und dem Lagerkommandanten Schwahl war es den Genossen des ILK gelungen, Krämer zum Lagerältesten zu 'machen.'"

[48] SAdK, Bruno-Apitz-Archiv 7, Mappe 2: 118.

[49] SAdK, Bruno-Apitz-Archiv 7, Mappe 2: 121. The German here is "gefahrdrohende Ruhe" and "ihr finsteres Schweigen hatte sich zwischen ihnen wie ein Riß aufgetan."

[50] SAdK, Bruno-Apitz-Archiv 7, Mappe 2. The German text of the insults is: "'Du alter Hosenschiß! Speckjäger, Muselmann! Mensch, wenn Du auch nur ein Wort nach außen quatschst, dann hauen wir dir die Jacke voll!'" Scenes involving disputes between Rose and the other prisoners have been either deleted or almost completely deleted on pages 16, 17, and 111 of the MDV typescript.

[51] SAdK, Bruno-Apitz-Archiv 7, Mappe 2: 346. The German here is "gut" and "tief menschlich."

[52] SAdK, Bruno-Apitz-Archiv 8: "Mitschrift einer Aussprache der Genossen Kurt Faustmann und Helmut Schulz mit dem Genossen Bruno Apitz," 10 April 1961.

[53] LHASA, Bestand Mitteldeutscher Verlag Halle, VHSt 140: Letter from Apitz to Schmidt, 5 April 1958.

[54] See Erich Loest, *Der Zorn des Schafes* (Munich: DTV, 1993), 43–44.

[55] For Schmidt's contribution, see Martin Gregor, *der mann mit der stoppuhr* (Halle-Saale: Mitteldeutscher Verlag, 1957). For a scathing critique of the "tangenten" series, see Eva Strittmatter, "'tangenten,'" *Neue Deutsche Literatur* 7 (1958): 124–30.

[56] Bundesbeauftragte für die Unterlagen des Staatssicherheitsdienstes der ehemaligen Deutschen Demokratischen Republik (henceforth BStU), Archiv-Nr. 5141/59: 000060: "Hauptabteilung II/4 — b: Abschlußvermerk. Betr.: Abbrechen der Verbindung mit der DA 'Brendel,'" 31 October 1959.

[57] BStU, Archiv-Nr. 5141/59: 000016: "Betrifft Republikflucht des [blacked out]," Berlin, 15 July 1958.

[58] See LHASA, Bestand Mitteldeutscher Verlag Halle, VHSt 140: Letter from Apitz to Noglik, 8 February 1958.

[59] LHASA, Bestand Mitteldeutscher Verlag Halle, VHSt 140: Letter from Apitz to Schmidt, 5 February 1958.

[60] The MDV typescript, on which Apitz and subsequently the MDV editors made many, largely (but not exclusively) stylistic, alterations, was the version of the novel sent to the Hauptverwaltung Verlagswesen and to MDV's printers. My interpretation of events is as follows. Apitz edited one copy of this typescript, while MDV made alterations to the other. Schmidt brought this latter copy to Apitz on 30 November 1957 to discuss possible editorial alterations with him. This copy Apitz at some point passed on to Walter Bartel. In a letter to Apitz of 3 February 1958, Schmidt asked for this copy back (Apitz had since sent his own copy back to MDV, duly edited), as two copies were needed and the changes on one had to be entered onto the other before one was sent to the printers and one to the Ministry for Culture. There can be little doubt that the typescript in the Apitz archive (SAdK, Bruno-Apitz-Archiv 7, Mappe 2) is one of these copies. When Apitz received the first proofs, he complained

to Schmidt that he had no copy of the typescript to compare the proofs with. Schmidt duly sent him the copy that had been set for printing. The copy in Mappe 2 has clearly been edited in preparation for printing. That the Mappe 2 typescript is the one used as a basis for publication is also clear from the exchange of letters between Apitz and Schmidt in 1957 and 1958. Both refer to page numbers that correspond to the page numbers of the document in Mappe 2. To take one example: on 7 April 1958, Apitz wrote to Schmidt complaining that, when comparing the proofs with the typescript, he had spotted a discrepancy. The sentence "sie glich der Stunde zwölf" had been deleted by MDV's editorial team. This sentence, he wrote, was on page 502 of the typescript on which the proofs were based; it can indeed be found on page 502 of the version of the novel contained in Mappe 2 of Bruno-Apitz-Archiv 7. Moreover, it has been crossed out as Apitz claimed.

[61] SAdK, Bruno-Apitz-Archiv 7, Mappe 2: 36. The German is "der Transport geht nach Bergen-Belsen."

[62] Apitz, *Nackt unter Wölfen* (2001), 35. The German is "der Transport geht ins Ungewisse."

[63] SAdK, Bruno-Apitz-Archiv 7, Mappe 2: 60. The German is "nur, um es noch sicherer dem Bergen-Belsener Tod zuzutragen."

[64] Apitz, *Nackt unter Wölfen* (2001), 56. The German is "nur, um es neuen, unbekannten Gefahren entgegenzutragen."

[65] For references subsequently omitted from the published version, see SAdK, Bruno-Apitz-Archiv 7, Mappe 2: 36, 58, 62, 63, 64, 71, 81, 121, 123.

[66] SAdK, Bruno-Apitz-Archiv 7, Mappe 2: 56. The German is " 'Das sind wieder tausend Leichen, die auf die Reise gehen. . . .' "

[67] Apitz, *Nackt unter Wölfen* (2001), 53. The German is " 'Das sind wieder tausend, die wir ins Ungewisse schicken müssen. . . .' "

[68] LHASA, Bestand Mitteldeutscher Verlag Halle, VHSt 140: Letter from Apitz to Schmidt, 5 February 1958.

[69] LHASA, Bestand Mitteldeutscher Verlag Halle, VHSt 140: Letter from Bressau to Apitz, 2 November 1955.

[70] SAPMO-BArch, DR1/1213: G. Hoffmann, "HA Verlage Aktennotiz," 28 January 1958. See also SAPMO-BArch, DR1/7794. For a discussion of the books that gave rise to the KdAW's concern, see Bill Niven, " 'Der Not gehorchend, nicht dem eignen Triebe, ich tu's der Werbung nur zuliebe!' The Genesis of Bruno Apitz's *Nackt unter Wölfen*," *German Studies Review* 28, no. 2 (May 2005): 265–83; here, 277.

[71] SAPMO-BArch, DR1/3941, Druckgenehmigungen Ang-Ar, 1954–1965: "EINZELOBJEKT NR. 10/58 ZUM PRODUKTIONSPLAN 1958."

[72] SAdK, Bruno-Apitz-Archiv 15: Letter from Rudolf Wunderlich to Bruno Apitz, 12 May 1958.

[73] SAPMO-BArch, DR1/3941, Druckgenehmigungen Ang-Ar, 1954–1965: "EINZELOBJEKT NR. 10/58 ZUM PRODUKTIONSPLAN 1958."

[74] DY57/49: "Beschlußprotokoll der Sitzung der Parteigruppe des Präsidiums des Komitees am 21. April 1958."

[75] SAPMO-BArch, DY30/ J IV 2/2/591: "Anlage Nr. 9 zum Protokoll Nr. 19/58 vom 28. April 1958."

[76] SAdK, Bruno-Apitz-Archiv 15: Letter from Robert Siewert to Rudi Wunderlich, 5 May 1958.

[77] SAdK, Bruno-Apitz-Archiv 15: Letter from Wunderlich to Apitz, 12 May 1958. This letter included a copy of Großkopf's report.

[78] Martin Gregor-Dellin, "Ich war Walter Ulbricht: die Entstehung des Romans *Nackt unter Wölfen* von Bruno Apitz — eine ungewöhnliche Geschichte," *Süddeutsche Zeitung*, 21/22 February 1987, 3 [Beilage].

[79] SAPMO-BArch, DR1/3941, Druckgenehmigungen Ang-Ar, 1954–1965: "EINZELOBJEKT NR. 10/58 ZUM PRODUKTIONSPLAN 1958."

[80] DHM, Bestand MfdG, Abt. Gedenkstätten: Veränderungen in Buchenwald 1958: Letter from Otto Halle to KdAW, 12 December 1956.

[81] DR1/7523: "Niederschrift über die Beratung des vom Ministerium für Kultur einberufenen Wissenschaftlich-Künstlerischen Beirates zum Zwecke der Begutachtung der Entwürfe für die Nationale Gedenkstätte Buchenwald (Ehrenhain) bei Weimar und Ravensbrück bei Fürstenberg/Havel."

[82] LHASA, Bestand Mitteldeutscher Verlag Halle, VHSt 15: "Auflagenhöhe/ Honorarzahlungen."

[83] See LHASA, Bestand Mitteldeutscher Verlag Halle, VHSt 123: "Hausmitteilung," 21 September 1983.

[84] See Deutsches Pädagogisches Zentralinstitut, ed., *Beiträge zum Literaturunterricht in den Klassen 8 bis 10* (Berlin: Volk & Wissen, 1960), 65–68.

[85] See SAPMO-BArch DR1/7859: "Zum 15. Jahrestag der Befreiung: Anleitungsmaterial für allgemeine Bibliotheken," 1960.

[86] See Archiv der Gedenkstätte Buchenwald, Nachlaß Walter Bartel, VS 12/1: "Nationale Mahn- und Gedenkstätte Buchenwald: Ferienkursus für Lehrer," 12–17 February 1962.

[87] Wolfgang Emmerich, *Kleine Literaturgeschichte der DDR* (Aufbau: Berlin, 2000), 135.

[88] See SAPMO-BArch DR1/7861: Alexander Abusch, text entitled "Die Veranstaltung, vom Börsenverein einberufen, findet Donnerstag, den 13.11. [1959] um 19 Uhr 30 im Neuen Rathaus in Leipzig statt."

[89] Alexander Abusch, "Bruno Apitz 60 Jahre: Glückwunsch des Ministers für Kultur," *Berliner Zeitung*, 28 April 1960.

[90] "Glückwunsch des ZK für Bruno Apitz," *Neues Deutschland*, 28 April 1965.

[91] StadtA Weimar, 000732/1659: "Vorlage zum Beschluß Nr. 64/61 der Stadtverordnetenversammlung Weimar vom 17. August 1961."

[92] See SAdK, Bruno-Apitz-Archiv 9: "Antifaschismus — eine Basis unserer Kunst," *Leipziger Volkszeitung*, undated, probably 1979.

[93] See *KL Bu: Konzentrationslager Buchenwald*, 43–45.

[94] See Apitz, *Nackt unter Wölfen* (2001), 106, 108, 115, 134, 136, 156, 166, and 204.

[95] Marcel Reich-Ranicki, "Ein ungewöhnlicher Publikumserfolg," *Die Zeit*, 27 October 1961 (repr. in Marcel Reich-Ranicki, *Ohne Rabatt: Über Literatur aus der DDR* (Stuttgart: Deutsche Verlagsanstalt, 1991), 25–27; here, 27).

[96] It is true that Stefan's guardian, Zacharias, is deported in the novel, but Apitz does his utmost to portray him as a bland, helpless, and timid figure, for whom the reader has little sympathy.

CHAPTER FOUR

THE CINEMA FILM OF *NAKED AMONG WOLVES*

The "Facting" of Fiction

AS THE LAST CHAPTER has shown, *Naked among Wolves* (*Nackt unter Wölfen*, 1958) constituted a foundational myth. Not that Apitz or indeed any GDR commentators on *Naked among Wolves* conceived of the novel in terms of myth, a term that, after all, suggests elements of the supernatural and fantastic, and even of pure invention. Apitz did, however, admit taking artistic liberties in his portrayal of real-life figures. While there really was a Walter Krämer, he was never Camp Elder; in fact, he was Kapo in the sick bay at Buchenwald, and he was murdered over three years before the action of the novel sets in. Höfel, in real-life, was indeed Kapo of the Personal Property Room but was released from Buchenwald in April 1939. As for the real-life Willi Pippig (not Rudi as in the novel), he was not murdered in Buchenwald. In fact, he died a peaceful death in the town of Dessau in 1988. And Herbert Bochow was, in real life, never even a Buchenwald prisoner. Bochow was a member of a resistance group in Dresden to which Karl Stein, Fritz Schulze, and Albert Hensel also belonged; he was executed at Berlin-Plötzensee in 1942.[1] "Every figure in the novel is a compendium of many of my former comrades," Apitz said in a 1973 interview.[2] *Naked among Wolves* was Apitz's personal tribute to a whole range of real-life figures, aspects of whose lives and personalities were combined in the novel's individual characters. Thus Bochow in the novel is as much a personification of Bartel as of the actual Bochow. It is also quite feasible that Stefan Cyliak, while clearly modeled chiefly on Stefan Zweig, personified the fate of a number of children.

Apitz also admitted that some events in the novel had not happened at all: the SS man Zweiling did not shoot the spy Wurach, the child Stefan did not arrive in the camp in the care of a man who was not his father, and Höfel and Kropinski, or the real-life figures they partly represented, were never incarcerated in a cell in the Bunker Building. But at the same time Apitz asserted that he had "written nothing that would not have been historically possible," and that "the principle 'as if' was a fact of my working method." Zweiling *could* have killed Wurach in real life; *others* had been incarcerated, if not the real-life equivalents of Höfel or Kropinski.[3] So where the novel had not portrayed individuals and events in precise accordance with the facts, it had described them in a manner that was *potentially* real. Thus in the same moment as he admitted elements of invention, Apitz sought to play down their fictional status. Indeed, in a sense he viewed his novel as more real than reality, given that it purportedly represented, in distilled form, the biographies of many antifascists and the essential truths about Buchenwald and the fascist era. And in one respect he did always insist that his novel followed the material facts, namely, in its portrayal of the ILK's resistance struggle and of self-liberation. Moreover, as time passed, Apitz proved more and more inclined to explain away elegantly the liberties he had taken with the facts, and to talk of the novel as if it were a mirror of reality — to the extent that, when Stefan Jerzy Zweig came to the GDR in 1964 and Apitz gave him a guided tour of Buchenwald, Apitz could be heard telling him about his arrival at the camp in a suitcase, contradicting the facts as Apitz surely knew them.[4]

Because the press and GDR cultural officials interpreted his novel as a statement on reality, and because it gradually became a kind of literary monument to antifascism, its credibility came to depend on its authenticity as history. This, in turn, made it, and Apitz, vulnerable to questions about its veracity. Apitz responded by shielding the text against such questions. Following the appearance of *Naked among Wolves* in 1958, Apitz embarked on countless reading tours, acquiring a car for the purpose. Usually, he claimed in a 1960 interview, readers wanted to know "what had become of the child," and "if everything is really true that you write in the book." While Apitz goes on to claim that such questions were not really an expression of "distrust of the author," but rather one of the inability of the reader to imagine the reality of the concentration camps, they surely proved unsettling nevertheless.[5] Hence it became a matter of some importance to Apitz — and not just to him — to corroborate his own text. Arguably, the making of the DEFA film of *Naked among Wolves* in 1962/63 was the expression of an official drive toward absolute authentification of the novel's portrayal of Buchenwald. The larger context for this desire was the wish to exploit, through further popularization, the propagandist potential of the novel's glorification of antifascist resistance — but this aim would only be achieved if it were perceived as being *more* than just a story.

Why Now?

Before examining the means deployed by DEFA to achieve maximum authentification, we have to answer one question. Why did the East German film company become so keen to make a film that, in 1954/55, it had had no interest in making? Certainly, prior to the 1960s DEFA's handling of the whole concentration camp topos had been gingerly and tangential, to say the least. In the very first German postwar film, *The Murderers are Among Us*, by Wolfgang Staudte (*Die Mörder sind unter uns*, 1946), Hildegard Knef plays Susanne Wallner, a former concentration-camp prisoner, but her past sufferings are not a theme of the film. The atrocity of mass annihilation forms only the background to Kurt Maetzig's *Council of the Gods* (*Rat der Götter*, 1950), which focuses on the production of poison gas by IG Farben. And in Heiner Carow's *They Called Him Amigo* (*Sie nannten ihn Amigo*, 1958/59), a group of boys in Berlin help an escaped concentration-camp prisoner; one of the boys, the son of a communist, is subsequently incarcerated in a camp. But it was not until Konrad Wolf's *Stars* (*Sterne*, 1959) that DEFA ventured to any significant degree into the world of the camps themselves. Wolf portrays a Bulgarian transit camp where Greek Jews are being held prior to deportation to Auschwitz; *Wehrmacht* corporal Walter Gericke falls in love with the Jewish prisoner Ruth, but he cannot save her from deportation, and he eventually deserts to join Bulgarian partisans. Nevertheless, it would be true to say that until the late 1950s DEFA had not overcome a reluctance to situate an entire feature film within the confines of a concentration camp. The reason, in all probability, was the feeling that it was too negative a setting. Acts of heroism, resistance, and solidarity often take place outside the camps, as in Carow's *They Called Him Amigo* and Wolf's *Stars* — as, indeed, in Anna Seghers's classic novel *The Seventh Cross* (*Das siebte Kreuz*, 1946). By contrast, the camps were still associated by DEFA largely with suffering and death.

It was the SED's drive to establish Buchenwald as a site of national memory between 1955 and 1958, and above all Apitz's novel, which demonstrated that a concentration camp *could* be portrayed positively as a site of socialist heroism and victory. And indeed it was after the novel's resounding success that DEFA approached Apitz in April 1959 to inform him that it wished to make a film of the novel — a request that nevertheless surprised Apitz, given DEFA's earlier rejection of his proposal.[6] DEFA's interest in the project was surely strengthened by two dramatizations of *Naked among Wolves* that demonstrated that its story could easily be transferred to other media. The first of these was Horst Liepach's radio play *Naked among Wolves*, for which Apitz himself wrote the script, and which was first broadcast on GDR radio on 14 September 1958. If anything, Liepach's radio play intensified the heroism in Apitz's novel; for example, at the end of the dramatization, as the prisoners storm the gates, their cries and shouts gradually give way to an orderly, yet impassioned, singing of the *Internationale*, the well-known communist song calling on victims of oppression to stand up, unite, and carry on the struggle. The conclusion of Apitz's novel is being quite explicitly interpreted here as a stage in the socialist defeat of capitalist barbarism. The second dramatization was Georg Leopold's film for GDR television, first broadcast on

10 April 1960. It begins with powerful images of evacuees from Auschwitz being driven mercilessly toward Buchenwald. We see a moving train, belching out black smoke. Images of Buchenwald's crematorium follow, also emitting dense black fumes, and of corpses being transported across the roll-call area at Buchenwald. The camera then zooms in on the face of a man who lies dying near the gates to the camp. But for two hours subsequently, the focus is on a narrative of resistance and survival. The final moving image is of the rescued child being held up in the air. Leopold's film describes the journey from annihilation to victory. It ends with a still showing Fritz Cremer's group of figures on the southern slopes of the Ettersberg (see chapter 2). This has the effect of underpinning affinities between the action of the film and Buchenwald's official memorial landscape. Indeed, this image of Cremer's statues serves to memorialize the action the viewer has just witnessed.

These two highly effective dramatizations surely proved to DEFA that its skepticism voiced in 1954/55 in response to Apitz's proposed film had been unfounded. Indeed DEFA was now only too keen to build on their success by transferring the action of the novel to the cinema screen.[7] That DEFA could not begin to fulfill this wish until late 1961 had to do partly with problems in finding a director. Wolfgang Langhoff, originally envisaged as director of *Naked among Wolves*, was overcommitted at the Deutsches Theater. The suggestion was then mooted that the young director Frank Beyer take over the film.[8] Although Beyer agreed, his cooperation with Apitz in writing the script did not start until November 1961.[9] Beyer had other commitments to fulfill first,[10] and Apitz's health had not been good. But when they finally put their heads together in November 1961, it was at a politically highly charged moment. The Wall had been built in August 1961. This increased ideological pressure on DEFA to produce films that emphasized the ever present threat of capitalist imperialism and brutality, and the need for effective self-defense on the part of the socialist collective. In the post-August 1961 climate, a film of *Naked among Wolves* could serve to highlight this threat, invite viewer identification with antifascism, and encourage GDR citizens to identify with the East German state, which was now fighting to maintain the antifascist legacy in a bitter struggle with West Germany.

Beyer had originally not wanted to make a film of *Naked among Wolves* — a novel he had not even read when first approached by DEFA.[11] After making two antifascist films set between 1933 and 1945, namely, *Five Cartridge Cases* (*Fünf Patronenhülsen*, 1960) and *Star-Crossed Lovers* (*Königskinder*, 1962), he would have preferred to make a film set in the present. This he made quite clear in a speech to a DEFA Party meeting in late 1962. In the same speech he launched what was in DEFA's history an unprecedented attack on its output and its failure to attract cinema audiences, which he put down to its being regarded by GDR citizens as the "extended arm of a politics the public does not subscribe to." Beyer's controversial speech, especially in its call for a contemporary, critical cinema that would confront the issue of "honesty and hypocrisy," could well have been a reaction to the ideological pressure he felt himself under when making *Naked among Wolves*.[12] In an interview, he told me that his uncle had been unjustly interned by the Soviets in postwar Buchenwald — and that he suffered a crisis of conscience because he knew that he would never be able to introduce a reference, however guarded, to the taboo subject of Buchenwald's second history into *Naked among Wolves*. As a member of the first Artistic Working Group (KAG) set up by DEFA in 1960, the "Red Circle" (*Roter Kreis*), Beyer arguably enjoyed a degree of autonomy. But the socialist filmmaking collectives such as the "Red Circle" were constantly subjected to ideological training and always under the watchful eye of DEFA's management. As a member of a socialist team, moreover, Beyer was always answerable to it. It was not until 1966, in his film *Trace of Stones* (*Spur der Steine*), that Beyer was able to turn his hand to a contemporary theme — namely, the difficulties surrounding a socialist building project. He promptly found himself at the center of official disapproval.[13]

Despite the concerns he might have had about "honesty," his film of Apitz's novel, because it remains largely faithful to the text, with the possible exception of the final scenes (see later in the chapter), reproduces what might be perceived as that novel's dishonesty. Both Apitz's novel and Beyer's film version play down the fact that Buchenwald was a site of (largely Jewish) suffering. Both glorify the communist underground at Buchenwald by promoting the myth of self-liberation and by focusing only on the beneficial aspects of its conduct: problematic topics such as the exchange of names on transport lists to save members of the communist cadre (*Opfertausch*), the possible collusion of communist prisoners with the SS (whether inevitable or not), and the questionable behavior of some communist Kapos (corruption and brutality) are not broached. Despite his concerns with "hypocrisy," then, Beyer's film does not touch on the problem that while some members of Buchenwald's communist resistance did indeed strive, as they later claimed they had, to uphold humanist values, this cannot be said to have applied to all. Of course it would have been hard to address these themes in public form at any point in the GDR's history, particularly during the period after the building of the Wall — even if Apitz or Beyer had wanted to. But as we shall see, both Beyer and Apitz appeared only too ready to support claims as to the film's uncompromised veracity.

The fetishization of authenticity in the film served as a kind of armor plating, and one can certainly see that this was necessary. As Frank Beyer said, "I know of no other DEFA film that shows us the concentration camp from the point of view of fighting antifascists."[14] With *Naked among Wolves*, the history of the concentration camps, that darkest chapter of the war, was finally reinterpreted as a positive history of socialist triumph. But such a reinterpretation was not without its risks. How credible would a positive image be, given that many Germans — despite the view of Buchenwald promulgated in the GDR — still thought of the camps as places of SS dominance, unmitigated brutality, and prisoner helplessness? Only a firm casing of verisimilitude could protect the DEFA film against possible charges of prettification.

Authenticity in the DEFA Film of *Naked among Wolves*

How, then, did this process of authentification proceed, and was it as effective as was clearly hoped? The most obvious aspect of this process was DEFA's use of the original site of Buchenwald for all outdoor scenes. Thus the scene of the arrival of prisoners from Auschwitz near the start of the film was shot outside the very building where the real prisoners' personal effects had been stored; mass scenes were shot at the very roll-call area where prisoners had been forced to gather; and Buchenwald's gatehouse and gate with the notorious slogan "To Each His Own" featured several times in the film, as did the Crematorium — its stack once more emitting smoke — and the SS buildings. While a few sequences of the television film had also been shot at Buchenwald (by DEFA, as it happened), the "Red Circle" team was far more systematic in its use of the site. Indeed for two months in the summer of 1962, Buchenwald was closed to the public and, as it were, became a "real" concentration camp once more. For DEFA did more than use the original site; it also reconstructed parts of Buchenwald as it had been during the Nazi period. It was in March 1962 that the head of the "Red Circle" collective, Hans Mahlich, wrote to DEFA's controller Zunft informing him that "large parts of Buchenwald concentration camp have to be rebuilt." "Construction of the whole set of 'concentration camp Buchenwald,'" Mahlich continued, "has to be finished by the time filming begins on 25 April." Mahlich envisaged that filming would be completed by about 10 June.[15]

As we saw in chapter 2, Buchenwald in the post-1950 period had been purged of many remnants of its concentration camp past — notably of the barracks used to house the prisoners. Now, these were to be erected again, albeit only for a short period. Barracks similar to those at Buchenwald concentration camp were brought in from other parts of the GDR with the help of the Ministry for Construction and placed in two to three rows immediately behind the roll-call area; behind these barracks, props resembling the sides of other barracks were set up in serried ranks, so that when the camera panned across the whole camp, the cinemagoer would gain an impression of the original extent and depth of the prisoner huts. Interestingly, Mahlich also told Zunft that, after filming, the set would have to be torn down "so that the camp can be opened to visitors again as soon as possible in its *original, clean condition* [my italics]."[16] Here, Mahlich uses the term "original" to refer to the camp's denuded condition as it was known to memorial-site visitors. Of course the NMGB Buchenwald did predate the reconstruction of the concentration camp by the "Red Circle" team. Moreover, this reconstruction was a film set, a "Dekoration," to use Mahlich's German term. Nevertheless, the GDR's Buchenwald was as much a creation, by deconstruction, as Beyer's Buchenwald was one by reconstruction. That Mahlich should see the GDR Buchenwald as the "original" to a degree reflects the SED view that Buchenwald's prime significance was as a symbol of the triumph of socialism over fascism, not as a relic of National Socialist atrocities. Buchenwald was reconstructed only for it to be deconstructed once again, a process that reinforces this symbolism.

Nevertheless, the evocation of Buchenwald concentration camp had to be convincing, for only then would the film's action, and above all the portrayal of communist resistance itself, appear convincing. It was for this reason that DEFA went to considerable lengths to trace and use real historical artifacts. Thus Mahlich requested from the Institute for Marxism-Leninism (IML) original Buchenwald documents for use in the film, such as lists of block inmates, block leaders' logbooks, and passes;[17] original items such as identity cards were acquired from the Museum for German History.[18] Where original items were not attainable, "Red Circle" took the next best. Thus the loan of 150 palliasses and 200 woolen blankets was requested from the prison authorities at Berlin-Lichtenberg.[19] While many indoor scenes were filmed at the Babelsberg studios in Potsdam rather than Buchenwald, here too every effort was made to preserve an authentic feel. DEFA's technical and production director Albert Wilkening wrote to the "Red Circle" group in April 1962 stating that the photographic style of the film required "shooting to be documentary in character," which meant "never using artificial light when shooting daytime scenes."[20] According to an interview I conducted with director Frank Beyer, a hut (with windows) similar to those erected at Buchenwald was brought to Babelsberg and placed outside the studios.[21] This made it possible to shoot the indoor scenes using natural light, thus reproducing the light conditions as they would have been in a Buchenwald barracks.

What also added to the impression of authenticity was Beyer's use of a number of actors who had actually *been* in concentration camps. Erwin Geschonneck, who played Krämer in *Naked among Wolves*, was a German communist who had survived Sachsenhausen, Dachau, and Neuengamme. He also survived the tragic sinking by the British of the *Cap Arcona*, a ship filled with evacuees from Neuengamme concentration camp; Geschonneck

Fig. 17: Bruno Apitz (far right) playing a prisoner in Beyer's Naked among Wolves. *Courtesy of the Bundesarchiv-Filmarchiv and the DEFA photographer Waltraut Pathenheimer (Berlin).*

clung to the ship's anchor until rescued by a British boat. Peter Sturm, who played Rose, was an Austrian communist who had survived Dachau and Auschwitz. He was also in Buchenwald briefly in 1938 and then again in early 1945. Krystyn Wójcik, who took the part of Kropinski, was never in a camp himself, but he had grown up near Maidanek and his father-in-law had been murdered by the Nazis. Apitz, a former Buchenwald prisoner, himself took a small part in the film.

Beyer and Apitz, who worked on the script together,[22] kept close to the original novel; that too was an aspect of the attempt at authenticity. Given that Apitz's *Naked among Wolves* was regarded in the GDR more as a historical report than as a novel, not to have followed it closely would have been, paradoxically, to risk accusations of fictionalization. That said, Beyer did include one short sequence of events that is not in the novel. Central to this sequence is the figure of an older prisoner who, in a number of very brief scenes, can be seen feeding Stefan Cyliak and protecting him from the probing glances of SS man Kluttig. While Bochow and other prisoners do protect Stefan from Kluttig in Apitz's *Naked among Wolves*, the figure of the older character is absent. But according to Beyer, the sequence with the older prisoner was based on an anecdote related to him by Apitz.[23] It was thus not really an invention. Its authentic feel is heightened by the fact that Apitz himself, in a cameo role, plays the older prisoner.

The author, as actor, develops his own text in line with his own experience, implicitly authenticating the additional scenes.

Beyer's use of foreign actors for foreign roles also served to heighten the impression of authenticity. The Polish actors Zygmund Malanowicz, Boleslaw Plotnicki, and Krystyn Wójcik took the parts of Pribula (a Polish member of the ILK in the novel and film), Jankowski, and Kropinski respectively; the Czech actor Jan Pohan played Kodiczek, while the well-known Soviet actor Viktor Avdjushko was Bogorski. Casting the foreign characters in this way was by no means self-explanatory; in his 1960 film *Five Cartridge Cases*, set during the Spanish Civil War, Beyer had used German actors for the parts of Soviet, Polish, Spanish, French, and Bulgarian characters. If the GDR television film of *Naked among Wolves*, which had used German actors, had been the chamber-music version of the novel, the version produced by the "Red Circle" collective was fully orchestrated. In March 1962, Jochen Mückenberger of DEFA wrote to Admiral Verner requesting the help of the GDR's National People's Army (NVA).[24] Between 3,000 and 4,000 soldiers subsequently took part in the film's crowd scenes; the hundreds of prisoners attending the roll call at the beginning of the film were played by NVA soldiers, as were the many prisoners who storm through the opened gates at the film's end. Large numbers of soldiers also took part in the scenes recreating an evacuation from Buchenwald. The television film's makers had not had the means, or perhaps not the desire, to create such mass scenes. But no effort was spared by DEFA in its attempt to convey an accurate impression of Buchenwald's roll calls, where huge numbers of prisoners stood for hours or were forced to do excruciating marches and exercises to the strains of the camp band — the sound and sight of which open Beyer's film.

The sets of the indoor scenes (created by set designer Alfred Hirschmeier) also seemed designed to persuade the viewer of the historical, documentary character of the screenplay. Some scenes in the SS quarters were shot against the background of maps on the wall. The progress of the Allies is an important theme in the novel and the DEFA film, but the visibility of large-scale maps also has the effect of authenticating the action. The viewers are invited to interpret what they are watching in the context of real cartographic representations of Europe as it was at the time. A radio is also a feature of the sets of the SS quarters — from which original news broadcasts can be heard. In the scenes shot in Krämer's office, the ticking of a clock can be heard, and shots of a clock-face can be seen as the hour approaches when the Camp Elder is supposed to have summoned the prisoners for evacuation. Scenes are measured out chronometrically, in "real" time, an idea Beyer seems to have borrowed from Georg Leopold's television film version.

The style of Marczinkowski's camerawork throughout the DEFA film is in large measure very discreet; techniques such as zooming in and out or following the movements of the characters are used sparingly. The camera's perspective often seems static; the emphasis is on the *what*, rather than the *how* of its recording — a style of filming associated more with documentary than with feature films. The camera shows respect for its object, seeks to preserve its "reality." The DEFA film of *Naked among Wolves* was filmed in cinemascope; this too enhances the impression of authenticity. The screenplays of both Leopold's and Beyer's films suggest an epic battle between the SS and the ILK, but only in Beyer's film is this suggestion borne out both by the mass scenes and the sheer scope of the perspective. The style of acting is often as restrained as the camerawork. By and large, except in some of the group or crowd scenes, and certainly in the first two-thirds of the film, the prisoners talk quietly; we are never allowed to forget that they are prisoners whose conspiratorial designs are constantly under threat of discovery by the SS. The scenes with the SS men present them not as screaming sadists but as altogether more pedestrian henchmen who go about the practice of violence with a cool, functional, at times almost bored, attitude. In one scene, Kluttig can be seen eating food from his lunch box, and Zweiling spends his evenings in the petit-bourgeois environment of his home. It certainly is one of the great achievements of Beyer's film that, for the first time in either East or West German feature films, the sheer ordinariness of many an SS man is conveyed. They are not exceptional figures any more: their banality makes them credible and their deeds all the more terrible. On the other hand, the characterization as petit-bourgeois puts the blame for Nazism firmly at the door of the (lower) middle classes and exculpates the workers. It confirms the Marxist understanding of Nazism as a symptom of crisis in capitalist society.

Authenticity and Propaganda

When DEFA began its advertising campaign for the film, it emphasized that "*Naked among Wolves* reflects authentic events."[25] In a 1963 radio interview, Apitz himself talked of the "frighteningly genuine atmosphere conveyed by the film both in its scenery and its representation of the character of the camp."[26] *Naked among Wolves* was premiered in Berlin's Colosseum on 10 April 1963, on the eve of the anniversary of Buchenwald's supposed self-liberation, a date carefully chosen to underpin the film's veracity. GDR newspaper reviews of the film the following day were full of praise for it; it was described again and again as "genuine" and "convincing." Former prisoners such as Robert Siewert lauded the actors for their realistic performances.[27] It was almost as if voices had been, or might be, raised to question the film's validity, so strong was the emphasis on its authenticity. The symbolic function of the child's rescue, its use therefore as a literary and filmic device, was not overlooked by commentators and critics. But then intriguingly casuistic interpretations were offered to reconcile this with the idea of realism.

In a DEFA advertising brochure, Helmut Ullrich wrote that Apitz "had not been content to merely provide a factual report, but gave the rescue of the child a metaphorical significance," namely, one that highlighted the "human substance of the antifascist struggle." Metaphor, then, occupied a deeper level of reality than fact; Ulrich went on, indeed, to suggest that Beyer's "powerful realism" actually embraced this "symbolic over-determination."[28] For all that the film had to be authentic, this authenticity was not to be regarded as simple respect for supposed facticity. Apitz himself asserted that the film was "completely genuine in its characters and milieu without being naturalistic";[29] Beyer too insisted that, while all important exterior and interior sets recreated the original milieu and the camp atmosphere conveyed was genuine, the film was not naturalistic.[30] Naturalism was often condemned in the GDR as realism without socialism — mimesis without an overarching sense of the unstoppable progress of history. Socialist realism required that the inherent dynamic of history be laid bare. In DEFA's *Naked among Wolves*, as in Apitz's novel, this "deeper" realism is visible in the triumph of socialist humanism over fascist bestiality.

Of course, as I have already pointed out, the problem with all this was that *Naked among Wolves*, both as DEFA film and as novel, represented a misrepresentation of history at many levels. But balanced truth was not the criterion when it came to representing the past in the GDR (or in any other state, for that matter). Indeed such a balance would have been quite unwelcome. What mattered above all was that the past be represented as it was convenient to see it, and that this view then be corroborated as the only true representation. The more convincingly the history of the Third Reich, including Buchenwald, was presented as one of unalloyed communist good against capitalist Nazi evil, the more legitimately the GDR could be presented as deriving from good and the Federal Republic as deriving from evil. Indeed the GDR's constant claims that it was continuing a long-standing antifascist struggle depended on the credibility of such a view of history.

The massive authentification process that played such a role in the making of *Naked among Wolves* and in the way the film was then presented to the GDR public provided the basis for the film's propaganda value; *Naked among Wolves* was deployed as a cultural weapon in the Cold War with more vehemence than any other DEFA film. Arguably, the political agenda with *Naked among Wolves* was written into its making. In March 1962, before filming had even begun, Jochen Mückenberger described the film as "politically and artistically the most important project of the year."[31] And in May of the same year, Apitz wrote in reference to the antifascist resistance struggle at Buchenwald: "this secret struggle, rooted in unshakeable solidarity, is the theme of this film, with which DEFA hopes to reach audiences even in capitalist countries, so that everyone can see what international community can achieve."[32]

One thing the DEFA film of *Naked among Wolves* did not do was draw *explicit* parallels between Buchenwald's fascism and West Germany — any more than Apitz's original novel did. But as the film was being made, events occurred that made it possible for such explicit parallels to be drawn. Apitz himself was at the center of these events. In late October 1962, he traveled to Dortmund to give a reading from *Naked among Wolves* at the invitation of a West German youth organization. He was promptly arrested by the West German police and shunted over the German-German border. The official reason for Apitz's forced return to the GDR was that he did not have a visa, but there was more to it than this. A few days earlier, the West German police had raided the offices of the West German weekly *Der Spiegel* following its publication of an article allegedly containing classified information about the West German army; the article's author, Conrad Ahlers, was arrested, as was the chief editor of *Der Spiegel*, Rudolf Augstein. Apitz's arrest, which provoked protest from the GDR's Writers' Union among others,[33] was symptomatic of the neurotic political climate at the time in West Germany, with Chancellor Adenauer warning against "an abyss of treachery."[34] Clearly, October 1962 was not a good month for a communist author such as Apitz to be visiting Dortmund. The West German police told him that, as a writer, he was a "functionary of the SED."[35]

No sooner had Apitz set foot in the GDR again than he began to compare his treatment at the hands of the West German police — described in the GDR press coverage of his arrest as "political police," evoking the Gestapo — with his treatment at the hands of the Nazis: "I was reminded, violently reminded, of what happened around 1933."[36] GDR newspaper articles, for their part, drew comparisons with Apitz's novel. One newspaper claimed that Apitz had found himself yet again "naked among wolves": "the offspring of the fascist wolves are alive and are pursuing . . . the limitless abuse of unlimited power in West Germany."[37] DEFA's press office, in its 1963 advertising brochure for the forthcoming release of *Naked among Wolves*, also drew parallels. Heinz Hofmann compared the West German police who had arrested Apitz to Zweiling and Kluttig, and claimed that "the Adenauer authorities" had demonstrated "the contemporary relevance of the struggle and the conflict in *Naked among Wolves*."[38]

Apitz's arrest was therefore interpreted as a timely and evocative validation of precisely that admonitory message that DEFA's officials, GDR cultural functionaries, the GDR press, and indeed Apitz himself hoped the film would convey. And when the film was finally made, Apitz was among the first to highlight this message and thus help set a framework for the film's reception. After *Naked among Wolves* had been previewed by journalists on 2 April 1963, Apitz, in connection with developments in West Germany, claimed in front of the assembled press representatives that "what we saw today is still there in the world."[39] Others were quick to take up this cue. On the occasion of the film's official first performance, Georg Spielmann of the KdAW, in a speech welcoming prominent premiere guests such as the GDR's Minister for Culture, Hans Bentzien, stressed the "contemporary relevance" of the film, "because in West Germany the Kluttigs, Mandrills, and Reineboths are up to their old tricks again."[40] It did not take long for the majority of film reviewers to follow suit. GDR film reviews made much, for instance, of the fact that the SS character Reineboth in the DEFA film can be seen changing his uniform for civilian clothes.[41] Writing in the Party newspaper *Neues Deutschland*, Horst Knietzsch contended that many of those responsible for Nazi crimes occupy important positions in West Germany, adding: "they no longer wear the old uniforms; they act as if they were democrats."[42]

The film's purported authenticity, then, was two-layered. It not only showed the past as it had been, but also, implicitly, the *present* as it really is, given that the fascist past was far from over. In a review, Fred Gehler claimed that "a Buchenwald film of 1963 cannot ignore the fact that the fronts existing in the camp in 1945 have since been incarnated politically in the two German states and their representatives."[43] In Gehler's view, both the film and the novel of *Naked among Wolves* succeed in depicting what he defines as the "convergence of problems and conflicts between 1945 and 1963." It bears repeating, however, that while there can be little doubt that Apitz did wish his novel to be understood as a comment on the Cold War, both it and Beyer's film eschew direct comparison; instead, cultural functionaries and reviewers encouraged GDR readers and viewers to make the desired inferences.

In defense of Beyer, it needs to be pointed out that GDR commentators routinely failed to take into account — or perhaps even notice — the film's slightly ambivalent ending, an ending that is differently nuanced from the ending of Apitz's novel. Whereas in the novel Kropinski, holding the child aloft as the prisoners charge through the opened gates, runs into the swirling mass, in Beyer's film the mass charges past him, and he struggles to keep up. And Kropinski's facial expression is hard to interpret: is he happy, as in the novel, or is he not a shade worried? Beyer also adds a brief scene in which the mass appears to charge past Bochow as he supports the injured Krämer. It would be possible to see in these alterations to the original novel a critique of contemporary *East* Germany — the individual is left behind in the stampede toward a better world.

There is evidence, moreover, that DEFA were concerned that the end of the film was generally too chaotic. Thus Hans Rodenberg, after viewing the original uncut version of *Naked among Wolves*, complained that the final scene seemed "fragmented and restless" and suggested cuts to make

Fig. 18: The prisoners storm the gates in Beyer's Naked among Wolves.
Courtesy of the Bundesarchiv-Filmarchiv and the DEFA photographer
Waltraut Pathenheimer (Berlin).

it appear "more disciplined and ordered."[44] I was not able to establish
whether these cuts were made. As the film stands, the charge of the prisoners
does indeed have something uncontrolled about it, and Beyer accompanies
it with almost sinister-sounding background music. Interesting, too, is the
fact that, shortly after liberation in the film, the character played by Apitz
dies, and the child, having dissolved into tears, appears anything but happy
as it is carried out of the camp. Were Beyer and Apitz, as Evelyn Preuss has
argued, hinting at the "death of the author," and the appropriation of his
material by the state?[45] Is the screaming child a symbol of discontented
youth coerced into the GDR socialist collective? Perhaps. The end is more
ambivalent than was ever recognized in the GDR. But I choose the word
ambivalent quite consciously. In Apitz's novel, the child also cries at liberation: its screams could indicate, simply, that he is at last able to give voice
to his suffering. He also appears calmer in the final moments of the film.
And while the character played by Apitz does indeed die, he does so with
a smile on his face. The author, perhaps, dies sure in the knowledge that
the novel — his "child" — is in safe hands. Finally, the impression of a
chaotic stampede toward freedom can be interpreted quite positively. The
rush through the gates represents an explosion of dynamic and creative
energy, and the weakness of Kropinski, Höfel, and Krämer in that moment

is the inevitable result of the efforts they have taken upon themselves to make that moment possible.

Beyer, we should also remember, was first and foremost an artist, not a politician. His making of the film was informed by certain aesthetic and ontological interests. Thus he admired Apitz's novel for its novella-like composition: that a small boy should find himself at the center of a life-and-death struggle between the resistance and the SS was, for Beyer, an "unheard-of event" in the Goethean sense.[46] What had also fascinated Beyer was the elemental conflict between reason (Bochow) and feeling (Krämer, Höfel).[47] It is the elemental force of emotion that appears to dominate at the end of the film. The *political* significance of this conflict and its outcome remains open to interpretation. Just as open to interpretation is Beyer's comment that the conflict is "of great significance for our society, which is building up socialism."[48] He thus appears to confirm the view that the heart versus reason dialectic was a contemporary issue that Apitz put into a historical setting in order to provide a persuasive didactic framework. But he does no more than that. In the end, in the absence of any explicitly articulated counter-interpretations of the conclusion in the GDR, the view that it uncomplicatedly asserted the glorious triumph of the socialist prisoner collective over the SS and therefore over capitalist imperialism dominated.

Deploying *Naked among Wolves* in West Germany

To reiterate: in general, give or take one or two changes whose significance can be debated, Beyer's film served to authenticate Apitz's novel. Thus corroborated, surrounded by what I referred to earlier as the "armor plating" of authenticity, it could be reliably deployed as propaganda by the GDR's cultural establishment. DEFA's production director Wilkening, who adjudged the "deployment" of the film in West Germany to be of "great political importance," even suggested that such a deployment might proceed "unofficially" if necessary by copying the film to a 16-millimeter format.[49] Obviously, however, it would be far preferable if *Naked among Wolves* could be shown quite legally on West German cinema screens. Attempts to bring the film to West Germany, however, were beset with problems.

The first problem was West German censorship. All eastern bloc films had to be passed by the West German "Interministerial Monitoring Committee for East/West Film Matters" before they could be shown in West German cinemas. The legal basis for the work of this committee was the 1961 Import Prohibition Law, which forbade the import to West Germany of films adjudged to constitute propaganda against the "free and democratic basic order." In practice, however, only a few films were banned.[50] In 1966, the DEFA film *The Sonnenbrucks* (*Die Sonnenbrucks*) was banned because it presented "West German universities as bastions of a renascent Nazism and as reactionary."[51] Another DEFA film, *Dead Men Don't Talk* (*Tote reden nicht*) was banned in 1966 because it implied that the West German pharmaceutical industry would even stoop to murder to hush up a health scandal.[52] In other words, the propaganda, whether in historical or contemporary form, had to be fairly explicit, even drastic, for a prohibition to be imposed. The propaganda in *Naked among Wolves* was obviously considered not so obtrusive, because the film, contrary to what was often claimed in the GDR, was never banned. But it had a checkered history for all that.

Applications to show an eastern bloc film always stood a better chance if they came from clubs or groups wishing to show the film only to club or group members, not as a public performance. The threshold they had to cross was lower. In the autumn of 1963, the Frankfurt branch of a group calling itself the *Naturfreundejugend Deutschlands* — roughly translatable as the "German Friends of Nature Youth Organization" — asked for the DEFA film of *Naked among Wolves* to be passed in West Germany for "club and internal" performances only.[53] The Interministerial Committee agreed to the *Naturfreundejugend*'s request.[54] The first West German performance of *Naked among Wolves* in Frankfurt was followed by a discussion organized by the *Naturfreundejugend* and the Frankfurt branch of the Buchenwald Committee. During this discussion, the GDR actor Erwin Geschonneck (who played Krämer in the DEFA film) and East German author Karl Barthel talked about the "lessons" that could be drawn from the *Naked among Wolves* film for the present. According to GDR newspapers, discussion centered not least around the "scandalous" issue that public performances of the film were not permitted in the FRG.[55] In fact, no one had applied for public showing rights.

Beyer's *Naked among Wolves* was subsequently viewed in several private performances in West German cities. It was shown in Munich's Arri cinema to Komma Club members in April 1964; the showing was followed by a vigorous discussion about the continuing fascism in West Germany and the important role of films such as *Naked among Wolves* in helping to fight this.[56] Frank Beyer and Günter Marczinkowski took part in this discussion. East German newspapers again made reference to a supposed prohibition of the film.[57] What these newspapers do not relate is that several people in the audience asked Beyer how he could justify making a film about a concentration camp when he himself was living in a country that had surrounded its inhabitants with a wall and fences.[58]

Leopold's TV film of *Naked among Wolves* was also shown on the other side of the border, although here there is some, albeit rather vague, evidence that the Interministerial Committee had its reservations. The Frankfurt branch of the West German League of Those Persecuted by the

Nazi Regime (VVN) was the first organization to apply for permission to show the television film.[59] On 29 May 1964, most members of the Interministerial Committee concluded that it did not constitute a violation of the "free and democratic basic order" as stipulated in Article 5 of the Import Prohibition Law.[60] One or two members, however, appear to have had lingering doubts, and the film was viewed again by the committee on 8 June 1964. Despite the fact that the doubts entertained by representatives of the Press and the Federal Ministry for Health could not be entirely dispelled, the committee granted the VVN the right to show the film.[61] Sadly, the archive material consulted here docs not reveal exactly *why* some committee representatives had concerns. What is certainly clear is that neither the TV film nor Beyer's film was ever banned in West Germany.

Indeed Beyer's *Naked among Wolves* appears to have been passed for general release in West Germany in 1964. In September of that year, Second German Television asked for permission to show DEFA's *Naked among Wolves* and *The Gleiwitz Case* (*Der Fall Gleiwitz*) on West German television. The committee discussed the application and decided that, because it had already ruled on 8 June that *Naked among Wolves* did not violate Article 5 of the 1961 law, ZDF's request had to be granted.[62] The puzzling thing here is that the 8 June ruling refers to Leopold's film, not Beyer's. Hoffmann of the Economics Ministry, in agreeing to the import of Beyer's film for public broadcast on ZDF, also refers to a decision of his from 11 June that applies only to the Leopold film. Whatever the source of this confusion, there can be little doubt that Beyer's feature film *Naked among Wolves* was passed for general viewing. A list of those DEFA films that the committee passed for showing between January and September 1964 includes *Naked among Wolves*.[63]

Yet it took another three to four years for *Naked among Wolves* to actually reach West German cinemas, although there is some evidence of distributor interest. For example, Cosmos Film and Television wrote to the Economics Ministry on 12 September 1964 to inquire about the situation regarding permission to show the film not just on West German television but also in cinemas. Cosmos repeated their inquiry on 13 November 1964. On 19 May 1965, the West German Film Studio Walter Leckebusch wrote to the Economics Ministry saying it had received copies of the films *Naked among Wolves* and *The Flying Dutchman* from DEFA, and that while these films were initially for "internal showings," the ultimate intention was to distribute them in West Germany generally. Leitreiter of the Economics Ministry has scribbled at the bottom of the Leckebusch Studio's letter that "*Naked among Wolves* does not violate Art. 5 of the Import Prohibition Law."[64] Leckebusch indicates in his letter that other firms had already brought the DEFA film of *Naked among Wolves* to West Germany (on a piecemeal basis).

In 1967, Pegasus Film, a representative of Sovexport, formally acquired the export rights from DEFA for West Germany. *Naked among Wolves* finally came to West German cinema screens in 1968. The three-to-four-year hiatus is difficult to explain. It cannot be ruled out that obstructions were placed in the way of distributor interest despite the committee's 8 June 1964 ruling. It is more likely, however, that distributors themselves, after showing initial interest, shied away from the film because of poor sales prospects. The interest in DEFA films in West Germany was generally not very strong in the post-1961 period. Between 1961 and 1968, only twenty-three DEFA films were actually sold to West Germany for general release. In 1962, the only DEFA film sold in this way was *Snow White*; in 1966 and 1968, not one DEFA film was sold. What interest there had been in showing *Naked among Wolves* in 1963 and 1964 — either Beyer's or Leopold's version — had come from left-wing organizations such as the *Naturfreundejugend*, which was not just interested in environmental issues but was also staunchly antimilitary and sympathized with socialism. The film may have passed the censors, but this did not necessarily mean that West German cinemas would have wanted to show it.

It would be easy to criticize the cultural interference of the Interministerial Committee. On the other hand, there can be little doubt that the showing of DEFA films in West Germany was part of the SED's propaganda campaign against the Federal Republic. The Section for Cultural Contact to West Germany within the East German Ministry for Culture was in large measure responsible for this campaign. The example of the planned activities for one year, 1965, will illustrate the way it worked. In the section's provisional plan, we read: "with the means of culture we have to intensify the struggle against militarism and revanchism and lend effective support to the popular movement against atomic armament in West Germany."[65] For the first half of 1965, the Section looked forward to the "deployment" in West Germany of DEFA films such as *Naked among Wolves* (in Lübeck, Munich, Frankfurt am Main, Hamburg, and other locations), *Divided Heaven*, and *The Adventures of Werner Holt*.[66] These film performances were usually to be followed by some form of discussion, involving a DEFA delegation and focusing critically on reactionary West German politics. Thus between February and May 1965, the section envisaged that there would be several showings of *Naked among Wolves* organized by West Germany's Buchenwald Committee, which would be followed by discussions on the issue of the statute of limitations for prosecution of the crime of murder in West Germany;[67] in the event, the West German parliament agreed to extend the twenty-year period by another five years.

Performances of plays by GDR theatre ensembles, concerts by GDR orchestras, and readings by GDR authors — such as Apitz himself in March 1965 in Remscheid and Düsseldorf, or Christa Wolf in Munich and

Augsburg in February 1965 — were also to be accompanied by some sort of discussion, petition, or protest focusing on political ills in West Germany. The Ministry for Culture, at some level, was clearly involved in steering the organization of the various venues. This is not quite the same thing as saying that the Munich Komma Klub, for instance, was an instrument of the SED, but it is certainly the case that there was "collaboration." Not that these cultural events in West Germany always went according to plan. It was not unusual, for instance, for East German orchestras to return to the GDR short of a member or two. The temptation to escape to the West was too great for some to resist. Thus the Section for Cultural Contact to West Germany, in its report on activities in 1964, commented that the GDR's cultural representatives had comported themselves "with dignity" in the West — "apart from a few exceptions in the area of our orchestras."[68]

Authentic or Inauthentic?
Naked among Wolves Abroad

DEFA had less difficulty promoting *Naked among Wolves* in other corners of the globe. As early as April 1963, the GDR's Cultural Cente in Warsaw organized a showing to mark the twentieth anniversary of the Warsaw Ghetto uprising. It was a grand occasion, attended by the GDR ambassador to Poland as well as by members of the Polish government and diplomatic corps, with Apitz himself also present. Given that *Naked among Wolves* focuses on communist resistance — the Jew is represented as the helpless child in need of rescue — this was a suggestive showing indeed, implicitly underpinning the communist position that there never would have been an uprising without the encouragement of communist resistance groups in Warsaw. A similarly grand first performance was organized by the GDR embassy in Sofia in June 1963; prominent Bulgarian guests from the diplomatic corps, as well as leading scientists and intellectuals, attended. In July 1963, the film was the GDR's official entry to the Moscow Film Festival, to which we will return a little later. It was also shown at the Edinburgh Film Festival in August 1963. In the spring and early summer of 1964, *Naked among Wolves* came on general release in Greece (March), Belgium (April), Holland (May), and Japan (June); it was also shown in Israel in Tel Aviv's Shderot cinema in April 1964, a showing attended by Zacharias Zweig and Stefan Jerzy Zweig (of whom more in chapter 5). In August 1964, it came on general release in Great Britain and in May 1967 it reached the United States. Reviews of the film were, on the whole, positive. *Time* magazine, while finding Alain Resnais's *Night and Fog* superior to Beyer's *Naked among Wolves*, praised the latter because it showed that "at a time of utmost degradation, man still has the will to endure, and to

Fig. 19: Armin Müller-Stahl (Höfel) and Jürgen Strauch (Stefan Cyliak) in Naked among Wolves. *Courtesy of the Bundesarchiv-Filmarchiv and the DEFA photographer Waltraut Pathenheimer (Berlin).*

prevail."[69] Beyer's film proved almost as successful the world over as Apitz's novel, upon whose rapidly established international reputation it was able to build.

But not all reviews in foreign newspapers were positive, and even quite a few of the positive ones had some reservations. There were, however, some interesting international contrasts between critical reactions. When the film ran in Edinburgh in 1964, the Scottish press thought it better to warn audiences that it made rather brutal viewing, and the *Glasgow Herald* found the "realism" in the subtitles excessive.[70] Greek critics, however, often found the film's portrayal of brutality understated and tendentious. The Greek newspaper *Ethnos* lamented the fact that Beyer's film showed "a nice, well-tended Buchenwald, where only the disobedient and the communists are punished severely." This criticism highlights a weakness of Beyer's film, namely, its sterile atmosphere; there is no real hint of disease, dirt, or disorder, let alone starvation, and not much sign of death, as a Dutch critic of the film pointed out.[71] Marczinkowski's shots of Buchenwald, whether they be of the roll-call area or the reconstructed barracks or the camp streets, seem like shots of a stage, despite the gesture of authenticity. *Ethnos*'s reviewer also expressed sardonic surprise at the ease with which the prisoners "hold discussions and meetings and get themselves organized under the noses of the Nazis; and all the Nazis can do is scream repugnantly."[72] Another Greek newspaper, *Ta Nea*, cast doubt on the film's veracity: "All the 'terrible things' that we see in the Buchenwald studio are not even a pale imitation of Buchenwald in reality." "Of course this film was made by Germans," the article continues. "But does this give them the right to talk about the noose in the house of the hanged without mentioning the victims?"[73] This highlights trenchantly another problem with both novel and film. In *Naked among Wolves*, it is not the Jews who are seen to suffer, but Germans — *for* a Jew. Resistance and victimhood reside with Pippig, Höfel, and Krämer.

But none of this criticism, often balanced with praise, not least for the acting and the suspenseful story, will have hurt DEFA or the SED as much as the failure of the film to win the main prize at the Moscow Film Festival in July 1963. Here, in the very heart of the socialist bloc and at the most prestigious international film festival in a socialist country, *Naked among Wolves*, the GDR's official entry for the festival alongside *The Russian Miracle* (*Das russische Wunder*), should have had its greatest success. It was enormously popular with the Moscow cinema-going public and received very positive reviews in the Soviet press. According to the GDR's Deputy Minister for Culture, Hans Rodenberg, in his report on the festival — sent to Walter Ulbricht among others — the general opinion among participants in Moscow had been that *Naked among Wolves* was the "only film deserving of the Grand Prize." Rodenberg also claimed that the jury originally intended to divide this prize between *Naked among Wolves* and a

Yugoslavian film.[74] But following a viewing of Federico Fellini's *8½*, and after thirty-six hours of debate, the jury decided to award the Grand Prize to Fellini. Not that the DEFA delegation, which included Rodenberg, Apitz, and Beyer, came away entirely empty-handed: Beyer was awarded a silver medal in recognition of his skilful direction of *Naked among Wolves*. But this did little to allay the feeling of disappointment, and indeed anger, at being upstaged by a Fellini film that Romanov, the head of the State Film Committee within the Soviet Council of Ministers, had allegedly decried in conversation with the GDR delegation as "extremely decadent and formalistic."[75] While *Naked among Wolves* had been popular with the Moscow public, the Fellini film had been a flop; of the 12,000 people who crowded into the Lushniki Sport Palace to watch *8½* on 21 July 1963, 9,000 walked out in the course of its showing. At least no one attacked the projectionist, as happened in Italy when *8½* was shown.

How was this volte-face in the jury to be explained? As jury discussions were conducted *in camera* and members were not supposed to disclose details of proceedings, we do not know for sure; and as the GDR for the first time did not have a member on the jury, Rodenberg had no one whom he could impose upon to be indiscreet. Nevertheless, there were rumors. One of these was that the American, Italian, and French members of the jury had threatened to walk out if *8½* did not win (the American jury member was Stanley Kramer, director of *Judgement at Nuremberg*). Rodenberg came close in his report to suggesting that there had been a capitalist conspiracy, and that socialist and neutral country jury members had allowed themselves to be dazzled by the array of Western stars at the festival such as Jean Marais, Ives Montand, and Tony Curtis. Rodenberg also attacked the Soviet members of the jury for giving in, and the socialist country members generally for failing to provide a united front, with each representative gunning for a film from his or her own country.

Rodenberg further condemned the award to *8½* as an "act of ideological coexistence."[76] This was a reference to Khrushchev's adoption of a non-combative policy of compromise toward the cultural values of the West. According to this argument, *Naked among Wolves* was sacrificed on the altar of foreign policy. The GDR cultural attaché in the GDR's Moscow Embassy, in turn, criticized Rodenberg's delegation for not doing enough to promote *Naked among Wolves* and other GDR films at the festival.[77] Rodenberg was so furious that he complained personally to Romanov, threatening to write to Ulbricht (which he did), and lambasting the Soviet jury members for their support of Fellini. Romanov was sympathetic. He praised *Naked among Wolves* and criticized Fellini's film, appearing genuinely baffled that the Soviet members had supported it despite the fact that they had had clear instructions from the Party to support *Naked among Wolves* — even in Moscow, then, Party directives were not always sacrosanct.[78]

It never seems to have occurred to Rodenberg that *8½* might actually be an artistically imaginative film; some consider it to be Fellini's best, indeed, one of the greatest films ever made, and it is often cited in other films (such as Tarantino's *Pulp Fiction*). It describes in evocative images the crisis of a successful film director, Guido, played by Marcello Mastroianni, who finds himself unable to put together a story for his next film. For Rodenberg, it reeked of decadence and experimentalism — quite in contrast to *Naked among Wolves*, which certainly had a story to tell and told it quite conventionally. There could hardly be a clearer example of the contrast between cultural systems than that provided by a comparison of Beyer's film with Fellini's, the former driven by a forward-moving, revolutionary dynamic, the latter portraying a kind of creative stagnation, while at the same time making of this portrayal a work of art. Of all the rumored reasons for the jury's decision not to award the main prize to *Naked among Wolves*, one of the most likely is arrogantly dismissed by Rodenberg. According to Rodenberg's report, the Polish jury representative Jan Rybkowski, during the jury's deliberations, complained that *Naked among Wolves* did not correspond to historical reality: "this film . . . varnishes over reality, it doesn't show how the mountains of corpses in Buchenwald were shifted with bulldozers." Rodenberg's response was to object vituperatively that none of the jury representatives from socialist countries protested against "this malicious rubbish."[79]

Rybkowski was a well-known filmmaker in the eastern bloc who had already enjoyed success at the Moscow Film Festival in 1961 with *The City Will Die Tonight*, a film about the bombing of Dresden. He had (voluntarily) endured forced labor in the Third Reich and had started his career as artistic supervisor for a celebrated film by Wanda Jakubowska, *The Last Stage* (1948), a seminal film about Auschwitz concentration camp.[80] Given this biography, his view will have carried weight in 1963, and in fact in the interview I conducted with him, Beyer surmised that Rybkowski's victim status may have lent him a certain authority. Be this as it may, Rybkowski's opinion may also have carried weight for the simple reason that it was perceived to be valid. Beyer's *Naked among Wolves* shows next to nothing of the Small Camp with its terrible suffering and mortality; it does put an antifascist shine on reality, displacing in the minds of viewers memories of images of concentration camps as death camps (as shown in postwar newsreels and documentaries), and substituting these with different images. Far from highlighting the truth about Buchenwald, then, Beyer's film was little more, if we follow Rybkowski, that a meretricious attempt to conceal that truth, hiding from view those bodies that Buchenwald had left behind. Its apparent authenticity was precisely that: a cheap illusion.

If Rodenberg reacted with acerbic oversensitivity to Rybkowksi's comments, then surely because Rybkowski had at one stroke exposed the falseness of a film into whose carefully constructed impression of authenticity so much hard work, energy, and rhetoric had been invested. He had, at the very heart of the Soviet empire, accused the GDR of lying. In criticizing *Naked among Wolves*, moreover, Rybkowski implicitly cast doubt on the antifascist GDR version of concentration camp history as a whole. That it was not an American or French or Italian member of the jury who spoke out most influentially against the film, but a Pole, a citizen of a fellow socialist country, made the criticism an even more bitter pill for the GDR to swallow. Attempts by Rodenberg to interpret the failure of *Naked among Wolves* in Moscow as the result of both capitalist conspiracy and ideological coexistence — a somewhat inconsistent interpretation — overlook the uncomfortable fact of Rybkowksi's influence. Despite the GDR's membership of the socialist bloc, there were those within that bloc, such as Rybkowski, who appeared to view with some suspicion its attempts to create for itself an antifascist past. In the end, the debate in Moscow was about whether or not East Germany should be allowed to get away with positioning itself *post hoc* on the side of the victims and liberators, instead of confronting the atrocities and murders committed by Germans at Buchenwald and elsewhere.

The rather crestfallen DEFA delegation returned home in late July 1963. But this return had its compensations. In October 1963, Beyer, Marczinkowski, Hirschmeier, and Apitz were awarded one of the GDR's highest cultural accolades: the National Prize, 1st Class, for Art and Literature. It was handed to them in person by Walter Ulbricht. The GDR press reported on this extensively. The award was almost certainly intended by the SED as a defiant rebuttal of the discrediting of *Naked among Wolves* in Moscow. The film, after its failure at the festival, was demonstratively feted — in protest, and in an attempt to repair the film's damaged reputation and restore its halo of authenticity. For while East German citizens knew nothing of the possible reasons as to why the film had not won the major award in Moscow, they might have wondered at its lack of success, given that the GDR press had firmly reckoned with this success, as indeed had DEFA. They thus needed to be reassured of the film's value.

But as it happened, Moscow had not been an entire waste of time for the GDR representatives. During the festival, two Soviet citizens came forward claiming that one of their relatives had undergone a fate similar to that of Stefan Cyliak in the film. This information was to trigger a search for Stefan Zweig, a search that, as we shall see in the next chapter, proved successful. That this search was launched is surely symptomatic of the impact of the film's failure in Moscow. Rypkowski had not questioned the authenticity of the story of the child's rescue by the antifascist prisoners; his criticism had been much more general in tone. Nevertheless, his remarks certainly implied that such heroic exploits either did not happen or were of limited historical significance in the general context of Buchenwald as a site of death. In finding Stefan, the GDR could prove to itself and the world that these exploits *did* happen, and that they mattered, asserting the right to remember Buchenwald as a location of effective resistance — precisely the view that Rybkowksi had dismissed as "varnish." Now it was Stefan himself who was to be used to authenticate both the GDR's version of his story and the GDR image of Buchenwald in general. It was he who was to prop up, as it were, the tottering foundation myth.

Notes

[1] For more on the biographies of these figures, see Archiv der Gedenkstätte Buchenwald (henceforth BwA), 52-11-77.

[2] Josef-Hermann Sauter, "Interview mit Bruno Apitz," *Weimarer Beiträge* 19/1 (1973): 26–37; here, 34.

[3] Stiftung Archiv Akademie der Künste (henceforth SAdK), Bruno-Apitz-Archiv 8: "Mitschrift einer Aussprache der Genossen Kurt Faustmann und Helmut Schulz mit dem Genossen Bruno Apitz," 10 April 1961.

[4] For more on this, see chapter 5.

[5] See Deutsches Rundfunkarchiv (henceforth DRA), 2005639X00: "Radio DDR II: Literarische Stunde: Zum 85. Geburtstag von Bruno Apitz." This contains excerpts from Apitz's 1960 interview.

[6] See Stiftung Archiv der Parteien und Massenorganisationen der ehemaligen Deutschen Demokratischen Republik im Bundesarchiv (henceforth SAPMO-BArch), DR117/1946: Letter from Apitz to Wilkening, 6 May 1959.

[7] See SAPMO-BArch, DR117/1946: Letter from Apitz to Wilkening, 6 May 1959.

[8] SAPMO-BArch, DR117/1946: "Aktennotiz" sent by Wilkening to Wischnewski and Zunft, 21 November 1960.

[9] SAPMO-BArch, DR117/1946: "Aktennotiz" sent by Wilkening to Wischnewski and Zunft, 21 November 1960.

[10] In a letter of 6 August 1961 to Apitz, Beyer informed him that problems with the filming of *Star-Crossed Lovers* had caused delays. See SAdK, Bruno-Apitz-Archiv 15.

[11] Interview with Frank Beyer, 2 February 2002.

[12] SAPMO-BArch, DR1/8919: "Diskussionsbeitrag Frank Beyer," 1962 (no date or location specified). Beyer was roundly criticized for these comments by Kurt Maetzig during a Party meeting of the "Red Circle" filmmaking collective in early 1963 (see SAPMO-BArch, DY30/IV A2/9.06/122: "Hausmitteilung" from Siegfried Wagner to Kurt Hager, 12 March 1963).

[13] See Ralf Schenk, ed., *Regie: Frank Beyer* (Berlin: Edition Hentrich, 1995), 106–51.

[14] Heinz Hofmann, "Nackt unter Wölfen," *Märkische Volksstimme*, 6 March 1963.

[15] SAPMO-BArch, DR117/1946: Letter from Hans Mahlich to Zunft, 14 March 1962.

[16] SAPMO-BArch, DR117/1946: Letter from Hans Mahlich to Zunft, 14 March 1962.

[17] SAPMO-BArch, DR1/0901/Film 369: Letter from Mahlich to IfML, 30 March 1962.

[18] SAPMO-BArch, DR1/0901/Film 369: Letter from Rost to Museum for German History, 10 June 1962.

[19] SAPMO-BArch, DR1/0901/Film 369: Letter from Mahlich and Rost to Berlin-Lichtenberg Prison, 2 July 1962.

[20] SAPMO-BArch, DR1/0901/Film 369: Letter from Wilkening to "Red Circle," 14 April 1962.

[21] Interview with Frank Beyer, 2 February 2002.

[22] The opening credits of Beyer's *Naked among Wolves* claim that Apitz alone was responsible for the film script, but while he provided the dialogues, he discussed the shape and length of the individual scenes in advance with Beyer (interview with Frank Beyer, 2 February 2002).

[23] Interview with Frank Beyer, 2 February 2002. One of Buchenwald's prisoners present during the making of the film, Paul Heilmann, recalled that the inmates really had formed a protective wall around a child when SS man Werner Berger drew a pistol and threatened to shoot him. See Christa Otten, "Denn weil der Mensch ein Mensch ist," *Wochenpost*, 26 May 1962.

[24] SAPMO-BArch, DR1/0901/Film 369: Letter from Jochen Mückenberger to Admiral Verner, 14 March 1962.

[25] Bundesarchiv-Filmarchiv, 12038: Helmut Ulrich, "Nackt unter Wölfen," *Progress Filmblatt* (undated).

[26] DRA, 200307000: "Der DEFA-Film 'Nackt unter Wölfen,'" *Berliner Rundfunk*, 7 April 1963.

[27] Horst Knietzsch, "Ein Lied vom wahren Menschen," *Neues Deutschland*, 11 April 1963.

[28] Bundesarchiv-Filmarchiv, 12038: Helmut Ulrich, "Nackt unter Wölfen," *Progress Filmblatt* (undated).

[29] Bundesarchiv-Filmarchiv, 12038: "Nicht Typen, sondern Menschen: Eine notwendige Korrektur; Nach einem Gespräch mit Bruno Apitz von Heinz Hofmann," *Progress-Dienst für Presse und Werbung* 14 (1963): 2–6; here, 2.

[30] Bundesarchiv-Filmarchiv, 12038: Heinz Hofmann, "Die Grundidee tiefer erfaßt," *Progress-Dienst für Presse und Werbung* 14 (1963): 6–8, here 7.

[31] SAPMO-BArch, DR1/0901/Film 369: Letter from Jochen Mückenberger to Admiral Verner, 14 March 1962.

[32] "Ein berühmter Roman wird verfilmt," *Thüringische Landeszeitung*, 8 May 1962.

[33] An open letter of protest signed among others by Franz Fühmann, Hermann Kant, Anna Seghers, and Arnold Zweig was sent to the West German literary group *Gruppe 47*. See "Westdeutsche verurteilen Schikane gegen Apitz," *Berliner Zeitung*, 4 November 1962.

[34] Quoted in *Die Fischer Chronik: Deutschland '49–'99* (Frankfurt am Main: Fischer, 1999), 307.

[35] Bundesarchiv-Filmarchiv, 12038: "Nicht Typen, sondern Menschen," 6.

[36] Horst Eckert, "Die Wölfe fürchten sich," *Berliner Zeitung*, 2 November 1962.

[37] "Wehrhaft gegen die Wölfe," *Neue Zeit*, 3 November 1962.

[38] Bundesarchiv-Filmarchiv, 12038: "Nicht Typen, sondern Menschen," 6.

[39] "Vor großem Filmerlebnis," *Berliner Zeitung am Abend*, 3 April 1963.

[40] "Nackt unter Wölfen," *Neuer Tag*, 14 April 1963.

[41] See, for instance, Rosemarie Rehahn, "Nackt unter Wölfen," *Wochenpost*, 27 April 1963.

[42] Horst Knietzsch, "Ein Lied vom wahren Menschen."

[43] Fred Gehler, "Nackt unter Wölfen," *Sonntag*, 14 April 1963.

[44] SAPMO-BArch, DR117/1946: "Rohschnittabnahme 'Nackt unter Wölfen' am 24.9.62."

[45] I am grateful to Evelyn Preuss for suggesting this interpretation to me. I would also like to express my thanks to Eve Rosenhaft for pointing out to me the problematic nature of the conclusion to the film.

[46] Interview with Frank Beyer, 2 February 2002.

[47] Bundesarchiv-Filmarchiv, 12038: Hofmann, "Die Grundidee tiefer erfaßt," 6.

[48] Bundesarchiv-Filmarchiv, 12038: Hofmann, "Die Grundidee tiefer erfaßt," 6.

[49] SAPMO-BArch, DR117/1946: "Rohschnittabnahme 'Nackt unter Wölfen' am 24.9.62."

[50] Thus between 1961 and 1965 only 25 films were found to be illegal under the terms of the Import Prohibition Law. Only four were banned in 1966, while none were banned between 1967 and 1969. By contrast, of the 2,878 films scrutinized, 2,850 were considered acceptable (see the lists of films in the documents contained in Bundesarchiv Koblenz B103/228).

[51] Bundesarchiv Koblenz, B102/144135: "Kurzprotokoll Nr. 16/66 über die Ressortbesprechung betreffend Überwachungsgesetz am Mittwoch, dem 22. Juni 1966," 23 June 1966.

[52] Bundesarchiv Koblenz, B102/144135: "Kurzprotokoll Nr. 17/66 über die Ressortbesprechung betreffend Überwachungsgesetz am Mittwoch, dem 7. September 1966," 8 September 1961.

[53] Bundesarchiv Koblenz, B102/144129: Letter from *Naturfreundejugend Deutschlands* to the Federal Press and Information Office, undated, probably October 1963.

[54] Bundesarchiv Koblenz, B102/144129: "Kurzprotokoll Nr. 19/63 über die Sitzung des interministeriellen Ausschusses für Ost/West-Filmfragen am Donnerstag, dem 7. November 1963," 11 November 1963.

[55] See, for instance, "Ein Film, der Lehren vermittelt," *Thüringer Tageblatt*, 19 March 1964.

[56] Karl Feuerer, "Nackt unter Wölfen in München," *Die Andere Zeitung*, 7 May 1964.

[57] See "Beifall in München," *Berliner Zeitung*, 26 April 1964.

[58] Interview with Frank Beyer, Berlin, 2 February 2002.

[59] While I was unable to find conclusive proof of the public nature of the VVN showing, the committee would not have needed to view the film had the planned showing been intended solely for VVN members as an "internal" event.

[60] Bundesarchiv Koblenz, B102/144130: "Kurzprotokoll Nr. 13/64 über die Sitzung des interministeriellen Ausschusses für Ost/West-Filmfragen am Freitag, dem 29. Mai 1964," 30 May 1964.

[61] Bundesarchiv Koblenz, B102/144130: "Kurzprotokoll Nr. 14/64 über die Sitzung des interministeriellen Ausschusses für Ost/West-Filmfragen am Donnerstag, dem 4. Juni 1964," 10 June 1964.

[62] Bundesarchiv Koblenz, B102/144131: "Kurzprotokoll Nr. 18/64 über die Sitzung des interministeriellen Ausschusses für Ost/West-Filmfragen am Donnerstag, dem 24. September, und Freitag, den 25. September 1964," 28 September 1964.

[63] Bundesarchiv Koblenz, B103/228: "Vom Ausschuß zugelassene DEFA-Filme."

[64] Bundesarchiv Koblenz, B102/144133: Letter from Film Studio Leckebusch to the Economics Ministry, 19 May 1965.

[65] See SAPMO-BArch, DY30/IV A 2/9.06/55, Fiche 1: "Sektor Kulturelle Arbeit mit Westdeutschland: Arbeitsplan I. Halbjahr 1965," Berlin, 21 January 1965.

[66] SAPMO-BArch, DY30/IV A 2/9.06/55, Fiche 1: "Maßnahmen 1965."

[67] SAPMO-BArch, DY30/IV A 2/9.06/55, Fiche 1: "Maßnahmen 1965."

[68] SAPMO-BArch, DY30/IV A 2/9.06/55, Fiche 1: "Informationen über die Arbeit des II. Halbjahres 1964."

[69] "In the Charnel House," *Time*, 6 May 1967, 65.

[70] For excerpts in German translation from reviews of the film in the *Glasgow Herald* (27 August 1963), the *Edinburgh Evening News* (28 August 1963) and the *Daily Worker* (31 August 1963), see SAdK, Bruno-Apitz-Archiv 96.

[71] "Nackt unter Wölfen," *Voor allen*, 16 November 1963 (my source here is a German translation of this article in SAdK, Bruno-Apitz-Archiv 96).

[72] "Nackt unter Wölfen," *Ethnos*, 10 March 1964 (my source here is a German translation of this article in SAdK, Bruno-Apitz-Archiv 96).

[73] "Nackt unter Wölfen," *Ta Nea*, 10 March 1964 (my source here is a German translation of this article in SAdK, Bruno-Apitz-Archiv 96).

[74] SAPMO-BArch, DR1/8907: Hans Rodenberg, "Bericht über das Internationale Moskauer Filmfestival," 24 July 1963.

[75] SAPMO-BArch, DR1/8907: Hans Rodenberg, "Bericht über das Internationale Moskauer Filmfestival," 24 July 1963.

[76] SAPMO-BArch, DR1/8907: Hans Rodenberg, "Bericht über das Internationale Moskauer Filmfestival," 24 July 1963.

[77] SAPMO-BArch, DR1/8907: Haida, "Botschaft der DDR Moskau: Bericht über das III. Moskauer Filmfestival 1963," 9 August 1963.

[78] SAPMO-BArch, DR1/8907: Dieter Heinze, "Aktennotiz über eine abschliessende Besprechung beim Vorsitzenden des Staatlichen Filmkomitees des Ministerrates, Genossen Romanov, am Montag, dem 22. Juli 1963 in Moskau," 26 July 1963.

[79] SAPMO-BArch, DR1/8907: Hans Rodenberg, "Bericht über das Internationale Moskauer Filmfestival," 24 July 1963.

[80] I am very grateful to both Marek Haltof and Paul Coates for providing me with detailed and helpful information about Jan Rybkowski.

CHAPTER FIVE

STEFAN JERZY ZWEIG AND THE GDR

Exploitation

FROM THE VERY MOMENT Stefan Zweig arrived on East German soil in early 1964, indeed even before he did so, the GDR sought to use him as "living proof" of the truth of the story behind the book and film of *Naked among Wolves* (*Nackt unter Wölfen*). Zweig's presence was also used more generally to confirm the effectiveness and humanity of communist-led antifascist resistance under Hitler. This chapter will examine in detail the process of this exploitation. First, the GDR presented Zweig's experience of Buchenwald as identical to that of Stefan Cyliak in *Naked among Wolves*. This had the added effect of framing this experience entirely within the typical GDR narrative of communist-led antifascist resistance — a framing that played down the specifically Jewish character of that experience. In the interests of such a framing, Zacharias Zweig's account of his son's rescue, serialized in February 1964 in the *Berliner Zeitung am Abend*, was, as we shall see, substantially altered.

The SED also attempted to use Stefan Zweig both as an example of its avowed philo-Semitism and as a mouthpiece for its anti-Zionist sentiment. This may appear inconsistent to us today, but according to East German readings of the Second World War, Nazi anti-Semitism served the interests of imperialist capitalism; Zionism, in the present, also served these interests. Only in the socialist countries, so the argument ran, could Jews, as socialists, truly be emancipated — at the unstated price of abandoning their Jewishness (according to a set of statistics for 1978, East Berlin's Jewish Community had a mere 340 members; yet at the same time some 4,000 GDR citizens living in East Berlin were recognized as racial victims of Nazism).[1] In something of a balancing act, then, Zweig's Jewishness had to be visible enough for him to be used in a variety of ways, yet never emphasized; his function, after all, was to serve primarily as a mirror reflecting communist courage, rather than the Jewish experience of discrimination and persecution under Nazism. As the chapter will show, Stefan's response to all this was ambivalent. Both Stefan and his father appeared content to attest to the glory of communist resistance. Yet in his own way Stefan also sought to draw attention to the fate of the Jews, and he resisted attempts to use him as a mouthpiece to criticize Israel.

Stefan, for a variety of reasons, left the GDR in 1972, although he did return on occasion for short visits. The final section of the chapter examines one last, related, stage in the only partly successful "authentification drive" explored in this chapter and the last — namely, the process of moving the main exhibition at Buchenwald's National Site of Warning and Commemoration (NMGB) away from the Disinfection Building to the Storage Building, a process finally completed in 1985. This move brought the exhibits into the immediate vicinity of the location of Zweig's initial rescue, a move that implicitly centered Buchenwald's history around the forces involved in that rescue, while at the same time lending it an air of "truth."

The Finding of Zweig

Ever since the publication of *Naked among Wolves* in 1958, readers had been curious to find out what became of Stefan after liberation in April 1945. In November 1963, Apitz told the newspaper *BZ am Abend*: "For years I've been getting letters from all over the world; women, mothers write to me, whole school classes turn to me. And again and again I have to tell them: I don't know anything." The newspaper also reported that, following the showing of *Naked among Wolves* in the GDR, which reached cinemas in April 1963, readers had assailed the newspaper with questions about the Buchenwald child.[2] There were various theories about his possible whereabouts, the most persistent of which was that he had been adopted by an American soldier and taken to the United States. Once, in the middle of the night, Apitz received a phone call from a newspaper claiming to have located Stefan Zweig in Cracow. The claim was true, but, as it turned out, it was a quite different Stefan Zweig. Apitz also relates that, during the inaugural ceremony held at Buchenwald's NMGB in September 1958, a rumor circulated that Stefan Zweig was attending the ceremony. This rumor triggered "such intense, joyful excitement among participants from all over the world that everyone took it to be true" — which, of course, it was not.[3]

That East German readers and filmgoers moved by *Naked among Wolves* should take an emotional interest in the child's post-camp life is only natural. However, the intensity of this interest does raise certain questions. For all the asseverations of authenticity issued by Apitz and others in connection with *Naked among Wolves*, doubts will have remained as to whether the story was a "real" one, and conceivably many East German citizens will have been eager to have these dispelled. In the wake of the Holocaust, there was a strong psychological and moral need for evidence of German decency toward Jews — as a salve to the German conscience. In Stefan's case, only "living proof" would suffice. On the other hand, it cannot be ruled out that such doubts were more a reflection of a residual cynicism toward communism. After all, under Hitler Germans had been taught to hate communism and to identify it as barbaric; fifteen years of

Soviet-style reeducation will not have overcome this negative stereotyping entirely. That the *BZ am Abend* set out to trace Zweig could be read as a response to a deep-seated unease; he had to be found because the legitimacy of the "humanist communist legacy" was at stake.

By his own account, it was *BZ am Abend* journalist Ewald Thoms who, as he was flying back to Berlin from the Moscow Film Festival in July 1963, resolved to start the search for Stefan.[4] During the festival, following an interview Apitz had given to Moscow Television, two Soviet citizens contacted the Film Festival magazine to say that, some ten years previously, documents pertaining to a case similar to that of Stefan Zweig's had circulated among their family members.[5] As it turned out, these relatives were Stefan's uncle Heinrich and his wife, who lived in Moscow.[6] This proved to be a crucial lead; soon Thoms had established that Stefan and his father had emigrated to Israel in 1949. But it proved impossible, from so far away, to find out where in Israel they were living. Ernst Hansch, chief editor of the *BZ am Abend*, decided to send someone to look for the Zweigs. Charlotte Holzer, a former resistance fighter in East Berlin, whose daughter lived in Israel and who was in possession of an entry visa, was entrusted with this mission in September 1963.[7] During the Nazi period, Holzer had been in the Herbert Baum resistance group, whose members — all Jews, most with a communist background — had attempted to burn down the anti-Soviet exhibition "The Soviet Paradise" in Berlin in 1942.

Through her son-in-law, who consulted the immigration records in Jerusalem, Holzer traced the Zweigs to an address in Tel Aviv. Two days later, she stood face to face with Zacharias Zweig. According to Holzer, he confirmed that Stefan had been rescued by Buchenwald's prisoners — "mainly German communists."[8] He did not know Apitz's novel. Holzer lent him a copy; after reading it, he told Holzer: "Yes, that's the way it was; never would I have believed that it would have been possible to bring that all back to life."[9] Zacharias, who informed Holzer that Stefan was studying in Lyon at the Institute for Applied Polytechnology, immediately sent his son a letter: "this Buchenwald boy, that's you . . . read this book by the German antifascist Bruno Apitz and you'll understand whom you and I owe our lives to."[10] Stefan got hold of a French translation of the novel and, on 10 January 1964, wrote to Apitz in French to express his thanks: "for many years I thought our past at Buchenwald had been forgotten. Your book *Naked among Wolves* was the strongest answer possible, and I am convinced that I was wrong."[11] Holzer, her mission accomplished, returned to the GDR in December 1963 with indubitable proof that Zacharias's son was the Stefan Jerzy Zweig upon whom Stefan Cyliak in Apitz's novel was based. She brought back with her, not only photographs of Stefan, but also photocopies of his Buchenwald registration card, of a pass issued to him by the American military authorities on 23 April 1945, and of Zacharias's 1961 Yad Vashem testimony.

All now seemed ready for the unveiling of a spectacular discovery, and on 3 February 1964, the *BZ am Abend* reported to its readers on the front page the finding of Stefan Jerzy Zweig.[12] But to a considerable extent, the newspaper, Apitz, Holzer, and the Committee of Antifascist Resistance Fighters (KdAW) had been upstaged by events in West Germany. For when the *BZ am Abend* broke the news, Zweig was in Stuttgart visiting Willi Bleicher, the former Personal Property Room Kapo involved in his rescue and now a regional head of the West German metalworkers' union, IG Metall. Bleicher had invited Zweig to Stuttgart to celebrate his, Stefan's, twenty-third birthday. Not only that: West German television had already reported on the meeting between Bleicher and Stefan on regional and national news on 2 February 1964. The *BZ am Abend* did tell its readers of Zweig's visit to Stuttgart; indeed it probably had little alternative. Ewald Thoms visited him there on 5 February. Bleicher then drove Stefan to Weimar to visit the memorial site at Buchenwald, where "Juschu" met with Apitz and Robert Siewert; the meeting was reported on GDR television and radio. While the *BZ am Abend* informed its readers that it was responsible for providing the Zweigs with Bleicher's Stuttgart address,[13] it did not inform them of the reason for this: namely that Zacharias had made this the precondition for giving Charlotte Holzer Stefan's address in France in the first place.[14] Stefan, moreover, insisted that he would only visit the GDR after first visiting Bleicher.[15] When the *BZ am Abend* announced the finding of Stefan on 3 February, it did not provide much detail; one gains the impression the newspaper felt compelled to make its announcement earlier than planned to prevent Bleicher stealing all of its thunder.

That Stefan chose, initially, to visit Bleicher implied that he regarded a *West* German Buchenwald survivor as the German to whom he owed the most. This was clearly a blow to the *BZ am Abend* and others in the GDR involved in tracing Stefan, who, they had hoped, would identify primarily, indeed exclusively, with those former Buchenwald prisoners who now lived in *East* Germany. As subsequent events were to show, East Germany believed *it* had the legitimate claim to Stefan, not West Germany. From an SED point of view, moreover, Bleicher's biographical data were not exactly ideal. As outlined in chapter 2, he had been a member of the renegade Communist Party Opposition (KPO); and while he rejoined the KPD in Buchenwald, he then returned to the west of Germany after the war — and became a social democrat. Nor was it ideal that Eugen Ochs had accompanied Bleicher and Stefan when they drove to Weimar on 6 February 1964. Ochs was another former KPO man who had had a hand in Stefan's rescue, and, like Bleicher, was a West German union representative. Stefan's trip with Bleicher and Ochs — "visiting" East Germany — rather seemed to imply that he identified first and foremost with a West German, "turncoat," social democrat group of former Buchenwald prisoners.

The *BZ am Abend*, and other GDR newspapers, responded to these problems by doing their best to reduce the significance of Bleicher's role in Stefan's rescue. In taking the initial decision to protect Stefan at Buchenwald, Bleicher probably acted without the explicit approval of the International Camp Committee (ILK). Yet Ewald Thoms, in the 3 February 1964 issue of the *BZ am Abend*, claimed that Willi Bleicher "took responsibility for the child on the orders of the Camp Committee." Horst Sievers in the East German *Berliner Zeitung* plowed a slightly different furrow. He sought to dissociate the West German trade union movement from the West German state, classifying the former as representing the tradition of antifascism, and the latter as peopled by officials and politicians "guilty of the worst deeds in the German past." By contrast, in the GDR, according to Sievers, the antifascist heroes had not only found a place in the workers' movement, but also acted as shop-floor managers and politicians. The implication of this piece of sophistry is that Stefan's visit to West Germany was not a visit to that state, but a visit to a *tradition* that existed in opposition to it; in the light of the view that this tradition, by contrast, had taken root in all areas of political and economic life in the GDR, Stefan's visit to West Germany was in effect a visit to an outpost of East German values on West German soil. Thus a trip to the West was reimagined as one to the East.[16]

When Stefan visited Weimar and Buchenwald between 7 and 9 February 1964, his "West German" rescuers Bleicher and Ochs were outnumbered by East German communist survivors of Buchenwald such as Bruno Apitz, Karl Barthel, Heinz Bausch, Carl Gärtig, and Robert Siewert. *BZ am Abend* reporter Günter Karau referred to the gathering of former Buchenwald prisoners as one of Juschu's "fathers," and to Juschu as the "prodigal son."[17] This reflects the tenor of all GDR newspaper reports on Stefan's Weimar visit. But the role, for instance, of Robert Siewert in rescuing Stefan — he hid him briefly in an air vent — can hardly be compared to that of Bleicher. GDR newspapers erased differences (deliberately or unwittingly) in their will to interpret the rescue act as the expression of a paternal collective in which the reader is also supposed to recognize a prototype of masculine GDR socialism. At the same time Stefan's life before his Weimar visit, while never explicitly invalidated (GDR newspapers acknowledged the assistance offered to Stefan by French antifascists), was nevertheless implicitly presented as an aberration that, with his return to Buchenwald, had come to an end. Stefan had come "home" to his "family." Former Buchenwald prisoners themselves contributed to the notion of a paternal collective by adapting their memories, or at least choosing to overlook inconsistencies. Accompanying Stefan on a tour of Buchenwald memorial site on 8 February 1964, Heinz Bausch pointed to the Storage Building and said: "Juschu, look up there, that's where we hid you for a long time."[18] Yet Heinz Bausch surely knew that, in his 1957 account of the hiding of a child in the Storage Building, he had dated this to 1942/43 and had referred to the rescued child as Josef Streich — not Zweig (see later in this chapter).[19]

Such adaptations were not an uncommon aspect of the reactions to Stefan's arrival. In the GDR, indeed, he was routinely treated not as the survivor Stefan Zweig but as the surviving Stefan Cyliak from Apitz's novel. Trailblazing in this respect was the 3 February 1964 edition of *BZ am Abend*. It showed, in juxtaposition, two photographs: one, dated 1946, of Zacharias Zweig holding Stefan Zweig aloft, and another, dated 1944, of the actor Gerry Wolff in the role of Bochow from the DEFA film of *Naked among Wolves*. Wolff is shown holding Cyliak in his arms. The visual correspondence between the two photographs and the tendentious use of dates posited an absolute equivalence of fiction with reality. In subsequent editions, the *BZ am Abend* featured photographs in which Stefan Zweig could be seen reading its 3 February 1964 headlines about his discovery, receiving a copy of *Naked among Wolves* from Ewald Thoms, and looking on as Willi Bleicher leafs through a special edition of *Naked among Wolves* with illustrations by Fritz Cremer.[20] Such photographs suggested self-discovery; Stefan Zweig was understood by the reader to be absorbing "the truth" about his past. This process involved plain distortion. Before Stefan was shown the DEFA film of *Naked among Wolves* in Weimar, Apitz, in an introductory address, told him he was about to witness how he was carried on the arms of the prisoners, "who fought their way . . . with courage and strength . . .," through the opened gates of Buchenwald toward freedom.[21] The reality had been very different: it was Zacharias who had ensured Stefan's survival immediately prior to liberation, and Stefan Zweig had never been carried through the gates as Stefan Cyliak was in the film.

In his address, Apitz also told Stefan that he was about to revisit his early childhood, "about which you surely — and thankfully — know very little."[22] Perhaps Apitz was assuming that Stefan's extreme youth at the time would have prevented him from acquiring too many horrific memories. On the other hand, Apitz must have known that Stefan was acquainted with his father's 1961 testimony. He therefore did know a lot about his childhood, even if he could not *remember* much. Apitz's comments thus could be read as an appeal to Stefan to accept the part he was expected to play in the GDR: that of a man whose mind on the subject of Buchenwald had been blank until he confronted "his" past in *Naked among Wolves*. In February 1964, a drama was acted out in Weimar in which Stefan, a smiling, polite, and reticent figure, appeared content to allow himself to be identified with Stefan Cyliak. Yet while Stefan's amenable and agreeable manner may have lent itself to attempts to create more or less precise equivalences,[23] Zacharias's Yad Vashem testimony did not. Apitz, Holzer, the *BZ am Abend*, and the KdAW had no doubt hoped that this testimony would serve to corroborate the story of rescue and resistance conveyed by *Naked among Wolves*. But it only partly corroborated it; in part, it contradicted it, or at least presented a much more complex picture.

Changes to Zacharias Zweig's Account of Stefan's Rescue

In the course of February 1964, the *BZ am Abend*, in twenty-four installments, serialized Zacharias Zweig's Yad Vashem testimony. For the first time, the GDR population had the chance to compare the story of Stefan's rescue as related in *Naked among Wolves* with the father's own version. Charlotte Holzer experienced problems when she attempted to persuade the Tel Aviv branch of Yad Vashem, which held Zacharias's testimony, to allow her to take a copy back with her to the GDR; there was concern it might "fall into the wrong hands," a concern that turned out, as we shall see, to be justified.[24] In early December 1963, the GDR's Committee of Antifascist Resistance Fighters and Buchenwald Committee wrote to Yad Vashem requesting a copy of the testimony "for our own documentation," and authorizing Zacharias to obtain it in their name. The letter was signed by both Holzer and Apitz.[25] Yad Vashem finally consented, and Holzer duly returned to the GDR with a copy later in December 1963. The Apitz archives contain a German translation of the testimony by one E. Walther;[26] this translation formed the basis of the *BZ am Abend* serialization and the later book *"Mein Vater, was machst du hier . . . ,"* published in West Germany in 1987.[27] So interested was the GDR public in the circumstances surrounding the finding of Zweig and in the serialization of the father's testimony that the *BZ am Abend* decided to issue a special supplement containing all parts of this serialization together with all the articles on the rescue that had been published in the newspaper throughout February; this supplement ran to at least three editions.

The publication of the testimony of a Holocaust survivor in the *BZ am Abend* may seem laudable, but it in fact represented a violation of what had been agreed between Zacharias Zweig and Yad Vashem on the one hand, and Apitz, Holzer, and the KdAW on the other — namely that the copy of Zacharias's testimony would be lodged in the Buchenwald archives for documentation purposes, but *not* published. Zacharias had made Apitz sign an affidavit to this effect.[28] In the event, moreover, it was serialized in heavily reduced form. Now, the father's testimony does run, in its German translation, to some 90 pages of typescript; cuts were inevitable. Moreover, editing was necessary here and there to smooth over excisions. Nevertheless, it is hardly a coincidence that the material omitted from the serialization was, in almost every instance, material that cast the rescue story in a different light from that of Apitz's novel; and editorial changes went further than the purely cosmetic. As none of the *BZ am Abend*'s correspondence from the period has survived, it is impossible to reconstruct precisely how these cuts came to be made and who was responsible for them. The Buchenwald Committee, to judge at least from a copy of three pages of the translated version of the testimony that has survived in KdAW archives, was surprised by the omissions. In the margins of these three pages, vertical lines have been drawn. A scribbled annotation reads: "in the *BZ am Abend* of 14 February 1964 these parts marked with an X were 'suppressed.' "[29] Nor is it likely that Walter Bartel was involved in the cuts; it was only on 14 February — long into the serialization — that Ewald Thoms sent Bartel, "as agreed," Zacharias's testimony for him to photocopy and return.[30] Stefan Zweig suspects Apitz himself of having had a hand in the alterations.[31] This is certainly possible, given that Apitz appears to have had access to a copy of the testimony in January, that is, before the *BZ am Abend* February serialization. Whoever it was who made the cuts must have had "precise knowledge of the camp," as Harry Stein of Buchenwald Memorial Site has claimed; as Stein rightly says, they affected "all formulations that raised questions regarding the social stratification of the camp and the role of the prisoner functionaries, as well as the relationship between prisoners and the SS."[32] It might be more exact, however, to maintain that someone with precise knowledge of how the camp was *represented in the GDR* undertook the cuts.

Behind the choice of excisions was the wish to make Zweig's testimony consistent with the view of Nazi ghettos and camps, and particularly with the view of Buchenwald and the Stefan Jerzy Zweig story prevalent in the GDR. According to this view, camp life was characterized by sharp divisions between the prisoners and the SS. It was clearly upon this view that the credibility of the antifascist resistance narrative rested. Such a view underpins, for instance, the novel and film of *Naked among Wolves*. For sure, there are passages in Zacharias's original testimony that appear to confirm the GDR view; equally, there are as many passages that demonstrate that divisions were not always absolute, indeed could not be if survival were to be possible. Thus Zacharias makes it clear he could never have saved Stefan's life in the Cracow ghetto or at Biezanow, Skarzysko, and Plaszow had it not been for his readiness, and that of prisoner-run administrative bodies, to approach and consult with the SS. All passages documenting such approaches were cut from the *BZ am Abend* version, such as the episode where Zacharias, at Plaszow camp, called in a favor owed to him by a Jewish doctor called Gross.[33] Also cut was the section describing how, on arriving at Skarzysko camp, Zacharias obtained permission from the SS camp commandant for himself and Stefan to go straight to his allocated block without first having to wait.[34] A passage describing how the political prisoners at Buchenwald negotiated with the camp commandant in an attempt to save Stefan from deportation likewise fell prey to excision.[35] And a key change was made to the section on attempts by German prisoners to get Stefan admitted to the sick bay; whereas, according to Zacharias's version, contact was made with an SS doctor, in the *BZ am Abend* version the word "SS" has been removed.[36] The established image in the GDR of Stefan's rescue was that it depended entirely on heroic resistance and solidarity between fellow prisoners, not on appeals to authority and consultation with the SS.

Zacharias's version also made it clear that the SS witnessed Stefan's arrival in the camp, and that some SS men, at least, knew of his whereabouts in the Main Camp; how, otherwise, could there have been those who brought him fruit and candies, and others who "looked askance" at the child?[37] Zacharias further related that, in the Small Camp, an SS man and a group of women forced into prostitution by the SS spent time with Stefan.[38] None of this featured in the *BZ am Abend* version, because it raised a number of questions. Was Stefan's presence tolerated in the camp, at least at certain points or by certain SS men? Did his survival depend as much on their willingness to turn a blind eye as on the resourcefulness of the political prisoners? Did the political prisoners bribe them in some way? When Stefan was hidden in the Small Camp, did his survival there depend on the discretion of an SS man and female prisoners? And if so, why did the SS man walk the streets of the Small Camp with Stefan and even take him outside it?[39] What, in other words, was the precise nature of the threat to Stefan's life, and did this threat vary in intensity?

It is clear that excisions in the *BZ am Abend* serialization affected both passages pointing to moments of SS tolerance and even indulgence *and* passages showing how the political prisoners were prepared to seek the cooperation of the SS in their attempts to save Stefan's life. In this respect, the most significant deletions were those made to sections of Zacharias's testimony that implied that Stefan's survival, at one point, depended on sacrificing the life of another prisoner. Bleicher's remark that he would be prepared to send another child to Auschwitz in Stefan's place if he had one to hand was excised, as was Zacharias's short reference to the Gypsies who were added to the transport to Auschwitz after Stefan had been taken into the sick bay.[40] Passages of Zacharias's testimony imply a grey area between SS and prisoners, between villainous perpetrators and heroic victims. These were cut because they contradicted the typical GDR view that the antifascist collective operated exclusively in an underground world and in accordance with a higher morality; there could be no point of contact between it and the SS, or of overlap with SS methods. References to the power of Buchenwald's political prisoners and to the fact that they enjoyed certain privileges were cut for the same reason.[41] What remained of Zacharias's testimony, in essence, in the *BZ am Abend* serialization, were passages highlighting the courage and solidarity of the political prisoners — and there certainly were *several* such passages in between the more ambivalent ones.

The newspaper also cut passages that point to Zacharias's role in Stefan's survival at Buchenwald — particularly on the eve of liberation. These elided passages include heart-rending moments when German prisoners in the Small Camp's prisoner self-administration insist that Zacharias return to the Main Camp with Stefan — thus exposing him to the danger of evacuation.[42] Zacharias calls into question the solidarity of *some* of the German political prisoners *some* of the time, and he also criticizes the resistance organization for its failure to take up arms against the evacuations from Buchenwald in early April 1945. He thus adopts a position similar to that of the figure of Pribula in Apitz's novel, who constantly presses for action, while others in the ILK feel that the uprising should be delayed until the Americans are nearer. But in *Naked among Wolves*, the policy of postponement is presented as a wise one: the ILK succeeds at least in delaying evacuations, and then stages a highly successful rebellion. In Zacharias's view, by contrast, the uprising was not postponed, it never took place. In his testimony, it is the Americans who liberate Buchenwald. Indeed he blames the ILK for *not* having broken down the gates of Buchenwald. Zacharias's critique of the ILK did not feature in the *BZ am Abend* version.[43] Alterations were made, moreover, to his description of events on 11 April. Whereas Zacharias had stated that the SS had fled as the Americans approached, this was changed to "were put to flight" in the *BZ am Abend* serialization.[44]

Zacharias's original testimony, then, was also problematic for the GDR because it suggested that Stefan's survival was as dependent on the individual initiative of the Jew Zacharias — on one occasion *against* the will of antifascist prisoner functionaries — as on German communist prisoners. It contrasts sharply with the typical GDR view that there had been "active" communists and "passive" Jews. Indeed Zacharias, arguably, embodies or at least advocates a more active form of resistance than the ILK, which opted to sit on its stockpile of weapons rather than use it. In the *BZ am Abend* serialization, by contrast, Zacharias's role at Buchenwald is reduced as far as possible to that of an onlooker. At the same time, episodes describing Jewish suffering were excised;[45] for while Jews were to be conveyed as passive victims, it was undesirable to dwell on their pain, lest this detract from the impression of the concentration camp as the site of struggle. Most empathy, moreover, was to be reserved for the communist prisoners.

A number of changes for the serialization can be ascribed to the influence of the Cold War, especially those to passages describing Willi Bleicher's involvement in Stefan's rescue. But these changes were not in *every* case motivated by the wish to play down the role of someone who was now a West German. One key example will illustrate this. Zacharias describes in his testimony how Bleicher turned down a request by an SS man for a pair of boots for his son (Stefan's boots, made by prisoners, had caught his eye); this man, in anger at being spurned by Bleicher, may have been responsible for triggering the order for Stefan's deportation. This passage was entirely cut by the *BZ am Abend* because, of course, it implied that the potentially fatal prospect of deportation was in part the result of a moment of fool-hardy defiance on the part of a communist prisoner.[46] Some changes to the Bleicher sections of Zacharias's testimony may seem defensible. Zacharias had mistakenly taken Bleicher to be the head of the resistance organization, and in the *BZ am Abend* serialization any phrases suggesting that he and other prisoners in Block 40 were amongst its leaders were either deleted or reformulated. Thus the phrase "Willi Bleicher, chief of the illegal organization" was altered to "member of the illegal organization."[47] Nevertheless, it would also have been quite unacceptable to convey the impression that a prisoner who had spearheaded resistance at Buchenwald was now an SPD member and union leader in West Germany — even if it had been true. It was also unacceptable to suggest that Bleicher's motives could have been Christian as well as communist, as Zacharias did; this reference was also deleted from the *BZ am Abend* serialization.[48]

Zacharias Zweig's testimony of his experiences was not the only memoir by a Holocaust survivor to be subjected to massive cuts prior to its publication in the GDR. Rolf Weinstock's account of his experience as a Jewish inmate of Auschwitz and Buchenwald, first published in west Germany under the title *The True Face of Hitler's Germany* in 1948, was reduced from some 80,000 words to about 50,000 before being published in the GDR as "*Chin Up, Rolf!*" in 1950.[49] Cuts affected *inter alia* Weinstock's descriptions of the horrors of Auschwitz. Even then the book was attacked for its "complete neglect of the illegal work of antifascists in the concentration camps,"[50] and immediately withdrawn by the VVN. Some years later, the KdAW even stepped in to completely prevent the publication in the GDR of Primo Levi's *If This Is a Man* (1947/58) and *The Truce* (1963), again because of the neglect of the theme of organized resistance (*If This Is a Man*), but also because of Levi's critical portrait of the Soviet liberators (*The Truce*) and his "anticommunism" and "Zionism."[51] In these cases and in the case of Zweig's testimony, deletions were made or prohibitions imposed to prevent the public dissemination of a view of concentration camps that differed from the standard GDR view of the camps in that it foregrounded Jewish experience rather than communist resistance, adopted an individual rather than a collective point of view, and even criticized the political prisoners (Levi). In short, alternative perspectives were blocked, thereby preventing the emergence of different discourses and the inevitable tensions, questions, and ambivalences that attend the coexistence of such discourses. In defending the monopoly of the antifascist discourse, the KdAW and the former Buchenwald prisoners in particular sought to protect the legitimacy of the high moral terms in which it was couched — and the moral authority enjoyed by former antifascists as a result of this discourse.

The Emergence of Discrepancies

In a 2004 interview, Stefan told me that his father was deeply upset, not just by the serialization of his testimony, but also by the changes described above.[52] Nevertheless, despite the truncation of Zacharias's testimony in the interests of using it as "objective" proof of the rescue story as known through Apitz's novel, not all discrepancies could be suppressed. The passage describing Stefan's arrival in the camp could not be removed entirely without running the risk of drawing attention to it through its very absence. As a result, the reader of the serialization was informed that Stefan walked into the camp at his father's side because the latter had not had time to hide him in a rucksack.[53] Despite this, the GDR press continued to report that Stefan was smuggled into the camp either in a rucksack, or in a suitcase.[54] Apitz himself, according to one newspaper report, even told Stefan when the latter was visiting Buchenwald in February 1964: "Your father brought you through this gate in a rucksack."[55] As an (unidentified) member of the Buchenwald Committee in whose files I found a clipping of this newspaper report has written at the bottom of it: "That's not true, and B. Apitz knows this perfectly well."[56]

Logically, the confusion in the GDR press about whether, and, if so, how, Stefan had been smuggled into the camp was complemented by a degree of confusion on the issue of whether or not he was a registered prisoner. The serialization in the *BZ am Abend* refers to the "precisely filled-out registration cards" that were waiting for Zacharias and Stefan.[57] This corresponded to the claim in a compilation of documents pertaining to Buchenwald, published in the GDR in 1960, that Stefan had been in the camp "legally."[58] When Zweig visited Willi Bleicher in January 1964, West German television, in keeping with the version in Apitz's novel, reported that Stefan was *not* a registered prisoner. Bartel, clearly sensing that contradictory versions might accompany Stefan's visit to the GDR, wrote to Rudolf Wunderlich of the KdAW on 4 February 1964 saying that Stefan had been in the camp "legally" and that a statement should be formulated so that "possible inquiries can be answered unambiguously."[59] I could find no evidence of this statement having been issued. If it had been, it is doubtful whether it would have been helpful. Despite the fact that the *BZ am Abend* had included a photograph of Stefan's prisoner registration card in its very first report on his discovery on 3 February 1964,[60] GDR newspapers continued to assume that Stefan had entered the camp secretly.

This confusion, in hindsight, might appear rather unimportant; after all, smuggled into the camp or not, registered or not, there had been a

Fig. 20: Bruno Apitz (left) and Stefan Zweig at Buchenwald in 1964. Courtesy of the Deutsches Historisches Museum (Berlin).

need to protect Stefan from the SS at certain times. But it has to be remembered that Apitz's novel, not least as a result of the DEFA film, had come to be regarded as an authentic statement on events at Buchenwald rather than as a work of fiction. The problem was probably compounded by reports in the West German press. Not surprisingly, these stressed the role of Bleicher in Stefan's rescue far more than the GDR press did, and pointed to the contributions of other prisoners now living in West Germany, such as Eugen Waller; Stefan, to a degree, was also claimed by West Germany as proof that *it* was heir to the antifascist tradition. West German newspapers, moreover, described episodes in Stefan's rescue that were suppressed in the GDR, such as the bribery of an SS doctor and the role of Zacharias in saving his son's life shortly before liberation.[61] There can be little doubt that some East Germans will have read these reports.

There is evidence, moreover, that the public was bemused by these contradictions and inconsistencies. When Apitz, Peter Edel, Ewald Thoms, Erwin Geschonneck, and Walter Bartel participated in a podium discussion on the subject of the Buchenwald child in Berlin-Pankow on 11 February 1964, the questions from the audience centered on the relationship between fiction and reality. "There were also such simple questions like: how did the child really come into the camp?" Bartel noted. He also observed that Apitz "made a somewhat nervous impression."[62] It seems too that some GDR citizens had spotted discrepancies between claims made in the GDR press, which unequivocally hailed Stefan as "the" Buchenwald child, and a report by the former Personal Property Room Kapo Heinz Bausch in the 1960 Buchenwald documentation. Here, Bausch referred to the hiding of the two-and-a-half-year-old Josef Streich in the Storage Building — a Pole who had been smuggled into Buchenwald in a rucksack by his father.[63] In February 1964, Edwin Borgner, at the time director of the NMG Buchenwald, expressed his concern about the fact that visitors had been wanting to know who the "real" Buchenwald child was — Stefan Zweig or Josef Streich.[64]

Visitors may also have been acquainted with another part of the 1960 Buchenwald documentation, in which it had been claimed — albeit in a footnote — that Apitz had conflated in his novel the stories of the rescue of both Zweig, "who had the number 67,509 and was in the camp legally," and Streich, "who was hidden illegally in the camp."[65] On the surface of it, this passage could have been regarded as helpful: after all, it asked the reader to accept that there was more than one Buchenwald child. But then if Streich had been "hidden illegally," and Stefan a registered prisoner, was *Naked among Wolves* not perhaps based more on Streich's rescue than on Stefan's survival? The publication of Zacharias's testimony in the course of February 1964 will surely have dispelled any doubts GDR citizens might have had as to the dangers faced by Stefan at Buchenwald — "registered" or not — and enhanced the impression that *Naked among Wolves* was based strongly on his fate. But one still suspects that some GDR citizens, at least, felt unable to accept entirely that it was really Stefan Zweig who had been the inspiration for Apitz's novel.

What GDR citizens did not know was that several ex-Buchenwald prisoners had long harbored doubts as to whether Streich ever existed. As early as December 1960, Walter Bartel mentioned in a letter to Otto Halle that there had been "criticism" of Bausch's testimony in the 1960 documentation and asked for the names and addresses of former Storage Building prisoners who might be able to help out with further information.[66] In January 1961, the former Buchenwald prisoner Richard Kucharzyk wrote to Bartel to say that Bausch, in his account, had got the name wrong: "here it should read Stefan Zweig, not Josef Streich."[67] And in February 1963, Bausch himself wrote to Bartel to say he was now convinced that he had wrongly remembered the name of the hidden child, and that "the boy Streich and Zweig are one and the same person."[68] But Bartel remained cautious. In an April 1964 letter to Siewert, he claimed that Bausch was making it "too easy for himself" in simply declaring that Streich's name was actually Zweig.[69] Not that Bausch was really able to make up his mind. Barely three months after his letter to Bartel, he claimed in a newspaper interview in May 1963 that "Juschu's" real name was Joseph Streich.[70]

Following a rumor that Streich might be living in Poland, Bartel contacted one Vaclav Szarnecki in Warsaw in February 1964 asking for his help in locating Streich. "It would be good for us (here I mean the Buchenwalder [former Buchenwald prisoners] in particular)," Bartel wrote, "if this matter could also be clarified, especially of course as some people are again asking questions about how it really was with the illegal child. Did he only exist in our fantasy, or did he really exist?"[71] Bartel does not specify who "some people" are, but it is not inconceivable that members of the public themselves were beginning to probe: if Stefan had not been smuggled into the camp, and if Streich were an invention of the ex-Buchenwald prisoners, then how reliable was Apitz's novel on the issue of "illegality"? Again, its authenticity was in doubt. For Bartel, the solution clearly lay in tracing Streich. If he could succeed in finding Josef Streich, perhaps even presenting him *in person* to an astonished GDR, this would have corroborated the existence of an "illegal" child and his rescue, and made it easier for GDR citizens to believe that there had been two "Buchenwald children" rather than one.

On the very same day that Bartel wrote to Szarnecki, namely on 14 February 1964, he also wrote a letter to the executive committee of the Club of Creative Artists in Berlin, asking it to organize an event around the theme of "fiction and historical reality" in relation to "Juschu-Jerzy."[72] Bartel decided, with Ewald Thoms, to "call upon Apitz" to take part, which Apitz agreed to do. Unfortunately I was not able to trace any record of the outcome of this event, which was planned for 11 March 1964.[73] Did Bartel hope to stage some sort of "resolution" of the apparent contradictions that had emerged between Zweig's rescue story and that of Stefan Cyliak in Apitz's novel? Or some clarification regarding Josef Streich? The question remains open. Streich was never found. Questions and contradictions continued to smolder beneath the surface of the success story of Stefan's discovery and his arrival in the GDR.

Bringing Stefan to the GDR

In the course of 1964, Stefan came to the GDR three times; in February, May, and September. When he came the third time, it was to stay; he took up his studies in Potsdam-Babelsberg, training to become a cameraman. It was a propaganda coup for the GDR. Not only had East Germans discovered Stefan and brought him to the GDR, but he had also been persuaded to move there. At a time when the Auschwitz trials in Frankfurt were exploring the depths of anti-Semitic atrocities during the Third Reich, the GDR was able to demonstrate its philo-Semitic credentials in the present, as well as the philo-Semitic nature of the antifascist legacy on which it was built. Stefan's presence helped to lend support to the argument that it was only West Germany that had an anti-Semitic past and present to face.

It has not proved possible to reconstruct in every detail the process by which Zweig came to be provided with the opportunity to study in the GDR. However, there are indications that certain individuals had a bearing on this process. According to Zweig himself, Robert Siewert and Willi Bleicher played their part.[74] Another possible influence was the *BZ am Abend* editor and journalist Ernst Hansch, who met Zacharias and Stefan in Israel twice: once when the DEFA film of *Naked among Wolves* was shown in Tel Aviv in April 1964,[75] and again in July 1964.[76] The role of the Free German Youth (FDJ), however, was probably more decisive. In February 1964, the FDJ's Central Council approached Stefan during his stay in Weimar and let him "know that I could study here; what I studied would be my decision."[77] Through its newspaper *Junge Welt*, the FDJ then issued to Stefan an invitation from the First Secretary of its Central Council, Horst Schumann, to attend the *Deutschlandtreffen* in May 1964.[78] This, as it turned out, was the last mass meeting of East and West German youth organized by the FDJ (the previous two had been in 1950 and 1954) in the interests of promoting the image of the GDR as a progressive and antifascist state (thus a showing of DEFA's film of *Naked among Wolves* was part of the program of events).[79] It was also the expression of a process of cautious liberalization and openness toward the West, particularly toward Western music.[80]

Stefan attended the *Deutschlandtreffen*, staying in the GDR from 15 to 28 May. He was treated to a very full program, partly ideological and partly touristic in character. Thus a visit to the Brandenburg Gate was combined with a meeting with GDR border guards. He attended a literature festival with Bruno Apitz, met youngsters from Hamburg and Rostock, as well as antifascist resistance fighters such as Walter Bartel, Otto Halle, and Peter Sturm, visited Eisenhüttenstadt, and attended a reception of the Central Council of the FDJ. On 17 May, Robert Siewert introduced Stefan to Walter Ulbricht, Otto Grotewohl, Albert Norden, Paul Verner, and other GDR notables. He was feted wherever he went, heaped with presents, and fussed over by the FDJ. His presence was noted by the GDR press and by GDR television.[81] But the FDJ not only chaperoned him; it also paid close attention to his response. After his departure, an anonymous eight-page report was compiled on Zweig and sent to Horst Schumann, Erich Rau, and the Youth Department of the Central Committee. Stefan, the report stated, did not see in the omnipresent blue of the FDJ a "uniforming" ("Uniformierung") of youth; rather he had experienced again and again, personally, the bonds linking youth in the GDR to the antifascist struggle, and how today's young people had fulfilled the oath of Buchenwald (in April 1945, Buchenwald's liberated prisoners vowed to continue the fight against fascism). The report also pointed to other positive responses on Zweig's part to the GDR.

But not all that the report had to say about Zweig was enthusiastic. While showing understanding for Stefan's desire not to be the center of attention at the festival, it pointed out that he had "often found it difficult to meet the demands of the program." Stefan asked his hosts not to expect any "official statements" from him on "West German imperialism and militarism" (not least, one assumes, out of consideration for Willi Bleicher in Stuttgart, whose association with Zweig could have been used against him by conservative sections of the West German press). Not only did he resist attempts to make propaganda out of his visit, but he also posed a number of awkward questions, such as why there were so many Arabs and so few Israelis studying in socialist countries, and generally criticized Arab policies toward Israel. He seems to have bombarded his hosts with questions about political and social aspects of life in the GDR, even asking them to tell him "what the state in the GDR was doing against striptease," and "how it had managed to stop prostitution." It would be hard to overlook a certain irony, even sarcasm, in these questions, which is palpable even in the starchy FDJ report. In the end, while making it clear that Stefan had temporarily decided against further university studies, and that this was the reason why the FDJ did not repeat its invitation to him to study in the GDR, the report also found that it would not be "appropriate" ("zweckmäßig") to invite Stefan at that time, given that he was liable to "very strong mood swings," and was "physically and mentally labile." Besides, having not yet taken the chance to study in the GDR, Stefan seemed not to want to "officially decide in favor of the workers' and farmers' state."[82]

Not that the FDJ had lost hope of bringing Stefan to the GDR, or of winning him over. The report indicated that contact was to be maintained with Stefan via Ernst Hansch, whose closer ties to the Zweigs were to be used "to continue following Jerzy's development." The FDJ was to help to create "fruitful contacts" between "progressive forces" in Israel and Stefan, and was to send material to him demonstrating "the fulfillment of the antimilitary and antifascist struggle of the forces of humanism in Germany" by the GDR.[83] The FDJ had therefore by no means permanently shelved the idea of bringing Stefan to the GDR. In fact, Stefan himself discussed such a move with his father when he returned to Israel.[84] In July, when Ernst Hansch, whose contacts to the Zweigs were being monitored by the FDJ, visited them in Israel, it would seem that the possibility of studying in the GDR was raised again. But it was not until Stefan Zweig went to France with the Israeli basketball team — of which he was a member — in the summer of 1964 that he finally decided in favor of moving to East Germany.

There were reasons why Stefan did not jump at the chance to study in the GDR. For one, both he and his father were well aware that taking up that opportunity would expose Stefan to attempts to manipulate him.[85] The changes to Zacharias's testimony had already alerted father and son to the danger of manipulation. Indeed the very decision to publish this testimony in the GDR demonstrated what little respect some in the GDR, at least, were prepared to accord to the wishes of Zacharias and Stefan. The FDJ's close chaperoning of Stefan at the *Deutschlandtreffen* and the precisely orchestrated program worked out for his visit, moreover, were an unmistakable sign that the SED would seek to make Cold War capital out of him. Stefan, in any case, had no desire to become the center of public and political attention; he has always felt, apart from anything else, that it was his father who deserved recognition and acknowledgment.

Last but not least, moving to the GDR meant moving to one half of the country that had unleashed the Holocaust. For all their praise of East Germany's cultivation of antifascist traditions, Zacharias and Stefan will hardly have been convinced — especially given the GDR's anti-Zionism — that it was a state free of anti-Semitism. Anti-Semitism, moreover, was a problem with a long history in the eastern bloc of which the GDR had become a part. Stefan's family had suffered from both Nazi *and* Soviet anti-Semitism. Ignaz Zweig, one of Zacharias's brothers, had been killed as a "Jewish intellectual" during Stalinist purges in 1936; another brother, Heinrich Zweig, had been imprisoned in a Gulag.[86] Having married a Russian (see below), Heinrich had not wanted to leave the Soviet Union — where he had fled in 1939 to escape the Nazis — when the war came to an end in 1945. He paid a heavy price for remaining: together with his family, he was sentenced to a twenty-five-year stint in a forced labor camp in Semipalatinsk (now Semey).[87] Amnestied following Stalin's death in 1953, he settled in Moscow, where he became a member of the Academy of Science.[88] While the GDR in the 1960s could not be compared to the Soviet Union in the 1950s, and while even in the Soviet Union anti-Semitism was less severe in the 1960s than it had been, the fact remained that East Germany had a genocidal past *and* was part of an anti-Zionist socialist bloc — hardly an inviting prospect.

What, then, prompted Stefan, after much prevarication, to decide in favor of studying in the GDR? Was it simply that, on reflection, he had decided that this opportunity — at the expense of the GDR — was just too good to pass up? This is possible. Certainly Stefan appears to have reached something of a crossroads in his life by the summer of 1964. In the winter of the previous year, partly as a result of illness, partly because of his problems with physics and math, he had decided to abandon his studies at the Institute of Applied Technology in Lyon;[89] financial difficulties also played a part.[90] Returning to Israel at a time of economic crisis, he was unable to find even temporary employment; instead, he was called up, very much against his will, for reserve military service.[91] His visit to France in the summer of 1964 brought this uncertain period to an end. Instead of traveling back to Israel with the basketball team, Stefan resolved to remain in France, staying with his aunt in Paris. It was here — finding himself with nothing but a hundred dollars in his pocket and a couple of suitcases stowed away in a cupboard — that he took the decision to accept the offer to study in the GDR.[92]

In some ways, then, Stefan's decision was not so much a decision *for* the GDR as one *against* the instability of his current existence. Of course, Stefan did feel a certain emotional pull toward the GDR, despite his reservations. He will have felt flattered by all the attention lavished upon him during his February and May visits. In Israel, Zacharias and Stefan were just two Holocaust survivors among many. In the GDR, by contrast, they were special.[93] There can also be no doubt that Stefan took up the chance at least partly out of gratefulness to his erstwhile "camp fathers," who, it seemed, were once more planning to adopt him. But, in the end, the circumstances of his personal life seem to have triggered his acceptance — that, perhaps, and a determination to make his decisions when *he* wanted to make them, and not when the FDJ and others in the GDR wanted him to.[94]

There was one other factor that played a part in Stefan's decision. Before following through on his plans, Stefan consulted with his father. While Zacharias was skeptical of them, he had no fundamental objections to Stefan moving to the GDR. But he did ask one thing of him: namely, that he look for a way when in East Germany of establishing contact to Heinrich Zweig and persuading him to emigrate with his family to Israel.[95] Zacharias had been worried about Heinrich Zweig's safety for many years. While Heinrich's Gulag experience was a thing of the past, he was still a Jew living in a state not well disposed toward Jews. Heinrich's threatened status as a Jew was not Zacharias's only cause for concern, however. Heinrich was married to Sorja Serebryakova, the daughter of Galina Serebryakova, a Russian writer probably best remembered for her biographies of Karl Marx and her erstwhile relationship to the composer Dmitri Shostakovich. She had been married in turn to two leading Bolsheviks, Leonid Serebryakov and Grigori Sokolnikov, both of whom were murdered in the course of Stalin's purges in the 1930s.[96] Serebryakova was caught up in these acts of Stalinist persecution. She was summoned repeatedly to the notorious Lubyanka prison in Moscow and interrogated;[97] subsequently, she was sentenced to twenty years imprisonment in a Gulag. If her survival of this experience was miraculous enough, so was her unbroken faith in communism. She also seems to have been accepted back into the Soviet establishment under Khrushchev; many books by her, including biographical works on Marx and Engels, were published in the Soviet Union in the 1960s. But given her suspect past she could never be sure of her future, any more than Heinrich could be sure of his. Zacharias's concerns were not without foundation.

Stefan Zweig moved to the GDR in September 1964. On 7 October 1964, the GDR celebrated the fifteenth year of its existence. Among the guests invited to this official celebration were Stefan Zweig and his father.

It was Zacharias's first visit to the GDR. According to his son, Walter Ulbricht wanted to meet him; and the Israeli flag was even hoisted in his honor near Berlin's Gendarmenmarkt.[98] But Zacharias came to the GDR with one particular goal in mind, namely, bringing about Heinrich's emigration. Clearly, this would have to be discussed with Heinrich directly — and at length. Thanks to the mediation of *BZ am Abend* journalist Ernst Hansch, who took care of the formalities, Heinrich Zweig was able to travel from Moscow to East Berlin in early October, where he was reunited with Zacharias on the ninth of that month.[99] They had not seen each other since the outbreak of war on 1 September 1939.[100] But the visit was to be a disappointment. Try as they might, Zacharias and Stefan could not persuade Heinrich to consider leaving the Soviet Union. His motives remained unclear. Perhaps he was concerned about the effect plans for emigration or emigration itself might have on the safety of his family. Perhaps, as Stefan has speculated, he really believed in the Soviet system, "or had been brainwashed."[101]

Zacharias and Stefan, of course, were absolutely discreet about their efforts to persuade Heinrich to emigrate. In the GDR, it was assumed that the sole motive for Heinrich's East Berlin visit was the emotional wish of the brothers to be reunited. The central irony of Stefan's and Zacharias's sojourn in the GDR remained concealed. Their visit to the GDR was to be used by the SED as proof both of communist wartime solidarity toward Jews and of East German philo-Semitism. They were to be used as counterpropaganda to any suggestion that the GDR's critical stance on Israel implied it was anti-Semitic. Yet they came to the GDR, partly at least in Stefan's case, and much more so in the case of Zacharias, because they hoped to use the GDR as a base to engineer the rescue of Heinrich Zweig from the perceived threat of Soviet and socialist anti-Semitism.

This is not to say that Zacharias's and Stefan's praise of the GDR's antifascist legacy in the second half of 1964 was purely tactical. Even in 1963, when Holzer met Zacharias near Tel Aviv for the first time, Zacharias apparently exclaimed: "I want to make one thing clear from the start, whether you like it or not: it was the Buchenwald prisoners who saved my child's life, the International Camp Committee, and that was made up largely of German communists!"[102] And in a February 1964 interview with Ewald Thoms, Stefan claimed that his father had told him: "You're not a hero. Don't let yourself be put on a pedestal. The heroes, the fighters for humanity at the time of its utmost violation, were the others . . . the brave antifascists."[103] Zacharias was not only playing down his own role in rescuing Stefan here; he also appeared to be making a distinction in terms of moral worth between "mere survivors" and "resistance fighters," a distinction that characterized both the Zionist narrative of the Shoah and the East German view of Nazism — except that in the latter case the distinction was one, not between Jews and other Jews, but between Jews ("the victims") and antifascists ("the heroes"). His self-deprecating praise of the *German* communists in particular will have been music to the ears of the GDR's former Buchenwald prisoners.

While genuine gratefulness for the actions of Bleicher and others at Buchenwald on behalf of Stefan may explain these effusive comments, they do relate exclusively to the antifascist *past*, not the socialist *present*. But when Zacharias came to the GDR in the late summer of 1964, he made even more effusive comments — about the GDR as well as about Buchenwald's antifascists. The best example of this is the almost embarrassingly sycophantic poem he wrote in the guestbook of the Town of Weimar during his visit there in early October 1964. According to this poem, the "wound" dealt to the town of Weimar by Nazism has been healed and its shame wiped away by the "heroes of the Ettersberg." The poem claims that the legacy of Weimar humanism was fulfilled through these heroes' deeds, and that this legacy "in today's new Germany is the basis for every action." Zacharias's poem concludes with the lines: "your spirit, Weimar, and the spirit of those who were 'naked among wolves' is, in the GDR, in the best of hands."[104] He thus precisely reproduces the typical GDR view that Weimar's humanist legacy as passed down from German Classicism and The Enlightenment had been preserved for posterity by Buchenwald's communists and, subsequently, by the GDR.

That Zacharias, seconded by his son, should have so enthusiastically corroborated the GDR's own view of itself *despite* his experience of the way his testimony had been doctored in the GDR in February and *despite* the FDJ's attempts to exploit Stefan's presence in May can only be explained by the wish to help Heinrich; clearly, the more positive the impression Zacharias and Stefan made, the more support they could win for their bid to bring Heinrich to East Berlin, and the less they needed to worry about the real motive behind this reunion being guessed at by anyone in the GDR. To a considerable extent, both played the roles allocated to them so willingly because they had a clear goal, just as those who invited them to the GDR had a clear goal.[105] They understood that they were expected to authenticate and reinforce the GDR's exclusively heroic view of communist resistance at Buchenwald. They will also have understood that, as outsiders, as Jews, as Israelis, their corroboration was enormously important to a state normally reliant on praising itself — and self-praise is of limited credibility, especially when repeated too often.

Stefan in the GDR

In 1964, Stefan took up his studies within the "Fakultät Kamera" at the *Deutsche Hochschule für Filmkunst* (literally, the German University for the

Art of Film).[106] As the publicity surrounding his discovery and adoption by the GDR gradually subsided, life became slightly more "normal" for him. He dedicated himself to his studies, completing them in 1968. There followed a practical year developing his skills as a cameraman, after which he was employed by GDR television (*Deutscher Fernsehfunk*) as a cameraman, initially for news broadcasts, then for sport and entertainment. He fell in love, had a son, and then married his partner Christa, a teacher at the *FDJ-Hochschule* (the Free German Youth University) on 22 August 1966.[107] He had never made a secret of his intention to leave the GDR one day. Thus in an interview with the GDR's state news service in 1966, Stefan said he wished to return to Israel to work as a cameraman "in the television studio that is currently being established."[108] But when he left the GDR with his family in January 1972, he decided to remain in Europe —in Vienna. It was planned that his father, Zacharias, would also come to Vienna, and that they would both settle there, beginning a new life "in a town that resembled Cracow a little."[109] But Zacharias never made it to Vienna;[110] he died in Tel Aviv in mid-May 1972. Stefan, after attending his father's funeral, decided to remain with his family in Vienna rather than return permanently to Israel. He eventually gained employment as a cameraman with Austrian television (ORF), where he worked for many years. Now retired, he still lives in Vienna to this day.[111]

But these in and for themselves rather unspectacular facts belie Stefan's continued special status as the "Buchenwald child." When he came to the GDR in February 1964, he was not *just* an instrument of communist propaganda, nor were *all* of those Thälmann Pioneers and other schoolchildren who welcomed him in Weimar there merely because they had been told to be. There was a degree of spontaneous popular enthusiasm. The GDR media carried reports of a twenty-two-year-old train conductor who spared no effort to bring Stefan greetings and a bouquet of flowers on behalf of her FDJ group. "How happy I am to have seen you," she said to him, "to have talked to you and kissed you, you, the Buchenwald child!"[112] The discovery of Stefan, for many GDR citizens, was an event of emotional and psychological significance, as the "basketfuls" of mail sent to Zacharias in Tel Aviv surely demonstrate.[113] It is not inconceivable that the welcome they gave him was the expression of a subconscious sense of guilt for Germany's racist past — a guilt that, in welcoming him, they were able to expiate. Throughout his time in the GDR, Stefan often talked to groups of schoolchildren about his experiences, remaining to a degree in the public eye. He was also a guest over the years at various events at the NMGB and at events organized by the KdAW. By his very appearance at such events he continued to serve as an icon of communist resistance at Buchenwald. GDR newspapers continued to print interviews with him in which he praised the GDR and sometimes condemned West Germany as a state run by unreconstructed Nazis.[114]

Stefan, then, continued to play the role he was expected to play. In the mid-1960s, for instance, he directed a short film to satisfy the assessment requirements for that year of his studies. He chose as his subject the Buchenwald communist Robert Siewert. The film shows Siewert giving a commemorative speech at Buchenwald and standing inside the bell tower on the Ettersberg; interspersed are various shots of commemorative activities at Buchenwald, of the Thälmann shrine at the Crematorium Building, and of the Bunker Building, where prisoners were tortured. The film is prefaced with a short dedication: "comrades in struggle who survived the concentration camps were, after liberation from fascism, the most active in the reconstruction of a democratic Germany. One of these was Robert Siewert, to whom this film is dedicated."[115]

The relationship between Stefan and the GDR, however, was not always as harmonious as newspaper reports might lead one to believe. By his own account, he was spied on by the GDR's notorious State Security Service, or *Stasi*, during his time as a student; only when he complained about this to Robert Siewert did the spying stop.[116] The *Stasi* archives contain no record of this, but what has been gathered or reconstructed in these archives since unification does not cover anything like the total range of *Stasi* activities. As an Israeli citizen and a former Israeli soldier, Stefan was, from the point of view of GDR ideology, a representative of a westernized, capitalist, and Zionist state. He would, therefore, have been an obvious target for the *Stasi*. During his time in the GDR, Stefan resisted repeated attempts to get him to speak out publicly against Israeli politics. And in 1967 he called on Albert Norden (who was Secretary of Agitation) to complain about GDR policy toward Israel, "but was not admitted."[117] Although himself of Jewish background, Norden followed Ulbricht's cue in 1967 by strongly condemning Israel's actions in the Six-Day War.[118] In 1970, Stefan got into difficulties for commenting cynically on the refusal of GDR television to report on the hanging of nine Jews as "Zionist agents" in Baghdad. As a result, he was transferred from filming news broadcasts to GDR television's sports and entertainment department.[119] As relations between Israel and eastern bloc countries deteriorated, and especially as of the Six-Day War, Stefan seems to have been less inclined to conceal his support for Israel.

Increasing frustration at the GDR's anti-Israeli politics perhaps explains the fact that Stefan's explicit praise of the GDR and of antifascism in newspaper interviews is more characteristic of the 1964 to 1966 period than of the post-1967 period. Yet even during the 1964 to 1966 period, Stefan very much sought to make his own mark on his public activities. When he first visited Buchenwald in February 1964, he laid a wreath of red carnations at the location of the barracks in which, between 1938 and 1939, thousands of Jews were incarcerated, of whom 600 were murdered.[120] During his second trip to the GDR in May 1964, he visited the

Jewish cemetery at Weißensee and laid a wreath on the memorial stone commemorating the antifascist resistance group headed by Herbert Baum; he was then formally welcomed by East Berlin's Jewish Community and shown around the reconstructed synagogue on the Rykestrasse.[121] While his relations to Berlin's tiny Jewish community were never close, he did, through these symbolic acts, seek to make *Jewish* suffering and *Jewish* communist resistance visible at the same time as serving as an icon of non-Jewish German communist resistance. There is no doubt that he did this quite explicitly. During his time in the GDR he was not only welcomed by members of the population; he also received anti-Semitic mail.[122] He was aware of the need to combat continuing anti-Semitism by trying to raise awareness of the Holocaust and the German legacy of guilt.

His film about Robert Siewert, moreover, is more than just another tribute to communists. After the war, Siewert was Minister for the Interior in Saxony; but in 1950, ostensibly because of his erstwhile membership of the KPO, he was downgraded to a relatively insignificant position within the GDR's Building Ministry.[123] When he talked to the GDR press about his short film, Stefan commented that "in a land governed by people like Robert Siewert and his comrades in struggle, who themselves suffered under fascism, there cannot be any fascists." Stefan surely knew that Siewert was hardly a significant force in GDR politics. His film on Siewert and his comments in press interviews on the film reveal his sympathy for the former Buchenwald prisoners and are an implied criticism of the SED's rather duplicitous policy of exploiting the achievements of Buchenwald's communists for propaganda purposes while simultaneously excluding them from real political power in the GDR.[124]

Stefan thus tried to find a way to articulate his own values and views, even where they ran counter to those he was expected to articulate. Gisela Karau, a GDR writer acquainted with Stefan in the 1960s, described him as someone who had little patience with importunate FDJ functionaries and dogmatic socialists,[125] while Bruno Apitz's wife, Kikki Apitz, claimed he could not "accept that training to become a maker of film documentaries was at the same time of necessity a political training."[126] His determination to go his own way led, on occasion, to direct conflict with the authorities. For example, when he formed an albeit very loose connection to the group led by Wolf Biermann and Robert Havemann, a group critical of the regime, in 1965, he was hauled before an impromptu three-man commission and warned that he would not be allowed to continue his studies in the GDR if he did not break off all contact with Biermann and Havemann. After returning briefly to Israel to consult with his father, he returned to the GDR and was able to avert the threat of expulsion from university. But he never really accommodated himself to the expectations of the authorities, and he has written of the "distrust" of some in the SED, and even of plans to replace him with another "Buchenwald child" should he prove too recalcitrant.[127]

After Stefan's Departure

There were thus ongoing, indeed intensifying tensions between Stefan and the SED. These certainly played a part in his decision to leave when he did. These tensions were not forgotten. Years later, in 1978, the GDR newspaper *Das Volk* wrote to the Director of the NMGB, Klaus Trostorff, asking for information on the fate of children incarcerated at Buchenwald. In his reply, Trostorff made reference to Stefan's years in the GDR, adding that he had "caused some difficulties": "we don't mention his life today unless there are special requests for information, because he didn't exactly provide the best example of someone with a clear attitude toward our development."[128] Yet for all this it should not be assumed that Stefan left the GDR entirely as *persona non grata*; indeed he visited Buchenwald several times subsequently and was present at major commemorative events there.[129] In Vienna, he quickly established links to the Austrian ex-Buchenwald prisoners and attended international Buchenwald meetings, where he met with former Buchenwald prisoners from the GDR. Erich Fein, moreover, an Austrian Buchenwald survivor, told Bartel in 1979 that Stefan had "never ever made any sort of negative comments about the GDR."[130] For all his difficulties in the GDR — and Stefan told me he had not been happy there[131] — he remained thankful to it for welcoming him, loyal to the East German ex-Buchenwald prisoners, and reluctant to participate in criticism of the SED. In a way, the GDR became more of a home to him in retrospect than it had been between 1964 and 1972, a reflection, no doubt, of the fact that his life in Vienna was not nearly as privileged as his life in East Berlin had been.[132]

In the GDR itself, the Buchenwald myth was not negatively affected by Stefan's departure, although there will have been some who wondered why he had elected to turn his back on his "true" home. In coming to the GDR and studying there, he (albeit imperfectly) served the purpose for which he had been brought, namely to corroborate the version of his rescue by communists that had been disseminated through Apitz's novel. *Naked among Wolves*, its canonical status more or less reinforced, remained *the* text on Buchenwald in the GDR right up until 1989/90. Indeed its success was certainly a contributory factor to a development at Buchenwald's National Site of Warning and Commemoration in the 1980s. In 1985, the main exhibition moved from its home (since 1964) in the Disinfection Building to a site associated with Stefan's rescue, namely, the Storage Building.

Naked among Wolves triggered considerable interest in Buchenwald among the GDR's population, as did Zweig's stay in the GDR. Thanks to the novel and film, GDR schoolchildren often visited the NMGB with the desired view of resistance in place, and with some interest in the camp. The NMGB in turn pointed in its brochures to the significance of Apitz's novel, implicitly treating it as a work of documentation rather than fiction. Thus in a 1960 brochure, reference was made not only to a small boy rescued by prisoners, but also to the "moving" description of his fate by Apitz in *Naked among Wolves*.[133] Teachers were encouraged in pedagogical courses run at the NMGB to prepare their schoolchildren for a visit to Buchenwald by integrating a reading of the novel or a viewing of the film into their teaching program. Indeed the NMGB itself used both the novel and the DEFA film, released in 1963, as an integral element of these courses. Thus a reading from *Naked among Wolves* featured on the program of the very first course for history and civic studies teachers at Buchenwald memorial site in 1962.[134] A reading of the novel was also a component of the first Pioneer Leaders' course in 1962.[135] In 1985, the DEFA film of *Naked among Wolves* was shown no less than ninety-four times to young visitors staying in the youth hostel.[136]

The filtering of public memory of Buchenwald through the *Naked among Wolves* story led to openly expressed dissatisfaction at the condition of the Storage Building. In 1960, the director of the NMGB at the time, Ludwig Eisermann, wrote to the Ministry for Culture pointing out that visitors were becoming more and more interested in the Storage Building as a result of Apitz's novel and were surprised that grain was being stored there.[137] At the second of the Thälmann Pioneer Leader courses in 1963, participants complained because the Storage Building was closed to public view.[138] This was all grist to the mill of Eisermann and others who had long wanted to move the exhibition to the Storage Building[139] but had repeatedly come up against the difficulty that the agricultural combine VEAB was contractually entitled to use it. There were also cost problems.[140] Eisermann persisted, however, and in the NMGB's plan for the 1960 to 1962 period explicit reference was made to the proposed construction of a small "cultural-historical" museum in the Storage Building. This museum would start with references to Goethe and Schiller and then focus on the artistic expression of antifascist resistance, featuring examples of literature, drawings, and sculptures produced by prisoners during their time at Buchenwald. It would also include a section with exhibits relating to Apitz's *Naked among Wolves*.[141] Again, the plan foundered because of the problems already outlined — and because some former Buchenwald prisoners were hostile to the notion of an art exhibition on the grounds that it would water down the impression of Buchenwald as an antihumanist institution.[142]

In the late 1970s, the VEAB finally evacuated the Storage Building, and plans were drawn up for a museum within it that would take account of recent research into the concentration camp and include an exhibition on the role played by art and culture in resistance, thus reviving ideas from the early 1960s. Again, the Museum for German History cooperated with the NMGB and the KdAW in developing the concept and layout plan for this new museum, which was opened in 1985 in the renovated Storage

Building over three floors. In a report issued by director Klaus Trostorff, we read that the choice of the Storage Building for the new museum was appropriate because it was here that the KPD, the ILK, and also the International Military Organization (IMO) and the People's Front Committee ("Volksfrontkomitee") held illegal meetings to discuss actions against the SS and measures to save lives.[143] Trostorff's presentation of the Storage Building as a cente of communist-led international resistance at Buchenwald as a whole was questionable. Walter Bartel, the leading German member of the ILK, could not recall a single meeting of the ILK in the Storage Building.[144] Yet in his opening speech during the inauguration ceremony for the new museum, Bartel essentially followed Trostorff's line in playing up the significance of the Storage Building. He claimed that many comrades in the Personal Property Room work detail had been involved in the antifascist resistance struggle at Buchenwald, and that the construction of a new museum in this historical building was a means of preserving the memory of all those who risked their lives in seeking to protect their comrades.[145]

When the Storage Building was finally opened as a museum, draped in long red flags in honor of the occasion,[146] it was far more significant than it had seemed in the 1950s. Then, it had survived dismantling due to chance, and one member of the KdAW, Horst Schumann, had simply dismissed it as "not typical of the concentration camp."[147] Now, it was associated not only with one specific and very heroic act of rescue but also, *pars pro toto*, with antifascist resistance at Buchenwald as a whole. Indeed, in the imagination of many it was more than a symbol of the total resistance: it was its physical center. Without Apitz's novel this would never have happened. It was Apitz who, in *Naked among Wolves*, interwove the rescue of the child with the larger strands of antifascist resistance, culminating in the supposed self-liberation of 11 April 1945. This conflation of individual rescue with general antifascist endeavor, of micro- with macronarrative, found its real-life correlative in the fitting out of the Storage Building in 1985 as the site of the new main exhibition. Both Bartel and Trostorff acknowledged the significance of Apitz's novel in the context of this development. But of course this framing of the Storage Building as the "center" of memory in 1985 would also not have happened had Apitz's novel — and Zweig himself — not touched the hearts of millions of readers in the GDR and elsewhere. Thus the NMGB sought to capitalize on the book's success by, as it were, pandering to its symbolism. To the credit of the new museum, however, explicit mention was made of the fact that Stefan Jerzy Zweig was not just a boy, and not just Polish, but also a Jew. But that the majority experience for Jews at Buchenwald was murder, not survival, and certainly not rescue at the hands of antifascists, was an issue left as under-investigated as it had been at the time the novel was written, and as it was at the time of Stefan's stay in the GDR.

Notes

[1] See Angelika Timm, "Juden in der DDR und der Staat Israel," in *Zwischen Politik und Kultur — Juden in der DDR*, ed. Moshe Zuckermann (Göttingen: Wallstein, 2002), 17–33; here, 19. See also Michal Bodemann, "A Reemergence of German Jewry?," in *Reemerging Jewish Culture in Germany: Life and Literature since 1989*, ed. Sander L. Gilman and Karen Remmler (New York and London: New York UP, 1994), 46–61; here, 49.

[2] See "Wie das Buchenwaldkind gefunden wurde," in *Stefan-Jerzy Zweig: Der große Bericht über das Buchenwaldkind. Beilage der BZ am Abend* (1964), 4–5; here, 4.

[3] "BZA-Interview mit Bruno Apitz," in *Stefan-Jerzy Zweig: Der große Bericht*, 10.

[4] Ewald Thoms, "Das Kind, um das Millionen bangten," *DDR-Revue* 6 (1964).

[5] See "Wie das Buchenwaldkind gefunden wurde," 4.

[6] See Zacharias Zweig and Stefan Zweig, *Tränen allein genügen nicht* (Vienna: Eigenverlag, 2005), 179.

[7] "Wie das Buchenwaldkind gefunden wurde," 4.

[8] Charlotte Holzer, "Dramatische Begegnung mit dem Vater, Dr. Zweig," in *Stefan-Jerzy Zweig: Der große Bericht*, 5.

[9] Holzer, "Dramatische Begegnung mit dem Vater, Dr. Zweig," 5.

[10] Ewald Thoms, "Erste Begegnung mit Stefan in Stuttgart," in *Stefan-Jerzy Zweig: Der große Bericht*, 9–10; here, 9.

[11] Stefan Zweig, "Stefan-Jerzy schreibt Bruno Apitz," in *Stefan-Jerzy Zweig: Der große Bericht*, 6.

[12] Ewald Thoms, "Gute Nachricht für Millionen: Der Junge aus 'Nackt unter Wölfen' lebt," *BZ am Abend*, 3 February 1964.

[13] Charlotte Holzer told GDR radio that Zacharias had asked her for Bleicher's address; Zacharias had written to Bleicher, and Bleicher had then invited Stefan to Stuttgart for his twenty-third birthday. Zacharias also assured Holzer that he and his son would then come to the GDR. See Deutsches Rundfunkarchiv (henceforth DRA), 2013611010: "Besuch bei Dr. Zacharias Zweig in Israel," production date 1963, date of first transmission not specified.

[14] Zweig and Zweig, *Tränen allein genügen nicht*, 181.

[15] Uri Bender, "Dieses Kind bin ich" (Interview with Stefan Jerzy Zweig), *Maariv*, 16 June 2000. A faxed copy of the article can be found in the Archiv der Gedenkstätte Buchenwald (henceforth BwA), Ordner Stephan-Jerzy-Zweig.

[16] Erich Sievers, "'Juschu' und die deutsche Gegenwart," *Berliner Zeitung*, 13 February 1964.

[17] "Bewegendes Wiedersehen in Buchenwald," in *Stefan-Jerzy Zweig: Der große Bericht*, 10–12; here, 11.

[18] "Bewegendes Wiedersehen in Buchenwald."

[19] Internationales Buchenwald-Komitee/Komitee der Antifaschistischen Widerstandskämpfer in der Deutschen Demokratischen Republik, eds.,

Buchenwald: Mahnung und Verpflichtung, Dokumente und Berichte (Berlin: Kongress-Verlag, 1960), 381.

[20] See *Stefan-Jerzy Zweig: Der große Bericht*, 8–9.

[21] "Einst Nackt unter Wölfen — heute Freunde in aller Welt," *Thüringer Tageblatt*, 10 February 1964.

[22] Horst Schiefelbein, "Unvergeßliche Begegnung," *Neues Deutschland*, 9 February 1964.

[23] Although, according to Stefan Zweig, Apitz remained mistrustful, fearing that Stefan might behave in a way that could do "damage" both to himself and to Apitz (see Zweig and Zweig, *Tränen allein genügen nicht*, 216). Both Stefan and his father were more than unhappy at the fact that Apitz had simply eradicated the figure of the father from his account of the rescue in *Naked among Wolves* (Zweig and Zweig, *Tränen allein genügen nicht*, 215). Another reason for resentment towards Apitz was that he, Apitz, had made a considerable sum of money out of what one might describe as the "commercialization" of the Zweig rescue story — whereas Zacharias had been living for years in very modest circumstances in Israel (Zweig and Zweig, *Tränen allein genügen nicht*, 327–28).

[24] "Endlich die Adresse des Buchenwaldkindes," in *Stefan-Jerzy Zweig: Der große Bericht*, 5 6; here, 5.

[25] Stiftung Archiv der Parteien und Massenorganisationen der ehemaligen Deutschen Demokratischen Republik im Bundesarchiv (henceforth SAPMO-BArch), DY57/235: Letter from the KdAW and Buchenwald Committee to Yad Vashem, 3 December 1963.

[26] See Stiftung Archiv Akademie der Künste (henceforth SAdK), Bruno-Apitz-Archiv 167.

[27] Berthold Scheller, ed. in cooperation with Stefan Jerzy Zweig, *"Mein Vater, was machst du hier . . .?" Zwischen Buchenwald und Auschwitz: Der Bericht des Zacharias Zweig* (Frankfurt am Main: dipa, 1987).

[28] Interview with Stefan Zweig, 28 March 2004. See also Zweig and Zweig, *Tränen allein genügen nicht*, 216.

[29] SAPMO-BArch, DY57/235: the three pages referred to follow a letter from the KdAW and Buchenwald Committee to Yad Vashem of 3 December 1963.

[30] BwA, Nachlaß Walter Bartel, Bu-Häftlinge: Letter from Ewald Thoms to Walter Bartel, 14 February 1964.

[31] Interview with Stefan Zweig, 28 March 2004. According to Sabine Stein of the Buchenwald Memorial Site Archive, Bartel, moreover, made no reference to any such involvement in his diary.

[32] Harry Stein, " 'Nackt unter Wölfen' — literarische Fiktion und Realität einer KZ-Gesellschaft," in *Sehen, Verstehen und Verarbeiten: KZ Buchenwald 1937–1945, KZ Mittelbau-Dora, 1943–1945*, ed. Thüringer Institut für Lehrerfortbildung, Lehrplanentwicklung und Medien (Saalfeld: Satz & Druck Centrum, 2000), 27–40; here, 28.

[33] Compare Scheller, *"Mein Vater, was machst du hier . . .?"* 24–25, and SAPMO-BArch, DY57/235: "Aus dem amtlichen Bericht des Dr. Zacharias Zweig (V): 'Vater, ich bin hier . . . ,' " *BZ am Abend*, 1964 (no precise date).

34 Compare Scheller, *"Mein Vater, was machst du hier . . .?"* 27–28, and SAPMO-BArch, DY57/235: "Aus dem amtlichen Bericht des Dr. Zacharias Zweig (VI): Als Zweijähriger vor dem Galgen," *BZ am Abend*, 1964 (no precise date).

35 Compare Scheller, *"Mein Vater, was machst du hier . . .?"* 58, and SAPMO-BArch, DY57/235: "Aus dem amtlichen Bericht des Dr. Zacharias Zweig (15): Höchste Gefahr," *BZ am Abend*, 1964, no precise date.

36 Compare Scheller, *"Mein Vater, was machst du hier . . .?"* 57, and SAPMO-BArch, DY57/235: "Aus dem amtlichen Bericht des Dr. Zacharias Zweig (15): Höchste Gefahr," *BZ am Abend*, 1964, no precise date.

37 Compare Scheller, *"Mein Vater, was machst du hier . . .?"* 50, and SAPMO-BArch, DY57/235: "Aus dem amtlichen Bericht des Dr. Zacharias Zweig (XII): Berührung mit deutschen Kommunisten," *BZ am Abend*, 1964, no precise date.

38 Compare Scheller, *"Mein Vater, was machst du hier . . .?"* 63–68, and SAPMO-BArch, DY57/235: "Aus dem amtlichen Bericht des Dr. Zacharias Zweig (16): Illegal im 'Kleinen Lager,'" *BZ am Abend*, 1964, no precise date.

39 Compare Scheller, *"Mein Vater, was machst du hier . . .?"* 64, and SAPMO-BArch, DY57/235: "Aus dem amtlichen Bericht des Dr. Zacharias Zweig (16): Illegal im 'Kleinen Lager,'" *BZ am Abend*, 1964, no precise date.

40 Compare Scheller, *"Mein Vater, was machst du hier . . .?"* 61, and SAPMO-BArch, DY57/235: "Aus dem amtlichen Bericht des Dr. Zacharias Zweig (16): Illegal im 'Kleinen Lager,'" *BZ am Abend*, 1964, no precise date.

41 Scheller, *"Mein Vater, was machst du hier . . .?"* 50, 53, and 56.

42 Compare Scheller, *"Mein Vater, was machst du hier . . .?"* 85, and SAPMO-BArch, DY57/235: "Aus dem amtlichen Bericht des Dr. Zacharias Zweig (22): 'Iß nur, Vati,'" BZ *am Abend*, 1964, no precise date.

43 Compare Scheller, *"Mein Vater, was machst du hier . . .?"* 92, and SAPMO-BArch, DY57/235: "Aus dem amtlichen Bericht des Dr. Zacharias Zweig (24): Frei, aber wo ist die Mutter?" *BZ am Abend*, 1964, no precise date.

44 Compare Scheller, *"Mein Vater, was machst du hier . . .?"* 90, and SAPMO-BArch, DY57/235: "Aus dem amtlichen Bericht des Dr. Zacharias Zweig (23): Tod oder Freiheit?" *BZ am Abend*, 1964, no precise date.

45 Examples of passages describing Jewish suffering that have been removed from the *BZ am Abend* version can be found in Scheller, *"Mein Vater, was machst du hier . . .?"* 20, 28–29, 30, and 42.

46 Compare Scheller, *"Mein Vater, was machst du hier . . .?"* 51–52 and SAPMO-BArch, DY57/235: "Aus dem amtlichen Bericht des Dr. Zacharias Zweig (XII): Berührung mit deutschen Kommunisten," *BZ am Abend*, 1964, no precise date.

47 Compare Scheller, *"Mein Vater, was machst du hier . . .?"* 41, and SAPMO-BArch, DY57/235: "Aus dem amtlichen Bericht des Dr. Zacharias Zweig (X): Die 'Politischen' in Aktion," *BZ am Abend*, 1964, no precise date.

48 Compare Scheller, *"Mein Vater, was machst du hier . . .?"* 39, and SAPMO-BArch, DY57/235: "Aus dem amtlichen Bericht des Dr. Zacharias Zweig (IX): Ankunft in Buchenwald," *BZ am Abend*, 1964, no precise date.

[49] Rolf Weinstock, *Das wahre Gesicht Hitler-Deutschlands* (Singen: Volksverlag, 1948) and Rolf Weinstock, *"Rolf, Kopf hoch!" Die Geschichte eines jungen Juden* (Berlin: VVN-Verlag, 1950).

[50] The attack came from Stefan Heymann. His article appeared in *Die Tat* (45) on 9 December 1950; a copy of the article can be found in SAPMO-BArch, DY 55/V 278/3/211.

[51] See SAPMO-BArch, DR1/2124a: Letter from Otto Funke to Klaus Höpcke, 24 November 1981.

[52] Interview with Stefan Zweig, 28 March 2004.

[53] "Ankunft in Buchenwald," *BZ am Abend*, 14 February 1964.

[54] Thus Ewald Thoms claimed that Stefan was smuggled into the camp in a case ("Das Kind, um das Millionen bangten").

[55] Horst Schiefelbein, "Unvergeßliche Begegnung."

[56] SAPMO-BArch, DY57/235: Annotated clipping of the article by Horst Schiefelbein, "Unvergeßliche Begegnung."

[57] "Ankunft in Buchenwald."

[58] Internationales Buchenwald-Komitee/Komitee der Antifaschistischen Widerstandskämpfer, *Buchenwald: Mahnung und Verpflichtung*, 123.

[59] SAPMO-BArch, DY57/235: Walter Bartel, "Eine Information über Stephan Zweig" (for Rudolf Wunderlich), Berlin, 4 February 1964.

[60] See Ewald Thoms, "Gute Nachricht für Millionen: Der Junge aus 'Nackt unter Wölfen' lebt."

[61] See, for instance, "Als dreijähriges Kind 'Nackt unter Wölfen,'" *Morgenpost*, 5 February 1964.

[62] BwA, Nachlaß Walter Bartel, Bu-Häftlinge: no title, 11 February 1964.

[63] Internationales Buchenwald-Komitee/Komitee der Antifaschistischen Widerstandskämpfer, *Buchenwald: Mahnung und Verpflichtung*, 381.

[64] See BwA, Nachlaß Walter Bartel, Bu-Häftlinge: Letter from Edwin Borgner to Heinz Bausch, 24 February 1964.

[65] Internationales Buchenwald-Komitee/Komitee der Antifaschistischen Widerstandskämpfer, *Buchenwald: Mahnung und Verpflichtung*, 123.

[66] BwA, Nachlaß Otto Halle, Korrespondenz: Letter from Bartel to Halle, 17 December 1960.

[67] BwA, Nachlaß Walter Bartel, VS 12/1: Letter from Richard Kucharcyzk to Bartel, 3 January 1961.

[68] BwA, Nachlaß Walter Bartel, Bu-Häftlinge: Letter from Heinz Bausch to Walter Bartel, 12 February 1963.

[69] BwA, Nachlaß Walter Bartel, Bu-Häftlinge: Letter from Walter Bartel to Robert Siewert and Harry Kuhn, 6 March 1964.

[70] "Ein Oberstleutnant umarmte ihn: ein ehemaliger Buchenwaldhäftling erzählt," *Sächsische Neueste Nachrichten*, 8 May 1963.

[71] BwA, Nachlaß Walter Bartel, Bu-Häftlinge: Letter from Walter Bartel to Waclaw Szarnecki, 14 February 1964.

[72] BwA, Nachlaß Walter Bartel, Bu-Häftlinge: "Chroniknotiz," 14 February 1964.

[73] BwA, Nachlaß Walter Bartel, Bu-Häftlinge: "Chroniknotiz," 23 February 1964.

[74] See Uri Bender, "Dieses Kind bin ich" (Interview with Stefan Jerzy Zweig), *Maariv*, 16 June 2000. A faxed copy of this article can be found in BwA, Ordner Stephan-Jerzy-Zweig. Zweig stressed the role of Siewert in an interview I conducted with him on 28 March 2004.

[75] See "Buchenwald-Film in Tel Aviv aufgeführt," *BZ am Abend*, 27 April 1964.

[76] Ernst Hansch, "Tel Aviv — Der Frühlingshügel," *BZ am Abend*, 11 July 1964.

[77] "Gestern und heute: Aus einem Interview mit dem als Buchenwaldkind bekannten Stephan J. Zweig," *Bauernecho*, 14 May 1966.

[78] "Jerzy Zweig: Ich habe viele neue Freunde gewonnen," *Junge Welt*, 29 May 1964.

[79] See SAPMO-BArch, DY24/4.613, Mappe 2: "Deutschlandtreffen: Organisationskomitee der Jugend in der Hauptstadt der DDR. Pressedienst, Nr. 9, Berlin, den 14.4.1964," and SAPMO-BArch, DY24/4.612, Mappe 2: "Zur Organisation des Deutschlandtreffens." The latter report indicates however that West German visitors complained about the inadequate number of tickets available for *Naked among Wolves*.

[80] For a good account of the *Deutschlandtreffen*, its political context, and the role of the FDJ, see Alan McDougall, *Youth Politics in East Germany: The Free German Youth Movement, 1946–1968* (Oxford: Clarendon Press, 2004), 163–68.

[81] Later publications on the *Deutschlandtreffen* also made reference to Zweig, e.g. Sarah Kirsch and Rainer Kirsch, *Berlin-Sonnenseite: Deutschlandtreffen der Jugend in der Hauptstadt der DDR Berlin 1964* (Berlin: Verlag Neues Leben, 1964), 109.

[82] See SAPMO-BArch, DY24/11103: "Deutschlandtreffen 64: Besuch von Stefan-Jerzy Zweig in der DDR," undated.

[83] SAPMO-BArch, DY24/11103: "Deutschlandtreffen 64: Besuch von Stefan-Jerzy Zweig in der DDR," undated.

[84] "Erinnerung im Herzen," *Freiheit*, 20 May 1966.

[85] Stefan's somewhat ambivalent claim in connection with his reluctance to move to the GDR that he "feared not being able to feel free if others were restricted in their freedom" implies anxiety, too, at becoming entrapped in a state walled off from the western world. See Zweig and Zweig, *Tränen allein genügen nicht*, 249.

[86] Interview with Stefan Zweig, 30 March 2004. See also Zweig and Zweig, *Tränen allein genügen nicht*, 249.

[87] Semipalatinsk became the site of a testing-ground for the Soviet Union's nuclear weapons; Gulag labor was used to construct the facilities.

[88] See Zweig and Zweig, *Tränen allein genügen nicht*, 245.

[89] See Zweig and Zweig, *Tränen allein genügen nicht*, 185.

[90] See Ewald Thoms, "Stuttgarter Begegnung 1964," *BZ am Abend*, 15 February 1964.

[91] Zweig and Zweig, *Tränen allein genügen nicht*, 221.

[92] Zweig and Zweig, *Tränen allein genügen nicht*, 224.

[93] The SED also tried to lure Zacharias to the GDR, offering him a pension, his own apartment, and even the chance to work as a lawyer. But Zacharias turned down this offer. See Zweig and Zweig, *Tränen allein genügen nicht*, 222.

[94] In fact Stefan delayed so long in making his decision that he incurred the irritation, even annoyance, of Bleicher and Siewert. See Zweig and Zweig, *Tränen allein genügen nicht*, 249.

[95] Interview with Stefan Zweig, 30 March 2004. See also Zweig and Zweig, *Tränen allein genügen nicht*, 224.

[96] See http://www.siue.edu/~aho/musov/fay/fayrev4.html. See also Zweig and Zweig, *Tränen allein genügen nicht*, 249.

[97] See Anne Applebaum, *Gulag — A History* (London: Penguin, 2003), 132.

[98] See Zweig and Zweig, *Tränen allein genügen nicht*, 240 and — for a photo of the Israeli flag hoisted in Zacharias's honor — 241.

[99] Interview with Stefan Zweig, 30 March 2004. See also Zweig and Zweig, *Tränen allein genügen nicht*, 245. For an East German newspaper report on the meeting of the two brothers, see "Es ist — mehr Licht: BZA-Gespräch mit Heinrich Zweig," *BZ am Abend*, 16 October 1964.

[100] "Juschus Vater traf Hans von der Effektenkammer," *Freie Presse Karl-Marx-Stadt*, 30 September 1964.

[101] See Zweig and Zweig, *Tränen allein genügen nicht*, 245.

[102] Holzer, "Dramatische Begegnung mit dem Vater, Dr. Zweig," 5.

[103] Thoms, "Stuttgarter Begegnung 1964."

[104] Stadtarchiv Weimar (henceforth StadtA Weimar), 00 07 31/1500: "Auffinden des Buchenwaldkindes Stephan Jerzy Zweig."

[105] One person who may have suspected Zacharias of a degree of posturing was Walter Bartel. Bartel described Zacharias as a "typical lawyer who quickly adapted his opinion to the circumstances, although he was an extremely pleasant man." See BwA, Nachlaß Walter Bartel, Nr. 51, Korrespondenz Buchenwald [Sch-Z]: Letter from Bartel to Geschonneck, 7 November 1984.

[106] According to Stefan, it was while visiting Bleicher in Stuttgart in February 1964 that he had hit upon the idea of training to become a cameraman. See Zweig and Zweig, *Tränen allein genügen nicht*, 214.

[107] Christa's childhood also had its tragic aspects: her parents were shot by Soviet soldiers near Königsberg in January 1945. Later, Christa and her brother made the long trek westwards as two of the many German fugitives and expellees from the former German territories. See Zweig and Zweig, *Tränen allein genügen nicht*, 452.

[108] "Gestern und heute: aus einem Interview mit dem als Buchenwaldkind bekannten Stephan J. Zweig."

[109] See Zweig and Zweig, *Tränen allein genügen nicht*, 140 and 254.

110 Zacharias decided not to leave Israel because his brother Leon fell ill. See Zweig and Zweig, *Tränen allein genügen nicht*, 140.

111 Certainly one of the reasons Stefan remained in Vienna was that his wife, Christa, preferred to remain in a German-speaking environment.

112 DRA, 2013612011: "Erstes Zusammentreffen von Stefan Jerzy Zweig mit seinen Lebensrettern aus Buchenwald," February 1964 (precise time and date of first broadcast not specified).

113 For examples of such letters, see Zweig and Zweig, *Tränen allein genügen nicht*, 168.

114 See, for instance, "Hier, wo Deutschlands Zukunft ist," *Schweriner Volkszeitung*, 7 October 1966.

115 The film was called *Erinnerung im Herzen* (*Memory in the Heart*); a copy can be found at the library and archive of the Hochschule für Film und Fernsehen at Potsdam-Babelsberg.

116 Interview with Stefan Zweig, 17 June 2002.

117 Interview with Stefan Zweig, 28 March 2005. Zweig claimed in another interview that it was a fellow student at Potsdam-Babelsberg, John Green, who spied on him (interview with Stefan Zweig, 30 March 2004). He backs up this claim in Zweig and Zweig, *Tränen allein genügen nicht*, 255.

118 Norden issued a memo to the East German press instructing newspapers to stress "that the Israelis are acting as Hitler did on June 22, 1941, when he attacked the Soviet Union in night and fog." Quoted in Jeffrey Herf, *Divided Memory: The Nazi Past in the Two Germanys* (Cambridge, MA, and London: Harvard UP, 1997), 198.

119 Interview with Stefan Zweig, 28 March 2005.

120 "Stephan kommt wieder," *Berliner Zeitung*, 10 February 1964.

121 "Besuch beim Landesrabbiner," *BZ am Abend*, 21 May 1964.

122 See Zweig and Zweig, *Tränen allein genügen nicht*, 359. Here Stefan provides an example of such mail, where he is denounced as an "old Jewish swine" and threatened with "a bullet between the ribs" if he does not soon leave the GDR.

123 See Lutz Niethammer, ed., *Der "gesäuberte" Antifaschismus: Die SED und die roten Kapos von Buchenwald* (Berlin: Akademie Verlag, 1994), 515.

124 "Hier, wo Deutschlands Zukunft ist," *Schweriner Volkszeitung*, 7 October 1966.

125 Interview with Gisela Karau, 9 January 2003.

126 Interview with Kikki Apitz, 5 January 2003.

127 See Zweig and Zweig, *Tränen allein genügen nicht*, 381.

128 Letter from Klaus Trostorff to *Das Volk*, 24 February 1978. A copy of this letter is on display in the new exhibition at Buchenwald Memorial Site, which documents the GDR's use (and abuse) of Buchenwald.

129 In the early 1980s, an interview with Zweig formed part of Peter Rocha's documentary film *Otherwise We Would Not Have Survived* (*Sonst wären wir verloren*, 1981), a film about children at Buchenwald. Clearly the interview with Zweig was radically cut in the course of editing the film. Rocha himself claimed

that "because Zweig had since left the GDR, the state hindered [him, i.e. Rocha]" in making the film (quoted in Thomas C. Fox, *Stated Memory: East Germany and the Holocaust* (Rochester, NY: Camden House, 1999), 135). But the cuts probably had to do with what Zweig said in the interview, and possibly also with his rather halting style of delivery. See also Thomas Heimann, *Bilder von Buchenwald: Die Visualisierung des Antifaschismus in der DDR (1944–1990)* (Cologne, Weimar, and Vienna: Böhlau, 2005), 120–24.

[130] BwA, Nachlaß Walter Bartel, Nr. 77, Bleicher: Letter from Bartel to Bleicher, 29 November 1976.

[131] Interview with Stefan Zweig, 30 March 2004.

[132] John Green, the British citizen whom Zweig suspected of spying on him and who studied in Zweig's class at Babelsberg — a class consisting of foreign nationals — has claimed in his autobiography that the official attention Zweig received rather went to his head. Zweig moved into an apartment shared by Green and others in 1965, but moved out after a week: "He [Zweig] is of the opinion that he is too important to simply live together with other students" (see John Green, *Anonym unterwegs: Ein Fernsehjournalist berichtet* (Berlin: Dietz, 1991), 19).

[133] *Buchenwald: Ein Führer durch die Mahn- und Gedenkstätte* (Weimar: Volksverlag, 1960), 9–10.

[134] BwA, Nachlaß Walter Bartel, VS 12/1: "Nationale Mahn- und Gedenkstätte Buchenwald: Ferienkursus für Lehrer," 12–17 February 1962.

[135] BwA Nachlaß, Walter Bartel, VS 12/1: "Nationale Mahn- und Gedenkstätte Buchenwald: 1. Pionierleiter-Kursus," 19–22 November 1962.

[136] SAPMO-BArch, DR1/7181a: "Bericht über die Erfüllung des Planes der Aufgaben 1985," Buchenwald, 4 February 1985.

[137] SAPMO-BArch, DR1/7537: Letter from Eisermann to Hirsch, 23 February 1960.

[138] SAPMO-BArch, DR1/7522: "Protokoll der Auswertung des 1. Pionierleiterkurses am 20.11.1963 von 16.00 bis 17.45 Uhr im großen Kulturraum der Nationalen Mahn- und Gedenkstätte Buchenwald."

[139] See SAPMO-BArch, DR1/7524: Letter from Siering to Hirsch, 6 May 1960.

[140] See SAPMO-BArch, DR1/7524: Letter from Rudi Wunderlich to Heese, 10 June 1960.

[141] SAPMO-BArch, DR1/7524: "Perspektivplan der Nationalen Mahn- und Gedenkstätte Buchenwald 1960–1962," 1 January 1960.

[142] When the first edition of the Buchenwald documentation was being compiled by members of the International Buchenwald Committee and the KdAW, several former prisoners objected to the idea of including a chapter on art in the volume as this might render unclear the antihumanist nature of the camp. See BwA, Nachlaß Otto Halle, Korrespondenz: Letter from Bartel to Halle, 6 January 1958.

[143] SAPMO-BArch, DR1/7183a: Klaus Trostorff, "Bericht über den Stand der politisch-ideologischen und baulichen Vorbereitung der Einrichtung eines Museums im ehemaligen Kammergebäude von Buchenwald," dated Buchenwald, 25 January 1983.

[144] SAPMO-BArch, DY57/253: Walter Bartel, "Bemerkungen zur Grundkonzeption der Nationalen Mahn- und Gedenkstätte Buchenwald über die 'Aufgabenstellung zur thematischen Aussage, zur Einordnung und zum Umbau des ehemaligen Kammergebäudes,'" Berlin, 15 October 1978.

[145] SAPMO-BArch, DR1/7181: "Begrüßungsansprache zur Eröffnung des Museums am 12. April 1985."

[146] SAPMO-BArch, DR1/7181: "Maßnahmeplan zur Vorbereitung und Durchführung der Eröffnung des Museums des antifaschistischen Widerstandskampfes in der Nationalen Mahn- und Gedenkstätte Buchenwald am 12. April 1985," 20 March 1985.

[147] SAPMO-BArch, DR1/7520: "Protokoll über die Sitzung vom 9.12.1953 im Museum für Deutsche Geschichte," 200–204. See also SAPMO DR1/7520: "Genehmigung des Stellenplanes der Nationalen Gedenkstätte Buchenwald," 4 February 1954.

CHAPTER SIX

THE DECONSTRUCTION OF THE BUCHENWALD CHILD MYTH

The Pedagogical Reception of *Naked among Wolves*

U NTIL THE COLLAPSE OF THE GDR in 1990, *Naked among Wolves* (*Nackt unter Wölfen*) remained a canonical text in East Germany, not least for schoolchildren of the ninth grade (in the 1960s) and then the tenth grade (in the 1970s).[1] Indeed as of the 1970s, in GDR classrooms it probably became *the* most important literary statement on antifascism. It certainly became more important than Seghers's *The Seventh Cross* (*Das siebte Kreuz*, 1946), and was rivaled perhaps only by Dieter Noll's *The Adventures of Werner Holt* (*Die Abenteuer des Werner Holt*, 1960). Often, Otto Gotsche's "Buchenwald Song" ("Das Buchenwaldlied")[2] was taught alongside it, a short story celebrating Robert Siewert's rescue at Buchenwald of the Austrian-Jewish composer Hermann Leopoldi. GDR children were also introduced to Robert Siewert through Gisela Karau's children's book *The Good Star of Janusz K.* (*Der gute Stern des Janusz K.*, 1963), which describes his rescue of children at Buchenwald.[3]

Indeed it would not be exaggerated to claim that *Naked among Wolves* was regarded in the GDR as the pinnacle of German literature — at least when viewed in terms of the emphasis on revolutionary socialism that shaped the GDR's understanding of literary traditions. As might be expected, GDR schoolchildren were treated to a strongly selective and tendentious reading of the German literary legacy. Thus Goethe's poem *Prometheus* was presented to them as an expression of the "strength of the rising bourgeoisie," whose historical role was ultimately, of course, to give way to socialism, while his drama *Egmont* was interpreted as illustrating the link between "the struggle of the people against social repression" and "the struggle for the liberation of the nation." Schiller's play *Wilhelm Tell* was also read as a "drama of national liberation" with protosocialist tendencies.[4] In the course of their school education, pupils were also introduced to the revolutionary tradition in German literature of the nineteenth century (the poet Heinrich Heine — despite his criticism of communism — as well as Georg Büchner and Georg Weerth featured here), post-1848 "bourgeois realism," the anti-imperialist dimension to twentieth-century bourgeois realism (Heinrich Mann, Arnold Zweig, and Kurt Tucholsky), and pre-GDR antifascist socialist literature (Erich

Weinert, Friedrich Wolf, Bertolt Brecht, and Johannes R. Becher). This literary tradition reached its apogee in *Naked among Wolves*, which enshrined all its socialist and revolutionary virtues in ideal form. It depicted the strength of the KPD, the force of international proletarian cooperation, the power of socialist humanism, the moral nobility of socialist ethics in principle and practice, the dialectical struggle between socialism and capitalism, and the triumph of the oppressed collective against fascism in an act of self-liberation that was simultaneously an act of foundation.[5]

In GDR classrooms there was little scope for a critical approach to Apitz's novel, one that might have focused, for instance, on discrepancies between the facts of Stefan Zweig's rescue and Apitz's portrayal of the rescue of Stefan Cyliak in *Naked among Wolves*. It was not until 1981 that these discrepancies were touched on in a GDR publication, namely, Heinz Albertus's booklet *Children in Buchenwald*, published as part of a series issued by Buchenwald's National Site of Warning and Commemoration (NMGB).[6] Albertus refers to the fact that Stefan was sometimes able to leave his hiding-place and go outside, that his presence was noted and reported by SS man Dombeck, that the SS doctor Schiedlausky also spotted him after he had been given a fever-inducing injection and hidden in the sick-bay unit, and that Zacharias remained in the camp until liberation (this last fact was known to readers of the *Berliner Zeitung am Abend*'s 1964 serialization of Zacharias's testimony, but will probably not have been known to subsequent generations of GDR schoolchildren).[7] However, with the exception of the last, none of these differences to *Naked among Wolves* rank among the most significant ones. The fact that Stefan entered the camp as a registered prisoner, a fact surely known to Albertus, was suppressed. Only in a later edition (1989) of the brochure was reference made to the possibility that Stefan may have been pampered; in that edition, it was also suggested that Stefan was not permanently in hiding at Buchenwald.[8] Until 1989 in East Germany, then, the question as to what extent the terms "hidden" or "rescued" did or did not apply to the communist prisoners' adoption of Stefan was not openly confronted — and it was not until after unification that the "swap" of the Sinto boy Willy Blum for Stefan became public knowledge. Certainly, as of 1980, publications providing guidelines to teachers did encourage them to discuss with pupils differences between *Naked among Wolves* and the actual facts that Albertus (in selected form) had provided to them, including Apitz's replacement of the father figure by Jankowski.[9] But of course teachers were expected to present these changes purely as Apitz's means of enhancing the aesthetic and moral force of his tale, an interpretation that in some cases will have been quite legitimate, but not in all. Whether teachers will have had the insight or courage to suggest that Apitz dispensed with the father figure — and even dispensed ultimately with the ersatz father — so as to be able to focus exclusively on the communists and to circumnavigate potential questions as to the morality of separating the child from his father must remain a matter for speculation.

Nor, in the GDR, were other aspects of the novel's putative authenticity ever critically addressed, at least not in published form. East German children were encouraged to imagine on the basis of the novel that Buchenwald, indeed concentration camps generally, were places where antifascists fought Nazis, not sites of mass suffering and death. The novel gave no real impression of the extent of Jewish persecution, and little indication of the plural nature of Buchenwald's prisoner composition. It was not until the collapse of the GDR in 1989/90 that the novel's one-sidedness, the complete story of Zweig's rescue, and the full picture of camp life at Buchenwald, as well as its postwar suppression in the GDR, became the subject of public attention and debate. This post-unification deconstruction of the Buchenwald child myth within the context of the general deconstruction of the GDR's view of antifascism and Buchenwald forms the focus of the final section of this chapter. Before this, however, it is necessary to demonstrate that, while no such deconstruction could ever take place in the form of open public or media debate in the GDR, indeed perhaps never took place explicitly unless behind closed doors, there were works of GDR literature that, in presenting camp or ghetto life differently than Apitz did, implicitly criticized the hegemonic status of *Naked among Wolves* as the definitive novel about imprisonment under Nazism. Indeed, the occasional discreet use of intertextuality in such GDR literary works hints at a quite conscious distancing from *Naked among Wolves* and constitutes an invitation to the observant reader to reconsider his or her understanding of this canonical novel.

Literary Portrayals of Life in Concentration Camps and Ghettos

Bruno Apitz's Buchenwald novel was by no means the first literary work by a German writer to focus on a concentration camp. Willi Bredel, a communist author, had published his novel about Fuhlsbüttel concentration camp near Hamburg, *The Test of Endurance* (*Die Prüfung*) as early as 1934. Although literary in its declared status, it was closely based on Bredel's own experience and on that of the German communist Matthias Thesen.[10] The actor and director Wolfgang Langhoff, a KPD member who was active in agitprop theatre before 1933, published a report about his imprisonment in Börgermoor concentration camp, *The Moor Soldiers* (*Die Moorsoldaten*) in 1935 that became as well-known as Bredel's novel; in 1937, he also wrote a short story based on events at Börgermoor and Esterwege concentration camps, "A Loadful of Wood" ("Eine Fuhre

Holz"). Much more renowned is Anna Seghers's novel *The Seventh Cross*. Seghers herself was never in a concentration camp and wrote *The Seventh Cross* while in exile in Paris. Arguably, moreover, *The Seventh Cross* is not so much about the fictional camp Westhofen (closely based on Osthofen concentration camp near Worms) as it is concerned with the fate of seven escapees from that camp, including the main character and, ultimately, the only one of the seven who survives — the communist Georg Heisler.

The first (semi-)literary treatment of the theme of Buchenwald was probably Ernst Wiechert's *The Forest of the Dead* (*Der Totenwald*). Wiechert, a German writer whose works betray a certain ideological closeness to the "blood and soil" pseudo-romanticism of National Socialism, nevertheless found the courage to protest against the arrest of Pastor Niemöller by the Nazis in April 1938; following a period of imprisonment in Munich, he was subsequently sent to Buchenwald for his pains in July 1938. Released at the end of August, he returned home and wrote down his memories of the camp — related not in the first person but through a figure called Johannes — before hiding the manuscript in his garden. It was first published in book form in Switzerland in 1946. Unlike Wiechert, Erich Maria Remarque was an emigrant from Nazism who had no experience of Nazi camps. His novel *Spark of Life* (*Der Funke Leben*) — set in a fictional camp called Mellern — nevertheless provides a chilling view of a "Small Camp" very much like Buchenwald's. Remarque based Mellern on Eugen Kogon's detailed depiction of Buchenwald in *The SS State*, which Remarque read during a transatlantic crossing in 1950.[11] Remarque's novel appeared — to a very mixed reception — in West Germany in 1952.[12]

When Apitz came to write *Naked among Wolves* in the mid-1950s, then, there already was a corpus of German literary works about the concentration camps — in addition to published documentation about the camps and published testimonies — providing a background for his own writing. In a 1973 interview he claimed that he had read the works by Bredel and Seghers (while stressing they had not influenced him, or at least not consciously),[13] and he presumably also knew Langhoff's book on Börgermoor, which was widely read in the GDR. He may well have known Wiechert's *The Forest of the Dead*. It was the eastern-zone cultural and political monthly journal *Aufbau* that had first published excerpts from this work in 1946,[14] before it was published in book form in Zurich and then Munich (although it did not appear in book form in the GDR until 1977). And there is evidence that Apitz also knew Remarque's *Spark of Life* (even though it was never published in East Germany). Indeed, one of the very first drafts of *Naked among Wolves* from 1956 bore the title *Spark of Life* — an exact, and surely not purely fortuitous, replication of the title chosen by Remarque.[15] If, then, *Naked among Wolves* was intended in part at least as a critical development of earlier works, what are the differences?

Bredel's *The Test of Endurance*, Langhoff's *The Moor Soldiers*, and Seghers's *The Seventh Cross* were wartime works written as antifascist protests against Nazi barbarism. While emphasizing the leading role of communists in resistance, they also portray the importance of forming a truly antifascist front. Langhoff's *The Moor Soldiers* depicts the developing empathy between the bourgeois actor Langhoff and the communist workers imprisoned at Börgermoor, and in "A Loadful of Wood," a politically disillusioned carpenter wins back faith in his own class when confronted with the defiant solidarity of Börgermoor prisoners. Toward the end of Bredel's *The Test of Endurance*, a novel that is as savagely critical of social democracy as of fascism, it is nevertheless a former social democrat turned communist, Otto Regers, who helps to bring Kreibel back into the resistance group.[16] The seven prisoners who escape Westhofen in *The Seventh Cross*, moreover, are not all communists; nor does Seghers dwell on the politics of the main character Georg Heisler, and he receives the most help arguably from the unpolitical Paul Röder.[17] Langhoff stresses in *The Moor Soldiers* that some social democratic prisoners such as Mierendorff and Leuschner enjoyed enormous respect among communist prisoners,[18] and Bredel at least allows social democracy — through its mouthpiece-prisoner Schneemann — to express its views. Moreover, both Bredel and Langhoff, like Seghers, give an impression of the diversity of prisoners. Jewish prisoners are a theme in the novels of both Bredel (in the figure of Gottfried Miesicke) and Langhoff;[19] Langhoff, furthermore, makes reference to the Jehovah's Witnesses among the inmates.[20]

Apitz's *Naked among Wolves* is a postwar work. His interest is not in helping to forge an antifascist front across the nation's different classes and political identities in the fight against Hitler, but in bolstering the authority of the communist GDR in its fight against "western imperialism." While *Naked among Wolves* has much in common with the above works, it is almost totally monoperspectival, because of its obsessive focus on communist heroism. Given that the percentage of German communists among the prisoners in Buchenwald in 1945 was very small — in contrast to the situation in the early years of the concentration camps as described by Langhoff and Bredel — Apitz's focus is all the more misleading. While Langhoff, Bredel, and Seghers stress the need for (albeit communist-led) cohesion in the struggle against Hitler, the *only* people offering resistance in *Naked among Wolves* are communists. This retrospective imposition of a historically inauthentic absolute equivalence (antifascism = communism) represents a cultural response to the wish of both former Buchenwald prisoners in the GDR and the SED for a rewriting of history. Because, in the 1950s, the communists in the GDR regarded themselves as the only anti-imperialist force in the present (the Social Democratic Party now being a West German phenomenon), history had to be manipulated to imply that this had also been the case in the past. An exclusive claim was made to the resistance tradition in order to legitimize the policies and practice of the day.

Whereas Apitz's novel represents a tendentious development of emphases already present in Langhoff, Bredel, and Seghers, it represents a complete shift of emphasis when compared with Wiechert's *The Forest of the Dead* and Remarque's *Spark of Life*. Both of these works depict the concentration camp largely from the vantage point of suffering, torture, and death. Wiechert's bleak perspective is that of the writer Johannes, whose cultural pessimism and ideological disdain are only slightly tempered by an ambivalent religiosity. Remarque's chosen perspective is that of prisoner "509," who ekes out a desperate existence among the starving, disease-ridden Jewish prisoners in Mellern's Small Camp. *Spark of Life* depicts the largely hopeless resistance against death by starvation and disease, not the heroic communist resistance against the SS.[21] The resistance organization plays a peripheral role in the lives of Remarque's characters; while it hides a comrade and some weaponry in the Small Camp, it takes little interest in the lives of the prisoners there and offers them little assistance. "509," like Johannes in *The Forest of the Dead*, is skeptical of ideology. He distances himself from the postwar communist scenarios sketched out by the communist prisoner Werner, who freely admits that the communists, once in power, will put their opponents in concentration camps as the Nazis have done.[22] The American émigré Remarque's antitotalitarianism in *Spark of Life* is a direct reflection of his pro-western sympathies in the developing Cold War of the late 1940s. Wiechert's portrayal of communism in *The Forest of the Dead* is, in places, as negative as Remarque's — although his mouthpiece Johannes does praise communists Josef Biesel and Walter Husemann.[23] While a tone of cultural pessimism predominates in *The Forest of the Dead*, Johannes's view of the camp is also characterized by a certain moral and cultural elitism. In publishing his report in 1946, Wiechert no doubt hoped to counter the complaints by some exile writers such as Thomas Mann that writers of the inner emigration were tarnished by having opted to continue writing under Hitler. *The Forest of the Dead* very much portrays Johannes alias Wiechert as a victim of Nazism.

Apitz's eulogy of communist resistance in *Naked among Wolves* can be read as a response, not just to criticism of Buchenwald's communists from within the GDR, but also to criticism of communism voiced by Wiechert and particularly by the "western" emigrant Remarque. Equally, Apitz's exclusive focus on suffering that results directly from interrogation methods employed by the SS against the resistance organization implies a rejection of the approach toward suffering adopted by Wiechert and Remarque. Whereas suffering in Apitz's novel is given meaning as a form of victorious martyrdom in the struggle between the SS and the ILK, in Remarque's novel it is no more and no less than the result of senseless bestiality, and it leads, not to martyrdom, but rather to unimaginable misery and a slow

death. Apitz's transfiguration of suffering into noble endurance is complemented in *Naked among Wolves* by a representation of the prisoners as a
robust fighting collective — quite in contrast to *Spark of Life*, where they
are portrayed as weak, even moribund, victims. And while Remarque's
novel ends with a fragile post-liberation vision of a romantic bond between
two prisoners, implying that hope for the future rests in the reconstruction
of society at the micro-level, *Naked among Wolves* concludes with a triumphant assertion of collective socialist values. For all that, *Naked among
Wolves* does share some similarities with *Spark of Life*, not least a style that
alternates awkwardly between the colloquial and the metaphorical. Both
novels include portrayals of the lives of the SS men, whom both authors
see as products of a decadent petty bourgeoisie. The relationship in
Remarque's novel between camp commandant Neubauer and his more
pragmatic wife Selma may well have inspired Apitz to create a similar relationship between Zweiling and Hortense — both Selma and Hortense are
quite prepared to leave their vacillating husbands as the Americans
approach.

While *Naked among Wolves* is in some respects a rewriting of previous
concentration camp literature, its portrayal of incarceration under Nazism
was itself subsequently revised in a number of important works of East
German literature. The key works in this respect are Hedda Zinner's drama
Ravensbrück Ballad (*Ravensbrücker Ballade*, 1961), Jurek Becker's novel
Jakob the Liar (*Jakob der Lügner*, 1969), and Fred Wander's collection of
stories *The Seventh Well* (*Der siebente Brunnen*, 1971). Each of these works
takes up motifs than can be found in *Naked among Wolves* and subjects
them to a noticeably different treatment. All were to varying degrees controversial — not least because they challenged the hegemonic communist
narrative that lies at the heart of *Naked among Wolves*. Hedda Zinner's
Ravensbrück Ballad, although it received favorable reviews after its first
performance by the East Berlin *Volksbühne* on 6 October 1961, did not
meet with universal approval in the GDR. When GDR television in the
mid-1980s set about making a film of the drama, the Committee of
Antifascist Resistance Fighters (KdAW) succeeded in having the production banned. Objections were raised to the perceived overemphasis in
Zinner's drama on criminal prisoners, and a corresponding underemphasis
on political prisoners.[24] Like *Naked among Wolves*, Becker's *Jakob the Liar*
— set in a Polish ghetto — owed its genesis to an idea for a DEFA film.
Unlike Apitz's 1955 idea for a film, however, Becker's was accepted by
DEFA and reached the project stage before it ran into difficulties — the
Polish cultural authorities refused to grant director Frank Beyer permission
to film in Cracow when they discovered that *Jakob the Liar* focused on
anti-Semitism, still a sensitive theme in mid-1960s Poland.[25] In mid-1966,
moreover, Beyer fell out of favor with the GDR cultural authorities (see
chapter 4).[26] Becker reworked the script into a novel, and Beyer was finally

able to complete the film in 1974. Fred Wander's collection of stories *The Seventh Well*, the only one of the three works mentioned here to focus on Buchenwald, came under fire from the KdAW before it was published because, in the final story of the collection, liberation is depicted from the less than uplifting perspective of Buchenwald's Small Camp.[27] But the committee was unable to hinder publication, possibly because Wander was supported by Anna Seghers.[28]

Hedda Zinner's *Ravensbrück Ballad* was first performed two years after the new memorial site at Ravensbrück was opened to the public (1959). It was the GDR's most important literary monument to the largely female camp of Ravensbrück, just as Apitz's novel was the GDR's principal literary memorial for the largely male camp of Buchenwald. As some GDR theatre critics observed, it took up and modified the very same motif at the heart of *Naked among Wolves* — namely, the hiding of a prisoner.[29] In the case of Zinner's drama, it is a Soviet prisoner Wera who is hidden by the communist underground (she assumes the identity of a Polish prisoner, Wanda Janowska). However, her whereabouts are betrayed by another political prisoner, the German Ellen; like the "treacherous" Rose in *Naked among Wolves*, Ellen exists at the margins of the collective of political prisoners and in no way identifies with their underground activities. Zinner's drama certainly makes heroes of the organized resistance, particularly the figure of Maria; just as Stefan survives thanks to Höfel and then the ILK, so Wera survives thanks to Maria and the communist underground. But Zinner does not simply reproduce the message of Apitz's novel, extending its validity to a female camp. She introduces significant differences, which are all the more striking because of the above-mentioned similarities.

One of these lies in the gradual wearing down of Ellen's resistance to attempts by the SS to make her reveal Wanda Janowska's real identity; Zinner's dramatic focus is as much on Ellen's response to this pressure as it is on Maria and her heroic exploits — quite in contrast to *Naked among Wolves*, where Rose is of secondary importance. The method used by the SS, moreover, is not physical torture so much as a mixture of threats and bribery, and in exchange for her freedom, Ellen finally succumbs. That she does may point to a certain susceptibility among some of the "Reds" (political prisoners) — to which category, according to Zinner's cast list, Ellen at least nominally belongs.[30] Rose's weakness in *Naked among Wolves* is his lack of courage, a surely more acceptable weakness to the KdAW than Ellen's. Another significant difference is that the underground in *Ravensbrück Ballad* is not only in conflict with the SS. Maria and her fellow-politicals are also engaged in a struggle to maintain their authority vis-à-vis the non-political prisoners, particularly the asocial ("Black") and criminal ("Green") prisoners. In fact the selfishness and petty squabbles among the latter threaten to undermine resistance. The major weakness of

Zinner's drama is its presumptuous tendency to portray the non-political prisoners as morally inferior. But at least it provides an impression of the diversity of Ravensbrück's prisoners and their conflicts, and of the precarious power of communist resistance — in contrast to *Naked among Wolves*. Zinner, to her great credit, also addresses the theme of the persecution of Gypsies in the drama. Toward the end, the political prisoner Mira describes how the Gypsy boy Jeschko, as well as other Gypsy and Jewish children, is tossed into a truck to be taken away for gassing[31] — this is a short scene, but it poignantly throws into stark relief the fate of most children in concentration camps. It is hard not to believe that Zinner intended the scene implicitly at least as a critique of the one-sided impression conveyed by the exclusive focus on the rescue of one child in Apitz's *Naked among Wolves*.

Zinner's drama, of course, is about Ravensbrück, not Buchenwald. Nevertheless, Apitz's novel was regarded in the GDR as the definitive statement on concentration camps generally. At the same time, it elevated Buchenwald to cult status. Zinner's Ravensbrück drama questions Buchenwald's right to dominate the concentration camp memory landscape, and indeed it questions the domination of male-determined and male-focused memory. Jurek Becker's novel *Jakob the Liar* (1969) represents an even greater challenge to hegemonic memory in the GDR. In setting his novel in a ghetto, Becker, who had himself spent part of his childhood in the Lodz Ghetto, emphasizes to his readers the need to remember the fact that National Socialist persecution and brutality took place not just in Germany but also in Poland. While Zinner asserts the right of Ravensbrück to be remembered as much as Buchenwald, Becker questions the dominance of the tripartite focus in the GDR on Buchenwald, Sachsenhausen, and Ravensbrück — whatever the hierarchical relation between these in official memory. More important, in my view, is Becker's focus on a site of exclusively *non-German* and *Jewish* suffering. Because Apitz and Zinner invite empathy with German communists, they make it possible for their readers and audience to imagine Germans to have been victims — something made all the easier by their portrayal of SS conduct as the expression of class and capitalist interests, rather than as anything specifically German. Such empathy is not possible for German readers of *Jakob the Liar*, because here victims and perpetrators are divided along the lines of Jews and Germans. *Jakob the Liar* also compels the reader to recognize anti-Semitism as a self-sufficient motive for Nazi persecution. In the case of the works by Apitz and Zinner, it is largely *communist* suffering that is foregrounded. With *Jakob the Liar*, Becker put Nazi anti-Semitism, with its system of ghettos and its policy of liquidation, on the GDR's literary map of memory. To be fair, *Jakob the Liar* appeared at a time when East German historians were also beginning to confront the persecution of Jews in major works of historiography.[32] But Becker's novel — and Beyer's film — reached many more people than these publications.

More specifically, *Jakob the Liar* enters into an often critical intertextual dialogue with Apitz's novel. At the beginning of *Jakob the Liar*, Becker's narrator expresses his regret at the absence of trees in the ghetto, informing us of the role that trees have otherwise played in his life.[33] By contrast, while the only tree left standing *within* Buchenwald was the Goethe Oak, the camp was surrounded by trees, its name evoked trees, and it is with a vision of trees that Apitz's *Naked among Wolves* begins.[34] But the main intertextual link is one that permeates Becker's entire novel, namely, the motif of concealment — only in *Jakob the Liar* it is not a child that is concealed (although Jakob acts as ersatz father for Lina, whose parents have been transported to certain death), but a radio. Whereas hope in *Naked among Wolves* is nurtured by the courageous protection of Stefan, it is nurtured in Becker's novel by Jakob passing on news. The difference, of course, is that whereas Stefan exists, Jakob's radio does not. Jakob invents the radio broadcasts, initially to get himself out of a dilemma, then to keep feeding the hopes of his fellow inmates. The implication of this is that hope, for those in the ghetto, depends on illusion. There could hardly be a starker contrast to *Naked among Wolves* with its portrayal of a robust underground. In Becker's novel, the narrator declares with explicit contrastive reference to Warsaw and Buchenwald: "there was no resistance where I was."[35] Thus it is that *Jakob the Liar* implicitly calls into question the universal applicability of Apitz's and indeed Zinner's literary portrayal of Nazi imprisonment as a breeding ground for antifascist resistance. The reader gains the impression that, in the world of the ghetto, resistance would have been much harder to stage than was obviously the case at Buchenwald. The lot of the communists at Buchenwald cannot truly be compared with the much worse lot of the Jews in the ghettos and camps in Poland.

Becker's intertextual play with *Naked among Wolves*, one that draws attention to the questionable validity of its heroic perspective, becomes particularly clear at the conclusion of *Jakob the Liar*. In fact, the narrator presents us with two conclusions: one imagined, one "real." In the imagined conclusion, Jakob, unable to tolerate the effect on his fellow ghetto inhabitants of his decision to stop passing on "news," tries to escape but is shot; shortly afterward the other ghetto inhabitants are liberated by the Russians. Jakob's death thus appears absolutely senseless. He has martyred himself — in contrast to Pippig (*Naked among Wolves*) and Maria (*Ravensbrück Ballad*) — for nothing. In the conclusion as personally experienced by the narrator, the ghetto inhabitants are transported to their deaths before the Russians arrive. There is no liberation, let alone self-liberation; there is only liquidation. At the same time, Becker's play with alternative conclusions draws attention to the essential *fictionality* of literature, as does his use of a narrator who freely admits that he does not know the whole truth, and his deployment of the motif of the invented radio broadcasts, which function as a fiction within a fiction. Literature, then, is a play of the imagination, not a work of historiography — a view that implicitly takes issue with the ascription of documentary status to literary works such as *Naked among Wolves*. In the end, Becker treads a fine line between raising awareness both of the harsh historical reality of anti-Semitism and of the problems we all face when trying to recreate the past, a problem that can be particularly well represented in the fictional world of the novel.

More than any GDR literary work, it was Fred Wander's collection of stories *The Seventh Well* (1971) that challenged the right of *Naked among Wolves* to dictate the way in which the Nazi past is remembered.[36] *The Seventh Well* is set principally in three concentration camps, Hirschberg, Crawinkel, and Buchenwald; it ends with the liberation of Buchenwald. Like Becker in *Jakob the Liar*, Wander, himself a former prisoner of Auschwitz and Buchenwald, focuses mainly on Jewish suffering. His focus is wide. Through a series of flashbacks interwoven into the text, the stories follow the trail of Jewish suffering at the hands of the Nazis across western and eastern Europe. These flashbacks focus on the lives of individual Jews living in France, Poland, Czechoslovakia, or the Soviet Union at the time of the Nazi invasion. Wander conveys a sense of the European-wide destruction of intact, thriving Jewish communities, of a cultural and ethnic tragedy on a grand scale. In his stories, the experience of persecution by the Nazis is an essentially Jewish experience; Old Testament imagery, the use of Yiddish, and references to Jewish songs and storytelling enhance this impression. Thus Wander extends Becker's focus, building into the microcosmic focus on three German concentration camps a perspective opening outward onto the European dimensions of the Holocaust.

That Wander presents Buchenwald from the point of view of Jewish suffering serves to counterbalance the preoccupation in Apitz's *Naked among Wolves* with the ordeal of communists. But he goes further than this. In the opening and closing stories in Wander's collection, the focus is on the fate of children. In "How to Tell a Story," the narrator tells of the slow death of a child, Jossl, after he has been covered in snow by SS guards; the prospect of liberation remains a rumor that can do nothing to prevent Jossl's death (14). In the final tale, "Joschko and his Brothers," the narrator relates how he experienced the liberation of Buchenwald surrounded by Jewish children in the children's block of the Small Camp (109–12). He describes the children as being in a dreadful condition, barely existing in the midst of excrement, fragments of thrown-away clothes, and the bodies of dead children and adults. In their struggle for food, the children pillage other blocks, hunting through the pockets of the dead and dying. According to the narrator, dissolution had set in: "the ordering hand of the illegal camp committee no longer reached out as far as the last huts of the quarantine camp (111–12)." When the struggle for liberation by the ILK comes, it takes place in the distance; and the children are hardly able to appreciate that they have been liberated. Wander does not call into question the significance of the ILK's struggle with the SS or its part in liberating Buchenwald. However, by presenting this struggle as a tangential phenomenon when viewed from the perspective of the Small Camp, he certainly does call into question the ILK's right to a dominant position in portrayals of Buchenwald.

Most interesting, perhaps, is the implication in "Joschko and His Brothers" that those children who did survive did so, not because of the ILK, but thanks to their own devices. It is this self-reliance that the narrator ultimately finds so moving; he sees hope for the future in the animal strength of family bonds such as those between Joschko and his brothers (115), not in the activities of the resistance organization. Nor indeed, in adults at all. The Joschko story ends with the description of an adult male corpse, and with the suggestion that the children will carry on where the dead man has left off: "Joschko and his brothers, without knowing it, had picked up the staff that the dead man had cast aside and carried it away with them" (117). The narrator adds that Joschko and his brothers had rifled through the dead man's pockets and stolen the narrator's tin spoon. Here, there is no respect for the elders. Authority and the future passes from old to young — quite in contrast to *Naked among Wolves*, where Stefan remains dependent on his protecting masters.

In conclusion, then, it would be false to say that the view of Nazi camps promoted by Apitz's novel, among other media, was not challenged in the GDR. It was — through literature. Essentially, it was the claim to the absolute validity of this view that was challenged. The focus on communist prisoners was counterbalanced by a focus on asocial and criminal prisoners (Zinner), or indeed abandoned entirely in favor of a focus on Jewish prisoners (Becker, Wander). The problems and limits encountered by the communist underground in their attempts to stage effective resistance were depicted (Zinner, Wander), while in *Jakob the Liar* there is no resistance (in the organized sense) at all. It was shown that women were persecuted as well as men (Zinner), and that, in contrast to Stefan Cyliak in *Naked among Wolves*, many children did not enjoy protection and suffered terrible deaths (Zinner, but particularly Wander). And questions were raised as to the right of any piece of fiction to declare itself, or be declared, authentic (Becker). But while these works certainly challenged Apitz's view in many ways, it was not possible in the GDR, not even in literature, to seek to cast the communist prisoners themselves in a truly critical light. Issues of privilege among the communist prisoners, or of their (however motivated or limited) collusion in murderous SS practices, were not really brought up. Not out of ignorance — there will have been authors, such as Wander, who were well aware of these issues. Nor was the truth of Apitz's version of the Buchenwald child's rescue called into serious question. That, as we shall now see, was a task undertaken only after 1990. One undertaken with full justification, if not always for the right reasons.

Antifascism since 1990

The shift in interpretations of the Zweig rescue story after 1990 must be seen, first, within the context of the general critique of antifascism that set in after the peaceful revolution in the GDR ("Wende") in autumn 1989. The immediate trigger to this critique was perhaps the discovery in 1990 of the mass graves of German internees who had died in captivity when Buchenwald and other sites in eastern Germany were used as "Special Camps" by the Soviets between 1945 and 1950.[37] In the heated atmosphere of the post-"Wende" period, these revelations were bound to strike at one of the founding pillars of the GDR. Given that the antifascists and socialists *par excellence*, namely the Soviets, had not only let thousands of Germans die in postwar camps, but had also interned many innocent Germans along with Nazis, what credibility could the humanity supposedly at the heart of their antifascism and socialism now have? It was not just the Soviets whose moral credibility was severely called into question. Following the dissolution of the Soviet Special Camps in 1950, some 3,400 former internees were sentenced at Waldheim by an East German court in what were effectively rigged trials. Thirty-two of them received death sentences, and twenty-five were actually executed. Regardless of whether those treated in this way were Nazis or not, the denial to them of basic judicial rights was scandalous.[38] East German newspapers in 1990 ran reports both on these trials[39] and on more recent SED plans for holding political opponents in internment camps.[40] Hardly a day went by between 1990 and 1992, moreover, without lurid reports on the activities of the *Stasi*. Bit by bit, the East Germans found themselves confronting a legacy of SED crime that stretched from the GDR's inception up to the "Wende." Although many GDR citizens knew antifascism was manipulated by their government, most nevertheless — partly because they had not wanted to, partly because they had not had the whole picture — had not come to recognize that antifascism as practiced by the SED often functioned as a smoke screen designed to conceal state crime.

The post-unification period witnessed the publication of many academic books and articles exploring SED injustice. Especially among west German historians and political scientists, there was a general tendency to equate the GDR with the Third Reich. The accompanying critique of antifascism naturally focused on its use as an ideological weapon by the

SED in its bid to secure dominance and legitimize its political praxis. While east Germans were generally reluctant, with hindsight, to equate East Germany with the Third Reich, they nevertheless added their voices to the criticism of antifascism. The historian Olaf Groehler, for example, argued that the emphasis on antifascist resistance, particularly in the early years of the GDR, had the effect of exonerating the mass of East Germans for their part in Nazism.[41] Ralph Giordano had already expressed a similar concern in 1987 when he pointed out that, as a result of "prescribed antifascism,"[42] the SED effectively declared the state and the population of the GDR to be "co-victors of the Second World War" and a "part of the anti-Hitler coalition."[43]

The main thrust of the critique of antifascism itself was that the SED, by virtue of its imposition of a semantic corset on "antifascist" so that it came to mean "communist," its repression of other parties such as the SPD, its absolute dominance in the National Front, its suppression of civil rights, its anti-Semitism, its persecution of political opponents, and its generally autocratic stance effectively violated the spirit of that antifascism it claimed to have embodied. It was pointed out too, not least by the West German political scientist Antonia Grunenberg, that there was little historical evidence that there had ever been much of an "antifascist front" either during the Weimar Republic or under Nazism, or indeed in the Spanish Civil War against Franco, when conflicts between communists, social democrats, anarchists, and Trotzkyists and the communist persecution of supposedly "antifascist comrades" pointed more to internecine strife than to unity.[44] While Grunenberg's definition of antifascism as a "German myth" was not meant only as a critique of the GDR, the term "myth" has been most frequently applied since 1990 to the SED's glorified and distorted view both of antifascism during the Hitler period and of its own supposed antifascism.[45]

While the criticism of the GDR's cult of antifascism is certainly justified, it would be wrong to claim that it had no positive value — even given its elements of hypocrisy and distortion. Herfried Münkler has argued that the "founding myth" of West Germany in the 1950s, namely the Economic Miracle, had a wider basis in real experience than the East German founding myth of antifascism. Thus the collective memory of the Federal Republic was based more on communicative memory, that of the GDR more on cultural memory.[46] This distinction appears convincing, but it overlooks the manner in which cultural memory can become communicative memory. For those GDR citizens who experienced the state promotion of antifascism in the 1950s and subsequently, antifascist thinking and symbols became part of their lived reality. It should not automatically be assumed, moreover, that because the SED betrayed antifascist values, their citizens did as well. Many may genuinely have sought to practice what was preached.

Buchenwald after 1990

While the above-described critique of antifascism provided the general context for the deconstruction of the GDR's version of the Zweig story, the more immediate context — itself influenced by that general context — was the post-1990 deconstruction of the history of communist resistance at Buchenwald, and of the GDR's tendency to view and present the history of Buchenwald through the constricting lens of antifascism. One should not imagine that such a deconstruction was entirely the work of West German pressure or influence. It was with the onset of the "Wende" that a process of differentiation set in at the NMGB itself. In November 1989, some of the memorial site's members criticized the SED's political influence and called for commemoration of all the various victim groups at Buchenwald, including Jews.[47] A few months later, between April and June 1990, the NMGB presented a new Buchenwald exhibition in West Berlin, which gave greater weight to the representation of these groups.[48] At Buchenwald, new guided tours were established in April 1991 under the title "Overgrown History": visitors were for the first time able to find out in detail about the fate of homosexual prisoners and of Sinti and Roma. In May 1991, an exhibit on Catholic resistance was shown in Buchenwald; and in 1992, a book on Jews at Buchenwald by a long-standing member of the Memorial Site staff, Harry Stein, was published — the result of a publication project that dated back to GDR days but had long been hindered in its realization by communist ex-Buchenwald prisoners such as Bartel.[49]

So when a Historians' Commission entrusted with the task of drawing up recommendations for further developments at Buchenwald began its work in September 1991 — a commission of west German historians convoked by Thuringia's Ministry for Science and Art — it was able to build on progress toward diversification made by the Memorial staff itself. And indeed it was the task of the existing staff to implement the commission's recommendations.[50] In 1995, a new exhibition on the concentration camp replaced the old one in the Storage Building. It gives due care and attention to all of Buchenwald's victim groups. It also seeks to project a more subtle and complex image of survival strategies at the camp; forms of self-assertion, by means for instance of religion, art, and writing, as well as of mutual assistance through solidarity committees and the like, are given as much focus as organized resistance. The facts of organized murder through the SS take center stage, and the SS structures within the camp are precisely described. The new exhibition does not ignore communist resistance, but it presents it as merely one facet of Buchenwald among many others.[51]

More significant from the point of view of the present book, perhaps, is the fact that the exhibition, and particularly the accompanying catalogue, cast the communist-led underground in a highly critical light, presenting its activities as self-interested. The (German) communists' dominance of the system of self-administration is seen as their way of protecting their own cadre at the cost of others.[52] German communists, the catalogue states, "became caught up in the racial hierarchy of the camp as created by the SS."[53] The exhibition that was opened in 1995, therefore, not only quite explicitly abandoned the GDR tradition of privileging one Buchenwald narrative over all others; it also took issue with the GDR tradition of casting this narrative in the form of a moral fable in which the evil SS was overcome by the ethically superior ILK. However, while this criticism of communist resistance and the GDR's focus on it was sorely needed, it goes too far by implying that the history of this resistance was *almost exclusively* one of group egoism and complicity. Nor is it commendable that, in the few cases where the catalogue does outline the positive effects of organized resistance, clear reference to communist involvement is omitted. Thus we are informed of the achievements of Wilhelm Hammann in saving the lives of children in Block 8 — but not that Hammann was a communist (indeed he had been a KPD regional parliamentarian in Hesse between 1927 and 1933).[54]

This gathering trend toward a predominantly negative, rather than merely differentiated, view of Buchenwald's communists was started, arguably, by the west German literary critic Wilfried Schoeller. Invited by the Buchenwald Memorial Site to deliver an address on 11 April 1993 at the opening of an exhibition on Erich Maria Remarque, Schoeller launched a stinging attack on what he called the conspiratorial "cryptomania" of Buchenwald's communists, claiming that this anticipated the "pathological obsession with secrecy" of the *Stasi*. Representatives of the International Buchenwald-Dora Committee (IKBD) left the room in protest.[55] In February 1994, the Thuringian edition of the *BILD* newspaper published excerpts from transcripts of the interviews with former Buchenwald prisoners conducted by the 1946 investigative commission (see chapter 2). These excerpts pointed to communist collaboration with the SS in administering fatal injections; "Communists Helped SS with Murder," ran the headline.[56] Later in 1994, Lutz Niethammer's volume documenting internal SED investigations into Buchenwald was published. Laudably, Niethammer stressed in the introduction that it could not be the task of "a new and more realistic view of the history of this camp to omit what was emphasized in the GDR and replace it with what was omitted."[57] Certainly the volume makes it clear that the communist-dominated camp self-administration was preferable to a self-administration run by the criminal prisoners, and it also makes it clear that such self-administration was the prerequisite for effective resistance; collaboration and defiance went hand in hand. But by and large the book sets out to demonstrate that there was too much self-protective collaboration with the SS on the part of the communists.

Two other new exhibitions at Buchenwald seek to highlight the problems both of Soviet communism and GDR antifascism. After its first meeting in September 1991, the Buchenwald Historians' Commission, while recommending that the chief emphasis at the memorial site should remain on the concentration camp history, nevertheless advocated that the history of the use of Buchenwald as a Soviet Special Camp between 1945 and 1950 should also be remembered — albeit not to the same extent, and not in proximity to the sites of memory of the concentration camp.[58] A permanent exhibition on the Special Camp was opened at Buchenwald in 1997. It rather gingerly picks its way between criticism of Soviet methods of internment, acknowledgement of the fact that most Special Camp inmates were linked in some way with Nazism, and recognition of the fact that innocent people were also interned — not least those of different political persuasions, such as social democrats. The rather awkward term "Stalinist denazification" reflects this approach. A third permanent exhibition opened at Buchenwald Memorial Site in 1999 — a mere matter of yards from the entrance to the massive memorial complex on the southern slopes of the Ettersberg (see chapter 2). This exhibition addresses the history of memorialization at Buchenwald and in Weimar from 1945 till the present. It concentrates particularly on the evolution of the memorial complex and of Buchenwald's National Site of Warning and Commemoration (inaugurated in 1958), but also introduces the visitor to the changes to the memorial site since 1990, and the reasons for them. Taken together, Buchenwald's three new exhibitions represent a triadic deconstruction. The 1937 to 1945 exhibition implicitly and explicitly takes issue with the one-sidedness and lacunae of the antifascist narrative; the 1945 to 1950 exhibition seriously questions the moral character of Soviet socialism; and the exhibition on the history of Buchenwald Memorial Site points out the political agenda that drove it and the historiographical distortions, omissions, and prejudices that informed it.

This new generation of exhibitions is in many respects impressive — and has been accompanied by the establishment, at what is now called the Buchenwald Memorial Site, of new memorials and memorial plaques to, for instance, Jews, Sinti and Roma, and Jehovah's Witnesses, as well as by much work of essential archaeological recovery. It reflects a commitment to representing all aspects of Buchenwald's history, an openness pursued most vigorously by the Site's current director Volkhard Knigge (who has been in the post since 1994). This openness has laid Knigge and his team open to criticism from all sides. Surviving concentration camp victims, Jewish and communist, have often expressed indignation at the representation of the postwar history of the camp; for some of them, it is unacceptable that Buchenwald is now a site describing not only their suffering but also that of the nation that persecuted them. Surviving antifascist prisoners and organizations such as the IKBD are particularly angry at the fact that Buchenwald's communists should suddenly have become, so it seems to them, the villains of the piece. Yet surviving inmates of the Special Camp and organizations such as the League of Those Persecuted under Stalinism (BSV) are equally unhappy. As they see it, Knigge has "insulted" the Special Camp inmates by suggesting that most of them were not free of some form of guilt or responsibility for Nazism.[59]

It would be easy to shrug off these objections as the self-interested expression of group sensitivities. Acceptance of the changes at post-1990 Buchenwald, after all, presupposed a far from self-explanatory preparedness on the part of victim groups to exercise a degree of historiographical self-criticism and tolerance toward other victim groups whose positions they found hard to understand, or whose victim status they did not accept. But not all objections resulted from self-defensive entrenchment. The agenda of openness at the new-look memorial site has not been consistently applied. In opening a window on the dubious aspects of communist behavior at Buchenwald, those responsible for the memorial site have simultaneously opted to close nearly all of those that opened onto examples of communist courage and solidarity. It is surely no coincidence that two of the three exhibitions focus not on the ills of Nazism but on those of communism and antifascism. Even the main exhibition on the Nazi period is not free of a critical focus on communism. It would therefore not be unreasonable to claim that, since 1990, the GDR shrine to antifascism has been deconstructed along anticommunist lines, and certainly with excessive zeal. Today's memorial site conveys the impression that the real significance of Buchenwald is as a site of seamless communist repression, beginning with the communist underground at Buchenwald during the Nazi period, and only ending in 1989/90. At the very least the visitor will come away understanding Buchenwald in terms of the totalitarian paradigm, namely as a site with a "double history" of National Socialism and Stalinism. This understanding would be consistent with (west German-led) post-unification attempts to place the history of concentration camps within a history of twentieth-century dictatorships and to celebrate the end of the GDR as an act of liberation by the West.

The Reception of Zweig's Rescue since 1990

How, then, did all the above developments shape the post-unification reception of Zweig's rescue? Like the pre-1990 GDR reception, the reception in united Germany has taken the form of media reporting, historiography, literature, film, and exhibits. But for the first time the reception has been truly an all-German one: while Apitz's *Naked among Wolves* and Beyer's film were known in West Germany, the theme of Zweig's rescue — despite the publication of Zacharias Zweig's testimony in West Germany in 1987 — remained of peripheral interest. Quite unlike the pre-1990 GDR reception, however, the post-1990 image has been predominantly critical, both of the communists involved in Zweig's protection and of the image of this protection in the GDR. This deconstructive image, while partly corrective in character, has often been projected with an air of indignation and scandalous revelation. It has, moreover, arguably gone too far, often being motivated not so much by an interest in establishing the truth as by a desire to discredit Buchenwald's communists and the GDR. It has thus been driven, in its positive and negative aspects, by the same mixed agenda that informs the general critique of antifascism and developments at Buchenwald itself.

One of the first and most trenchant post-1990 criticisms of both Buchenwald's communists and the GDR's representation of Zweig's rescue can be found in Ruth Klüger's widely read memoir of her imprisonment at Terezin concentration camp, first published in Germany in 1992.[60] In the course of her memoir, Klüger describes a visit to Buchenwald Memorial Site. She takes offence at the plaque commemorating the rescue of Stefan Zweig, claiming that it obscures the largely negative nature of the relationship between the political and Jewish prisoners: "the political prisoners, who in part themselves came from an anti-Semitic background, despised the Jews because they regarded themselves as morally superior; after all, they had been imprisoned because of their beliefs, the Jews on the other hand for no reason at all." Klüger goes on to accuse those who had mounted the plaque of infantilizing and making kitsch out of the "enormous genocide, the Jewish 20th century catastrophe." She also dismisses Apitz's *Naked among Wolves* as "kitsch."[61] For Klüger, the novel and the plaque imply a philo-Semitic attitude on the part of the communist prisoners that was not borne out by historical fact; elitism and snobbery toward Jewish inmates were rather the norm. In his 1993 lecture at Buchenwald Memorial Site, Wilfried Schoeller likewise saw in Apitz's novel evidence, albeit unintended, of the "elitist consciousness" of the communist prisoners. In *Naked among Wolves*, he pointed out, only communists stage resistance; there is no reference to Christians, social democrats, or liberals.[62]

While Schoeller's position — despite his brief criticism of totalitarianist theory — is determined by a characteristically west German combination of deconstruction and anticommunist daemonization, Klüger's is that of the Holocaust survivor whose experience of the camps is diametrically different from that of Apitz. She is absolutely right to point to communist disdain for Jews in the camps, and to the fact that even politically active Jews were regarded in the first instance as Jews.[63] That one might mistakenly infer from the Storage Building plaque and Apitz's novel that the communists were programmatically committed to helping Jews is also true. Nevertheless, not all communists were disdainful, and there are many examples of courageous and selfless acts on the part of communists toward Jews, not least Jewish children. Again, the deconstruction goes too far.

Klüger also points out that the text of the plaque, while naming Zweig, does not *state* that he was Jewish. In a similar vein, Volkhard Knigge argues that Cremer's figure of a small child in the memorial complex at Buchenwald transforms Zweig into a resistance fighter without acknowledging his Polish-Jewish origins.[64] In other words: what was important was not Zweig's Jewishness but rather his symbolic value as an icon of communist resistance. On the other hand, as Klüger is clearly aware, Zweig's Jewishness must have been visible enough for the desirable inference of communist support for the Jews to be drawn. While Klüger and Knigge comment sensitively on the question of Zweig's (non)-visibility as a Jew, they do rather overstate the degree to which his Jewishness was downplayed at the NMGB or in the GDR generally.[65] Of course it was often downplayed; Zweig's identity was frequently left studiously vague. But, equally, there were occasions when it *was* explicitly referred to, even if the background of Jewish persecution was rarely set out clearly. And of course all of the GDR will have known of Stefan Zweig's Jewishness at the latest by 1964. This does not invalidate the basic point that his Jewishness was always less important than his symbolic value as above defined. Nevertheless, the intense publicity in 1964 surrounding a Holocaust survivor from Israel will have done something to raise the GDR population's awareness of Nazi anti-Semitism and the extent of Jewish suffering.

In early 2000, the Buchenwald Memorial Site removed the plaque describing Stefan's rescue and replaced it with a more detailed information board describing the function of the Storage Building and highlighting the fact that thousands of youths and children passed through it on their way to the Small Camp and the various armaments work details.[66] The new text does mention the hiding of a child in the building as well; but while the original plaque claimed that the prisoners in the Personal Property Room work detail had risked their lives to save Stefan Zweig from annihilation, the new text merely claims that "one of the youngest" children was hidden in the Storage Building by political prisoners, adding that some 900 other children survived in the children's blocks 8 and 66.[67] The new text not only broadens the context; it also subtly takes issue with the old plaque by avoiding making heroes of the communist prisoners who hid Stefan, and not making any explicit reference to their having thereby saved his life. That the new text eschews lofty rhetoric is certainly a reaction to the glorification of the communist version of Zweig's rescue in the GDR. But there is more to it than that, for in the early 1990s, staff at the memorial site became aware that Stefan had survived because a Sinto boy, Willy Blum, had been sent to Auschwitz in his place. This fundamentally called into question the idea that his protection had been a heroic act. Volkhard Knigge pointed out that the full story of Zweig's rescue, one of a "victim

Fig. 21: The new information board in front of the Storage Building. Author's own photograph.

swap," had been suppressed: "out of every catastrophe we somehow make nice stories, and that's got to stop."[68]

The fact of this exchange is now common knowledge in Germany. In a 1997 article on Apitz's *Naked among Wolves,* Susanne zur Nieden drew attention to it.[69] In a footnote, she refers to copies of transport lists shown to her by Sabine and Harry Stein of the Memorial Site.[70] Harry Stein himself, in reference to documents held at Washington's National Archives, pointed to the exchange in an article published in 2000.[71] Visitors to Buchenwald Memorial Site were able to read about it as of 1999; an exhibit in the new exhibition on the history of the memorial site refers to the substitution of Willy Blum for Stefan. And visitors to Berlin's newly opened permanent exhibition at the Jewish Museum can also read about the substitution — as could visitors to an exhibition entitled "Myths of the Nation," which ran in Berlin's German Historical Museum between 2 October 2004 and 27 February 2005.[72] And in October 2004, Second German Television (ZDF) included a feature on the exchange in their regular programme on aspects of German culture. The feature was titled "Willy's Last Journey," and was directed by Nina Gladitz, who has been researching the fate of Sinti and Roma under the Nazis for some time.

The retelling of the tale of Stefan's survival as one of "victim exchange" and death (Willy was murdered in Auschwitz) appeared to discredit the notion of heroic rescue once and for all. The text of the voiceover in Gladitz's "Willy's Last Journey" does refer to Zweig's "rescue," but it is made clear that this was a rescue undertaken at an intolerable price. The film voiceover also implies that the term "rescue" could only apply in this situation, not when Stefan first entered the camp: "no-one had to hide him or put themselves in danger as the film [of *Naked among Wolves*] suggests." In fact, the voiceover claims, the communists separated the child from his father because they recognized in him an "instrument of propaganda."[73] This is a strong claim, but, as we saw earlier in the book, Zacharias does quote the communist prisoners as saying that Stefan, having become through his father's protection a symbol of resistance against Hitler, deserved to be saved.[74]

Effectively, then, what had formerly been perceived as an act of heroic rescue has been recast as a murderous one. Objections can be raised to this reframing, some more weighty than others. It could be argued that it is not possible precisely to reconstruct the process that led to the substitution of Stefan's name and those of eleven others on the transport list in question. But Zacharias himself reports that Stefan was given a fever-inducing injection to make him unfit for transport;[75] those communist prisoners responsible for this injection certainly knew that, if Stefan could not travel, then another prisoner would have to do so in his place. It may have been an SS doctor who authorized the injection. It will in all probability have been the camp doctor August Bender who authorized the striking off of Stefan's name and its replacement with Willy Blum. It cannot be conclusively proved that one or both of these doctors were bribed or otherwise influenced by communist prisoners in their attempts to save Stefan's life. But it remains highly probable. To defend the swap, as the journalist Helga Wagner has done, by arguing that communist Kapos might have thought the sixteen-year-old Willy Blum had a better chance of escaping during transport than Stefan, is unconvincing.[76] His chances were as non-existent as anyone else's — as the communist functionaries well knew.[77] Nor can the implication in the reframing of the Zweig story that communists shared SS prejudices against Sinti and Roma, thus making the exchange easier for them to contemplate, be easily dismissed. It is an extremely positive aspect of the reframing that it has brought to public attention the neglected fate of Sinti and Roma at Buchenwald, and the existence of racial and racist hierarchies among prisoners as well as SS members.

Yet while the reframing's focus on the "victim swap" highlights hitherto neglected facts, it sidelines others. Thus the exchange, terrible as it was, represents only *one* of the situations in which Stefan was protected at Buchenwald. Does Blum's deportation invalidate *all* these other situations, in which individual communists were often involved? And were communists the only people to force through such exchanges? How much were they a fact, albeit terrible, of concentration camp life — and death (see later in the chapter)? The "victim swap" focus is as narrow as the GDR focus on Stefan because, like the latter, it ignores the courageous resourcefulness of Zacharias Zweig in saving his son's life over and again. That Stefan was saved at the expense of Willy certainly does not invalidate all the acts of courage on Zacharias's part *before* he arrived at Buchenwald, and probably not even after. It is my concern that these acts of Jewish resistance should consistently be left out of the frame: before 1990, because reference to them would have watered down the impression that resistance was communist-driven, and after 1990 because reference to them might (re)invigorate a *positive* interest in a story that now must serve as a *negative* example of communist meddling. No attempt has been made to reframe Zweig's story as one of family tragedy, paternal love, and Jewish courage. It must also be said that the narrative reframing since 1990 is not balanced by a recognition of the positive aspects of communist resistance in other areas. It is true that the GDR, with hindsight, can be said to have rather shot itself in the foot by promoting the Zweig rescue as emblematic of all that was noble in communist resistance. But it is not judicious to respond to this by promoting the reframed version, *pars pro toto*, as a general statement on communist resistance as a whole. This constitutes a remythification.

Deconstructing the Myth, Forgetting the Man?

Stefan Zweig himself has followed the changes at the Buchenwald Memorial Site and the accompanying discussions with some misgivings. It is true, as I pointed out in chapter 5, that he never really felt at home in the GDR. On display at the Buchenwald exhibition on the history of the memorial site and at the Jewish Museum in Berlin are facsimiles of a 1978 letter by Buchenwald's director at the time, Klaus Trostorff, in which he points out that Zweig "didn't exactly provide the best example of someone with a clear attitude toward our [i.e. the GDR's] development."[78] The citation of this letter implies the existence of a long-concealed schism between Zweig and the state that had temporarily adopted him. In 1995, Volkhard Knigge approached Zweig by letter, asking him if he would like to participate in a feature for MDR television that aimed to investigate Zweig's biography and its misrepresentation in *Naked among Wolves*.[79] Such implicit and explicit attempts to free Zweig's biography from its GDR misrepresentations and indeed give back to Stefan his "real" self may be well-meaning. But Zweig has not taken kindly to them.[80] He suspects ulterior motives — namely the wish to exploit him for particular purposes, comparable *mutatis mutandis* to what he was exposed to in the GDR.

Whereas in the GDR he and his father were dragooned into corroborating the supposed veracity of *Naked among Wolves*, now he feels pressured to speak out against it; whereas in the GDR he was constantly expected to say how much he approved of SED communism, now he is expected to condemn it. He is not prepared to do so, however, because despite his difficulties with the GDR, he retained an interest in its socialist program, and he also retained an enormous respect for certain of Buchenwald's communists whose lives were very much bound up with that program. His reluctance to collaborate in the reframing of his biography since 1990 is also not surprising, given the emphasis on the "victim exchange." Since the emergence in the public realm of details about Blum, he has complained that he, Stefan, was being made to feel he should not have survived; indeed he was being made to feel as if it were *he* who had murdered Blum.

The emphasis on the "victim exchange" took on particularly pointed and controversial form in the 2003 novel *Different* (*Anders*, 2003) by the (former East) German writer Hans-Joachim Schädlich. Here Schädlich not only presents the rescue story as one of "victim exchange" in line with the post-unification paradigm but also has his narrator say: "the East German communists have robbed Jerzy Zweig of his true story."[81] This more or less equates Zweig's "true story" with that of Blum's deportation and death. Zweig objected to Schädlich's novel in the strongest possible terms and in 2005 took up legal action against him through his lawyer, Hans Jürgen Groth; Zweig is demanding payment of damages.[82] Zweig's indignation was particularly fueled by a set of questionable juxtapositions in Schädlich's novel, where two retired meteorologists and their lady-friend Ida discuss case studies designed to illustrate the archetypical process by which individuals transform their identities and discard their previous biographies in order to adapt to new circumstances. Two key examples provided in the novel will suffice here as illustration. One is Gregor Gysi, who, despite his dubious role in the GDR as a lawyer who simultaneously defended dissidents and collaborated with the SED and *Stasi*, was able after the "Wende" to progress to being a representative of democracy and a much-wanted talk-show guest. Another case is that of Hans Ernst Schneider, a high-profile member of the SS *Ahnenerbe*, who disseminated racist propaganda and procured medical equipment for use in lethal experiments at Dachau. After the war, he became Hans Schwerte, launching a new career as a Germanist and eventually gaining an influential professorship at the Westfälische Technische Hochschule in Aachen.

It would perhaps be a mistake to read into *Different* an attempt on the part of Schädlich to equate unequivocally the biographies of Zweig, Gysi, and Schneider. After all, while Gysi and Schneider actively seek to discard their pasts in the novel, the suggestion in the case of Zweig is rather that his has been denied to him. Moreover, the novel's framework invites the reader to understand the narrator and his friend Awa as more obsessed

with their case studies than is good for them. That they are retired meteorologists is not without ironic significance; now that they are no longer
able to practice their profession, namely studying shifting weather patterns,
they switch their attention to the changeability of *homo sapiens*. Toward
the end, the narrator emancipates himself from this near-obsession during
a trip to Australia, where he learns that nothing will ever be achieved by
telling stories, and where a Jewish zoologist (and *Kindertransport* survivor) makes him aware that some creatures change color quite naturally in
accordance with their environment. In abandoning Awa, Ida, and his own
story-telling past, the narrator himself demonstrates his own mutability.

That Stefan Zweig was upset at the novel's use of juxtaposition is
nevertheless understandable. My reading above seeks to do justice to
Schädlich's aim in the novel; whether he succeeds is another matter. The
novel's main weakness is its thinly-layered irony, which is so inconspicuous
that most reviewers missed it. The post-unification reframing of the Zweig
story implies an absolute equivalence between the SS and the communists
at Buchenwald. The process of collaboration — for instance, in the drawing up of transport lists — is presented as evidence of the ideological similarities between communism and National Socialism. In the public realm,
Schädlich's novel has served, unintentionally perhaps, to reinforce this
reading through its juxtaposition of Schneider's story with that of Zweig.
Certainly Zweig feels he is being asked to accept that his biography is "like
that of a Nazi." Schädlich's novel has also led critics and readers to assume
that Stefan Zweig refused to face the fact that a Sinto had died in his place,
preferring to embrace Apitz's version of his rescue because it was a nicer
story than the real one.[83] Yet as we have seen in chapter 5, Stefan was aware
of discrepancies between his father's testimony and Apitz's version. If he
opted to conceal his concern at these discrepancies, this was at least in part
because open criticism of them would have been detrimental to his and
Zacharias's plan to bring about Heinrich Zweig's emigration from the
Soviet Union. To interpret Zweig's silence on the subject of the substitution as the result of willful blindness is presumptuous and unfair. Most
unfair of all is the subtle and nefarious implication that Zweig, in staying
silent, can be adjudged to have "colluded" *post hoc* in the deportation of
Blum. It is deeply problematic that a persecuted Jew who lost most of his
family in the Holocaust or the Gulags should be made to feel responsible
for the cost of his own rescue, a cost of which he was not even aware at the
time.

Stefan Zweig also reacted angrily to the removal of the plaque commemorating his rescue from the wall of the Storage Building. In a letter to
the newspaper *Neues Deutschland*, Zweig interpreted this as a sign that
memories no longer wanted today are being expunged — "if that is the
case," Zweig went on, "then I want all other references to me and my
family at Buchenwald to be removed."[84] Volkhard Knigge pointed out in

response that the old plaque had been replaced with a new text setting the story of Zweig in relation to the history of all children imprisoned at Buchenwald.[85] This is certainly true. Nevertheless, as already pointed out, the new text makes no explicit reference to Zweig. In this sense, the non-naming of Zweig anonymizes his story, "robbing" him of it, as Schädlich's narrator believes the GDR to have done. Perhaps the non-naming is meant to reflect the uncertainty surrounding whether it was Josef Streich or Zweig who was hidden in the Storage Building. Perhaps it is motivated by a policy of ensuring that equal weight is given, in memory, to all of Buchenwald's children, rather than to one particular name. Whatever the motive, the removal of Zweig's name was always going to be difficult for him to accept without protest.

Stefan Zweig is deeply concerned that the post-unification reframing of his story is expressive of a trend toward renewed anti-Semitism in Germany.[86] According to his reading, it is not just the communist underground and self-administration that are the critical butt of the reframing, but the Jewish prisoners as well: the reframing is perceived by Zweig to imply that his father and even he himself were somehow in cahoots with the communists. This, in turn, implies that Jewish and communist prisoners were "privileged." This implication, to follow Zweig's argument further, calls into question the victimhood of Jews. Zweig also takes virulent exception to the post-unification emphasis on the fact that he, Stefan, was in Buchenwald "legally" ("legal" or "offiziell").[87] His indignation is understandable, given the inflationary use of these terms in the public realm in recent years. He was certainly a registered prisoner, but the term "legally" suggests, perversely, that the Nazis had every right to incarcerate him, while "officially," equally perversely, suggests that he was paying some kind of formal visit. In any case, Stefan's registration would not have protected him against the SS. The post-unification deconstruction of the GDR Zweig narrative, it seems to me, does run the risk of casting Zweig himself in a negative light.

Of course it would be inappropriate simply to assume in all cases an anti-Semitic subtext to the reframing. After all, the Jewish Museum, which features an exhibit on the exchange of Willy for Stefan, can hardly be accused of anti-Semitism. In fact, in juxtaposing as it does the story of Zweig's rescue with that of Anne Frank's hiding, the Jewish Museum wishes to point out that, while the latter at least acknowledges by its end the fact of the Holocaust, the former — in the version in which it was known in the GDR — did not. And in pointing out that Willy Blum was sent to Auschwitz in place of Stefan, the Jewish Museum seeks to reframe the Zweig story as a story that points to another Holocaust, namely that committed against Gypsies. Thus it is that one victim group appears to acknowledge another in a gesture of solidarity often lacking in the entrenched debates on Berlin's Holocaust Memorial. But while the Jewish

Museum cannot be accused of anti-Semitism — indeed it implicitly criticizes the GDR's handling of Zweig himself — it can be accused of pro-
Westernism. The text board introducing the room featuring the Zweig
exhibit claims that in the GDR memory of the Holocaust and the Jews played
only a marginal role at concentration camp memorial sites. While this statement is basically true, if overstated, the next set of statements is more questionable. For example, it is emphasized that West Germany took over all
the legal and moral consequences of its role as legal successor to the Third
Reich, and that "conciliation became the central slogan." While admitting
that a true confrontation with Nazi crimes only set in later in West
Germany (above all in cultural forms of expression), the Jewish Museum
nevertheless generally gives too much credit to West Germany, and the suspicion must be voiced that the Anne Frank story is being framed in the
museum as evidence of the truth of the claim that the West Germans confronted the fate of the Jews more openly than the East Germans. While this
may be true of the 1970s and 1980s, it is less true of the earlier period of
West German history. And while this book has provided evidence of the
marginalization of the Holocaust in East Germany, the fate of Jews *was*
focused on in East German memorial sites — albeit within a Marxist interpretative framework that blamed capitalism rather than racism.

     I have argued in this chapter that the post-unification deconstruction
of the Zweig rescue story as told in the GDR was informed not just by a
spirit of critical enquiry but also, to a considerable degree, by a wish to
discredit communism. Demonization, in fact, paraded itself as objectivity.
I personally do not believe, in contrast to Stefan Zweig, that anti-
Semitism has played as significant a role as the wish to delegitimize
antifascism. But that it has played a part to a degree may well be true. In
my view, moreover, those who utilize the facts of the "victim swap" to
discredit communism — an undertaking that is problematic enough in
itself — appear oblivious to the possibility that their motive might be
misunderstood as anti-Semitic. One would have wished for more sensitivity on this issue.

     It is against the background of the deconstruction of the GDR's ver-
sion of Zweig's rescue that the attack on the Buchenwald Memorial on the
Ettersberg must be understood. On 28 July 1998, a visitor alerted the
Memorial Site to the fact that someone had tried to saw through one of
the legs of the boy in Cremer's prisoner group, possibly with a view to sev-
ering the figure completely from the rest of the sculpture. Knigge compared this act of vandalism to the burning down of the Jewish barracks at
Sachsenhausen Memorial Site in 1992, suggesting an anti-Semitic
motive.[88] The vice-president of Germany's Central Council of the Jews
at the time, Paul Spiegel, believed the "infamous deed" showed that the
"barbarism of the Holocaust should never be forgotten."[89] The VVN, the
organization representing former prisoners, placed the responsibility rather

at the door of "those who through their attempts at delegitimizing anti-fascist memory work in the GDR paved the way for the desecration of this memorial."[90] In the end, it transpired that three building-trade apprentices from Weimar had hit upon the idea of attacking the sculpture in a moment of drunken abandon.[91] The police and state prosecutors were quick to point out that the apprentices had no links to the right-wing radical scene and that there was no political motive for the deed.[92] In my view, it was overhasty to rule out a political motive. As Raimund Sauter, state prosecutor in Erfurt, observed, the apprentices had attempted to saw through the leg of the "Buchenwald child Stefan J. Zweig."[93] The three youths, in attacking a figure so closely associated with Zweig, certainly committed an act of vandalism that seemed to add a violent dimension to the anti-communist and, perhaps, even anti-Semitic thrust of the post-unification reframing of the Zweig story.

Conclusion

Unfortunately, the chance of a fair deconstruction of the GDR's reception of Zweig's rescue has not been taken. It is important that suppressed facts should come to light; it is also important to know how the Zweig rescue was used and abused in the GDR in the interests of myth-building and self-legitimation. The function of my book has been to follow the stages in this construction. But in this final chapter, while welcoming the general trend toward a more complex view of Buchenwald that has set in since 1990, I have felt bound to criticize the post-unification reframing, because of its self-serving one-sidedness. Nor are all the necessary facts being as clearly presented in the public realm as they should be. In all the post-unification discussions of Zweig and Blum, few questions have been asked about the other eleven prisoners whose names were substituted on the 25 September 1944 transport list. One exception is the suggestion by Schädlich's narrator in *Anders* that these eleven might have been saved because they were the sexual playmates of the political prisoners.[94]

That such sexual interests played a part in changes to transport lists is surely true. Former Buchenwald prisoner Colin Burgess, who has provided a graphic description of a deportation of Gypsy boys that could well have been the 25 September transport, suggests that, in addition to reasons of compassion, "sexual gratification" may also have played a part in the protection of Sinti and Roma children.[95] But one should also nevertheless be wary of making such accusations. Thus the name of Karl Stojka, a thirteen-year-old Roma boy from the Burgenland in Austria, was crossed off the 25 September transport list because his Roma uncle intervened on his behalf, claiming to the SS that he was older than he looked.[96] His name was replaced by that of one W. Schubert.[97] Unfortunately, the motives behind other changes to the transport list from which Zweig's name was crossed off, or indeed behind changes to such lists generally, have not been a subject of discussion — principally because any such discussion would detract from the image of communists as villains of the piece.

This book has told the story of how, in the GDR, a myth was made of a rescue by consistently representing it as a heroic act, a process only possible by neglecting its questionable aspects. It has shown how this myth was "authenticated" and how the facts — such as those in Zacharias's testimony — were distorted to fit the myth. The book has also described the deconstruction of this myth after 1990, and its mixed motives. Given the one-sidedness of the manner in which this deconstruction has frequently been implemented, it would be fair to claim that the GDR myth of the Zweig rescue has been replaced by a new myth, one whose underlying message is its exact opposite. The GDR Zweig rescue myth was a positive foundation myth, because it implied that the communist heroism and humanity that led to Stefan's rescue were exemplary of the tradition upon which the pillars of the new East German state rested. The post-unification reframing of the Zweig rescue is a negative foundation myth, because its function is to legitimize the exclusion of the communist heritage from the basis of the new German state. This paves the way for the domination of west German historical inheritances such as the resistance of Stauffenberg and the 20 July circle. To say the least, this is an unfortunate development. Zweig, one might say, is thrice a victim: first of the Nazis, then of the GDR's manipulation of his rescue, and now of united Germany's redefinition of it.

Notes

[1] There was a only brief period where, as far as I can see, *Naked among Wolves* did not feature on the school curriculum, namely between 1966/67 and 1970. Certainly the novel does not feature in the prescribed list published in 1967 (see Archiv der Bibliothek für Bildungsgeschichtliche Forschung des Deutschen Instituts für Internationale Pädagogische Forschung (henceforth BBF/DIPF/Archiv): Ministerium für Volksbildung, ed., *Lehrplan für das Fach Deutsche Sprache und Literatur der Vorbereitungsklassen 9 und 10* (Berlin: Volk & Wissen, 1967)). It does, however, reappear in the curriculum lists that applied as of September 1970 (see BBF/DIPF/Archiv: Ministerium für Volksbildung, ed., *Lehrplan Deutsche Sprache und Literatur, Klasse 9* [Berlin: Volk & Wissen, 1972], 48–50).

[2] See Otto Gotsche, "Das Buchenwaldlied," *neue deutsche literatur* 4 (1966): 102–4.

[3] Gisela Karau, *Der gute Stern des Janusz K.* (Berlin: Der Kinderbuchverlag, 1963). There was also a DEFA film based on Karau's novel. Directed by Celino Bleiweiß, it bore the title *My Blue Bird Flies* (*Mein blauer Vogel fliegt*, 1975). For a discussion of this film, see Thomas Heimann, *Bilder von Buchenwald: Die Visualisierung des Antifaschismus in der DDR (1945–1990)* (Cologne, Weimar, and Vienna: Böhlau, 2005), 125–27.

[4] See BBF/DIPF/Archiv: Ministerium für Volksbildung, ed., *Lehrplan für das Fach Deutsche Sprache und Literatur, Klassen 6 bis 10* (Berlin: Volk & Wissen, 1966), 42–43.

[5] See, for instance, BBF/DIPF/Archiv: Ministerium für Volksbildung, ed., *Lehrplan Deutsche Sprache und Literatur, Klasse 9* (Berlin: Volk & Wissen, 1972), 48–50.

[6] Heinz Albertus, *Kinder in Buchenwald: Verbrechen an Kindern und Jugendlichen im KZ Buchenwald und der Kampf der illegalen antifaschistischen Widerstandsorganisation um ihre Rettung*, 1st ed. (Weimar: Nationale Mahn- und Gedenkstätte Buchenwald, 1981).

[7] Albertus, *Kinder in Buchenwald*, 1st ed., 49–53.

[8] See Heinz Albertus, *Verbrechen an Kindern und Jugendlichen im KZ Buchenwald und der Kampf der illegalen antifaschistischen Widerstandsorganisation um ihre Rettung*, 5th ed. (Weimar-Buchenwald: Druckhaus Weimar, 1989), 51–58; here, 57.

[9] See Herausgeberkollektiv, ed., *Unterrichtshilfen Deutsch: Literatur, Klasse 9* (Berlin: Volk & Wissen, 1980), 120; and Autorenkollektiv, ed., *Unterrichtshilfen Deutsche Sprache und Literatur: Literatur, Klasse 9* (Berlin: Volk & Wissen, 1987), 121.

[10] See "Schlussbemerkung," in Willi Bredel, *Die Prüfung* (Berlin: Aufbau, 1954), 365–68; here, 365–66.

[11] See Thomas F. Schneider, "Mörder, die empfindlich sind: Zur Entstehung von *Der Funke Leben*," in *"Reue ist undeutsch": Erich Maria Remarques "Der Funke Leben und das Konzentrationslager Buchenwald,"* ed. Thomas F. Schneider und Tilman Westphalen (Bramsche, Germany: Rasch, 1992), 14–20, here, 18–19.

[12] See Claudia Glunz, "'Eine harte Sache': Zur Rezeption von Erich Maria Remarques *Der Funke Leben*," in Schneider and Westphalen, *"Reue ist undeutsch,"* 21–27.

[13] Josef-Hermann Sauter, "Interview mit Bruno Apitz," *Weimarer Beiträge: Zeitschrift für Literaturwissenschaft, Ästhetik und Kulturtheorie* 19/1 (1973): 26–37; here, 32–33.

[14] See Eike Middell, "Nachwort," in *Der Totenwald: Ein Bericht*, by Ernst Wiechert (Berlin: Union, 1977), 192–203; here, 192.

[15] Thus Fritz Bressau writes in a letter of 28 September 1956 to Apitz: "we have assessed your manuscript 'The Spark of Life' and would ask you if you can to visit us here at our publishing house next Friday (5th October)" (see Landeshauptarchiv Sachsen-Anhalt, Bestand Mitteldeutscher Verlag Halle, VHSt 140).

[16] Bredel, *Die Prüfung*, 351–52.

[17] See Alexander Stephan, *Anna Seghers "Das siebte Kreuz": Welt und Wirkung eines Romans* (Berlin: Aufbau, 1997), 46–48.

[18] Wolfgang Langhoff, *Die Moorsoldaten* (Essen: Neuer Weg, 1995), 239–43.

[19] Langhoff, *Die Moorsoldaten*, 166–69 and 172–74.

[20] Langhoff, *Die Moorsoldaten*, 311–13.

[21] In the GDR, Remarque's *Spark of Life* was often contrasted negatively with Apitz's *Naked among Wolves*. Thus an official (W. Zirwick) from the department within the East German Writers' Union concerned with literary studies complained in 1959 about a possible overestimation of Remarque in the Soviet Union. Zirwick lauds the prisoners in Apitz's novel because they "possess a clear image of the future, of what must follow fascism," whereas "the thoughts and wishes of Remarque's heroes in his KZ novel *Spark of Life* never go beyond the desire for survival . . . lack of perspective is a characteristic of all of Remarque's works" (Stiftung Archiv der Parteien und Massenorganisationen der ehemaligen Deutschen Demokratischen Republik im Bundesarchiv, DR1/1216: "Erich Maria Remarque").

[22] Erich Maria Remarque, *Der Funke Leben* (Cologne: Kiepenheuer und Witsch, 1998), 301.

[23] Ernst Wiechert, *Der Totenwald* (Frankfurt am Main and Berlin: Ullstein, 1988), 139–41.

[24] See "Protokoll der Diskussion zu 'Ravensbrücker Ballade' von Hedda Zinner am 21. Februar 1985 im DDR-Fernsehen, Berlin-Adlershof," in *Ravensbrücker Ballade oder Faschismus-Bewältigung in der DDR*, ed. Klaus Jarmatz (Berlin: Aufbau, 1992), 79–89; here, 83.

[25] See Frank Beyer, *Wenn der Wind sich dreht* (Munich: Econ, 2001), 184 and 187.

[26] For more on the early film script and changes made to it, see Sandor L. Gilman, *Jurek Becker: Die Biographie* (Berlin: List, 2004), 86–92.

[27] See Simone Barck, *Antifa-Geschichte(n): Eine literarische Spurensuche in der DDR der 1950er und 1960er Jahre* (Cologne, Weimar, and Vienna: Böhlau, 2003), 191.

[28] According to Thomas Taterka, conversation of 9 January 2005.

[29] See, for instance, Henryk Keisch, "Sie sind nicht mehr entblößt," *Neues Deutschland*, 10 October 1961.

[30] See Hedda Zinner, *Ravensbrücker Ballade* (Berlin: Henschelverlag, 1961), 7.

[31] Zinner, *Ravensbrücker Ballade*, 151.

[32] See, for instance, Helmut Eschwege, ed., *Kennzeichen J: Bilder, Dokumente, Berichte zur Geschichte der Verbrechen des Hitlerfaschismus an den deutschen Juden, 1933–1945* (Berlin: Deutscher Verlag der Wissenschaften, 1966); and Klaus Drobisch, Rudi Goguel, and Werner Müller, eds., *Juden unterm Hakenkreuz* (Berlin: Deutscher Verlag der Wissenschaften, 1973).

[33] Jurek Becker, *Jakob der Lügner* (Frankfurt am Main: Suhrkamp, 1982), 7–9.

[34] Bruno Apitz, *Nackt unter Wölfen* (Berlin: Aufbau, 2001), 7.

[35] Apitz, *Nackt unter Wölfen*, 99.

[36] Fred Wander, *Der siebente Brunnen* (Frankfurt am Main: Fischer, 1997). Further references to this work will be made in the text using page numbers alone.

[37] See Hasko Zimmer, *Der Buchenwald-Konflikt* (Münster: agenda Verlag, 1999), 13.

[38] See Falko Werkentin, *Recht und Justiz im SED-Staat* (Bonn: Bundeszentrale für politische Bildung, 1998), 12–17.

[39] "Gnadenlose Justiz," *Der Morgen*, 31 March/1 April 1990.

[40] "SED plante KZs für Sozialdemokraten, Grüne und Christen," *BILD-Zeitung*, 29 March 1990.

[41] Olaf Groehler, "Antifaschismus — vom Umgang mit einem Begriff," in *Zweierlei Bewältigung: Vier Beiträge über den Umgang mit der NS-Vergangenheit in den beiden deutschen Staaten*, by Ulrich Herbert and Olaf Groehler (Hamburg: Ergebnisse Verlag, 1992), 29–40; here, 30.

[42] Ralph Giordano, *Die zweite Schuld oder Von der Last, Deutscher zu sein* (Munich: Droemersche Verlagsanstalt Th. Knaur, 1990), 215–28.

[43] Giordano, *Die zweite Schuld*, 219.

[44] Giordano, *Die zweite Schuld*, 66.

[45] See, for example, Raina Zimmering, *Mythen in der Politik der DDR* (Opladen: Leske & Budrich, 2000); Zimmering's second chapter is entitled "Antifascism — Foundation Myth of the GDR"; see 37–168.

[46] See Herfried Münkler, "Das kollektive Gedächtnis der DDR," in *Parteiauftrag: Ein Neues Deutschland*, ed. Dieter Vorsteher (Berlin: Koehler & Amelang, 1996), 458–68.

[47] Archiv der Gedenkstätte Buchenwald (henceforth BwA), Handapparat: "Stationen der Neukonzeption der Gedenkstätte Buchenwald, A: Konzentrationslager Buchenwald 1937–1945."

[48] See Nationale Mahn- und Gedenkstätte Buchenwald, ed., *Konzentrationslager Buchenwald, Post Weimar/Thür: Katalog zu der Ausstellung aus der Deutschen Demokratischen Republik* (Erfurt: Dewag, 1990).

[49] Harry Stein, *Juden im Konzentrationslager Buchenwald, 1938–1942* (Gedenkstätte Buchenwald: Weimardruck, 1992).

[50] For the Commission's recommendations, see BwA, Handapparat: "Zur Neuorientierung der Gedenkstätte Buchenwald" (Weimar-Buchenwald, 1992).

[51] See Gedenkstätte Buchenwald, ed., *Konzentrationslager Buchenwald, 1937–1945: Begleitband zur ständigen historischen Ausstellung* (Göttingen: Wallstein, 1999).

[52] Gedenkstätte Buchenwald, *Konzentrationslager Buchenwald, 1937–1945*, 214.

[53] Gedenkstätte Buchenwald, *Konzentrationslager Buchenwald, 1937–1945*, 148.

[54] Gedenkstätte Buchenwald, *Konzentrationslager Buchenwald, 1937–1945*, 216.

[55] See Wilfried Schoeller, "'Doppelgedächtnis — in diesem Wort liegt der Anspruch': Eine Rede im ehemaligen Konzentrationslager Buchenwald, die Anstoß erregte," *Frankfurter Rundschau*, 15 April 1963.

[56] "So halfen Kommunisten den Nazis beim Morden," *BILD Thüringen*, 23 February 1994.

[57] Lutz Niethammer, ed., *Der gesäuberte Antifaschismus: Die SED und die roten Kapos von Buchenwald* (Berlin: Akademie, 1994), 24.

[58] "Zur Neuorientierung der Gedenkstätte Buchenwald," 10.

[59] In an open letter to the "Initiative Group Buchenwald 1945–1950" in Weimar, Volkhard Knigge asserted that the "majority of the prisoners [of the Special Camp] were civil functionaries of the NS system" (see "'Speziallager hatte Funktion,'" *Thuringische Landeszeitung*, 4 December 1995). In response to this, the president of the "Victims of Stalinism" (ODS) in Thuringia, Manfred Wettstein, started legal proceedings against Knigge on the grounds of "incitement of the people." But the state prosecutors in Erfurt, after a preliminary investigation, dropped the case.

[60] Ruth Klüger, *weiter leben: Eine Jugend* (Göttingen: Wallstein, 1992). Klüger's book later appeared, much modified, in English under the title *Landscapes of Memory: A Holocaust Girlhood Remembered* (London: Bloomsbury, 1999).

[61] Klüger, *weiter leben*, 74–75.

[62] Schoeller, "'Doppelgedächtnis.'"

[63] Klüger, *weiter leben*, 74.

[64] Volkhard Knigge, "Antifaschistischer Widerstand und Holocaust: Zur Geschichte der KZ-Gedenkstätten in der DDR," in *Erinnerung: Zur Gegenwart des Holocaust in Deutschland-West und Deutschland-Ost*, ed. Bernhard Moltmann et al. (Frankfurt am Main: Haag & Herchen Verlag, 1993), 67–77; here, 76.

[65] In fact, the 1985 exhibition in the Storage Building did make explicit reference to Stefan's Jewishness, even if the plaque did not.

[66] According to Stefan Zweig, the decision to remove the plaque was taken after he sent a long satirical poem to Knigge in 1999. This satirical poem, entitled "Schriftprobe" (literally meaning "Handwriting Sample" or "Attempt at Writing"), takes the memorial site to task on a number of counts, accusing Knigge in particular of turning Buchenwald into a memorial to the victims of Stalinism (see Zacharias Zweig and Stefan Zweig, *Tränen allein genügen nicht* (Vienna: Eigenverlag, 2005), 398).

[67] The German of the original plaque reads: "In diesem Gebäude befanden sich die Effektenkammer, die Häftlingsbekleidungskammer und die Gerätekammer. In der Effektenkammer versorgten Häftlinge den zwischen Säcken versteckten dreijährigen Stefan Zweig. Unter Einsatz ihres Lebens retteten sie das Kind vor der Vernichtung." The new text reads: "In diesem Depot ließ die SS die zivile Bekleidung und Habseligkeiten (Effekten) der Häftlinge sowie im Lager verwendete Häftlingskleidung, Schuhe und Blechgeschirr einlagern. Zehntausende Menschen wurden vom Bahnhof durch das Lagertor zur Desinfektion und in das Kammergebäude getrieben. Die meisten mussten den Weg in das kleine Lager und in eines der Rüstungskommandos antreten. Unter ihnen waren auch Tausende von Jugendlichen und Kindern. Einer der Jüngsten, ein vierjähriger polnischer jüdischer Junge, wurde hier von politischen Häftlingen versteckt. Über 900 andere überlebten in den Kinderbaracken 8 und 66."

[68] See the interview with Knigge, "Die Toten sind tot," *Neues Deutschland* (Beilage), 23/24 October 1999.

[69] Susanne zur Nieden, "'. . . stärker als der Tod': Bruno Apitz' Roman *Nackt unter Wölfen* und die Holocaust-Rezeption in der DDR," in *Bilder des Holocaust: Literatur — Film — bildende Kunst*, ed. Manuel Köppen and Klaus Scherpe (Cologne, Weimar, and Vienna: Böhlau, 1997), 97–108; here, 106.

[70] zur Nieden, " '. . . stärker als der Tod,' " 108.

[71] Harry Stein, " 'Nackt unter Wölfen' — literarische Fiktion und Realität einer KZ-Gesellschaft," in *Sehen, Verstehen und Verarbeiten: KZ Buchenwald, 1937–1945, KZ Mittelbau-Dora, 1943–1945*, ed. Thüringer Institut für Lehrerfortbildung (Bad Berka: Das Land Thüringen, 2000), 27–40; here, 32–33.

[72] The substitution is referred to in the catalogue; see Monika Flacke and Ulrike Schmiegelt, "Aus dem Dunkel zu den Sternen: Ein Staat im Geiste des Antifaschismus," in *Mythen der Nation: 1945 — Arena der Erinnerungen*, ed. Monika Flacke (Berlin: Deutsches Historisches Museum, 2004), 173–89; here, 183 (the article refers in turn to that of zur Nieden, " '. . . stärker als der Tod' ").

[73] Nina Gladitz, "Willys letzte Reise," in *Aspekte* (Zweites Deutsches Fernsehen), 29 October 2004.

[74] Berthold Scheller, ed. (in cooperation with Stefan Jerzy Zweig), *"Mein Vater, was machst du hier . . . ?" Zwischen Buchenwald und Auschwitz: Der Bericht des Zacharias Zweig* (Frankfurt am Main: dipa, 1987), 38.

[75] Scheller, ed., *"Mein Vater, was machst du hier . . . ?"* 61.

[76] Helga Wagner, "Streit um das Kind von Buchenwald," *Leipziger Volkszeitung*, 7 April 2000.

[77] In a conversation with Zweig on 27 March 2005, he asked if I had never heard of the principle that, on a sinking ship, it is always the youngest children who are placed in the lifeboats first. Thus the swap could be justified by "the survival of the youngest" principle.

[78] Letter from Klaus Trostorff to *Das Volk*, 24 February 1978.

[79] I am grateful to Stefan Zweig for providing me with a copy of Knigge's letter to him of 7 March 1995.

[80] Stefan Zweig told me that Knigge asked a friend, a London rabbi, to approach Zweig and mediate between him and Knigge — something to which Zweig did not take kindly (interview with Zweig, 27 March 2005). See also Zweig and Zweig, *Tränen allein genügen nicht*, 400–401.

[81] Hans-Joachim Schädlich, *Anders* (Berlin: Rowohlt, 2003), 93.

[82] See Stefan Zweig's own website at http://www.stefanjzweig.de/news.htm

[83] See, for instance, Helmut Böttiger, "Die Tragik der Metereologen," *Die Zeit*, 9 October 2003.

[84] Stefan Jerzy Zweig, "Die Tafel mit meinem Namen ist abgerissen worden," *Neues Deutschland*, 18 April 2000.

[85] Volkhard Knigge, "Die Gedenkstätte Buchenwald sieht sich als Anwalt aller Häftlingsgruppen," *Neues Deutschland*, 23 May 2000.

[86] Interview with Stefan Zweig, 28 March 2004.

[87] The term "legally" was also used in the GDR in discussions of Stefan's presence at Buchenwald, but not to the same extent, and more "behind the scenes" (see chapter 5).

[88] Quoted in "KZ-Mahnmal in Buchenwald geschändet," *Süddeutsche Zeitung*, 29 July 1998.

89 Quoted in "Mahnwache an der Figur des jüdischen Jungen," *Neues Deutschland*, 30 July 1998.

90 "Mahnwache an der Figur des jüdischen Jungen."

91 See "Denkmalschändung: Polizei nahm drei Jugendliche fest," *Thüringer Allgemeine*, 1 August 1998.

92 "Denkmalschändung: Polizei nahm drei Jugendliche fest."

93 See "Tatwerkzeug im Flußbett einbetoniert," *Thüringer Allgemeine*, 1 August 1998.

94 Schädlich, *Anders*, 73.

95 Colin Burgess, *Destination: Buchenwald* (Kenthurst, Australia: Kangaroo Press, 1995), 115.

96 See USHMM, ed. *The Story of Karl Stojka: A Childhood in Birkenau* (Washington: USHMM, 1992), 10. See also Karl Stojka and Reinhard Pohanka, *Auf der ganzen Welt zu Hause: Das Leben und Wandern des Zigeuners Karl Stojka* (Vienna: Picus, 1994), and http://www.Holocaust-trc.org/kstojka.htm

97 A copy of the transport list and the substitutions is held at the Buchenwald Memorial Site archive.

EPILOGUE

SHORTLY AFTER I HAD SENT what I took to be the final typescript of the current book to Camden House for publication, a book appeared entitled *Tears Alone Are Not Enough* (*Tränen allein genügen nicht*, 2005).[1] This book, compiled and written by Stefan Jerzy Zweig, had a long gestation period, much longer than that of my own book. I had begun to think it would *not* appear, at least not in time for me to include other than the briefest reference to it in my own book. I know that Zweig approached several publishers, without success, before deciding to finance the publication of the book himself. Given the fact that his book is devastatingly critical of post-unification developments at Buchenwald, not least of Volkhard Knigge himself, it is probably not surprising that no German-language publisher would be eager to publish it. That he published it under his own auspices has, however, meant that he in no way needed to make compromises in the tone and content of his book. It is certainly the most uncompromising statement on Buchenwald's post-1990 development that I have read. I am most grateful to Jim Walker of Camden House for allowing me, in what will be a brief epilogue, to say something about Zweig's book. I am grateful to him, too, for allowing me to make some last-minute changes and additions to earlier chapters. There are not many of these changes and additions, but I was glad I had the chance to make them: I was thus able to take account of what was, for me, new information gleaned from *Tears Alone Are Not Enough*, particularly with respect to Zweig's time in the German Democratic Republic.

Stefan Zweig published *Tears Alone Are Not Enough* under the name of Zacharias Zweig and Stefan Zweig. While the first part of the book reproduces Zacharias's Yad Vashem testimony, the second half consists of Stefan's own largely autobiographical writings. Interestingly, Stefan has chosen to portray his own life and express his own thoughts in the third person; he thus ensures that the only first-person narrator in the book is his father, and indeed the whole book is an expression of deep and lasting indebtedness toward and love for Zacharias. The long central second part of *Tears Alone Are Not Enough*, in fact, is called "Epilogue — In My Father's Debt" (138–306). In it Zweig allows us new insights into the life of his father. We learn from the testimonies of other Holocaust survivors that Zacharias saved the lives, not just of his own family, but also of many other Jews, both in the Cracow ghetto and in surrounding work camps (143–48). We learn too of Zacharias's difficulties in finding appropriate employment as a lawyer in Israel and his struggle to attain compensation for his past sufferings from the West German government (141–42). And we learn about Zacharias's support for Willi Bleicher, whose reputation, following attempts by the political right to sully it during the embittered tariff conflicts of the 1963 to 1964 period, was enormously enhanced when Zacharias's testimony became public knowledge in 1964. It was because of Zweig's report, too, that Yad Vashem honored Bleicher by allowing a tree to be planted in his name on the Avenue of the Righteous. "Overnight," Stefan writes, "the attacks on Bleicher stopped" (151).

Tears Alone Are Not Enough is also a tribute to Willi Bleicher, who not only helped to save Stefan's life at Buchenwald but also welcomed him in Stuttgart in 1964, and later successfully petitioned the regional government in Mainz to grant compensation to Zacharias (142). Bleicher, we learn, also helped to bring about the release and emigration of former Buchenwald prisoner Heinz Brandt, who had been imprisoned in the GDR for political reasons (196–97). Stefan's book demonstrates particularly clearly that the postwar story of the Zweigs is also a *West* German one, not just an East German, Israeli, and Austrian one. And in paying his respects to Bleicher, Stefan seeks to protect him against what he perceives to be the attack upon him represented by the "victim swap" focus of the Zweig rescue narrative since 1990. It is not unreasonable, indeed, to assume that the critical thrust of the new version of that narrative, while principally directed against communism and the GDR, is also aimed at trade union traditions in West Germany, traditions very much personified by the radical and uncompromising Bleicher. While Stefan feels the need to defend Bleicher in the new millennium, his father, as *Tears Alone Are Not Enough* demonstrates, felt the need to defend him in the 1960s and early 1970s (Zacharias died in 1972). That this was so is clear from the slightly amended version of Zacharias's Yad Vashem testimony published by Stefan in *Tears Alone Are Not Enough.*

According to Stefan — although this is not something he relates in his book — his father, after lodging his testimony with Yad Vashem, subsequently made amendments to it. He planned to turn this amended version into a book, but died before he could do so.[2] Stefan has included these amendments, as well as other thoughts of his father's, in the testimony as it stands in *Tears Alone Are Not Enough.* Its main difference from the Yad Vashem testimony is a number of additions. I can only focus here on some particularly significant ones. Amongst these are several new passages that highlight the role of Bleicher at Buchenwald. We read that Bleicher threatened the camp commandant in his attempt to save Stefan from deportation, telling him that the prisoners would "take his [Stefan's] fate into their own hands" and "accompany him to pay their last respects" (71). Later, we read that Zacharias, after liberation, told members of the resistance organization that, had "Willi Bleicher and others" still been in the camp in April 1945, the rebellion against the SS would have taken place a few days before 11 April, and it would have been started by the Personal Property Room work detail (96). Zacharias's praise of Bleicher's courage and resilience in his adapted testimony resulted, surely, from his wish to defend the moral character of a union leader much attacked by the right in West Germany.

Some of the new passages seem to imply that the issue of Stefan's threatened deportation from Buchenwald was a matter of concern, not just to Bleicher and other prisoners who knew of the child, but also to a large section of the prisoner community as a whole. This leads Zacharias to surmise that the SS may have wanted to deport rather than simply murder the child there and then because they were afraid of a prisoner uprising (73). A passage has also been added in which Zacharias claims that the SS action against the child was simultaneously one against the secret resistance organization (71). It has to be said that Zacharias's thoughts here appear speculative. My personal impression is that he has allowed himself, in one respect at least, to be influenced by Apitz's *Naked among Wolves* (*Nackt unter Wölfen*), where the SS's search for the child becomes intimately bound up with a campaign against the ILK. Certainly the above-mentioned additions owe much to a desire to praise Bleicher. They implicitly serve to underpin the emotional and symbolic importance of rescuing Stefan, and therefore the importance of Bleicher's role. In the post-unification context of the preoccupation with the "victim swap," moreover, the publication of these additions could help somewhat to rehabilitate Bleicher. The fact remains, however, that this swap took place; nor does it become less problematic, in my view, when one takes into account the "universal principle . . . that the youngest prisoners should be rescued when there is a threat to life" (71). The age difference between Willy Blum and Stefan Zweig was too small a one for the swap to be justified with reference to this universal principle.

But, as I stated in chapter 6 of my book, it is one thing to argue that the GDR's framing of the rescue story — which overlooked this swap — was blinkered and one-sided, and another to argue that the story should be reframed by focusing exclusively on that swap. The Zweig rescue story is complex: neither the wish to show communism as heroic nor the wish to demonize it are helpful analytical tools. *Tears Alone Are Not Enough* is a sardonic, sarcastic, satirical, and very angry book that reveals how much Stefan has suffered emotionally through the focus on the "victim swap" in recent years. But it is also always a clear book that states its objections sharply. Stefan Zweig accuses Knigge of seeking to "trivialize German Nazi crimes while blaming these instead on the Red Kapos" (366). In this connection, he writes of the recent "criminalization" of the communist prisoners at Buchenwald instead of the National Socialists, a process he sees as one of historical falsification, "if not worse" (264). He believes this process to be particularly visible in the reframing of his own rescue. Indeed he sees this reframing as paradigmatic: "the whole resistance staged by political prisoners at Buchenwald has been reduced to the rescue of Zweig — which, according to Knigge, was not really a rescue, but a rather a 'victim swap'" (364). Zweig also argues, as I pointed out in my final chapter, that he too is being criminalized: "it requires a good deal of shamelessness and cold-bloodedness . . . to pillory a three-year old child who was incarcerated in Buchenwald and was to be sent to Auschwitz" (166). Zweig interprets the "victim swap" focus as implying that he, Stefan, should have been killed; he had, in other words, no right to survive. And he deplores the fact that, in his eyes, the fate of a Gypsy is being played off against that of a Jew, sowing dissent among former victims (269).

Much more can be said about Zweig's book: for example, that it relentlessly attacks the focus at Buchenwald's new-look memorial site on the "victims of Stalinism" (a phrase Zweig routinely places in inverted commas), claiming that the attention paid to victims of the Nazis has paled by comparison (265). Some of Zweig's relatives were victims of both Stalinism and Nazism; he is therefore well aware of the similarities between these. But he is skeptical as to whether those interned in Buchenwald after 1945 really were victims of Stalinism, and as to the possible motives for making such equations in this case: the wish to blame the Soviets for the ills of the twentieth century, to detract from German criminal responsibility, and to present Germans more as victims than as perpetrators. The effect of this focus on post-1945 Buchenwald has been, according to Zweig, the marginalization of the pre-1945 victims at the Buchenwald Memorial Site itself (see particularly 420–21, and 399–418). Toward the end of *Tears Alone Are Not Enough*, Zweig attacks Schädlich for the juxtapositions made in his novel *Different* (see chapter 6). Here, as throughout the book, Zweig expresses concern at what he sees as the motive of anti-Semitism behind the reframing of his rescue as a "victim swap" (441–49). The most bitter, often sarcastic, expression of his indignation is undoubtedly the tract he sent to Knigge entitled "Tract on the Question: Is Dr. Knigge an Anti-Semite?" (see 433).

Knigge himself claimed in an interview with the *Süddeutsche Zeitung* that Zweig had sent him emails calling him an anti-Semite, an allegation he utterly refutes. "If it had been someone else," Knigge went on to say, "I would have reported him to the police." From the same interview it becomes clear that he had not taken the decision to display the information on the exchange of names at the memorial site lightly. But while wanting to protect Zweig, he did not wish to "let the legend have the last word." He understood that people wanted to hear there had been hope in the concentration camps, "but there was none, none without a price, people have to accept that."[3] To judge from this interview, Knigge does not wish to expose Zweig, but feels he has an obligation to tell the historical truth. This is a position one can understand. What is unfortunate is that Buchenwald Memorial Site has not told the whole historical truth in its reframing of the Zweig story. It has told an absolutely essential part of it, but opted to ignore the other parts, parts that show that there was indeed hope (not always at a price), that Zacharias generated it, and that he was supported by a number of communists. The exchange of names is the most negative moment of a story with other dimensions, some deeply problematic, others genuinely positive. That there *was* some small hope at concentration camps, moreover, is demonstrated by the new information board outside the Storage Building, which points to the rescue of other children in Blocks 8 and 66 — a rescue brought about largely by communists, a fact, however, not displayed on this new board.

In the final analysis, Zweig perceives in post-unification developments at Buchenwald, particularly with respect to his own story, the influence of a camarilla of anti-Semitic, anticommunist, and second-rate west German historians with a determined interest in discrediting the entire East German antifascist tradition, excluding Jews from the ambit of memory and relativizing German crime under Nazism. My own book has trodden a more cautious interpretative path, although I agree entirely with Zweig about the unfortunate and thoroughly unhelpful influence of anticommunism. And that Zweig has felt so angry and pained as to deliver this devastating riposte — one that includes caustic satirical drawings of Niethammer and Knigge — is symptomatic of a severe breakdown of communication between the Buchenwald Memorial Site and a former Nazi victim, one which could, one feels, have been avoided.

We should leave the last word, perhaps, to Nobel Prize winner Elfriede Jelinek, who has written the postscript to Zweig's book (458–65). It is she who, with characteristic analytical acuity, draws a parallel between the crossing out of Zweig's name on the controversial transport list and the removal of the plaque from the Storage Building wall, simultaneously, of course, a removal of Zweig's name itself (460). Jelinek points out that, for a Jew, the removal of a name is tantamount to the annulment of life (462) — and, in Zweig's case, she also sees the removal of the plaque as a way of erasing him "from collective memory" (460). Her postscript suggests, too, that this erasure represents an attempt to silence a surviving victim of Nazi anti-Semitism, indeed even expresses the wish that he were no longer alive, in order to ensure that the "silence of these millions of annihilated people keeps to its silence" (461). In the preoccupation with the "victim swap," for which Jelinek takes Schädlich in particular to task, Jelinek sees an insistence on the idea that Zweig still "owes his life" (461): "an eye for an eye, a Jew for a Sinti and Roma; everything must have its order" (463). She identifies a German obsession with the settling of accounts, and does not shrink, in reference to this, from quoting the phrase emblazoned on the gates of Buchenwald: "To Each His Own" ("Jedem das Seine"; 463).

Jelinek suggests that it is hypocritical to criticize the striking out of a name in the past and then remove one in the present. Where the Buchenwald Memorial Site emphasizes the continuity of communist machinations and repression, Jelinek, turning the tables, identifies continuities between the National Socialist era and the present, which appear linked by their dismissiveness of the Jewish right to life. One does not need to agree with this view — and I personally find it really does go too far — to recognize that it is a *thinkable* interpretation. It seems astonishing that the removal and replacement of the plaque in early 2000, and indeed the whole focus on the "victim swap," did not go hand in hand with a realization on the part of those responsible for these developments that such a reading *could* be made. One would have expected more sensitivity to the feelings of a Jewish victim, and a clear attempt to ensure that the deconstruction of the GDR's telling of the Zweig rescue story could not be construed simultaneously as an attack on Zweig himself. I will take from my reading of *Tears Alone Are Not Enough* one abiding impression. Stefan Zweig does not tell the story of his and father's lives chronologically, but instead connects events "on different levels" (140). Effectively, the narrative alternates sometimes abruptly from a focus on events at Buchenwald to one on the Zweigs' postwar lives, and here too the focus switches back and forth between Israel, the GDR, and contemporary Germany. For Zweig, the layers of his past, and of the present, are connected at a deep level; one of these connections, sadly, is provided by the continuity of discrimination, injustice, and manipulation. It is not to the credit of united Germany that Zweig continues to feel ostracized.

Notes

[1] Zacharias Zweig and Stefan Jerzy Zweig, *Tränen allein genügen nicht* (Vienna: Eigenverlag, 2005). Page-number references to this book are provided in parentheses throughout the text of the epilogue.

[2] Interview with Stefan Zweig, 23 June 2006.

[3] See Marcus Jauer, "Schwerelos in den Abgrund," *Süddeutsche Zeitung*, 11 April 2005. I tried to arrange an interview with Professor Knigge, who agreed to meet me, but then had to decline because of other commitments. I sincerely regret not having had the opportunity to speak with him, and am therefore dependent for his views on newspaper articles.

BIBLIOGRAPHY

Archival Sources

a. Archiv der Bibliothek für Bildungsgeschichtliche Forschung des Deutschen Instituts für Internationale Pädagogische Forschung, Berlin
b. Archiv der Gedenkstätte Buchenwald, Buchenwald, Weimar
c. Bundesarchiv-Filmarchiv, Berlin
d. Bundesarchiv, Koblenz
e. Bundesbeauftragte für die Unterlagen des Staatssicherheitsdienstes der ehemaligen Deutschen Demokratischen Republik, Berlin
f. Deutsches Historisches Museum, Berlin
g. Deutsches Rundfunkarchiv, Berlin
h. Landeshauptarchiv Sachsen-Anhalt, Magdeburg
i. National Archives and Records Administration (NARA), Washington
j. Stadtarchiv Weimar
k. Stiftung Akademie der Künste, Berlin
l. Stiftung Archiv der Parteien und Massenorganisationen der DDR im Bundesarchiv, Berlin
m. Thüringisches Hauptstaatsarchiv, Weimar
n. United States Holocaust Memorial Museum, Washington

Works Consulted

Abmayr, Hermann G. *Wir brauchen kein Denkmal: Willi Bleicher; Der Arbeiterführer und seine Erben.* Tübingen and Stuttgart: Silberburg Verlag, 1992.

Albertus, Heinz. *Verbrechen an Kindern und Jugendlichen im KZ Buchenwald und der Kampf der illegalen antifaschistischen Widerstandsorganisation um ihre Rettung.* 1st edition. Weimar-Buchenwald: Druckhaus Weimar, 1981.

———. *Verbrechen an Kindern und Jugendlichen im KZ Buchenwald und der Kampf der illegalen antifaschistischen Widerstandsorganisation um ihre Rettung.* 5th edition. Weimar-Buchenwald: Druckhaus Weimar, 1989.

Apitz, Bruno. "Esther." In *Die Verwischte Photographie: Sozialistische Erzähler über den Widerstand in Deutschland, 1933–1945*, edited by Gerda Zschocke, 120–39. Berlin: Militärverlag der DDR, 1983.

———. *Nackt unter Wölfen.* Berlin: Aufbau, 2001.

———. *Nackt unter Wölfen.* Halle: Mitteldeutscher Verlag, 1958.

Applebaum, Anne. *Gulag — A History.* London: Penguin, 2003.

Arbeitsgemeinschaft Junge Historiker. *Das Treptower Ehrenmal: Geschichte und Gegenwart.* Berlin: Staatsverlag der Deutschen Demokratischen Republik, 1980.

Autorenkollektiv, ed. *Unterrichtshilfen Deutsche Sprache und Literatur: Literatur, Klasse 9.* Berlin: Volk & Wissen, 1987.

Barck, Simone. *Antifa-Geschichte(n): Eine literarische Spurensuche in der DDR der 1950er und 1960er Jahre.* Cologne, Weimar, and Vienna: Böhlau, 2003.

Bartel, Walter, and Stefan Heymann, eds. *Konzentrationslager Buchenwald, Band 1: Bericht des Internationalen Lagerkomitees.* Weimar: Thüringer Volksverlag, 1945.

Barthel, Karl. *Die Welt ohne Erbarmen.* Rudolstadt: Greifenverlag zu Rudolstadt, 1946.

Becker, Jurek. *Jakob der Lügner.* Frankfurt am Main: Suhrkamp, 1982.

Beckert, W. A. *Die Wahrheit über das Konzentrationslager Buchenwald.* Weimar: Rudolf Borkmann, 1946.

Berke, Hanns. *Buchenwald: Eine Erinnerung an Mörder.* Salzburg: Ried-Verlag, 1946.

Beyer, Frank. *Wenn der Wind sich dreht.* Munich: Econ, 2001.

Bodemann, Michal. "A Reemergence of German Jewry?" In *Reemerging Jewish Culture in Germany: Life and Literature since 1989,* edited by Sander L. Gilman and Karen Remmler, 46–61. New York and London: New York UP, 1994.

Bredel, Willi. *Die Prüfung.* Berlin: Aufbau, 1954.

Buchenwald: Ein Führer durch die Mahn- und Gedenkstätte. Weimar: Volksverlag, 1960.

Bunzol, Alfred. *Erlebnisse eines politischen Gefangenen im Konzentrationslager Buchenwald.* Weimar: Thüringer Volksverlag, 1946.

Burgess, Colin. *Destination: Buchenwald.* Kenthurst, Australia: Kangaroo Press, 1995.

Burney, Christopher. *The Dungeon Democracy.* New York: Duell, Sloan & Pearce, 1946.

Carlebach, Emil. *Tote auf Urlaub: Kommunist in Deutschland; Dachau und Buchenwald, 1937–1945.* Bonn: Pahl-Rugenstein, 1995.

Carlebach, Emil, Paul Grünewald, Hellmuth Röder, Willy Schmidt, and Walter Vielhauer. *Buchenwald: Ein Konzentrationslager.* Berlin: Dietz, 1986.

Conter, Claude D. *Bruno Apitz: Eine Werkgeschichte* (MA thesis, University of Bamberg, 1997).

Cremer, Fritz. "Über die Arbeit an den plastischen Entwürfen meiner Buchenwald-Gruppe." *Das Blatt des Verbandes Bildender Künstler Deutschlands* 7 (July 1954).

Deutsche Akademie der Künste, ed. *Das Buchenwald Denkmal.* Dresden: Verlag der Kunst, 1960.

Deutsches Pädagogisches Zentralinstitut, ed. *Beiträge zum Literaturunterricht in den Klassen 8 bis 10*. Berlin: Volk & Wissen, 1960.

Dietmar, Udo. *"Häftling . . . X . . . in der Hölle auf Erden."* Weimar: Thüringer Volksverlag, 1946.

Drobisch, Klaus. *Widerstand in Buchenwald*. 4th edition. Berlin: Dietz, 1989.

Drobisch, Klaus, Rudi Goguel, and Werner Müller, eds. *Juden unterm Hakenkreuz*. Berlin: Deutscher Verlag der Wissenschaften, 1973.

Edel, Peter. "Das Kind vom Ettersberg: Gedanken über ein kleines Bild und einen großen Film." *Die Weltbühne*, 8 May 1963: 595–601.

———. *Wenn es ans Leben geht*. 5th edition. Berlin: Verlag der Nation, 1979.

Emmerich, Wolfgang. *Kleine Literaturgeschichte der DDR*. Berlin: Aufbau, 2000.

Epstein, Catherine. *The Last Revolutionaries: German Communists and Their Century*. Cambridge, MA, and London: Harvard UP, 2003.

Eschwege, Helmut, ed. *Kennzeichen J: Bilder, Dokumente, Berichte zur Geschichte der Verbrechen des Hitlerfaschismus an den deutschen Juden, 1933–1945*. Berlin: Deutscher Verlag der Wissenschaften, 1966.

Fein, Erich, and Karl Flanner. *Rot-Weiss-Rot in Buchenwald*. Wien and Zürich: Europaverlag, 1987.

Finkelmeier, Konrad. *Die braune Apokalypse*. Weimar: Thüringer Volksverlag, 1947.

Die Fischer Chronik: Deutschland '49–'99. Frankfurt am Main: Fischer, 1999.

Flacke, Monika, and Ulrike Schmiegelt. "Aus dem Dunkel zu den Sternen: Ein Staat im Geiste des Antifaschismus." In *Mythen der Nation: 1945 — Arena der Erinnerungen*, edited by Monika Flacke, 173–89. Berlin: Deutsches Historisches Museum, 2004.

Fox, Thomas. *Stated Memory: East Germany and the Holocaust*. Rochester, NY: Camden House, 1999.

Gedenkstätte Buchenwald, ed. *Konzentrationslager Buchenwald, 1937–1945: Begleitband zur ständigen historischen Ausstellung*. Göttingen: Wallstein, 1999.

Geve, Thomas. *Youth in Chains*. Rubin, MA: Jerusalem, 1958.

Gilman, Sander L. *Jurek Becker: Die Biographie*. Berlin: List, 2004.

Giordano, Ralph. *Die zweite Schuld oder Von der Last, Deutscher zu sein*. Munich: Droemersche Verlagsanstalt Th. Knaur, 1990.

Glunz, Claudia. "'Eine harte Sache': Zur Rezeption von Erich Maria Remarques *Der Funke Leben*." In *"Reue ist undeutsch": Erich Maria Remarques* Der Funke Leben *und das Konzentrationslager Buchenwald*, edited by Thomas F. Schneider und Tilman Westphalen, 21–27. Bramsche: Rasch, 1992.

Gotsche, Otto. "Das Buchenwaldlied." *neue deutsche literatur* 4 (1966): 102–4.

Green, John. *Anonym unterwegs: Ein Fernsehjournalist berichtet.* Berlin: Dietz, 1991.

Gregor, Martin. *Der mann mit der stoppuhr.* Halle-Saale: Mitteldeutscher Verlag, 1957.

Groehler, Olaf. "Antifaschismus — vom Umgang mit einem Begriff." In *Zweierlei Bewältigung: Vier Beiträge über den Umgang mit der NS-Vergangenheit in den beiden deutschen Staaten,* by Ulrich Herbert and Olaf Groehler, 29–40. Hamburg: Ergebnisse Verlag, 1992.

Hackett, David, trans. and ed. *The Buchenwald Report.* Boulder, San Francisco, and Oxford: Westview Press, 1995.

Halbwachs, Maurice. *On Collective Memory.* Edited and translated by Lewis A. Coser. Chicago and London: U of Chicago P, 1992.

Heimann, Thomas. *Bilder von Buchenwald: Die Visualisierung des Antifaschismus in der DDR (1945–1990).* Cologne, Weimar, and Vienna: Böhlau, 2005.

Heimler, Eugene. *Night of the Mist.* London: Love & Malcomson, 1961.

Hemmendinger, Judith, and Robert Krell. *The Children of Buchenwald.* Jerusalem and New York: Gefen, 2000.

Herausgeberkollektiv, ed. *Unterrichtshilfen Deutsch: Literatur, Klasse 9.* Berlin: Volk & Wissen, 1980.

Herf, Jeffrey. *Divided Memory: The Nazi Past in the Two Germanys.* Cambridge, MA, and London: Harvard UP, 1997.

Holzer, Charlotte. "Dramatische Begegnung mit dem Vater, Dr. Zweig." In *Stefan-Jerzy Zweig: Der große Bericht,* 5.

Internationales Buchenwald-Komitee und das Komitee der Antifaschistischen Widerstandskämpfer in der Deutschen Demokratischen Republik, eds. *Buchenwald: Mahnung und Verpflichtung.* Berlin: Kongress-Verlag, 1960.

Jarmatz, Klaus, ed. *Ravensbrücker Ballade oder Faschismus-Bewältigung in der DDR.* Berlin: Aufbau, 1992.

Karau, Gisela. *Der gute Stern des Janusz K.* Berlin: Der Kinderbuchverlag, 1963.

Kautsky, Benedikt. *Teufel und Verdammte.* Vienna: Verlag der Wiener Volksbuchhandlung, 1947.

Kirsch, Sarah, and Rainer Kirsch. *Berlin-Sonnenseite: Deutschlandtreffen der Jugend in der Hauptstadt der DDR, Berlin 1964.* Berlin: Verlag Neues Leben, 1964.

KL Bu: Konzentrationslager Buchenwald: Bericht des internationalen Lagerkomitees Buchenwald. Weimar: Thüringer Volksverlag, 1945.

Klüger, Ruth. *Landscapes of Memory: A Holocaust Girlhood Remembered.* London: Bloomsbury, 1999.

———. *weiter leben: Eine Jugend.* Göttingen: Wallstein, 1992.

Knigge, Volkhard. "Antifaschistischer Widerstand und Holocaust: Zur Geschichte der KZ-Gedenkstätten in der DDR." In *Erinnerung: Zur*

Gegenwart des Holocaust in Deutschland-West und Deutschland-Ost, edited by Bernhard Moltmann, Doron Kiesel, Cilly Kugelmenn, Hanno Loewy, and Dietrich Neuhaus, 67–77. Frankfurt am Main: Haag + Herchen Verlag, 1993.

———. "Opfer, Tat, Aufstieg: Vom Konzentrationslager Buchenwald zur Nationalen Mahn- und Gedenkstätte der DDR." In *Versteinertes Gedenken: Das Buchenwalder Mahnmal von 1958, Band 1*, edited by Volkhard Knigge, 5–95. Spröda: Edition Schwarz Weiss, 1997.

Kogon, Eugen. *Der SS-Staat: Das System der deutschen Konzentrationslager.* Munich: Heyne, 2001.

Kommunistische Partei Deutschlands Stadt und Kreis Leipzig, ed. *Das war Buchenwald! Ein Tatsachenbericht.* Leipzig: Verlag für Wissenschaft und Literatur, 1945.

Konzentrationslager Buchenwald: Geschildert von Buchenwalder Häftlingen. Vienna: Stern-Verlag, 1945.

Kuhirt, Ullrich. "Die Stelen." In *Das Buchenwald Denkmal*, edited by the Deutsche Akademie der Künste, 37–49. Dresden: Verlag der Kunst, 1960.

Kühn, Günter, and Wolfgang Weber. *Stärker als die Wölfe.* Berlin: Militärverlag der Deutschen Demokratischen Republik, 1976.

Kuratorium für den Aufbau Nationaler Gedenkstätten, ed. *Buchenwald: Aus Vergangenheit und Gegenwart des Ettersbergs bei Weimar.* Reichenbach: VEB Volkskunstverlag, 1956.

Langhoff, Wolfgang. *Die Moorsoldaten.* Essen: Neuer Weg, 1995.

Leibbrand, Robert. *Buchenwald: Ein Tatsachenbericht zur Geschichte der deutschen Widerstandsbewegung.* Stuttgart: Europa Verlag, 1946.

Loest, Erich. *Der Zorn des Schafes.* Munich: DTV, 1993.

McDougall, Alan. *Youth Politics in East Germany: The Free German Youth Movement, 1946–1968.* Oxford: Clarendon Press, 2004.

Meuschel, Sigrid. "Antifaschistischer Stalinismus." In *Erinnern, Wiederholen, Durcharbeiten: Zur Psycho-Analyse deutscher Wenden*, edited by Brigitte Rauschenbach, 163–71. Berlin: Aufbau, 1992.

Middell, Eike. "Nachwort." In Ernst Wiechert, *Der Totenwald: Ein Bericht*, 192–203. Berlin: Union, 1977.

Münkler, Herfried. "Das kollektive Gedächtnis der DDR." In *Parteiauftrag: Ein Neues Deutschland*, edited by Dieter Vorsteher, 458–68. Berlin: Koehler & Amelang, 1996.

Nationale Mahn- und Gedenkstätte Buchenwald, ed. *Konzentrationslager Buchenwald, Post Weimar/Thür: Katalog zu der Ausstellung aus der Deutschen Demokratischen Republik.* Erfurt: Dewag, 1990.

Nationale Mahn- und Gedenkstätte Buchenwald/Lagergemeinschaft Buchenwald-Dora beim Komitee der Antifaschistischen Widerstandskämpfer der DDR, eds. *Buchenwald: Mahnung und Verpflichtung, Dokumente und Berichte.* 4th edition. Berlin: VEB Deutscher Verlag der Wissenschaften, 1983.

Niethammer, Lutz, ed. *Der "gesäuberte" Antifaschismus: Die SED und die roten Kapos von Buchenwald.* Berlin: Akademie Verlag, 1994.

Niven, Bill. "'Der Not gehorchend, nicht dem eignen Triebe, ich tu's der Werbung nur zuliebe!' The Genesis of Bruno Apitz's *Nackt unter Wölfen*." *German Studies Review* 28, no. 2 (2005): 265–83.

Ochs, Eugen. *Ein Arbeiter im Widerstand.* Stuttgart: Editions Cordelier, 1984.

Overesch, Manfred. *Buchenwald und die DDR oder die Suche nach Selbstlegitimation.* Göttingen: Vandenhoeck & Ruprecht, 1995.

Peters, Ulrich. *"Wer die Hoffnung verliert, hat alles verloren": Kommunistischer Widerstand in Buchenwald.* Cologne: PapyRossa, 2003.

Pflugk, Gernot, and Dietrich Schuckmann. "Zur Behandlung des Romans 'Nackt unter Wölfen' von Bruno Apitz." In *Zur schöpferischen Arbeit im Literaturunterricht,* edited by Wilfried Bütow, 51–71. Berlin: Volk & Wissen, 1974.

Poller, Walter. *Arztschreiber in Buchenwald.* Hanover: Verlag für Literatur und Zeitgeschehen, 1960.

Reichel, Peter. *Erfundene Erinnerung: Weltkrieg und Judenmord in Film und Theater.* Munich and Vienna: Carl Hanser, 2004.

Reich-Ranicki, Marcel. "Ein ungewöhnlicher Publikumserfolg." In *Ohne Rabatt: Über Literatur aus der DDR,* 25–27. Stuttgart: Deutsche Verlagsanstalt, 1991.

Remarque, Erich Maria. *Der Funke Leben.* Cologne: Kiepenheuer und Witsch, 1998.

Reuter, Elke, and Detlef Hansel. *Das kurze Leben der VVN von 1947 bis 1953.* Berlin: edition ost, 1997.

Sapunow, Juri. "Die Getreuen der Heimat." In *Kampf hinter Stacheldraht,* edited by M. Wilenski and N. Kjung, 39–59. Moscow: Staatlicher Verlag für die Veröffentlichung politischer Literatur, 1960.

Sauter, Josef-Hermann. "Interview mit Bruno Apitz." *Weimarer Beiträge* 19/1 (1973): 26–37.

Scheller, Berthold, ed., in cooperation with Stefan Jerzy Zweig. *"Mein Vater, was machst du hier . . .?" Zwischen Buchenwald und Auschwitz: Der Bericht des Zacharias Zweig.* Frankfurt am Main: dipa, 1987.

Schenk, Ralf, ed. *Regie: Frank Beyer.* Berlin: Edition Hentrich, 1995.

Schneider, Thomas F. "Mörder, die empfindlich sind: Zur Entstehung von *Der Funke Leben.*" In Schneider and Westphalen, *"Reue ist undeutsch,"* 14–20.

Schneider, Thomas F., and Tilman Westphalen, eds. *"Reue ist undeutsch": Erich Maria Remarques "Der Funke Leben und das Konzentrationslager Buchenwald."* Bramsche, Germany: Rasch, 1992.

Schneider, Wolfgang. *Kunst hinter Stacheldraht: Ein Beitrag zur Geschichte des antifaschistischen Widerstandskampfes.* Weimar: Buchdruckerei Weimar, 1973.

Seghers, Anna. *Das siebte Kreuz.* Berlin: Aufbau, 1946.

Semprun, Jorge. *Der Tote mit meinem Namen.* Frankfurt am Main: Suhrkamp, 2002.

Sereny, Gitta. *The German Trauma: Experiences and Reflections, 1938–2001.* London: Penguin, 2000.

Sofsky, Wolfgang. *Die Ordnung des Terrors: Das Konzentrationslager.* Frankfurt am Main: Fischer, 1997.

Stefan-Jerzy Zweig: Der große Bericht über das Buchenwaldkind. Supplement to *BZ am Abend,* 1964.

Stein, Harry. *Juden in Buchenwald, 1937–1942.* Weimar: Weimardruck, 1992.

———. " 'Nackt unter Wölfen' — literarische Fiktion und Realität einer KZ-Gesellschaft." In *Sehen, Verstehen und Verarbeiten: KZ Buchenwald, 1937–1945, KZ Mittelbau-Dora, 1943–1945,* edited by the Thüringer Institut für Lehrerfortbildung, 27–40. Saalfeld: Satz & Druck, 2000.

Stephan, Alexander. *Anna Seghers "Das siebte Kreuz": Welt und Wirkung eines Romans.* Berlin: Aufbau, 1997.

Stojka, Karl, and Reinhard Pohanka. *Auf der ganzen Welt zu Hause: Das Leben und Wandern des Zigeuners Karl Stojka.* Vienna: Picus, 1994.

Stolpmann, Günther, and Helga Tille and Lothar Tille. "Bruno Apitz: *Nackt unter Wölfen.*" In *Literaturunterricht 9./10. Klasse (Teil I): Fachwissenschaftliche und methodische Anleitung zum Lehrplan 1970.* Berlin: Volk & Wissen Verlag, 1974.

The Story of Karl Stojka: A Childhood in Birkenau. Washington: USHHM, 1992.

Strittmatter, Eva. "tangenten." *Neue Deutsche Literatur* 7 (1958): 124–30.

Thoms, Ewald. "Erste Begegnung mit Stefan in Stuttgart." In *Stefan-Jerzy Zweig: Der große Bericht,* 9–10.

———. "Das Kind, um das Millionen bangten." *DDR-Revue* 6 (1964).

Timm, Angelika. "Juden in der DDR und der Staat Israel." In *Zwischen Politik und Kultur — Juden in der DDR,* edited by Moshe Zuckermann, 17–33. Göttingen: Wallstein, 2002.

Tschesno-Hell, Michael. *Eine Ziffer über dem Herzen: Erlebnisbericht aus zwölf Jahren Haft von Jakob Boulanger.* Berlin: Volk & Welt, 1957.

Union OSE, ed. *Les enfants de Buchenwald.* Geneva: OSE, 1946.

Unsdorfer, S. B. *The Yellow Star.* New York and London: Thomas Yoseloff, 1961.

USHMM, ed. *The Story of Karl Stojka: A Childhood in Birkenau.* Washington: USHMM, 1992.

Wander, Fred. *Der siebente Brunnen.* Frankfurt am Main: Fischer, 1997.

Weinstock, Rolf. *"Rolf, Kopf hoch!" Die Geschichte eines jungen Juden.* Berlin: VVN-Verlag, 1950.

———. *Das wahre Gesicht Hitler-Deutschlands.* Singen: Volksverlag, 1948.

Werber, Jack, with William B. Helmreich. *Saving Children: Diary of a Buchenwald Survivor and Rescuer.* New Brunswick and London: Transaction Publishers, 1996.

Werkentin, Falko. *Recht und Justiz im SED-Staat.* Bonn: Bundeszentrale für politische Bildung, 1998.

Wiechert, Ernst. *Der Totenwald*. Frankfurt am Main and Berlin: Ullstein, 1988.

————. *Der Totenwald: Ein Bericht*. Berlin: Union, 1977.

Wiesel, Elie. *Night*. London: Penguin, 1981.

Wilenski, M., and N. Kjung, eds. *Kampf hinter Stacheldraht*. Moscow: Staatlicher Verlag für die Veröffentlichung politischer Literatur, 1960.

Zahnwetzer, M. *KZ Buchenwald: Ein Erlebnisbericht*. Kassel-Sandershausen: Verlag M. Zahnwetzer, 1946.

Zimmer, Hasko. *Der Buchenwald-Konflikt*. Münster: agenda Verlag, 1999.

Zimmering, Raina. *Mythen in der Politik der DDR*. Opladen: Leske & Budrich, 2000.

Zinner, Hedda. *Ravensbrücker Ballade*. Berlin: Henschelverlag, 1961.

Zur Nieden, Susanne. "'. . . stärker als der Tod': Bruno Apitz' Roman *Nackt unter Wölfen* und die Holocaust-Rezeption in der DDR." In *Bilder des Holocaust: Literatur — Film — bildende Kunst*, edited by Manuel Köppen and Klaus Scherpe, 97–108. Cologne, Weimar, and Vienna: Böhlau, 1997.

Zweig, Arnold. *Fahrt zum Acheron*. Berlin: VVN Verlag, 1951.

————. *Im Feuer vergangen: Tagebücher aus dem Ghetto*. Berlin: Rütten & Loening, 1968.

Zweig, Zacharias, and Stefan Zweig, *Tränen allein genügen nicht*. Vienna: Eigenverlag, 2005.

INDEX

Bill Niven is Professor of Contemporary German History at the Nottingham Trent University, UK.